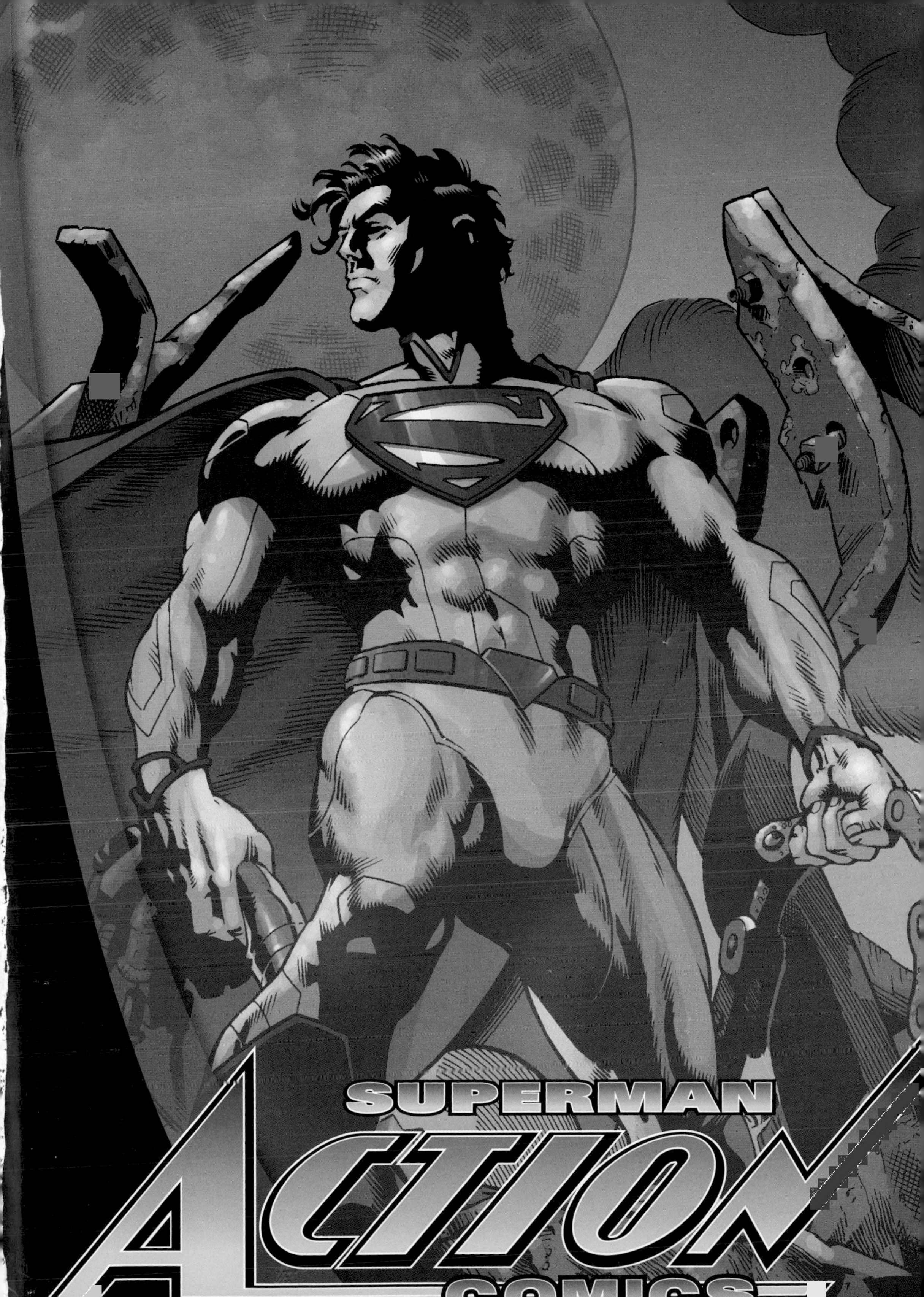
SUPERMAN
ACTION
COMICS

VOLUME 3 AT THE END OF DAYS

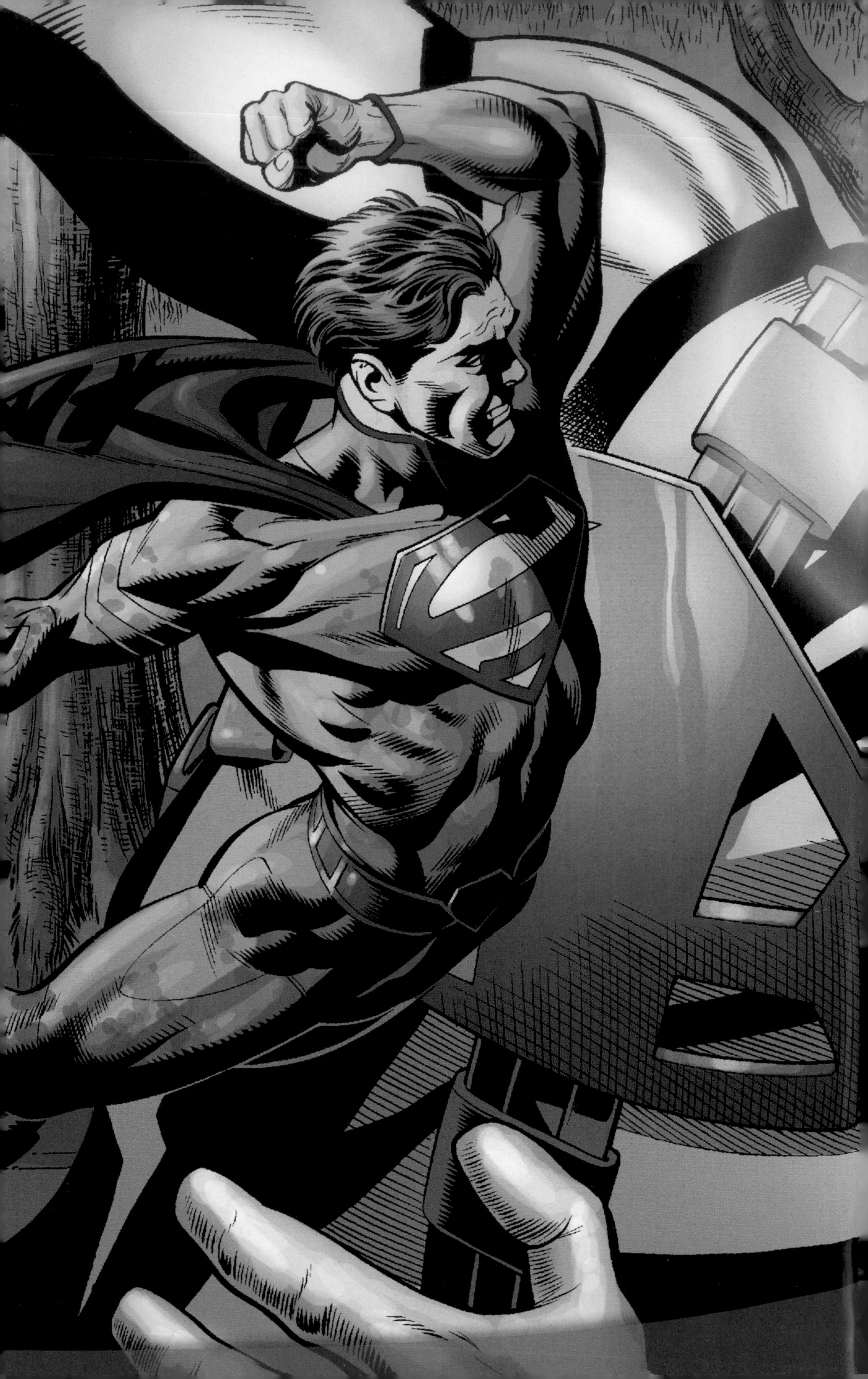

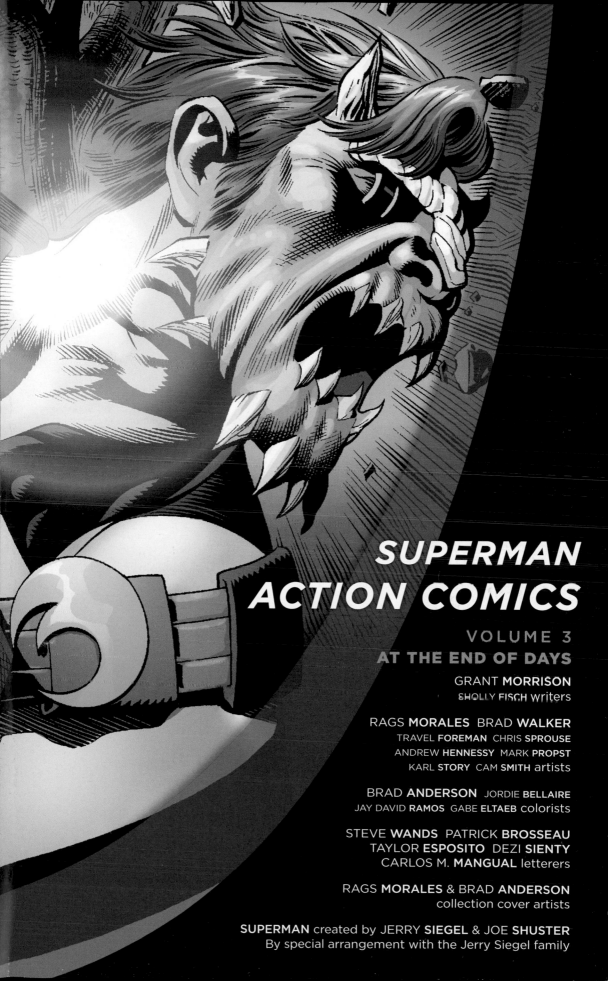

SUPERMAN
ACTION COMICS

VOLUME 3
AT THE END OF DAYS

GRANT **MORRISON**
SHOLLY FISCH writers

RAGS **MORALES** BRAD **WALKER**
TRAVEL **FOREMAN** CHRIS **SPROUSE**
ANDREW **HENNESSY** MARK **PROPST**
KARL **STORY** CAM **SMITH** artists

BRAD **ANDERSON** JORDIE **BELLAIRE**
JAY DAVID **RAMOS** GABE **ELTAEB** colorists

STEVE **WANDS** PATRICK **BROSSEAU**
TAYLOR **ESPOSITO** DEZI **SIENTY**
CARLOS M. **MANGUAL** letterers

RAGS **MORALES** & BRAD **ANDERSON**
collection cover artists

SUPERMAN created by JERRY **SIEGEL** & JOE **SHUSTER**
By special arrangement with the Jerry Siegel family

MATT IDELSON Editor – Original Series WIL MOSS Associate Editor – Original Series PETER HAMBOUSSI Editor
ROBBIN BROSTERMAN Design Director – Books ROBBIE BIEDERMAN Publication Design

BOB HARRAS Senior VP – Editor-in-Chief, DC Comics

DIANE NELSON President DAN DIDIO and JIM LEE Co-Publishers
GEOFF JOHNS Chief Creative Officer
JOHN ROOD Executive VP – Sales, Marketing and Business Development
AMY GENKINS Senior VP – Business and Legal Affairs NAIRI GARDINER Senior VP – Finance
JEFF BOISON VP – Publishing Planning MARK CHIARELLO VP – Art Direction and Design
JOHN CUNNINGHAM VP – Marketing TERRI CUNNINGHAM VP – Editorial Administration
ALISON GILL Senior VP – Manufacturing and Operations HANK KANALZ Senior VP – Vertigo and Integrated Publishing
JAY KOGAN VP – Business and Legal Affairs, Publishing JACK MAHAN VP – Business Affairs, Talent
NICK NAPOLITANO VP – Manufacturing Administration SUE POHJA VP – Book Sales
COURTNEY SIMMONS Senior VP – Publicity BOB WAYNE Senior VP – Sales

SUPERMAN – ACTION COMICS VOLUME 3: AT THE END OF DAYS

DC Comics, 1700 Broadway, New York, NY 10019
A Warner Bros. Entertainment Company.
Printed by RR Donnelley, Salem, VA, USA. 11/08/13. First Printing.
HC ISBN: 978-1-4012-4232-9

Library of Congress Cataloging-in-Publication Data

Morrison, Grant.
Superman - Action Comics. Volume 3, At the End of Days / Grant Morrison.
pages cm. — (The New 52!)
Summary: "The New York Times best-selling creative team Grant Morrison and Rags Morales' landmark run on SUPERMAN: ACTION COMICS
ends here in SUPERMAN: ACTION COMICS VOLUME 3: AT THE END OF DAYS! Five years ago, Clark Kent moved to Metropolis.
Alone but hopeful, he donned a simple t-shirt laden with a giant S, beginning the career of one of the greatest heroes this—or any other—
world has seen. Superman has grown with the city around him, and though he is feared by the public, there's no doubt they need him to
protect them from this universe's gravest threats. But when the multiverse sends it's deadliest villains against the Man of Steel,
can even he turn them back? — Provided by publisher.
"Superman created by Jerry Siegel and Joe Shuster."
ISBN 978-1-4012-4232-9 (hardback)
1. Graphic novels. I. Title. II. Title: At the End of Days.
PN6728.S9M734 2013
741.5'973—dc23
2013031446

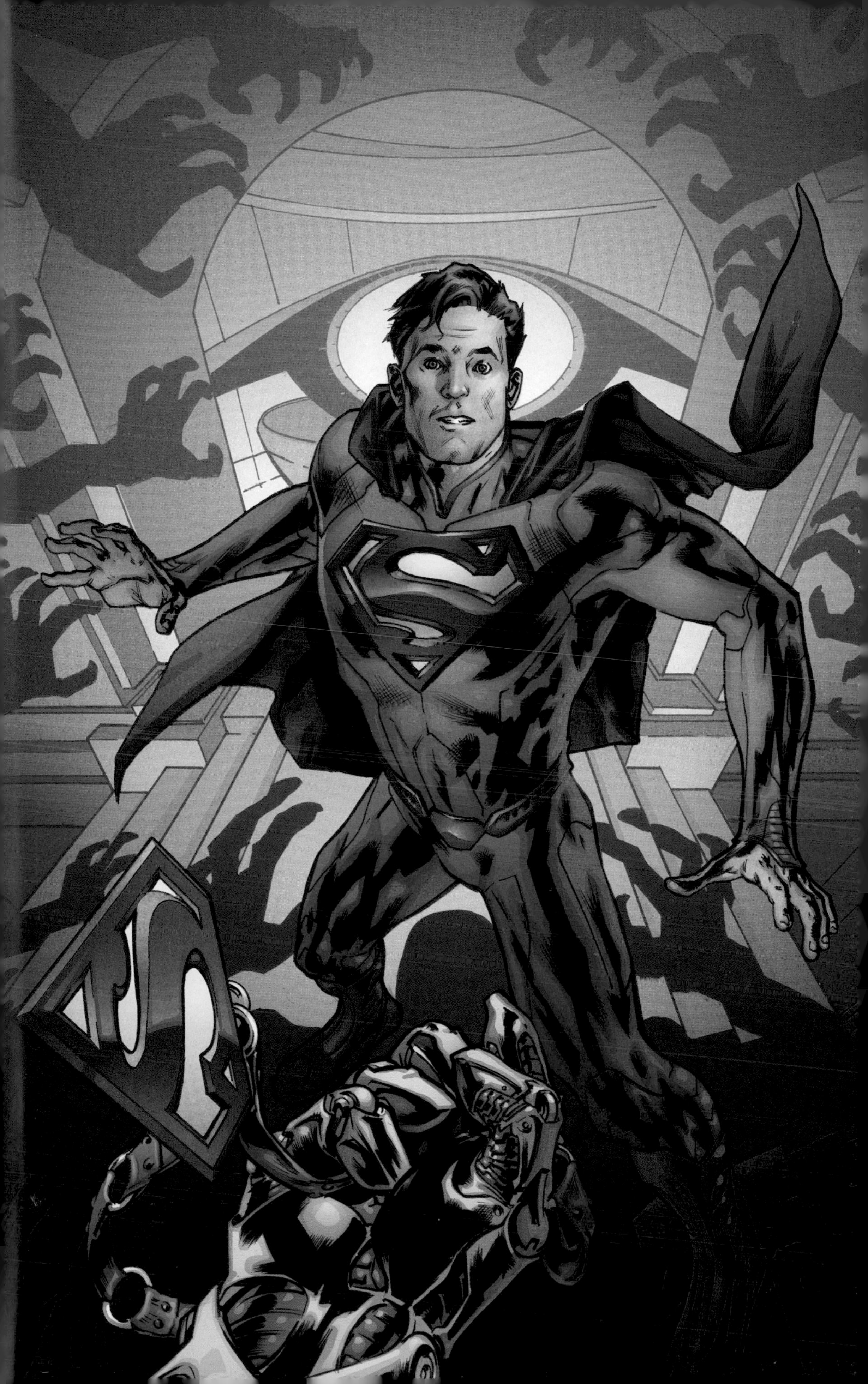

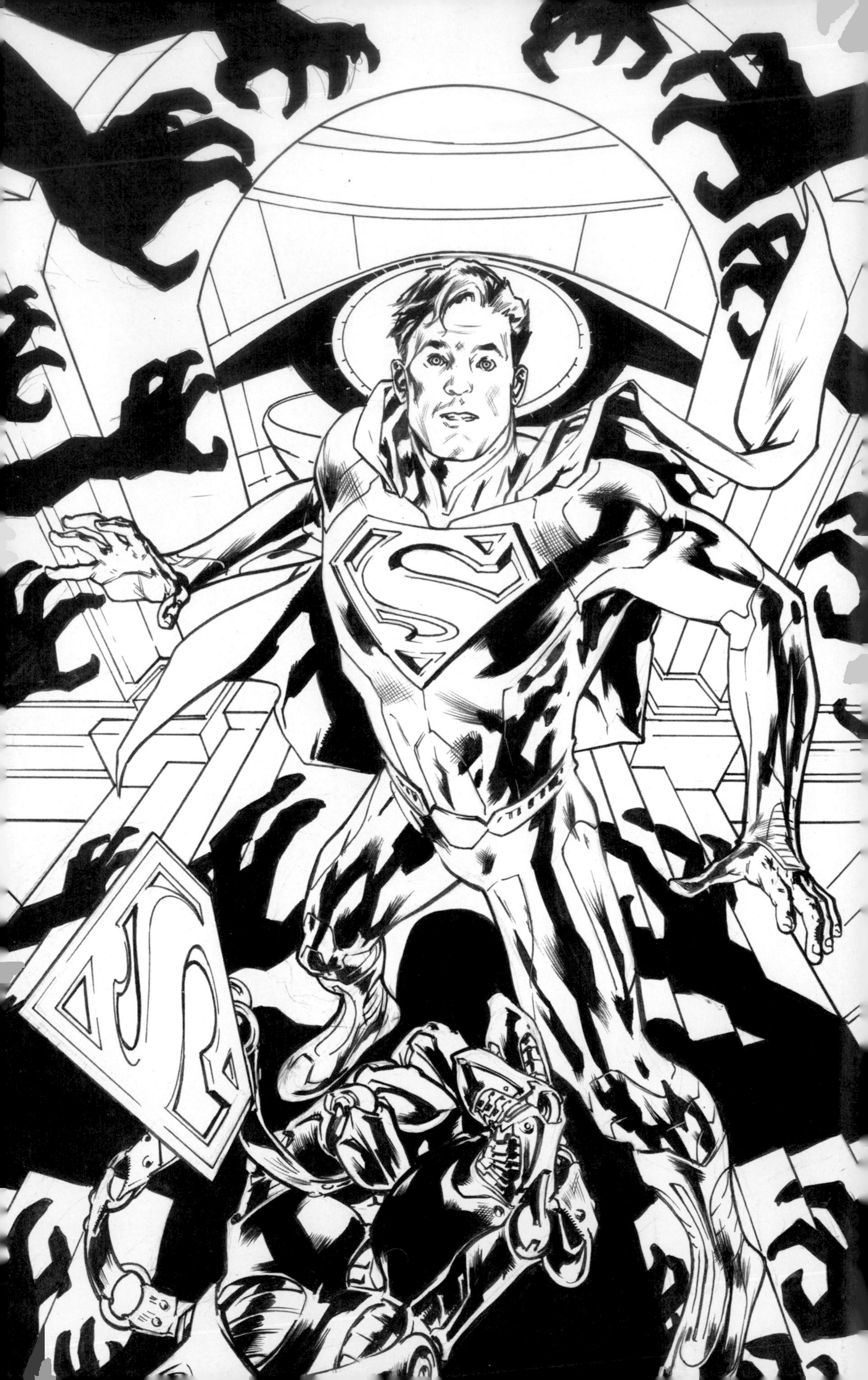

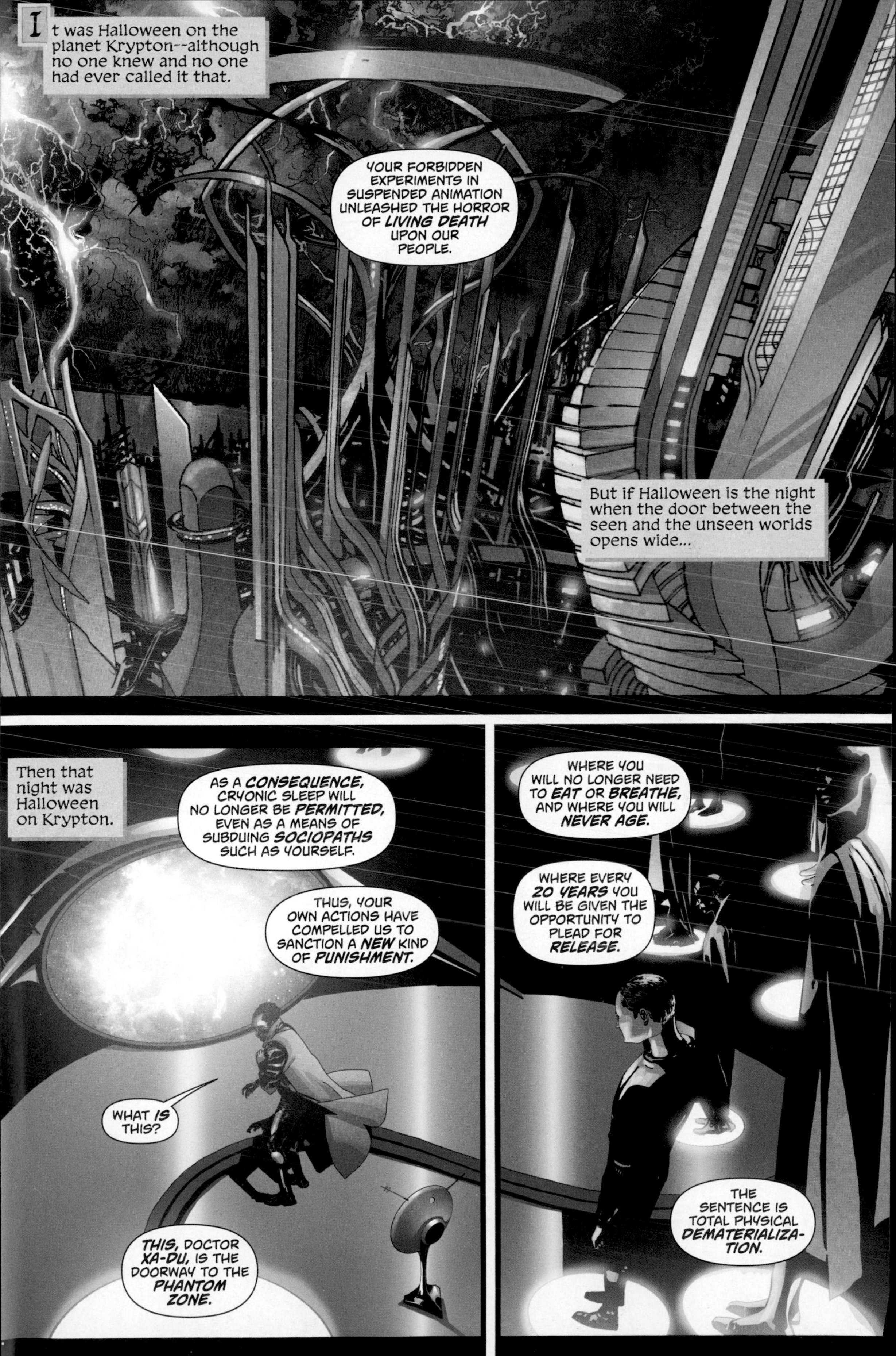
It was Halloween on the planet Krypton--although no one knew and no one had ever called it that.
YOUR FORBIDDEN EXPERIMENTS IN SUSPENDED ANIMATION UNLEASHED THE HORROR OF LIVING DEATH UPON OUR PEOPLE.
But if Halloween is the night when the door between the seen and the unseen worlds opens wide...
Then that night was Halloween on Krypton.
AS A CONSEQUENCE, CRYONIC SLEEP WILL NO LONGER BE PERMITTED, EVEN AS A MEANS OF SUBDUING SOCIOPATHS SUCH AS YOURSELF.
THUS, YOUR OWN ACTIONS HAVE COMPELLED US TO SANCTION A NEW KIND OF PUNISHMENT.
WHAT IS THIS?
THIS, DOCTOR XA-DU, IS THE DOORWAY TO THE PHANTOM ZONE.
WHERE YOU WILL NO LONGER NEED TO EAT OR BREATHE, AND WHERE YOU WILL NEVER AGE.
WHERE EVERY 20 YEARS YOU WILL BE GIVEN THE OPPORTUNITY TO PLEAD FOR RELEASE.
THE SENTENCE IS TOTAL PHYSICAL DEMATERIALIZA-TION.

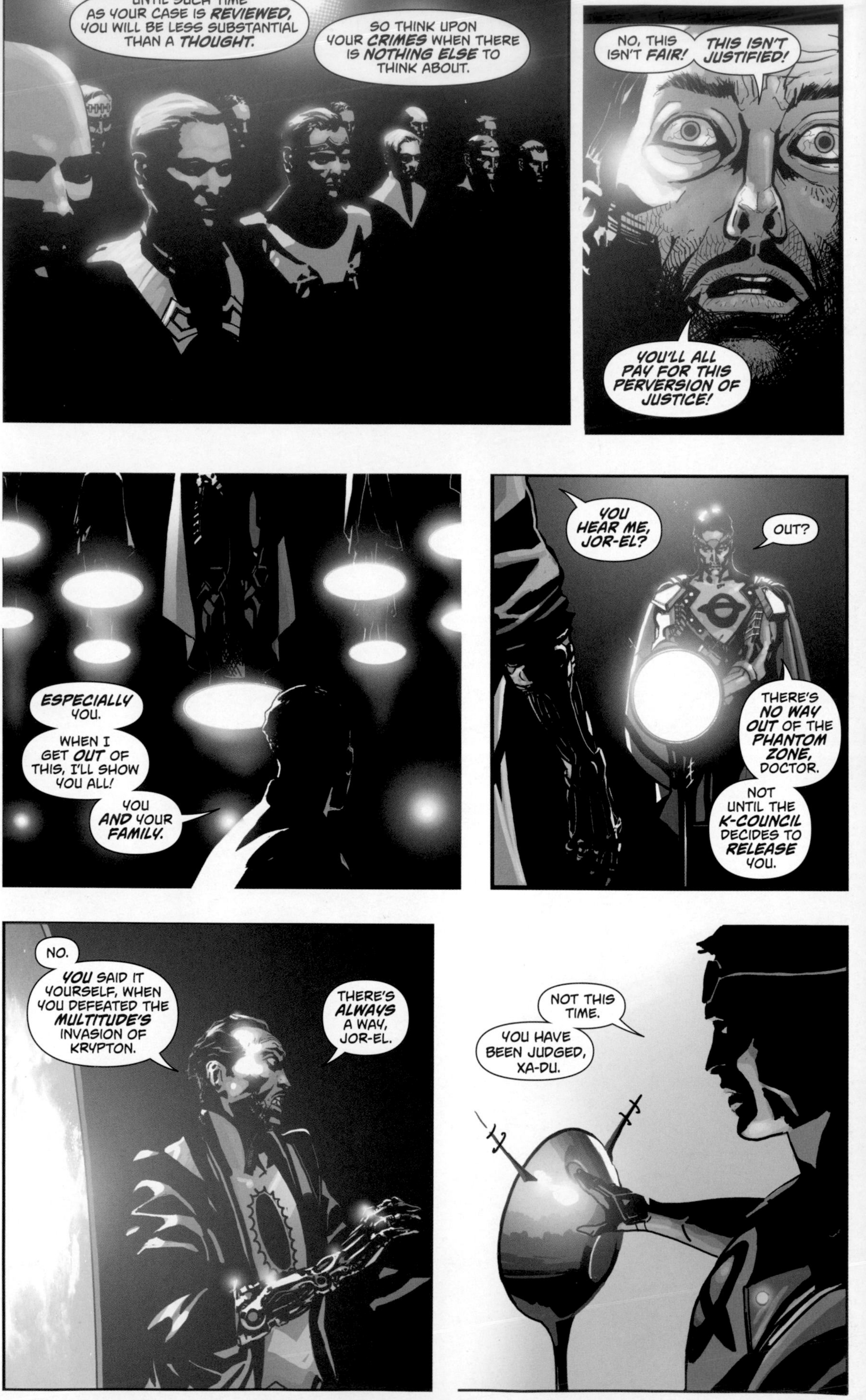
UNTIL SUCH TIME AS YOUR CASE IS REVIEWED, YOU WILL BE LESS SUBSTANTIAL THAN A THOUGHT.
SO THINK UPON YOUR CRIMES WHEN THERE IS NOTHING ELSE TO THINK ABOUT.
NO, THIS ISN'T FAIR!
THIS ISN'T JUSTIFIED!
YOU'LL ALL PAY FOR THIS PERVERSION OF JUSTICE!
ESPECIALLY YOU.
WHEN I GET OUT OF THIS, I'LL SHOW YOU ALL!
YOU AND YOUR FAMILY.
YOU HEAR ME, JOR-EL?
OUT?
THERE'S NO WAY OUT OF THE PHANTOM ZONE, DOCTOR.
NOT UNTIL THE K-COUNCIL DECIDES TO RELEASE YOU.
NO.
YOU SAID IT YOURSELF, WHEN YOU DEFEATED THE MULTITUDE'S INVASION OF KRYPTON.
THERE'S ALWAYS A WAY, JOR-EL.
NOT THIS TIME.
YOU HAVE BEEN JUDGED, XA-DU.

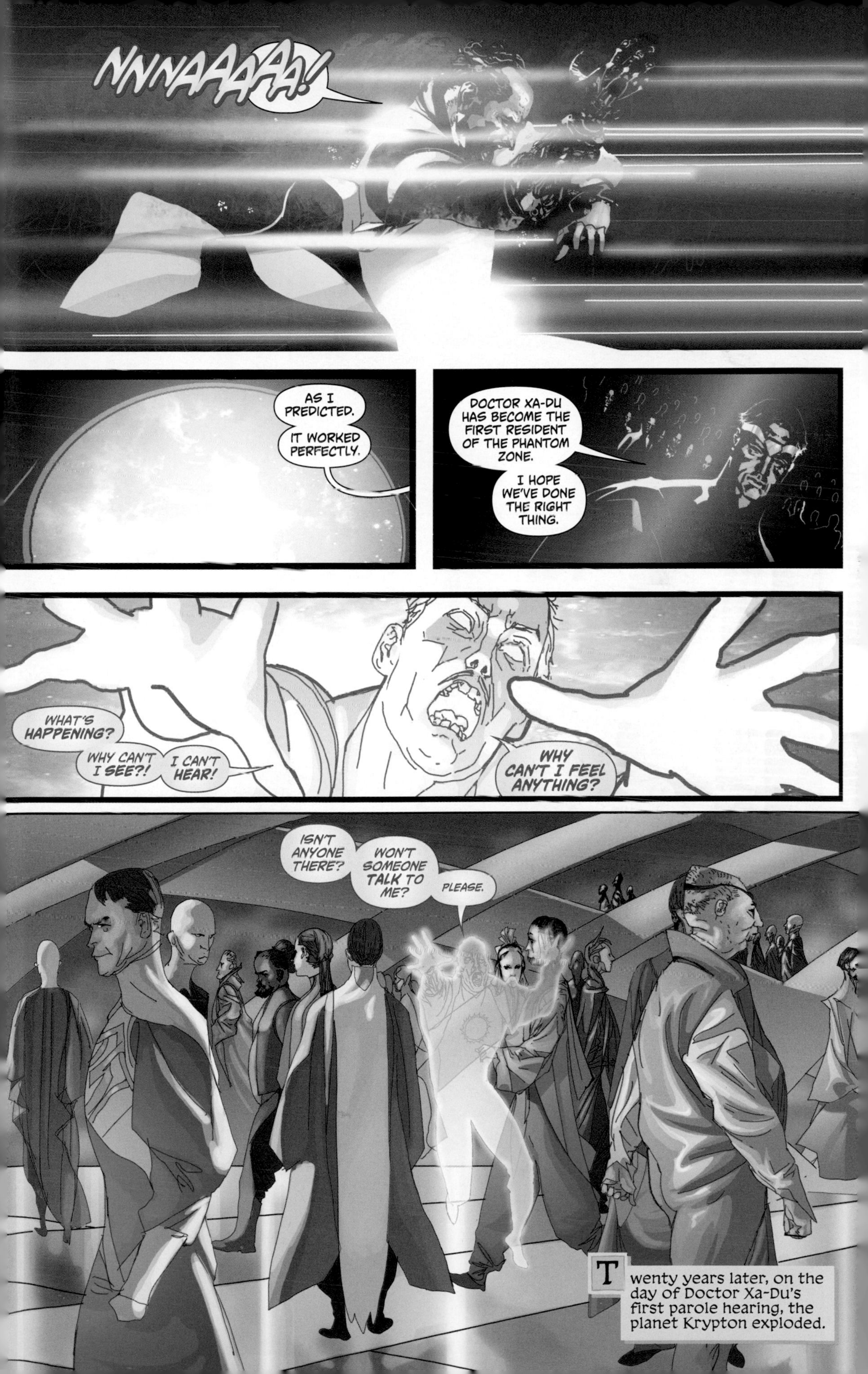
NNNAAAAAA!
AS I PREDICTED.
IT WORKED PERFECTLY.
DOCTOR XA-DU HAS BECOME THE FIRST RESIDENT OF THE PHANTOM ZONE.
I HOPE WE'VE DONE THE RIGHT THING.
WHAT'S HAPPENING?
WHY CAN'T I SEE?!
I CAN'T HEAR!
WHY CAN'T I FEEL ANYTHING?
ISN'T ANYONE THERE?
WON'T SOMEONE TALK TO ME?
PLEASE.
Twenty years later, on the day of Doctor Xa-Du's first parole hearing, the planet Krypton exploded.

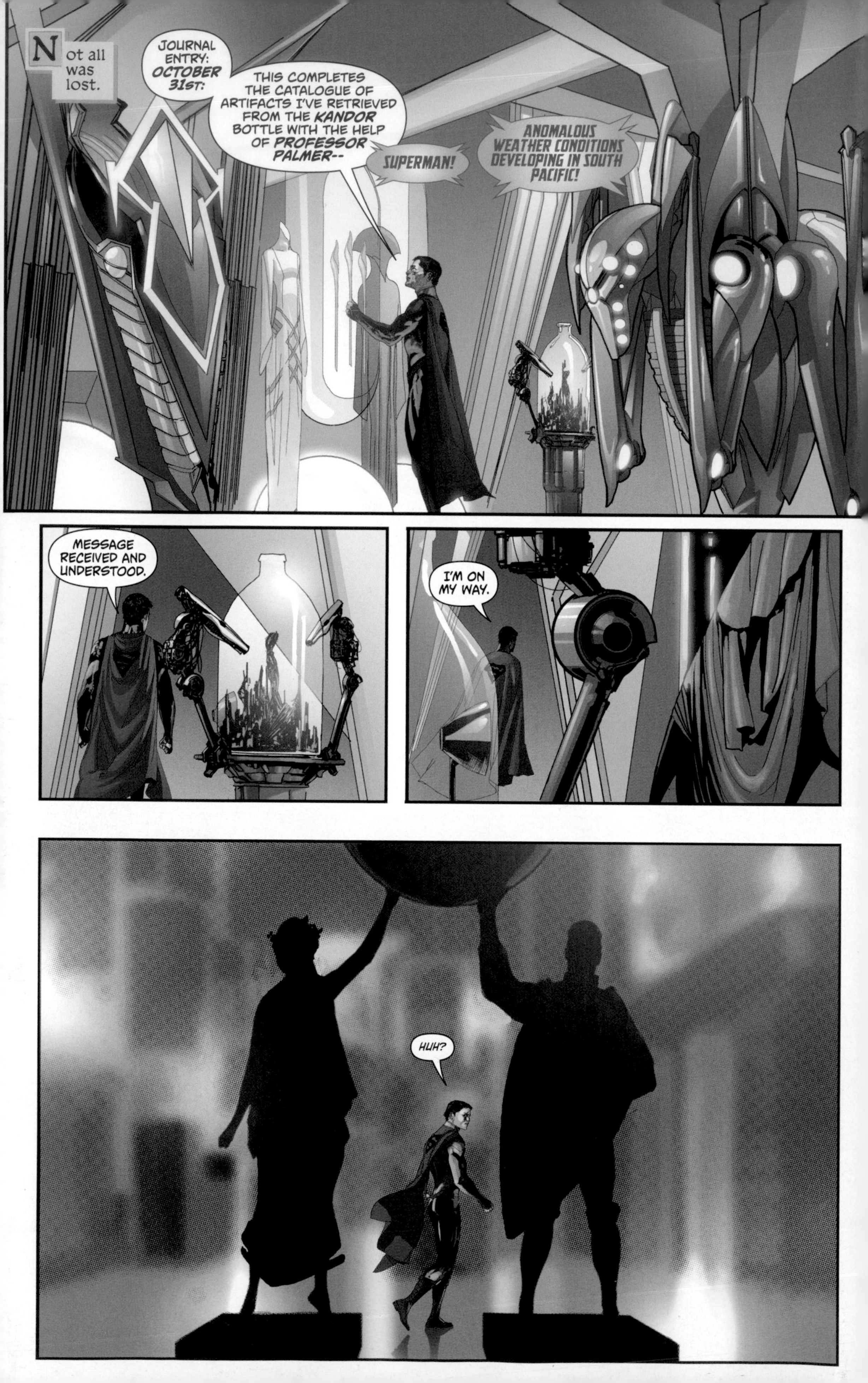
Not all was lost.
JOURNAL ENTRY: OCTOBER 31st:
THIS COMPLETES THE CATALOGUE OF ARTIFACTS I'VE RETRIEVED FROM THE KANDOR BOTTLE WITH THE HELP OF PROFESSOR PALMER--
SUPERMAN!
ANOMALOUS WEATHER CONDITIONS DEVELOPING IN SOUTH PACIFIC!
MESSAGE RECEIVED AND UNDERSTOOD.
I'M ON MY WAY.
HUH?

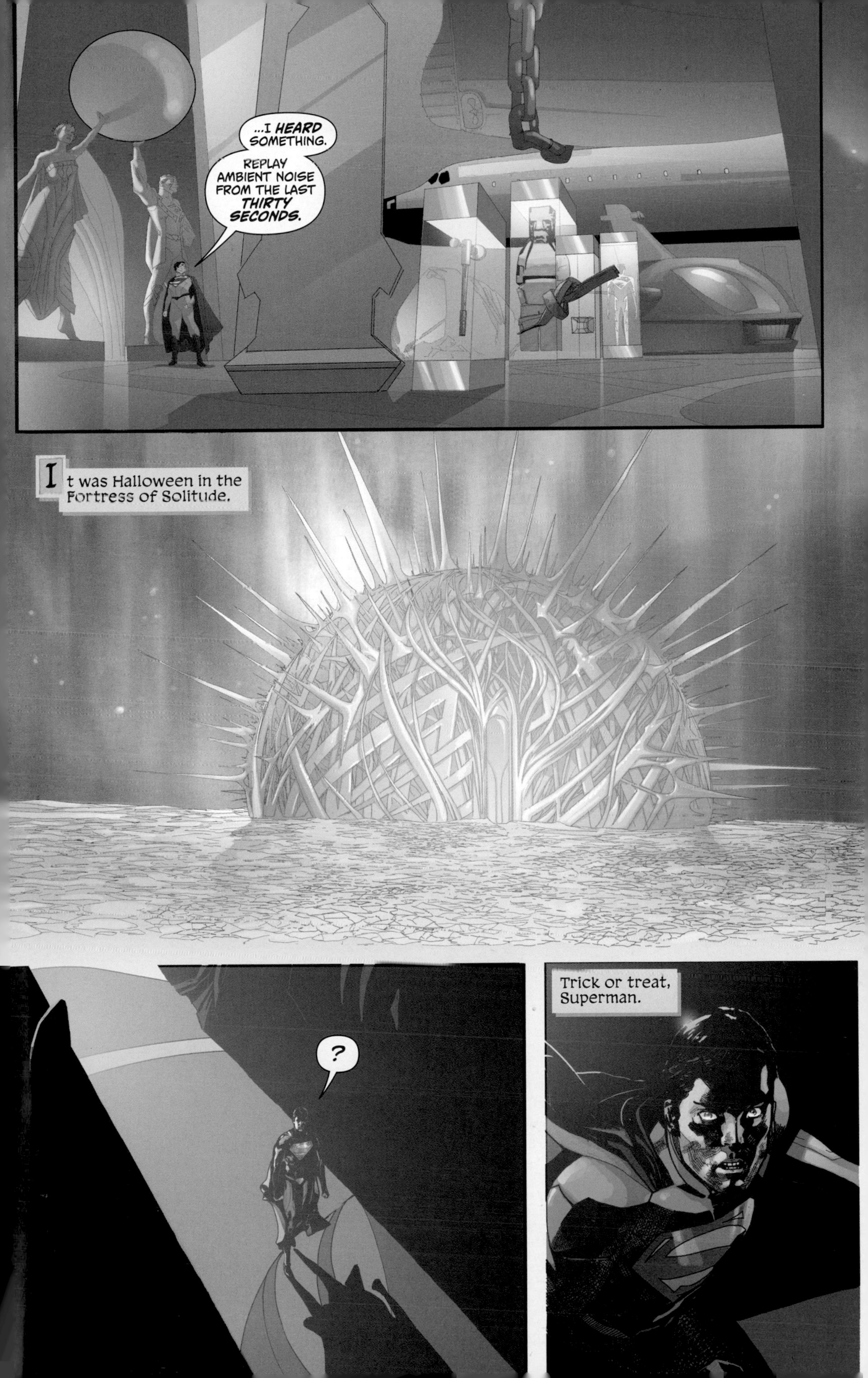
...I HEARD SOMETHING.
REPLAY AMBIENT NOISE FROM THE LAST THIRTY SECONDS.
It was Halloween in the Fortress of Solitude.
?
Trick or treat, Superman.

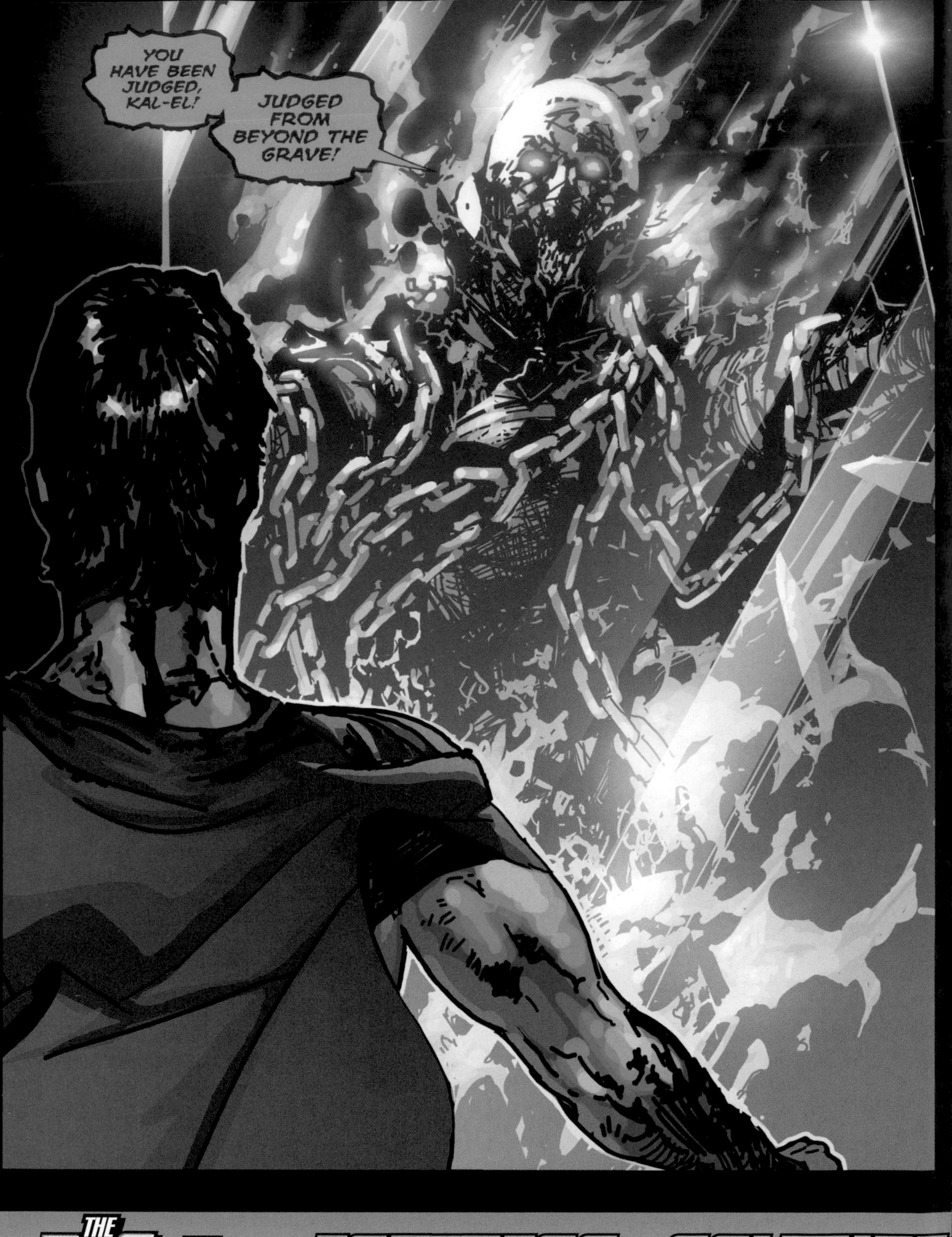
YOU HAVE BEEN JUDGED, KAL-EL!
JUDGED FROM BEYOND THE GRAVE!

THE GHOST IN THE FORTRESS OF SOLITUDE

GRANT MORRISON WRITER
TRAVEL FOREMAN ARTIST BRAD ANDERSON COLORIST STEVE WANDS LETTERER
BRYAN HITCH & DAVID BARON COVER RAGS MORALES & ANDERSON VARIANT COVER
WIL MOSS ASSOCIATE EDITOR MATT IDELSON EDITOR
SUPERMAN CREATED BY JERRY SIEGEL & JOE SHUSTER

DEDICATED TO THE GREAT RAY BRADBURY

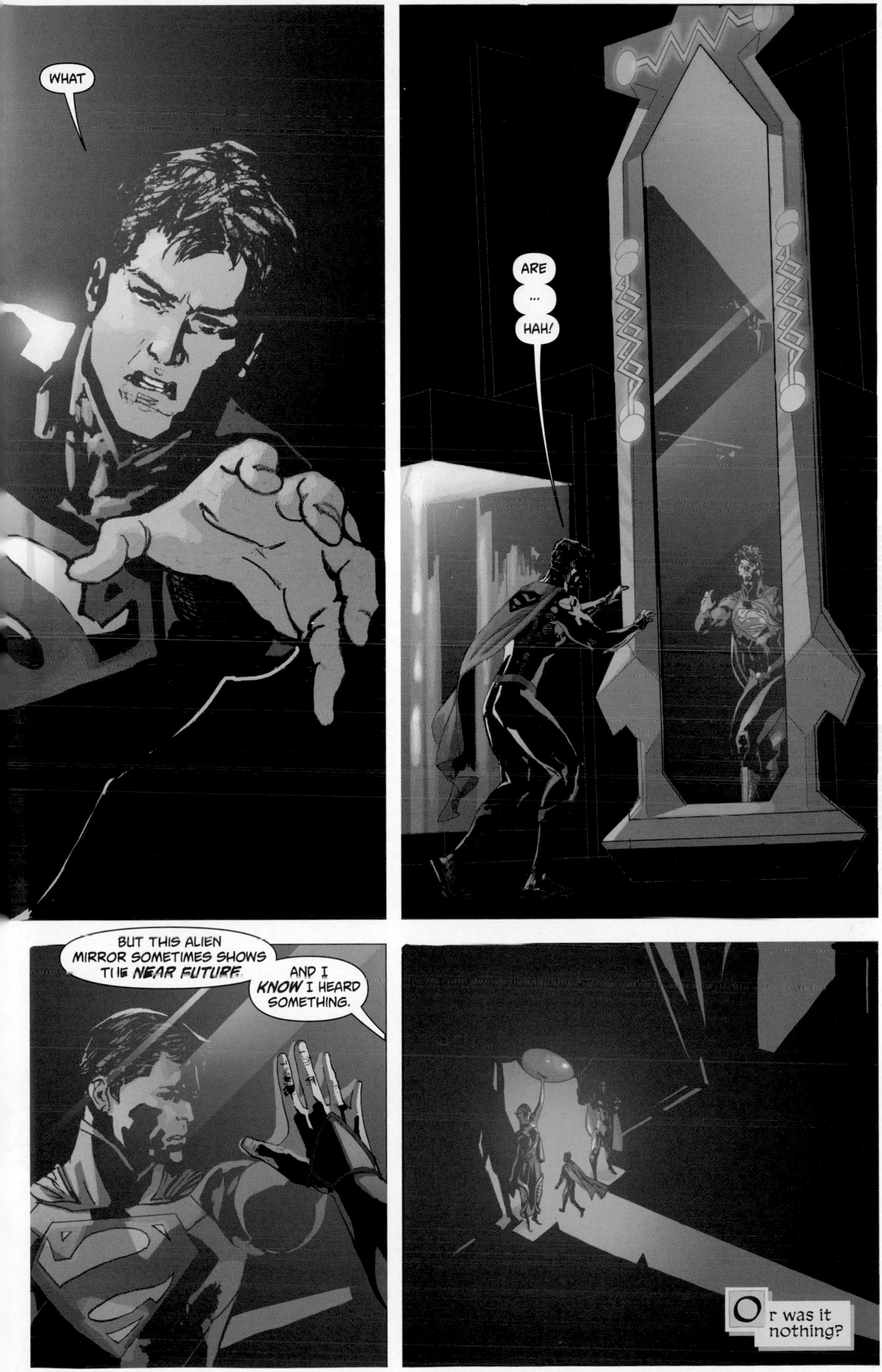
WHAT
ARE
...
HAH!
BUT THIS ALIEN MIRROR SOMETIMES SHOWS THE *NEAR FUTURE*.
AND I *KNOW* I HEARD SOMETHING.
Or was it nothing?

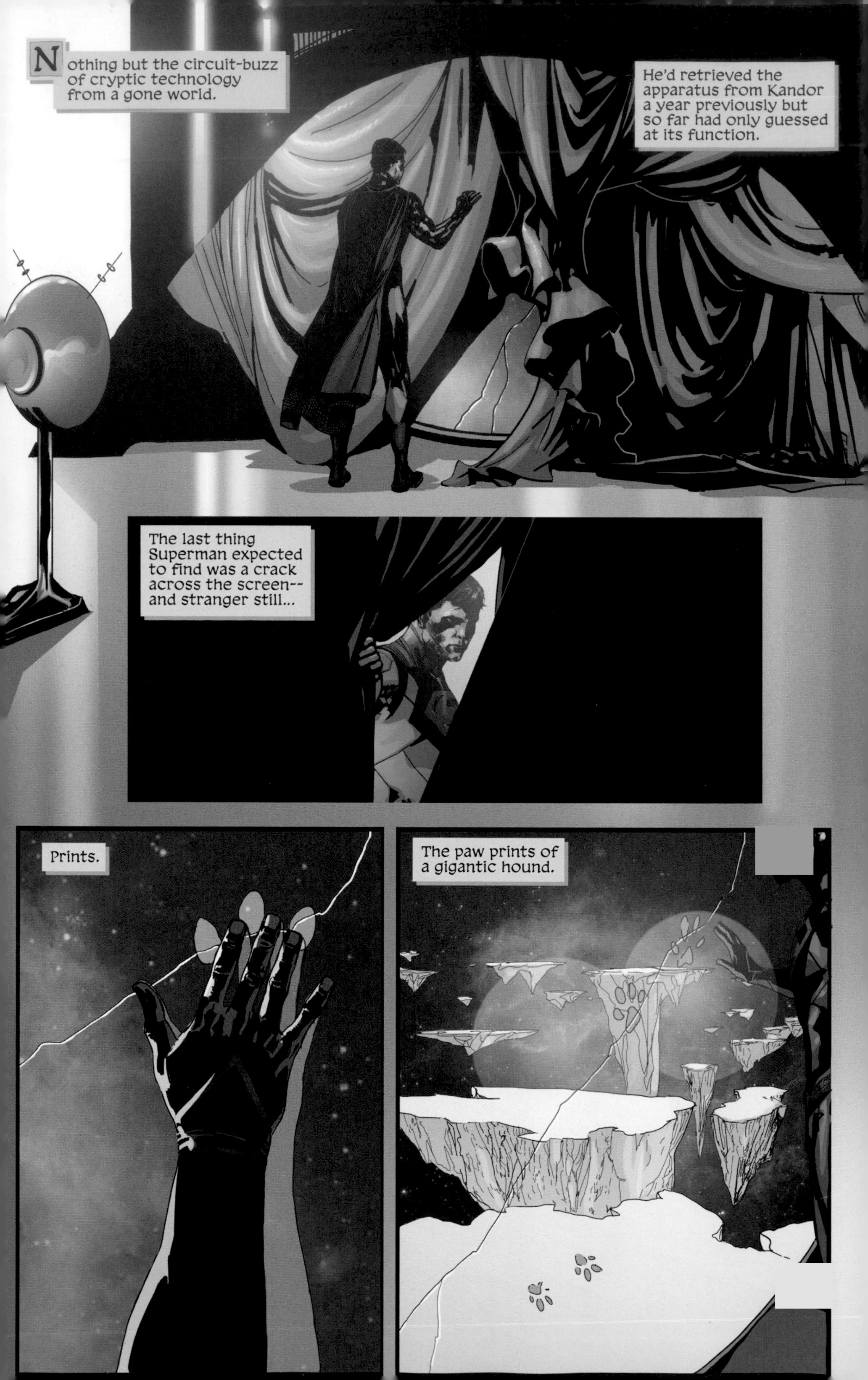
Nothing but the circuit-buzz of cryptic technology from a gone world.
He'd retrieved the apparatus from Kandor a year previously but so far had only guessed at its function.
The last thing Superman expected to find was a crack across the screen-- and stranger still...
Prints.
The paw prints of a gigantic hound.

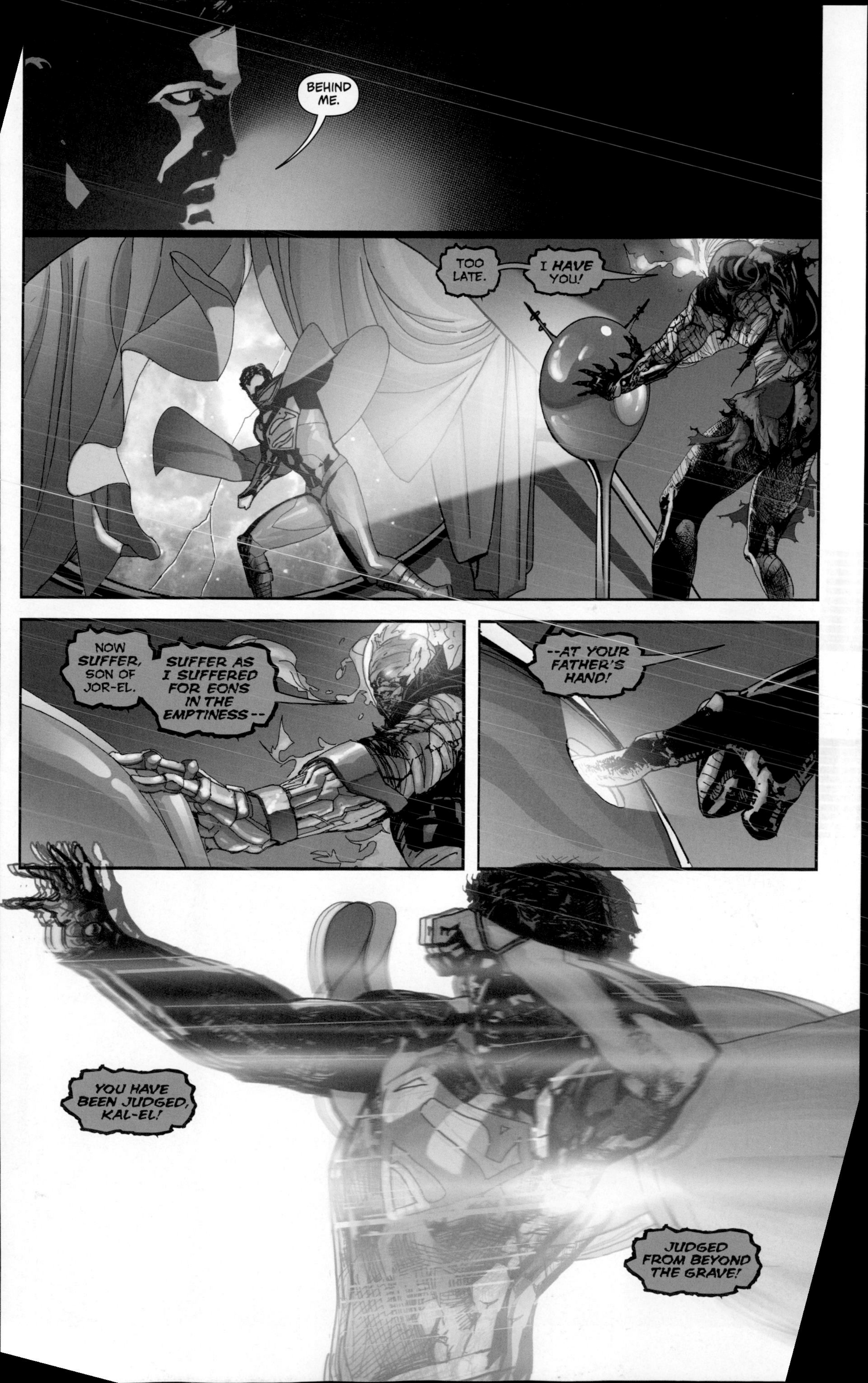
BEHIND ME.
TOO LATE.
I HAVE YOU!
NOW SUFFER, SON OF JOR-EL.
SUFFER AS I SUFFERED FOR EONS IN THE EMPTINESS--
--AT YOUR FATHER'S HAND!
YOU HAVE BEEN JUDGED, KAL-EL!
JUDGED FROM BEYOND THE GRAVE!

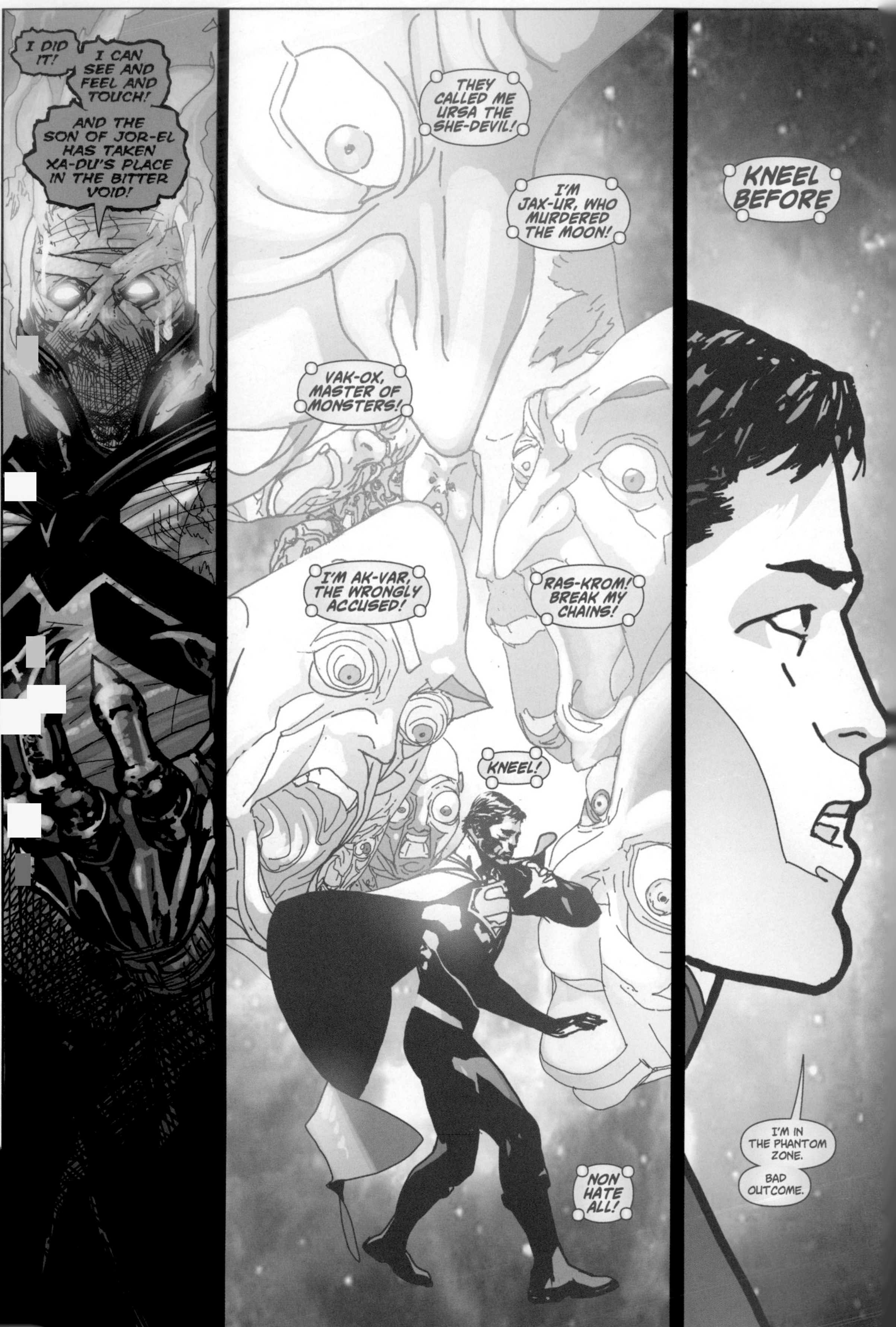
I DID IT!
I CAN SEE AND FEEL AND TOUCH!
AND THE SON OF JOR-EL HAS TAKEN XA-DU'S PLACE IN THE BITTER VOID!
THEY CALLED ME URSA THE SHE-DEVIL!
I'M JAX-UR, WHO MURDERED THE MOON!
VAK-OX, MASTER OF MONSTERS!
I'M AK-VAR, THE WRONGLY ACCUSED!
RAS-KROM! BREAK MY CHAINS!
KNEEL!
NON HATE ALL!
KNEEL BEFORE
I'M IN THE PHANTOM ZONE.
BAD OUTCOME.

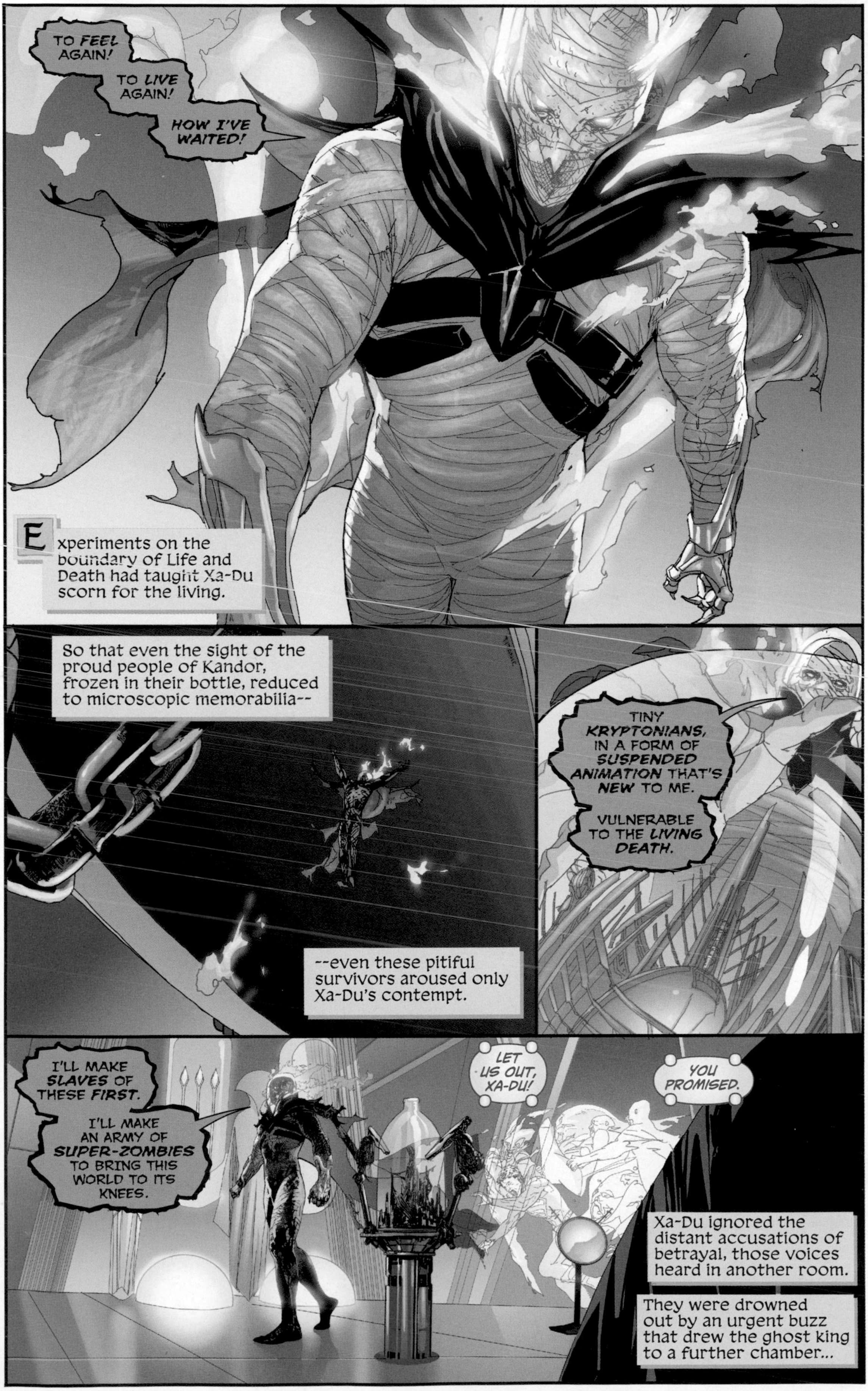
TO FEEL AGAIN!
TO LIVE AGAIN!
HOW I'VE WAITED!
Experiments on the boundary of Life and Death had taught Xa-Du scorn for the living.
So that even the sight of the proud people of Kandor, frozen in their bottle, reduced to microscopic memorabilia--
--even these pitiful survivors aroused only Xa-Du's contempt.
TINY KRYPTONIANS, IN A FORM OF SUSPENDED ANIMATION THAT'S NEW TO ME.
VULNERABLE TO THE LIVING DEATH.
I'LL MAKE SLAVES OF THESE FIRST.
I'LL MAKE AN ARMY OF SUPER-ZOMBIES TO BRING THIS WORLD TO ITS KNEES.
LET US OUT, XA-DU!
YOU PROMISED.
Xa-Du ignored the distant accusations of betrayal, those voices heard in another room.
They were drowned out by an urgent buzz that drew the ghost king to a further chamber...

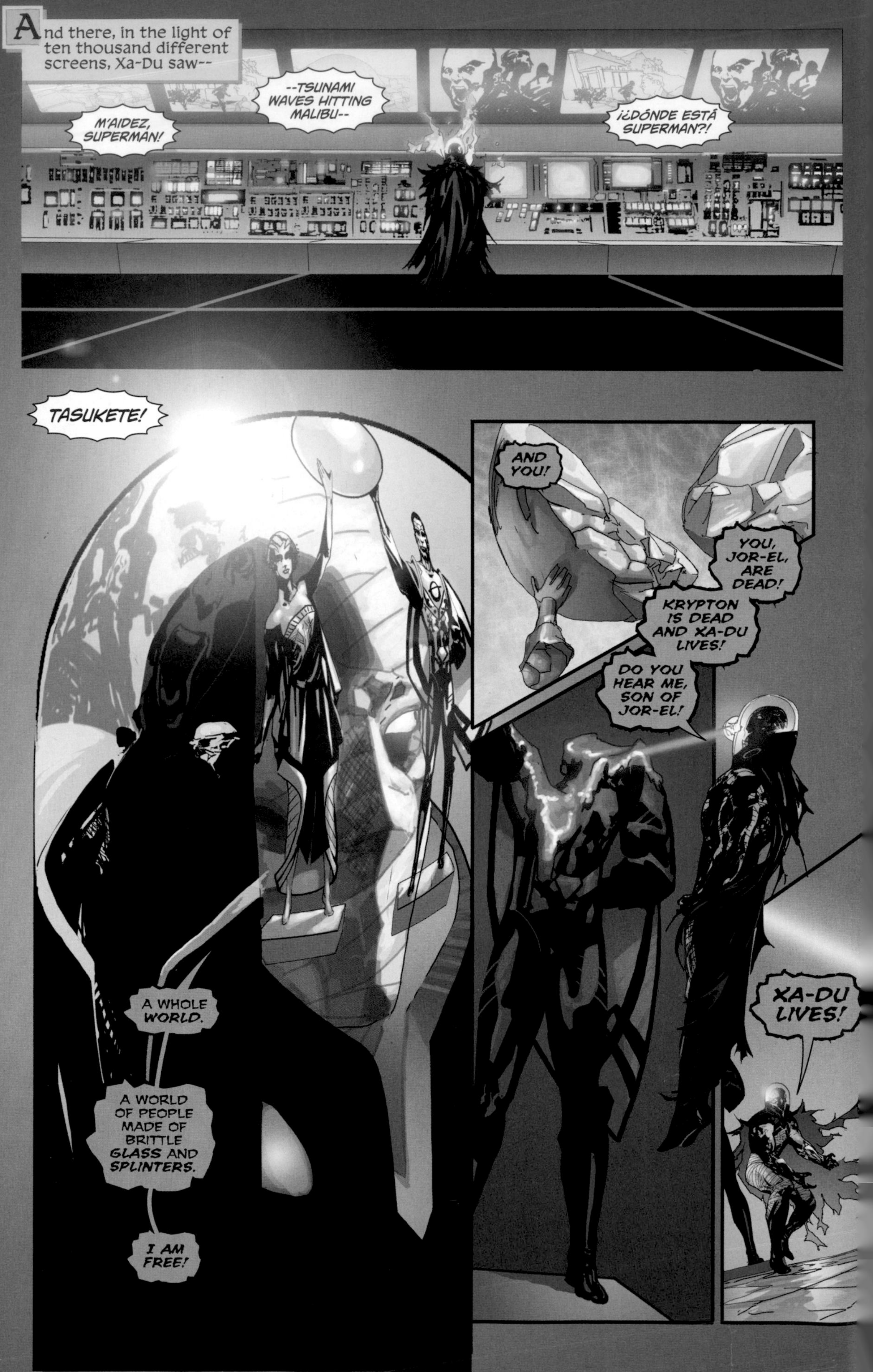
And there, in the light of ten thousand different screens, Xa-Du saw--
M'AIDEZ, SUPERMAN!
--TSUNAMI WAVES HITTING MALIBU--
¡¿DÓNDE ESTÁ SUPERMAN?!
TASUKETE!
A WHOLE WORLD.
A WORLD OF PEOPLE MADE OF BRITTLE GLASS AND SPLINTERS.
I AM FREE!
AND YOU!
YOU, JOR-EL, ARE DEAD!
KRYPTON IS DEAD AND XA-DU LIVES!
DO YOU HEAR ME, SON OF JOR-EL!
XA-DU LIVES!

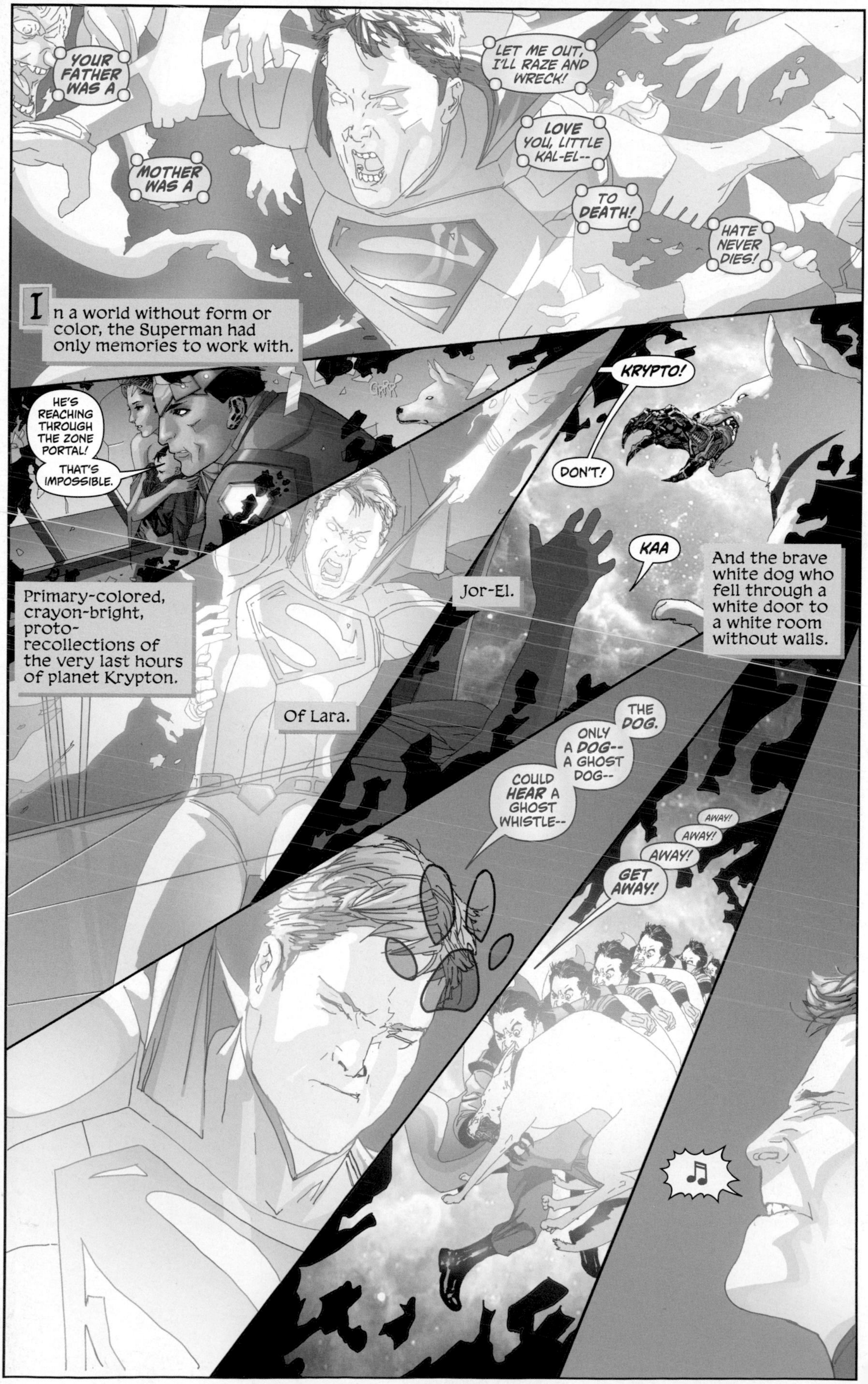
YOUR FATHER WAS A
LET ME OUT, I'LL RAZE AND WRECK!
LOVE YOU, LITTLE KAL-EL--
MOTHER WAS A
TO DEATH!
HATE NEVER DIES!
In a world without form or color, the Superman had only memories to work with.
HE'S REACHING THROUGH THE ZONE PORTAL!
THAT'S IMPOSSIBLE.
GRRR
KRYPTO!
DON'T!
Primary-colored, crayon-bright, proto-recollections of the very last hours of planet Krypton.
Jor-El.
KAA
And the brave white dog who fell through a white door to a white room without walls.
Of Lara.
THE DOG.
ONLY A DOG-- A GHOST DOG--
COULD HEAR A GHOST WHISTLE--
AWAY!
AWAY!
AWAY!
GET AWAY!
♫

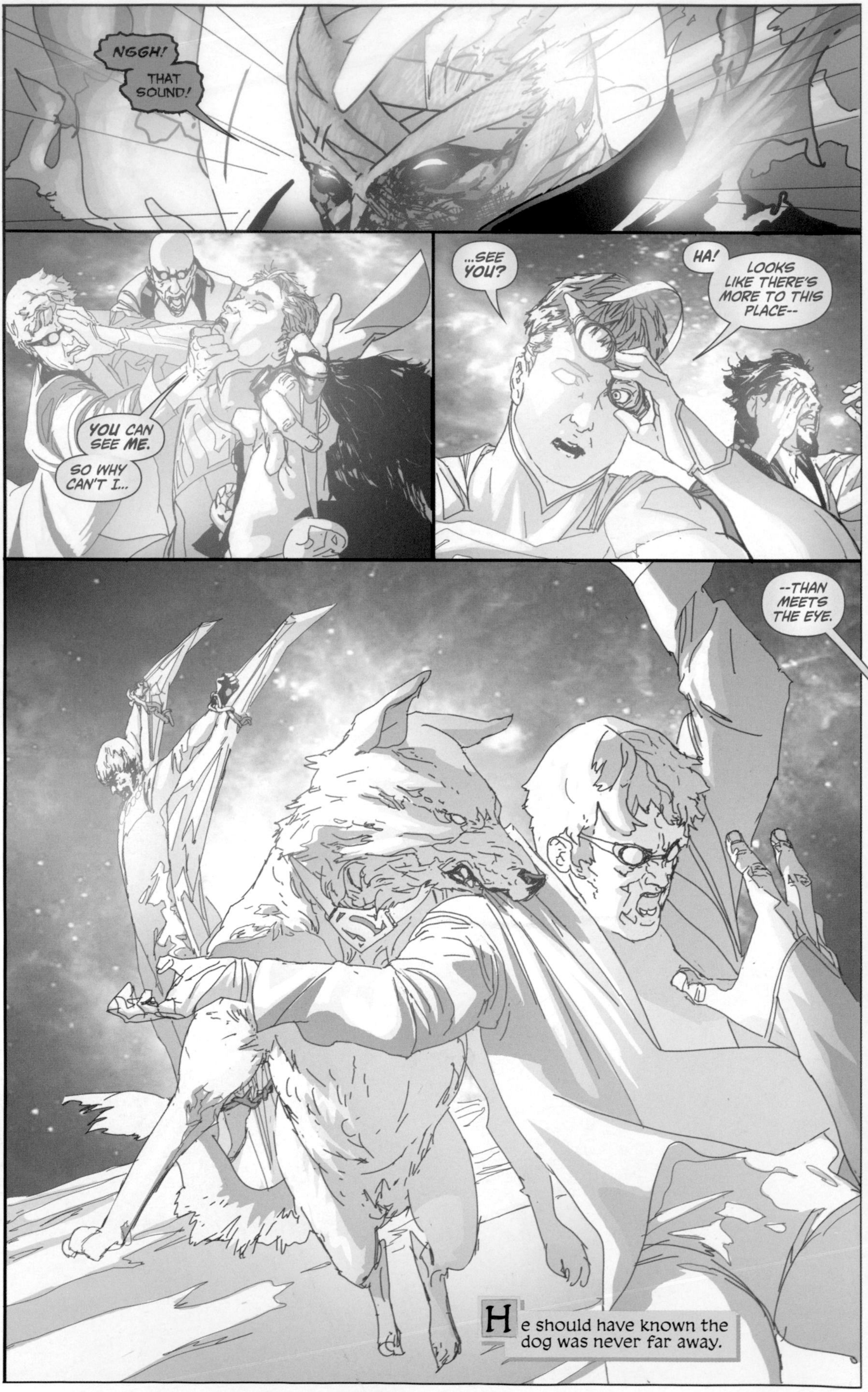
NGGH!
THAT SOUND!
YOU CAN SEE ME.
SO WHY CAN'T I...
...SEE YOU?
HA!
LOOKS LIKE THERE'S MORE TO THIS PLACE--
--THAN MEETS THE EYE.
He should have known the dog was never far away.

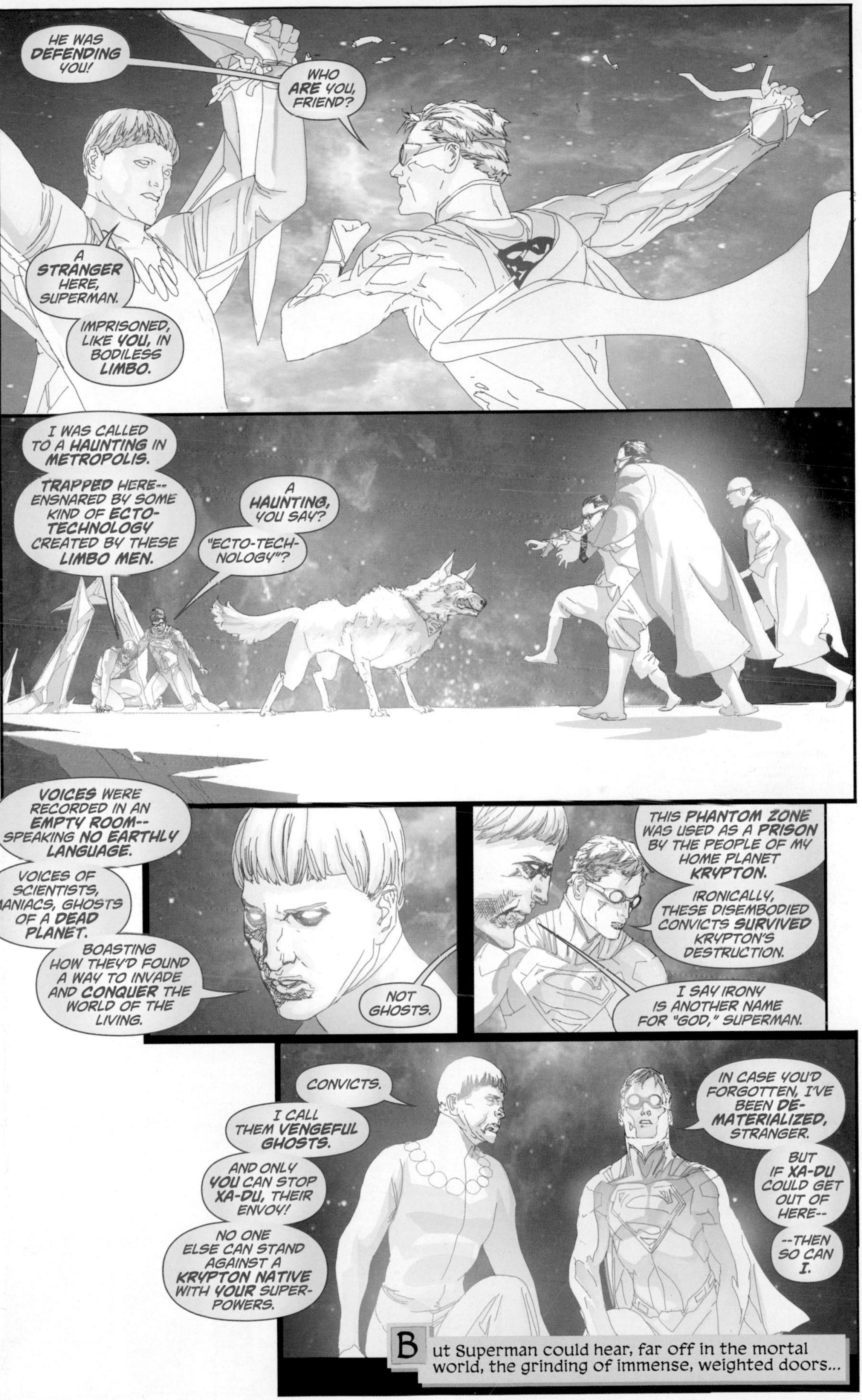
HE WAS DEFENDING YOU!
WHO ARE YOU, FRIEND?
A STRANGER HERE, SUPERMAN.
IMPRISONED, LIKE YOU, IN BODILESS LIMBO.
I WAS CALLED TO A HAUNTING IN METROPOLIS.
TRAPPED HERE-- ENSNARED BY SOME KIND OF ECTO-TECHNOLOGY CREATED BY THESE LIMBO MEN.
A HAUNTING, YOU SAY?
"ECTO-TECH-NOLOGY"?
VOICES WERE RECORDED IN AN EMPTY ROOM-- SPEAKING NO EARTHLY LANGUAGE.
VOICES OF SCIENTISTS, MANIACS, GHOSTS OF A DEAD PLANET.
BOASTING HOW THEY'D FOUND A WAY TO INVADE AND CONQUER THE WORLD OF THE LIVING.
NOT GHOSTS.
THIS PHANTOM ZONE WAS USED AS A PRISON BY THE PEOPLE OF MY HOME PLANET KRYPTON.
IRONICALLY, THESE DISEMBODIED CONVICTS SURVIVED KRYPTON'S DESTRUCTION.
I SAY IRONY IS ANOTHER NAME FOR "GOD," SUPERMAN.
CONVICTS.
I CALL THEM VENGEFUL GHOSTS.
AND ONLY YOU CAN STOP XA-DU, THEIR ENVOY!
NO ONE ELSE CAN STAND AGAINST A KRYPTON NATIVE WITH YOUR SUPER-POWERS.
IN CASE YOU'D FORGOTTEN, I'VE BEEN DE-MATERIALIZED, STRANGER.
BUT IF XA-DU COULD GET OUT OF HERE--
--THEN SO CAN I.
But Superman could hear, far off in the mortal world, the grinding of immense, weighted doors...

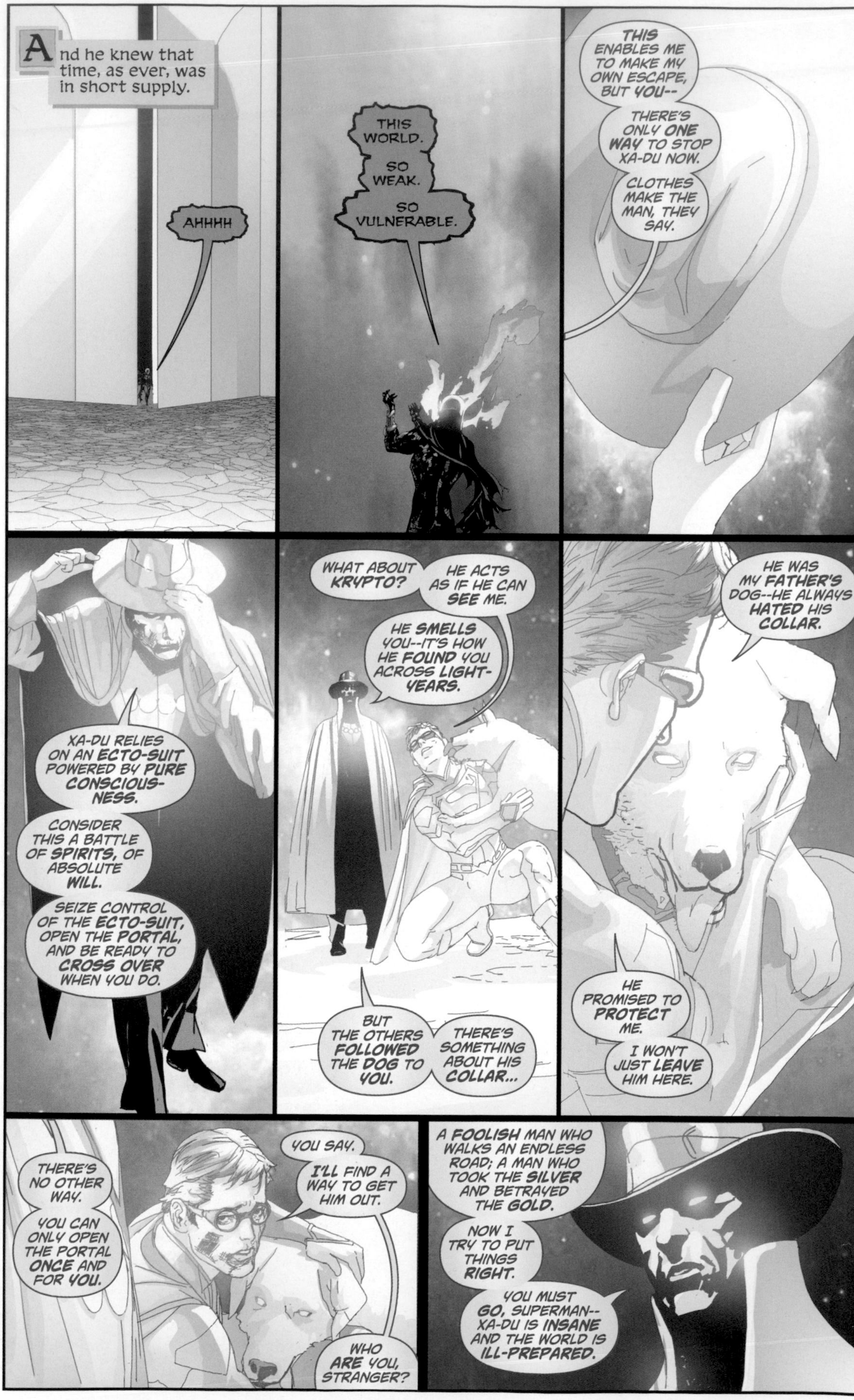
And he knew that time, as ever, was in short supply.
AHHHH
THIS WORLD.
SO WEAK.
SO VULNERABLE.
THIS ENABLES ME TO MAKE MY OWN ESCAPE, BUT YOU--
THERE'S ONLY ONE WAY TO STOP XA-DU NOW.
CLOTHES MAKE THE MAN, THEY SAY.
XA-DU RELIES ON AN ECTO-SUIT POWERED BY PURE CONSCIOUS-NESS.
CONSIDER THIS A BATTLE OF SPIRITS, OF ABSOLUTE WILL.
SEIZE CONTROL OF THE ECTO-SUIT, OPEN THE PORTAL, AND BE READY TO CROSS OVER WHEN YOU DO.
WHAT ABOUT KRYPTO?
HE ACTS AS IF HE CAN SEE ME.
HE SMELLS YOU--IT'S HOW HE FOUND YOU ACROSS LIGHT-YEARS.
BUT THE OTHERS FOLLOWED THE DOG TO YOU.
THERE'S SOMETHING ABOUT HIS COLLAR...
HE WAS MY FATHER'S DOG--HE ALWAYS HATED HIS COLLAR.
HE PROMISED TO PROTECT ME.
I WON'T JUST LEAVE HIM HERE.
THERE'S NO OTHER WAY.
YOU CAN ONLY OPEN THE PORTAL ONCE AND FOR YOU.
YOU SAY.
I'LL FIND A WAY TO GET HIM OUT.
WHO ARE YOU, STRANGER?
A FOOLISH MAN WHO WALKS AN ENDLESS ROAD; A MAN WHO TOOK THE SILVER AND BETRAYED THE GOLD.
NOW I TRY TO PUT THINGS RIGHT.
YOU MUST GO, SUPERMAN--XA-DU IS INSANE AND THE WORLD IS ILL-PREPARED.

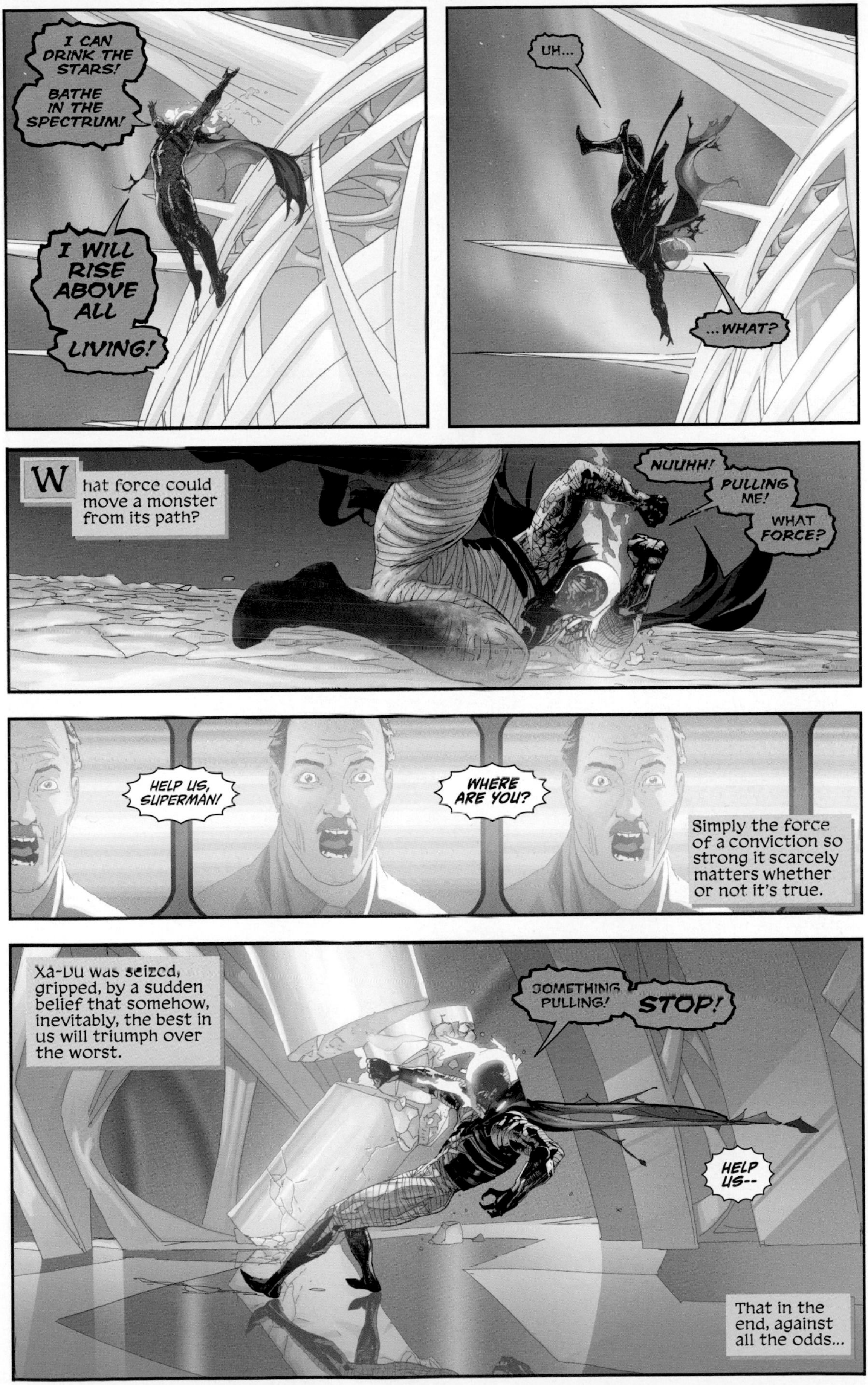

I CAN DRINK THE STARS!
BATHE IN THE SPECTRUM!
I WILL RISE ABOVE ALL LIVING!
UH...
...WHAT?
What force could move a monster from its path?
NUUHH!
PULLING ME!
WHAT FORCE?
HELP US, SUPERMAN!
WHERE ARE YOU?
Simply the force of a conviction so strong it scarcely matters whether or not it's true.
Xa-Du was seized, gripped, by a sudden belief that somehow, inevitably, the best in us will triumph over the worst.
SOMETHING PULLING!
STOP!
HELP US--
That in the end, against all the odds...

...Good is stronger than evil.

MY SUIT!

WHAT HAVE YOU DONE?

I CAN'T GO BACK!

DON'T MAKE MEEEEEE EEE--

HARD...TO ...MOVE...

AIR...LIKE GLUE...

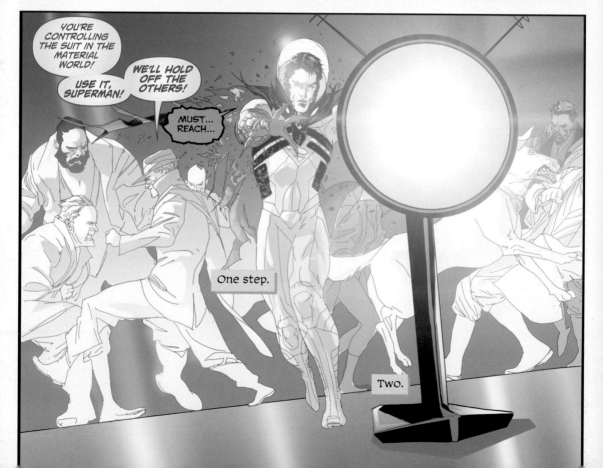

YOU'RE CONTROLLING THE SUIT IN THE MATERIAL WORLD!

USE IT, SUPERMAN!

WE'LL HOLD OFF THE OTHERS!

MUST... REACH...

One step.

Two.

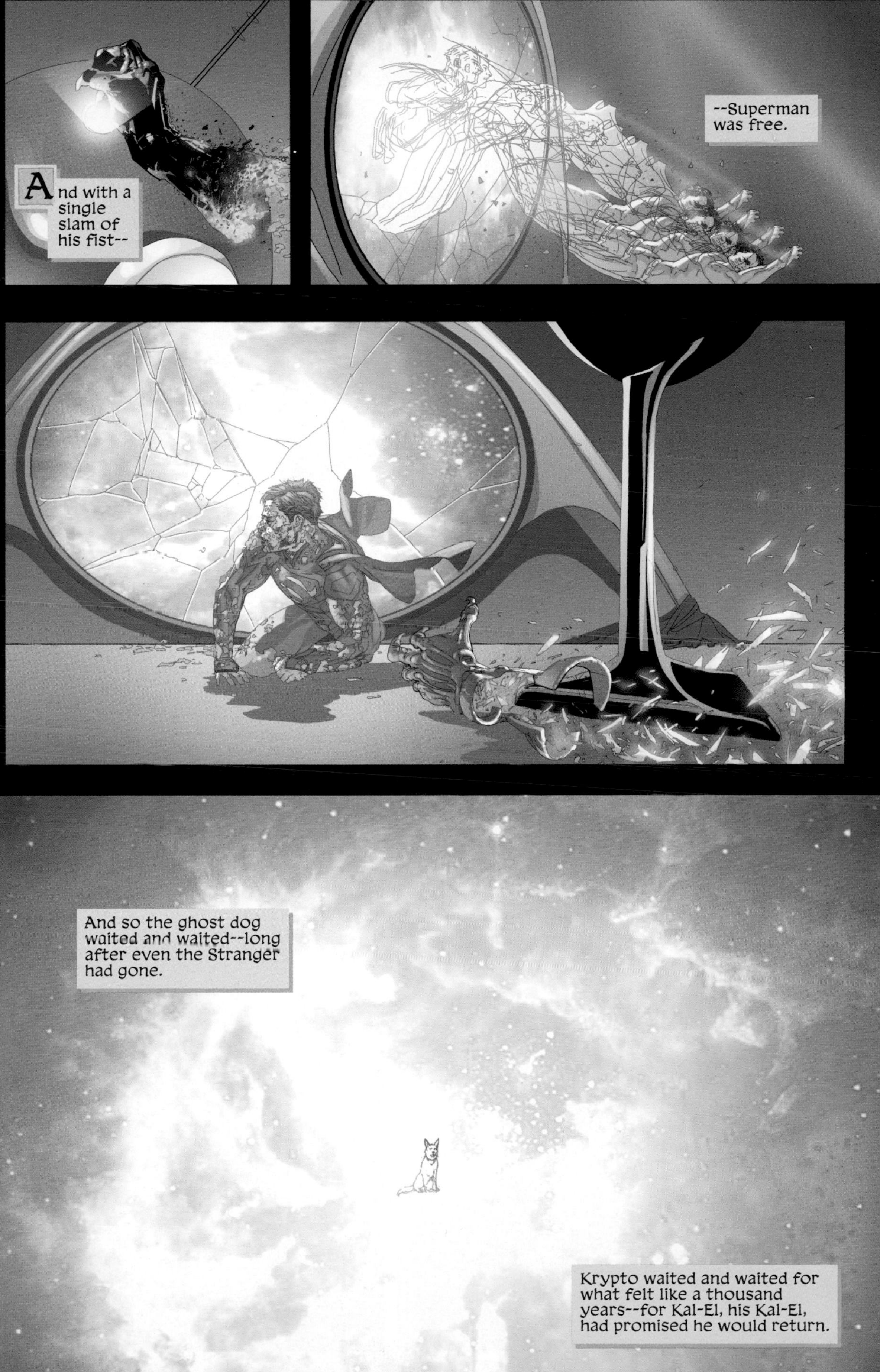
And with a single slam of his fist--
--Superman was free.
And so the ghost dog waited and waited--long after even the Stranger had gone.
Krypto waited and waited for what felt like a thousand years--for Kal-El, his Kal-El, had promised he would return.

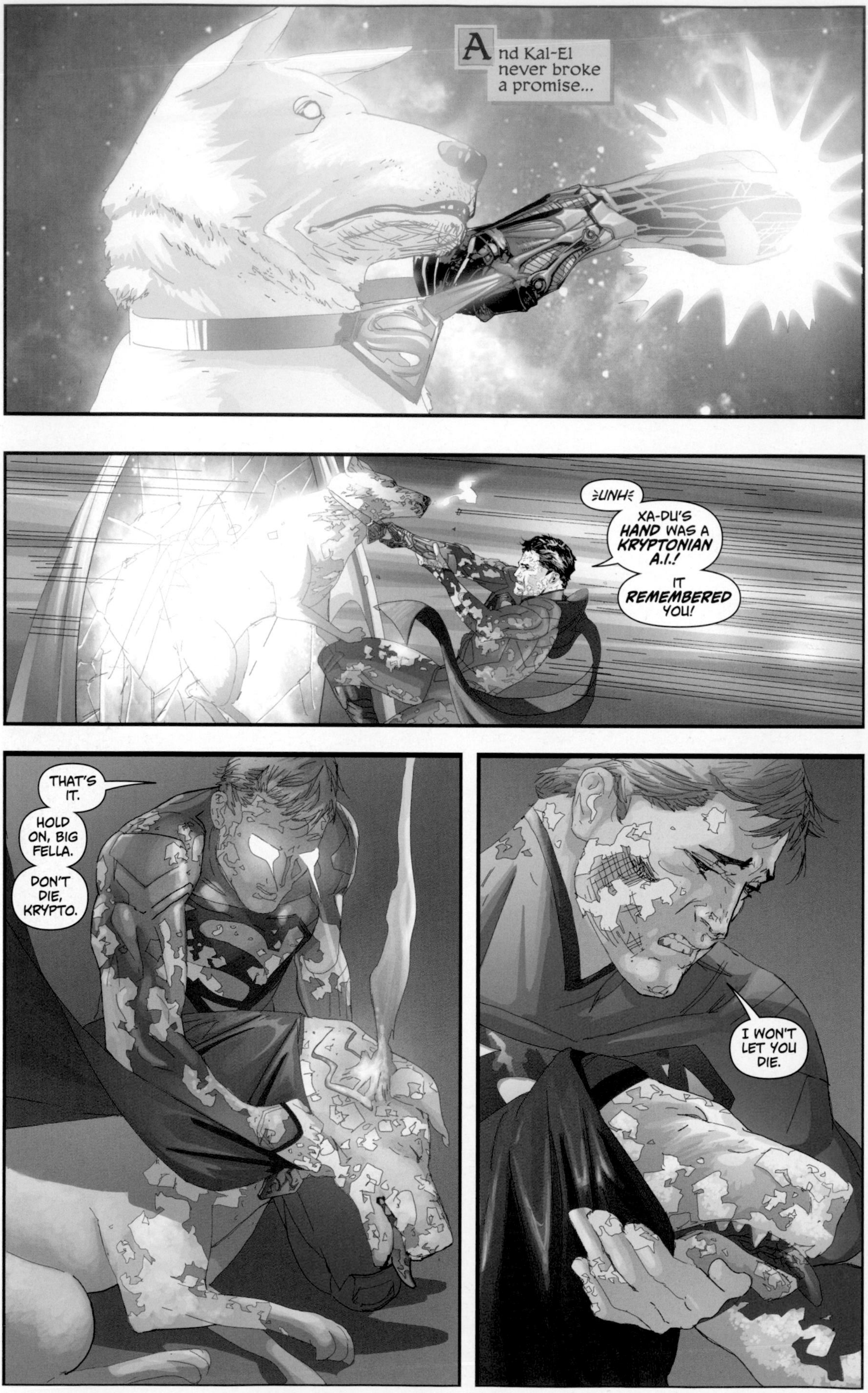
And Kal-El never broke a promise...
UNH
XA-DU'S HAND WAS A KRYPTONIAN A.I.!
IT REMEMBERED YOU!
THAT'S IT.
HOLD ON, BIG FELLA.
DON'T DIE, KRYPTO.
I WON'T LET YOU DIE.

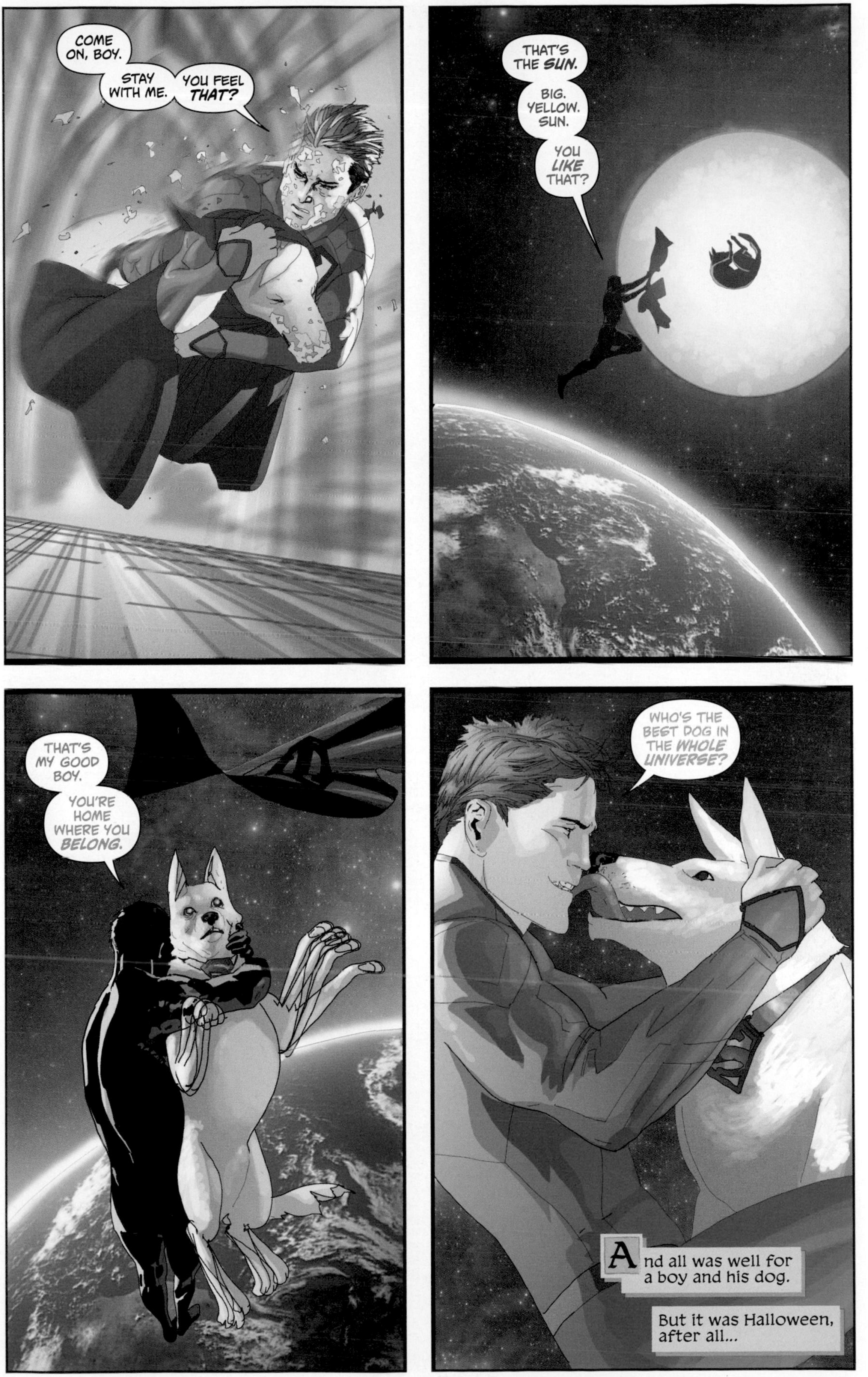
COME ON, BOY.
STAY WITH ME.
YOU FEEL THAT?
THAT'S THE SUN.
BIG. YELLOW. SUN.
YOU LIKE THAT?
THAT'S MY GOOD BOY.
YOU'RE HOME WHERE YOU BELONG.
WHO'S THE BEST DOG IN THE WHOLE UNIVERSE?
And all was well for a boy and his dog.
But it was Halloween, after all...

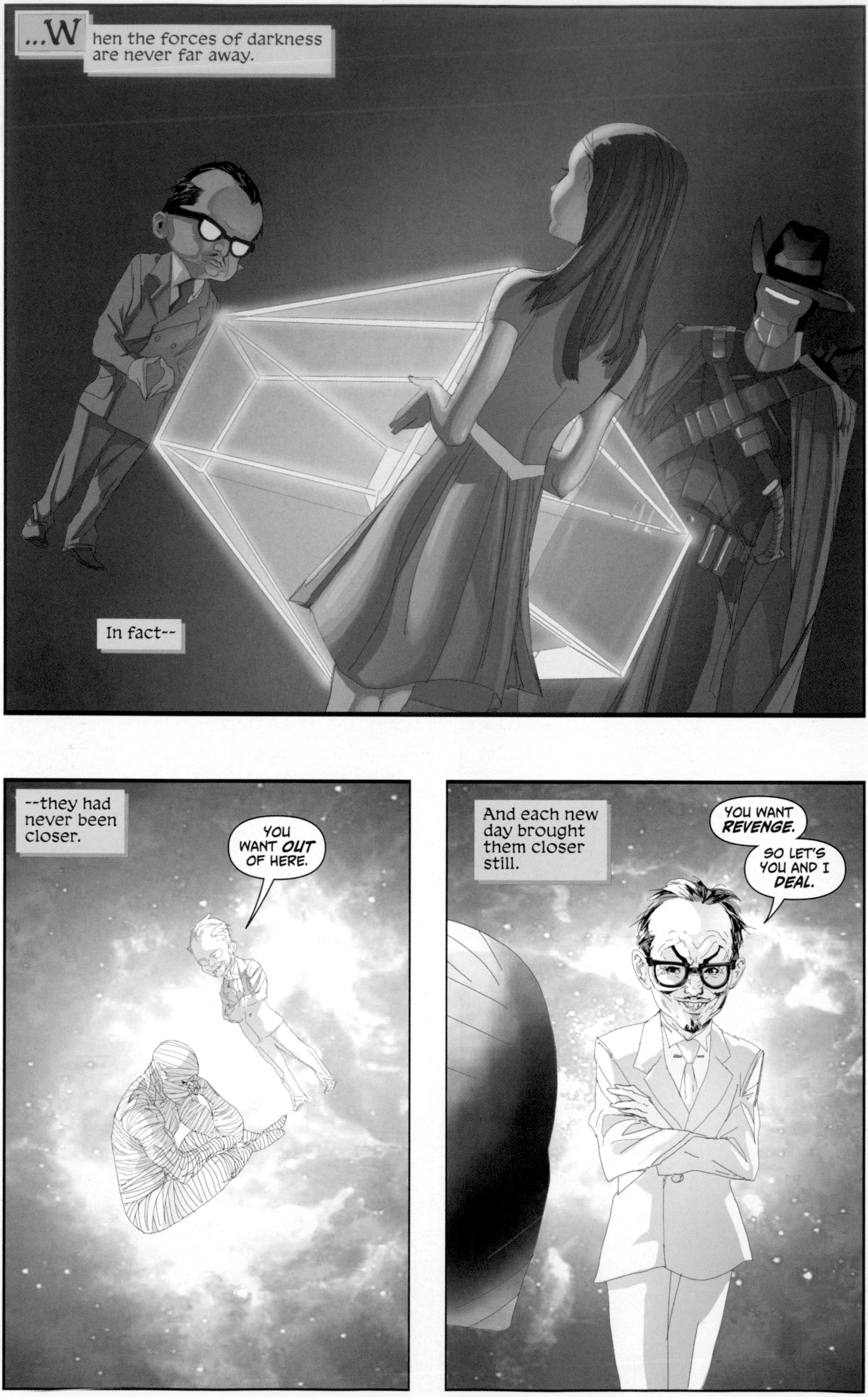
...When the forces of darkness are never far away.
In fact--
--they had never been closer.
YOU WANT OUT OF HERE.
And each new day brought them closer still.
YOU WANT REVENGE.
SO LET'S YOU AND I DEAL.

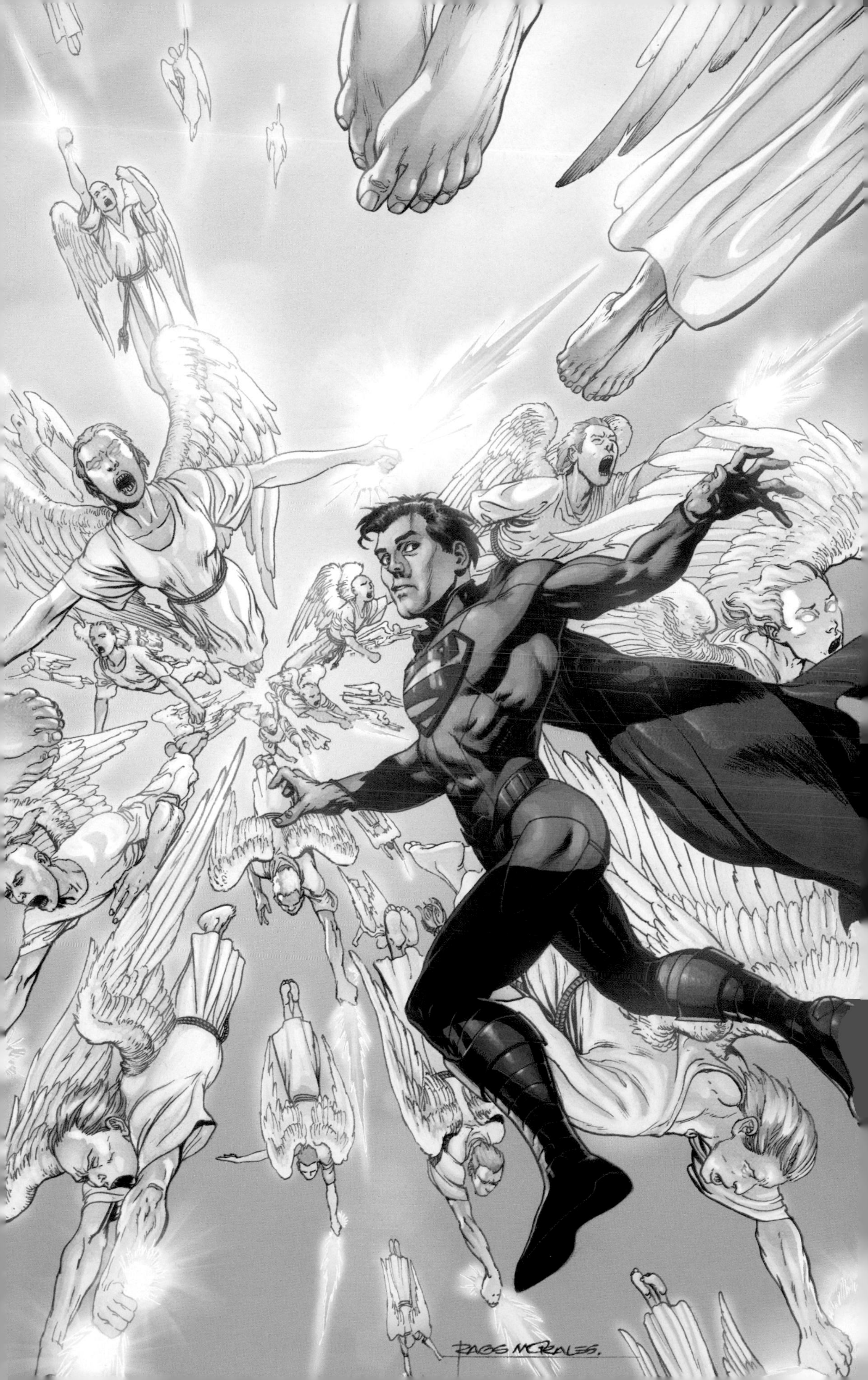
RAGS MORALES.

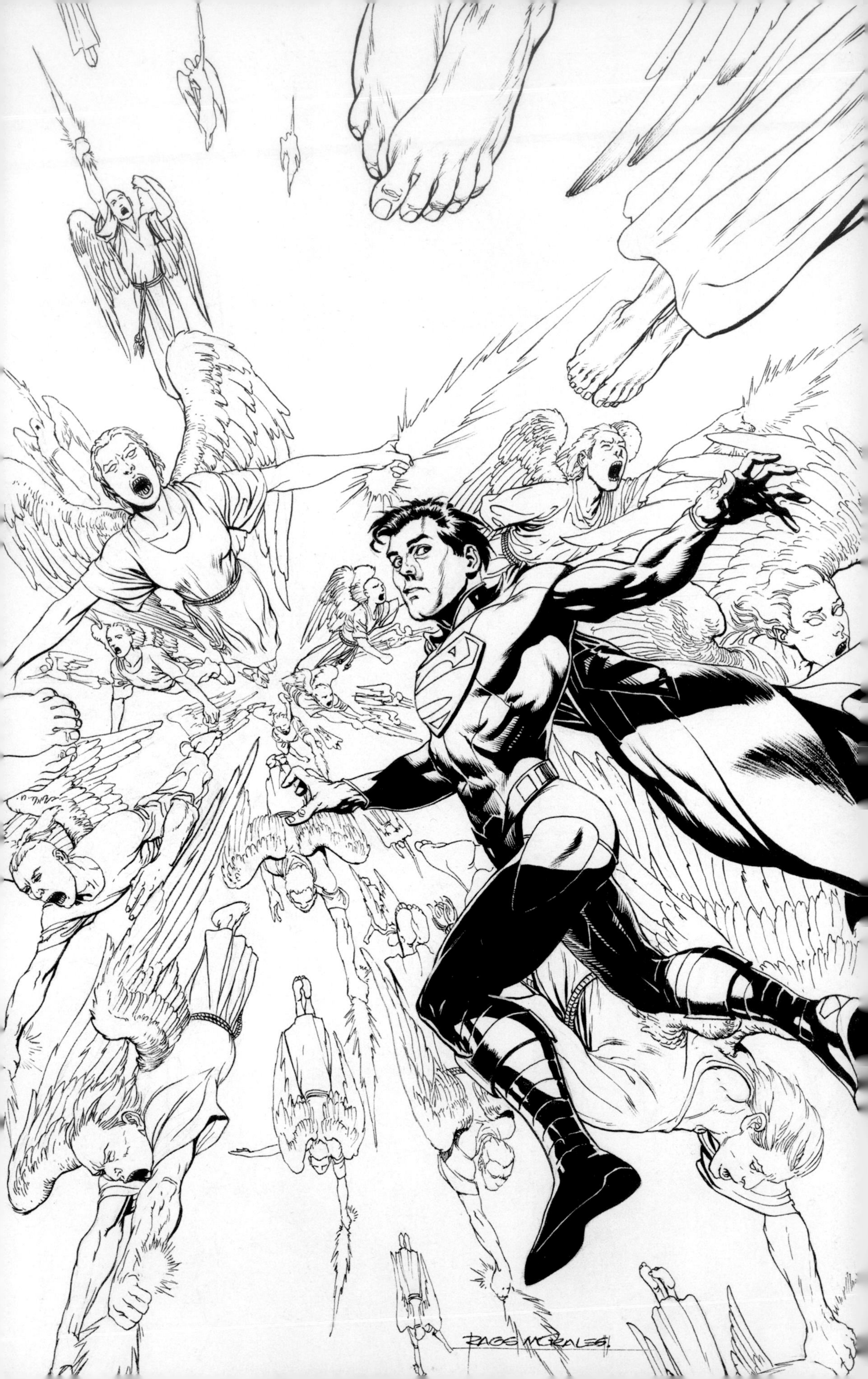
RAGS MORALES

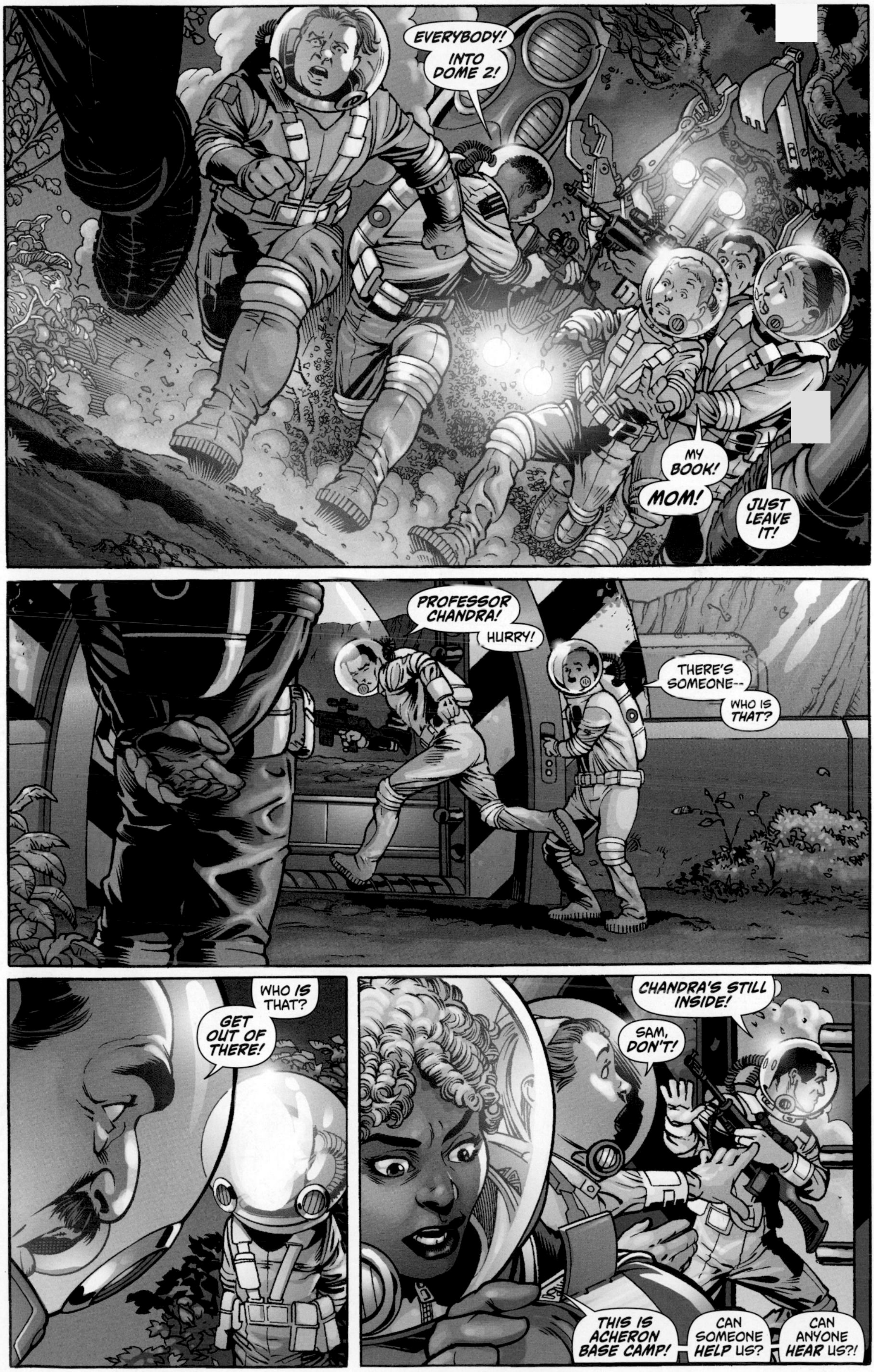
EVERYBODY!
INTO DOME 2!
MY BOOK!
MOM!
JUST LEAVE IT!
PROFESSOR CHANDRA!
HURRY!
THERE'S SOMEONE--
WHO IS THAT?
WHO IS THAT?
GET OUT OF THERE!
CHANDRA'S STILL INSIDE!
SAM, DON'T!
THIS IS ACHERON BASE CAMP!
CAN SOMEONE HELP US?
CAN ANYONE HEAR US?!

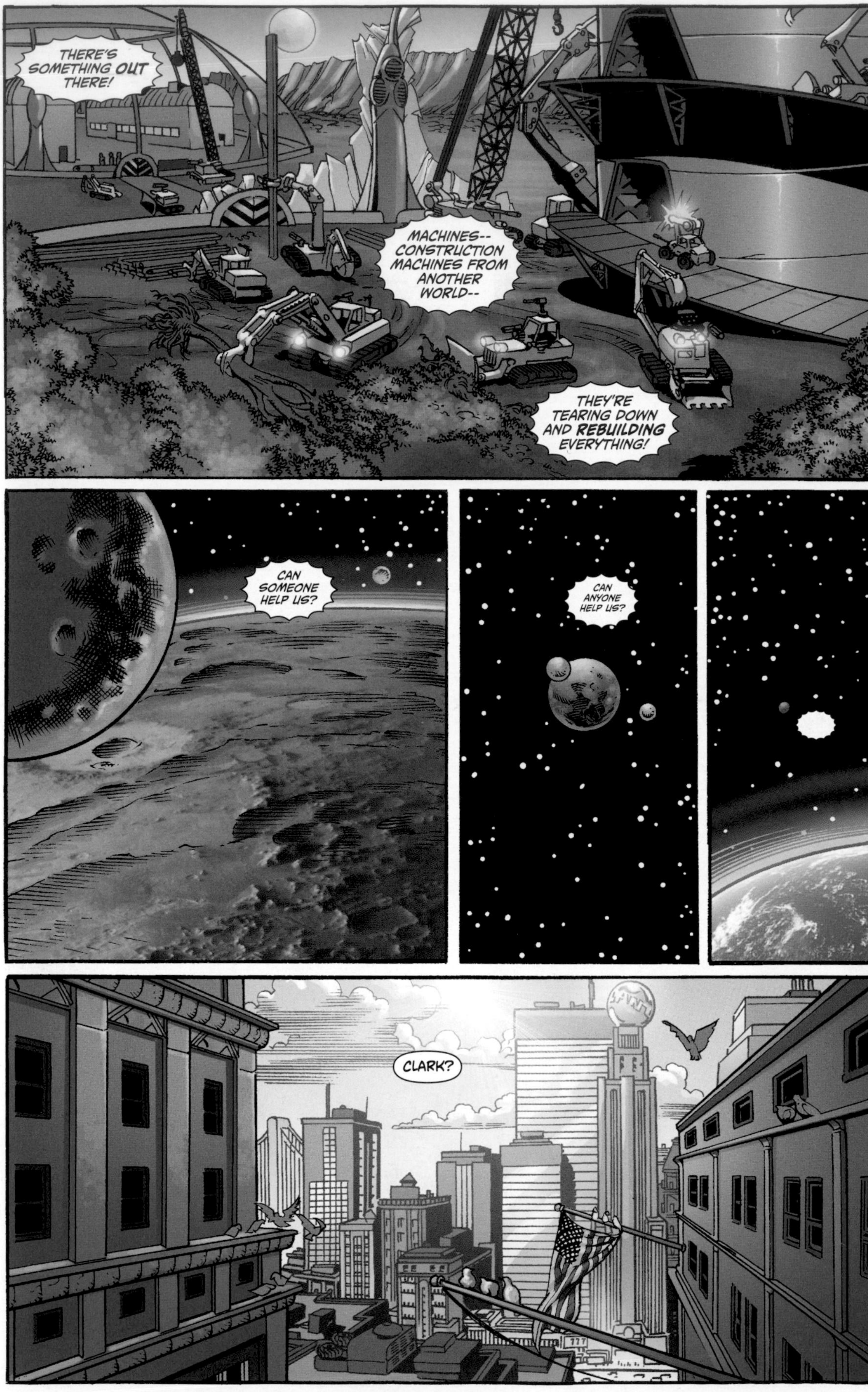
THERE'S SOMETHING OUT THERE!
MACHINES-- CONSTRUCTION MACHINES FROM ANOTHER WORLD--
THEY'RE TEARING DOWN AND REBUILDING EVERYTHING!
CAN SOMEONE HELP US?
CAN ANYONE HELP US?
CLARK?

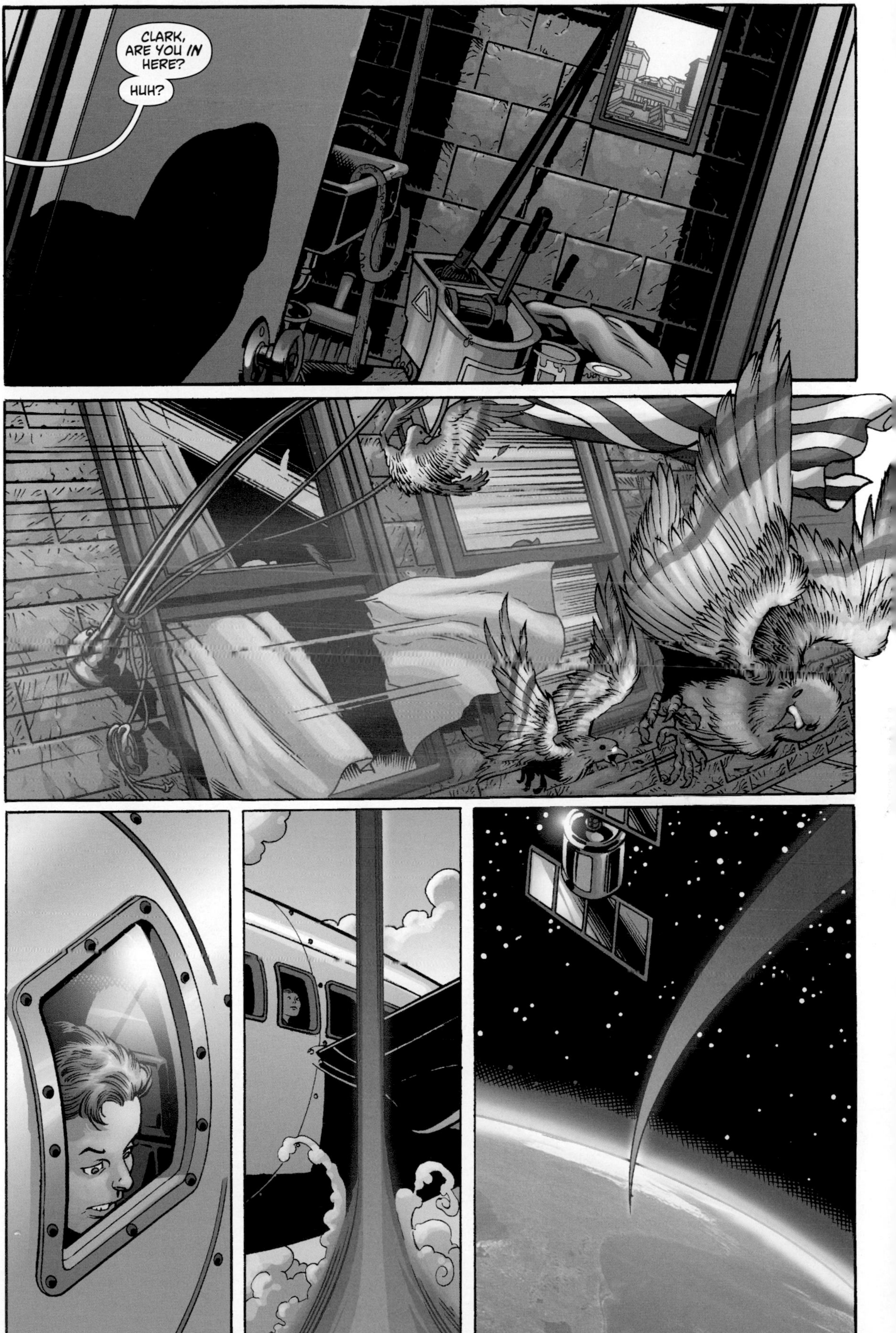
CLARK, ARE YOU *IN* HERE?
HUH?

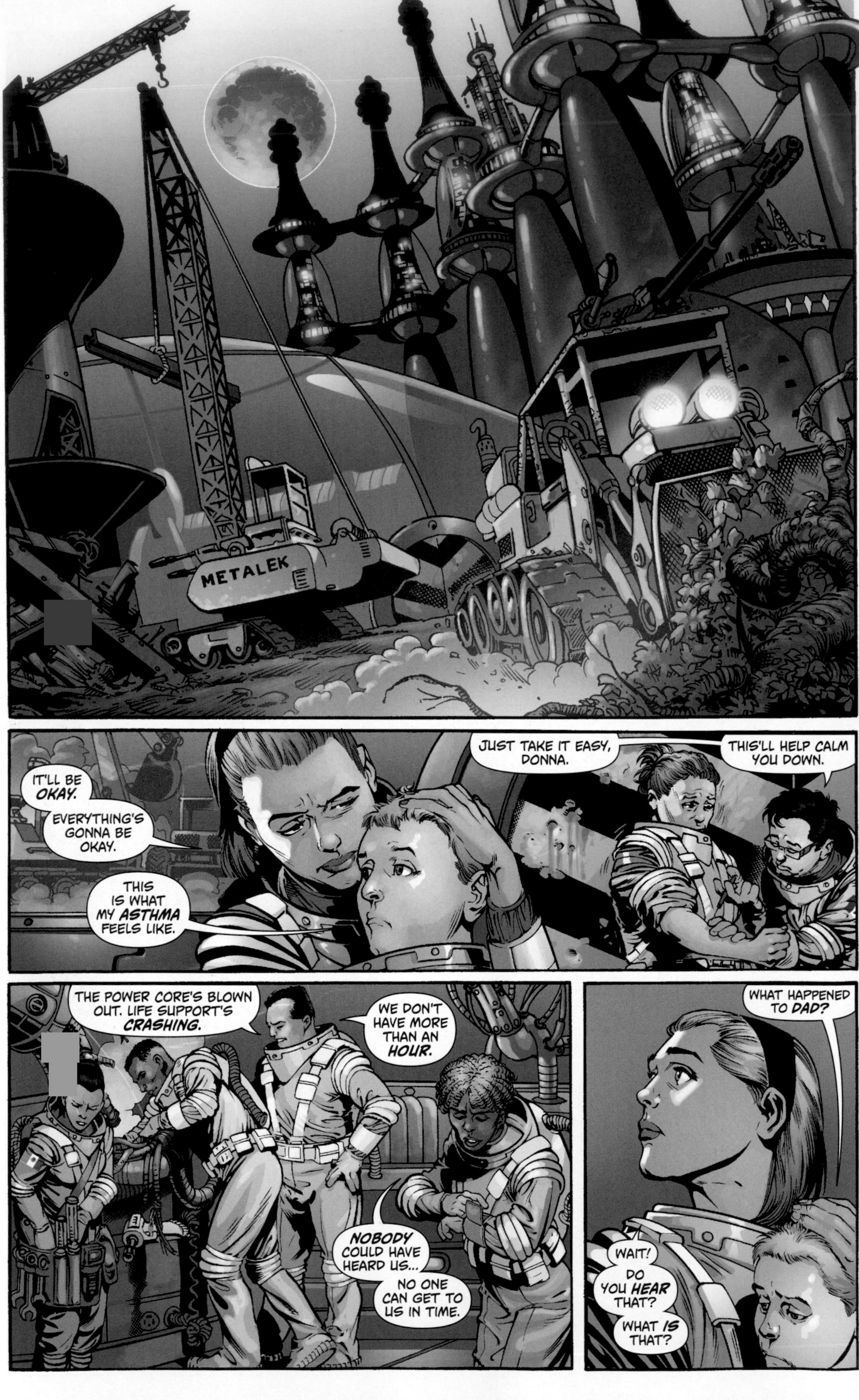
METALEK
IT'LL BE OKAY.
EVERYTHING'S GONNA BE OKAY.
THIS IS WHAT MY ASTHMA FEELS LIKE.
JUST TAKE IT EASY, DONNA.
THIS'LL HELP CALM YOU DOWN.
THE POWER CORE'S BLOWN OUT. LIFE SUPPORT'S CRASHING.
WE DON'T HAVE MORE THAN AN HOUR.
NOBODY COULD HAVE HEARD US...
NO ONE CAN GET TO US IN TIME.
WHAT HAPPENED TO DAD?
WAIT!
DO YOU HEAR THAT?
WHAT IS THAT?

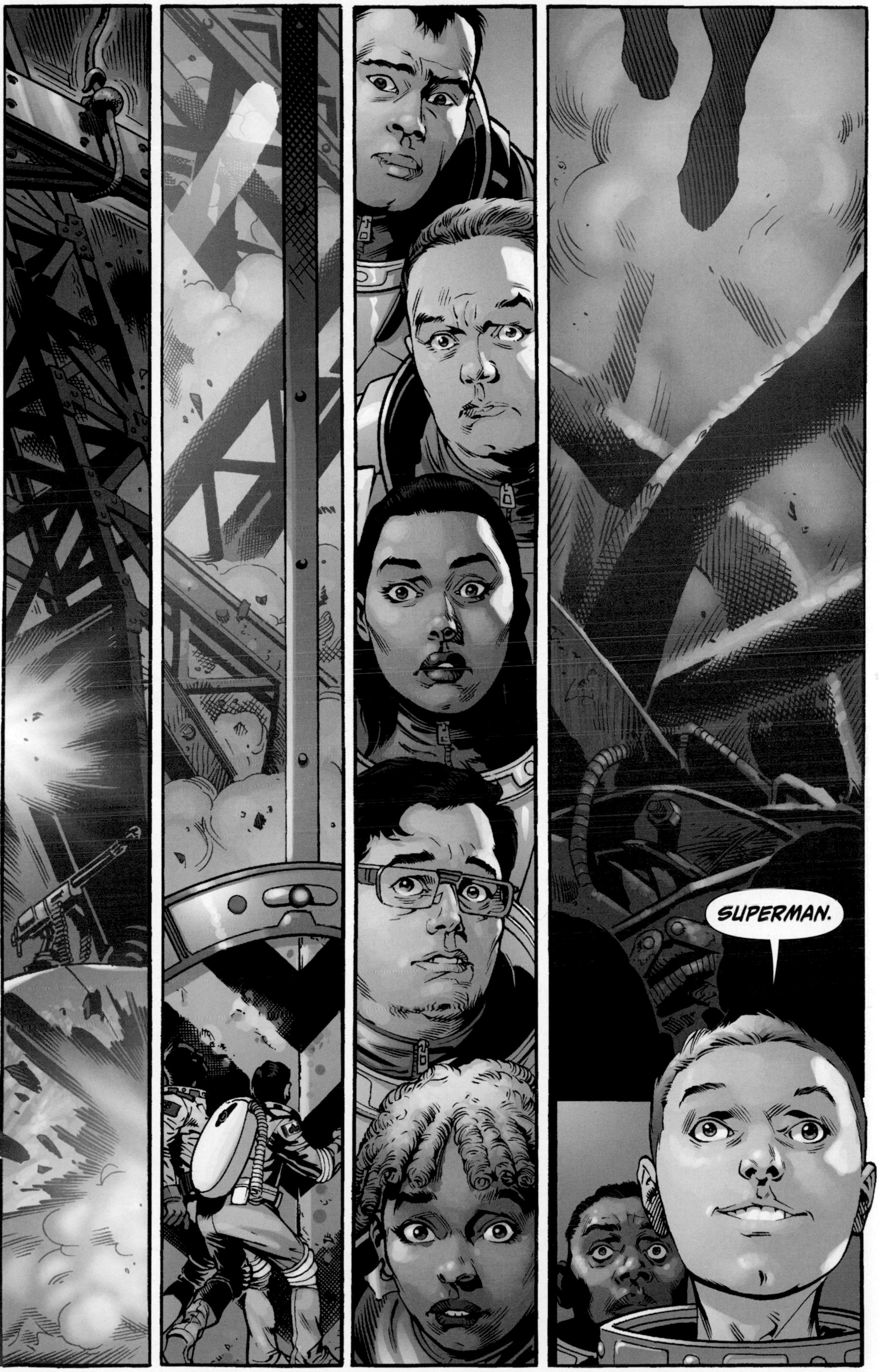
SUPERMAN.

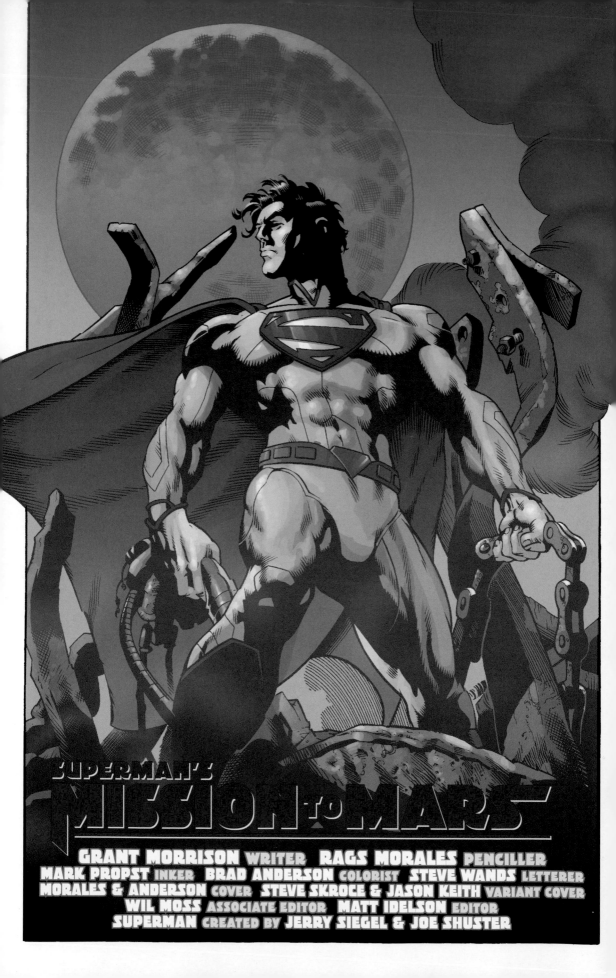

SUPERMAN'S MISSION TO MARS

GRANT MORRISON WRITER   **RAGS MORALES** PENCILLER
MARK PROPST INKER   **BRAD ANDERSON** COLORIST   **STEVE WANDS** LETTERER
MORALES & ANDERSON COVER   **STEVE SKROCE & JASON KEITH** VARIANT COVER
WIL MOSS ASSOCIATE EDITOR   **MATT IDELSON** EDITOR
SUPERMAN CREATED BY **JERRY SIEGEL & JOE SHUSTER**

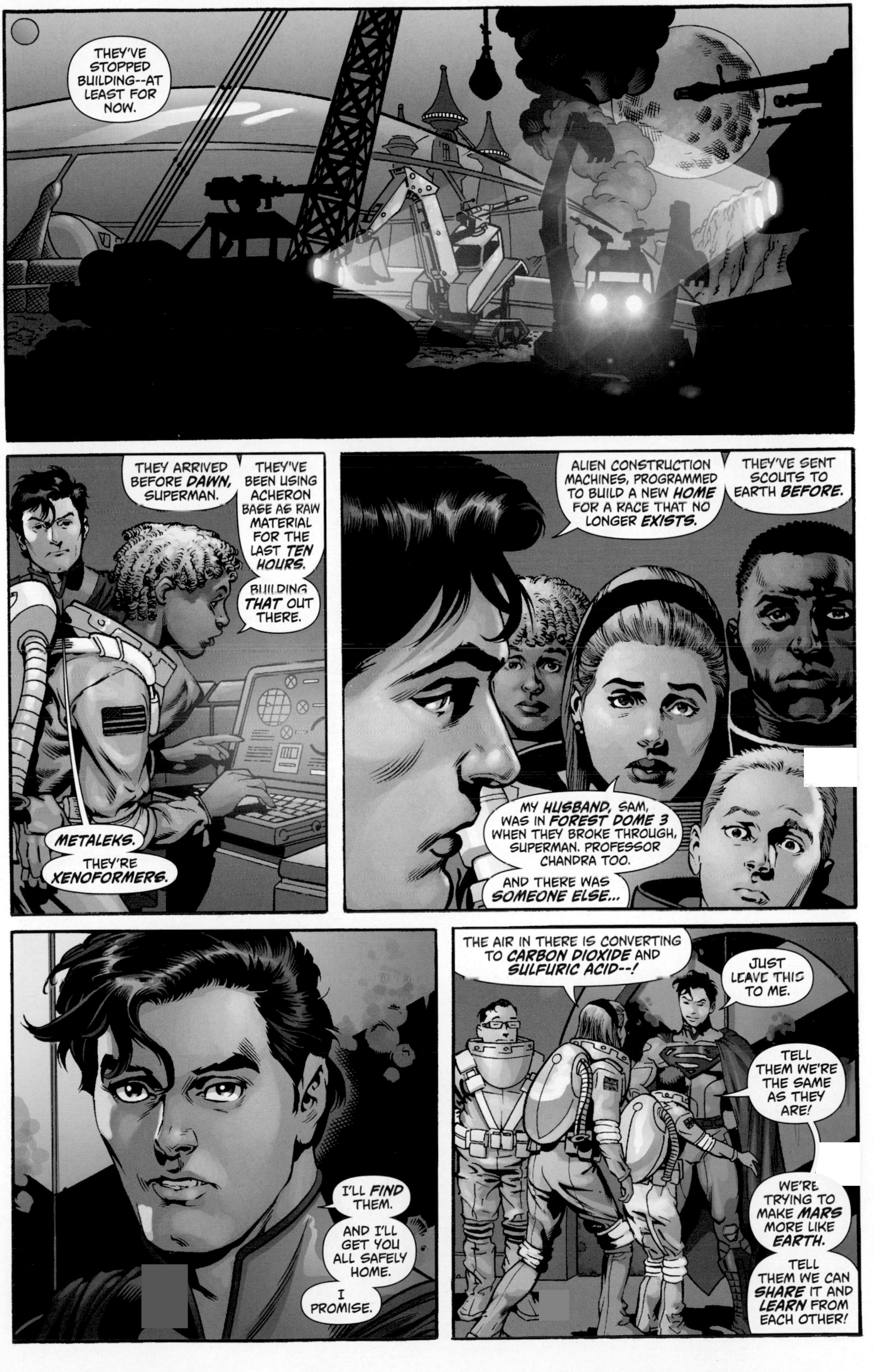
THEY'VE STOPPED BUILDING--AT LEAST FOR NOW.
THEY ARRIVED BEFORE DAWN, SUPERMAN.
THEY'VE BEEN USING ACHERON BASE AS RAW MATERIAL FOR THE LAST TEN HOURS.
BUILDING THAT OUT THERE.
METALEKS.
THEY'RE XENOFORMERS.
ALIEN CONSTRUCTION MACHINES, PROGRAMMED TO BUILD A NEW HOME FOR A RACE THAT NO LONGER EXISTS.
THEY'VE SENT SCOUTS TO EARTH BEFORE.
MY HUSBAND, SAM, WAS IN FOREST DOME 3 WHEN THEY BROKE THROUGH, SUPERMAN. PROFESSOR CHANDRA TOO.
AND THERE WAS SOMEONE ELSE...
I'LL FIND THEM.
AND I'LL GET YOU ALL SAFELY HOME.
I PROMISE.
THE AIR IN THERE IS CONVERTING TO CARBON DIOXIDE AND SULFURIC ACID--!
JUST LEAVE THIS TO ME.
TELL THEM WE'RE THE SAME AS THEY ARE!
WE'RE TRYING TO MAKE MARS MORE LIKE EARTH.
TELL THEM WE CAN SHARE IT AND LEARN FROM EACH OTHER!

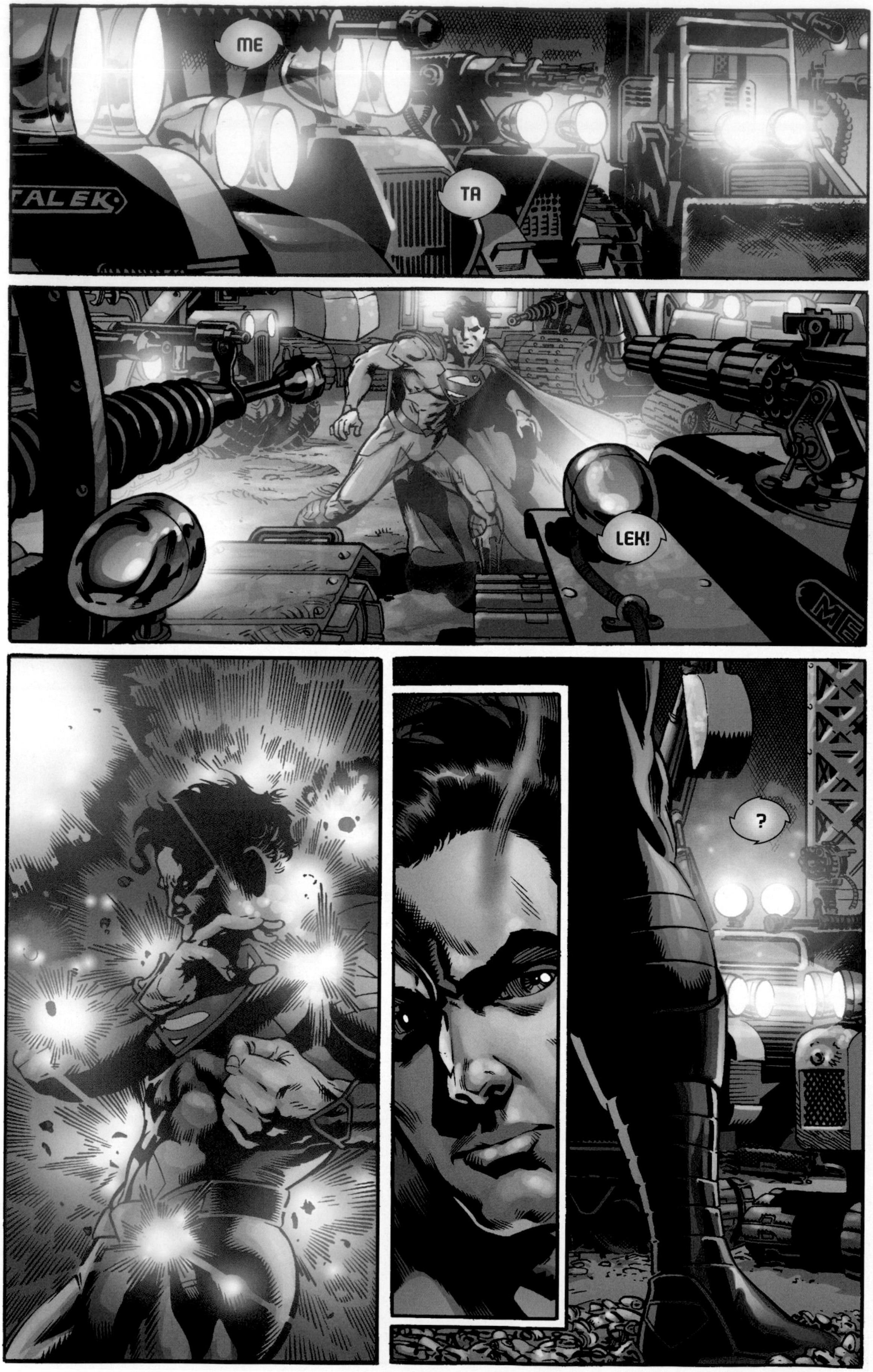
ME
TA
LEK!
?

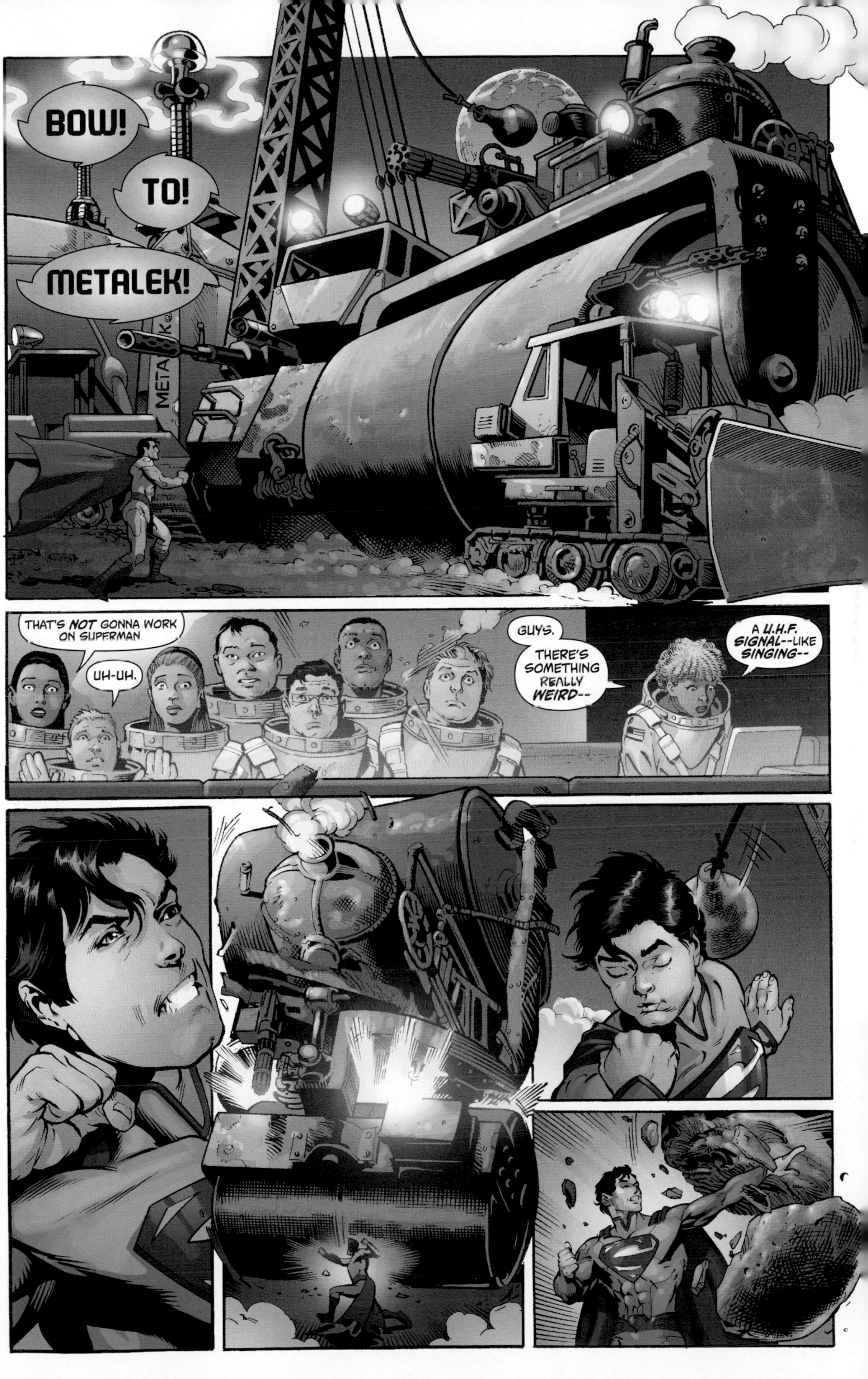
BOW!
TO!
METALEK!
THAT'S NOT GONNA WORK ON SUPERMAN.
UH-UH.
GUYS. THERE'S SOMETHING REALLY WEIRD--
A U.H.F. SIGNAL--LIKE SINGING--

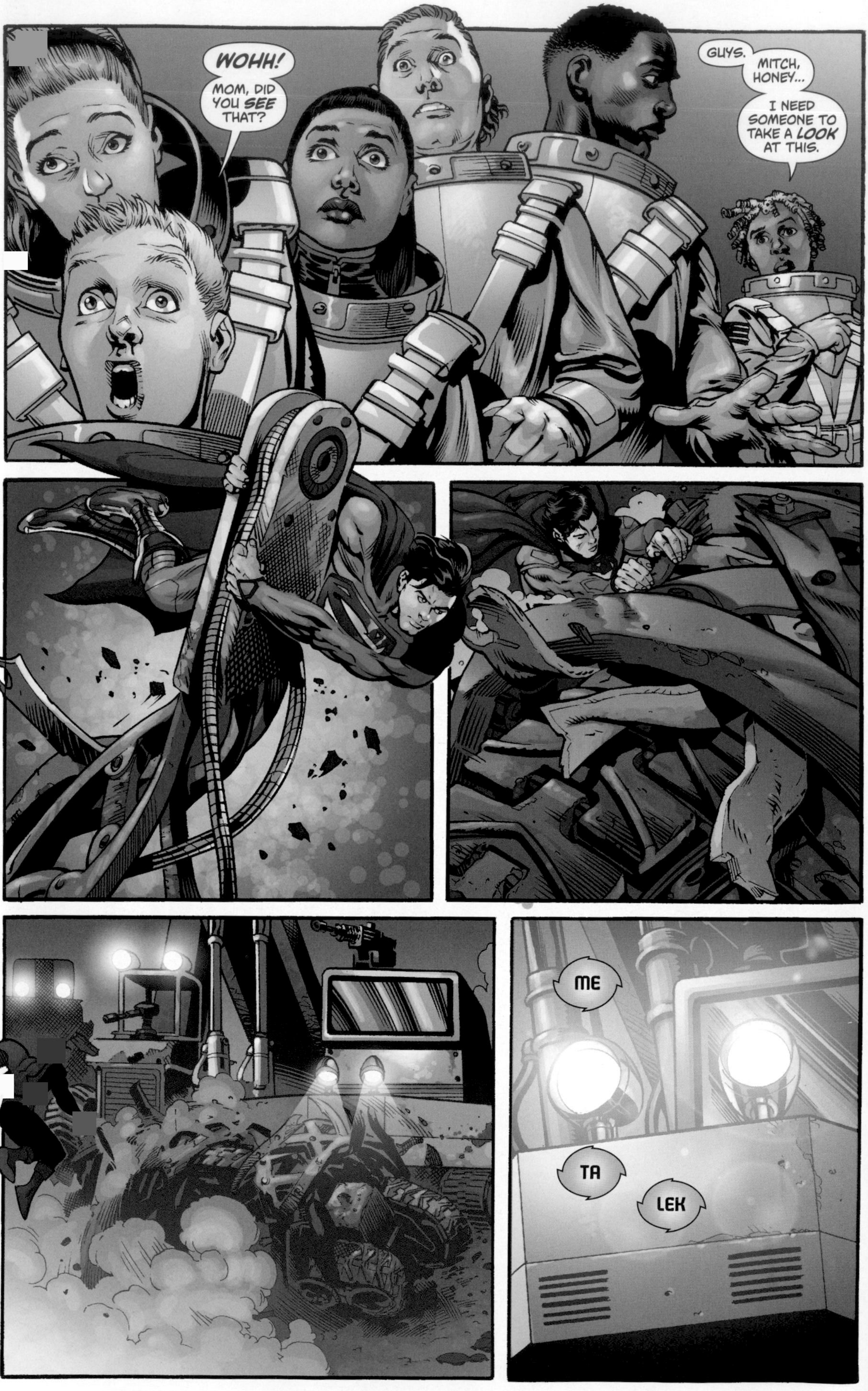
WOHH!
MOM, DID YOU SEE THAT?
GUYS.
MITCH, HONEY...
I NEED SOMEONE TO TAKE A LOOK AT THIS.
ME
TA
LEK

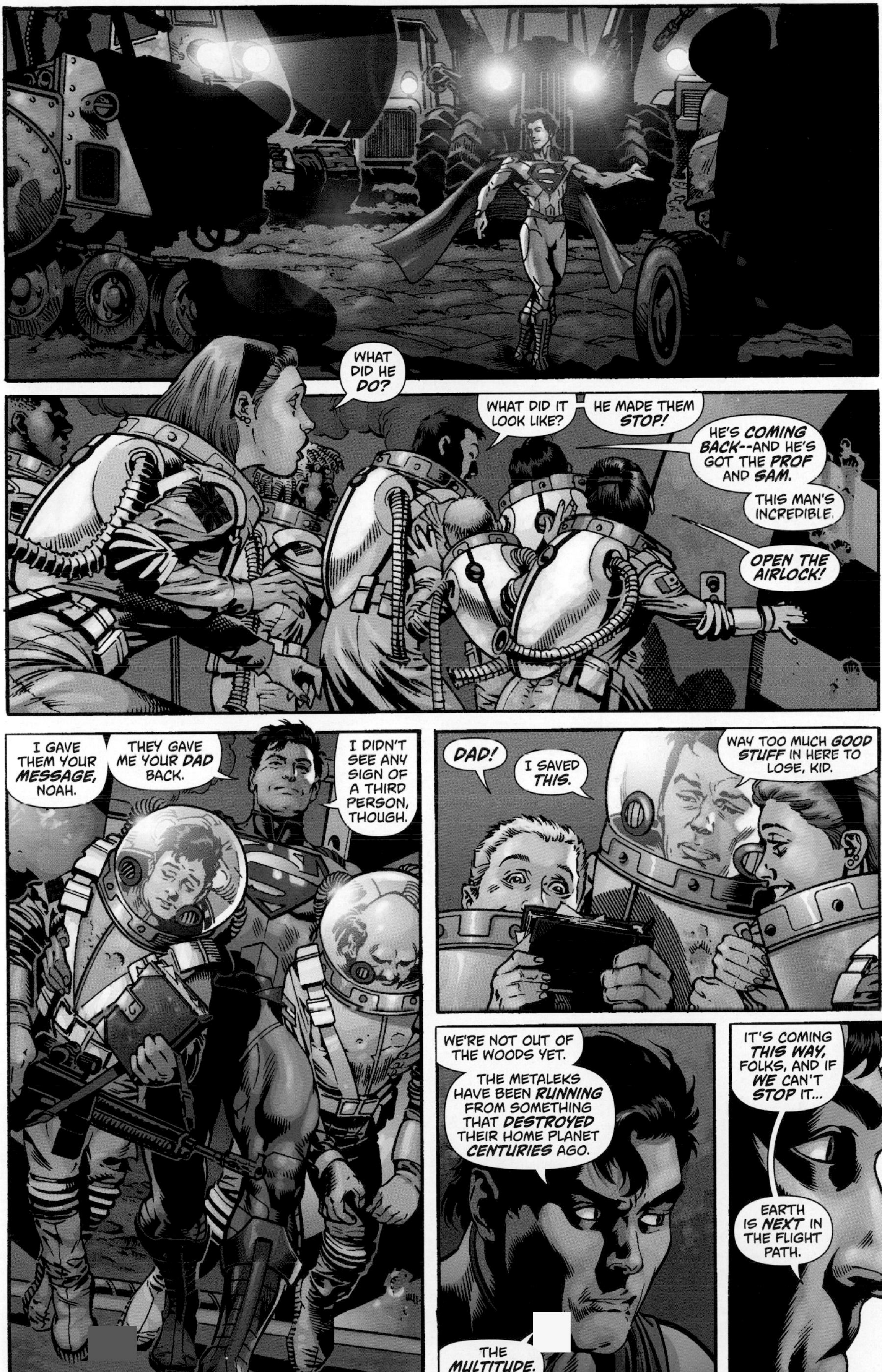
WHAT DID HE DO?
WHAT DID IT LOOK LIKE?
HE MADE THEM STOP!
HE'S COMING BACK--AND HE'S GOT THE PROF AND SAM.
THIS MAN'S INCREDIBLE.
OPEN THE AIRLOCK!
I GAVE THEM YOUR MESSAGE, NOAH.
THEY GAVE ME YOUR DAD BACK.
I DIDN'T SEE ANY SIGN OF A THIRD PERSON, THOUGH.
DAD!
I SAVED THIS.
WAY TOO MUCH GOOD STUFF IN HERE TO LOSE, KID.
WE'RE NOT OUT OF THE WOODS YET.
THE METALEKS HAVE BEEN RUNNING FROM SOMETHING THAT DESTROYED THEIR HOME PLANET CENTURIES AGO.
THE MULTITUDE.
IT'S COMING THIS WAY, FOLKS, AND IF WE CAN'T STOP IT...
EARTH IS NEXT IN THE FLIGHT PATH.

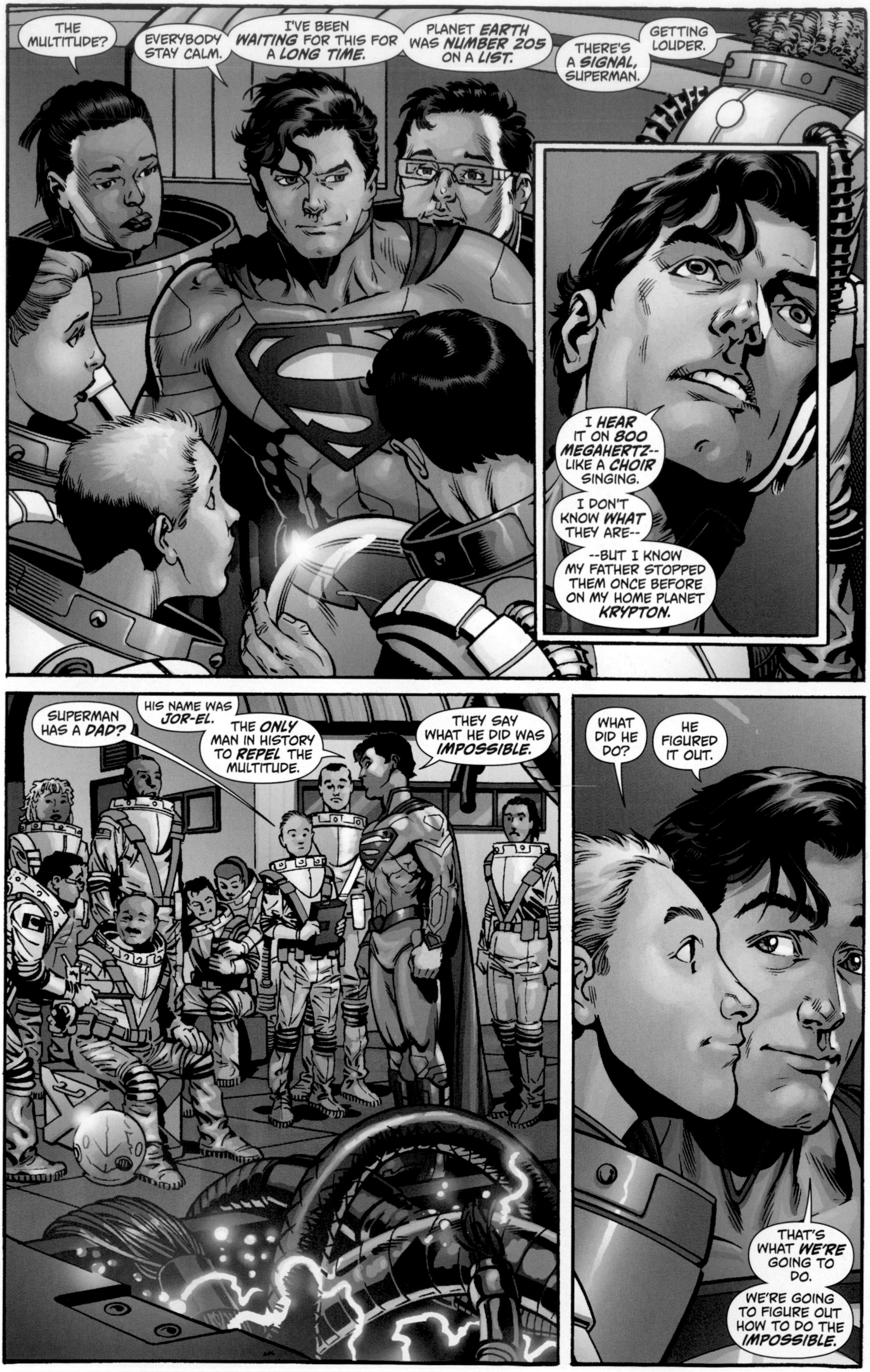
THE MULTITUDE?
EVERYBODY STAY CALM.
I'VE BEEN WAITING FOR THIS FOR A LONG TIME.
PLANET EARTH WAS NUMBER 205 ON A LIST.
THERE'S A SIGNAL, SUPERMAN.
GETTING LOUDER.
I HEAR IT ON 800 MEGAHERTZ-- LIKE A CHOIR SINGING.
I DON'T KNOW WHAT THEY ARE--
--BUT I KNOW MY FATHER STOPPED THEM ONCE BEFORE ON MY HOME PLANET KRYPTON.
SUPERMAN HAS A DAD?
HIS NAME WAS JOR-EL.
THE ONLY MAN IN HISTORY TO REPEL THE MULTITUDE.
THEY SAY WHAT HE DID WAS IMPOSSIBLE.
WHAT DID HE DO?
HE FIGURED IT OUT.
THAT'S WHAT WE'RE GOING TO DO.
WE'RE GOING TO FIGURE OUT HOW TO DO THE IMPOSSIBLE.

THERE MUST BE SOME WAY *WE* CAN HELP, SUPERMAN.

DEFEND YOURSELVES AS BEST YOU CAN.

I'M GOING BACK *OUT* THERE TO SEE EXACTLY WHAT WE'RE UP AGAINST.

TAKE CARE, SUPERMAN.

WHAT IS IT? WHAT'S COMING?

I LOVE YOU, NOAH.

THERE ARE HUNDREDS-- *THOUSANDS*--

MITCH. THEY'RE COMING OUT OF *NOWHERE*.

FROM *EVERYWHERE* AT ONCE.

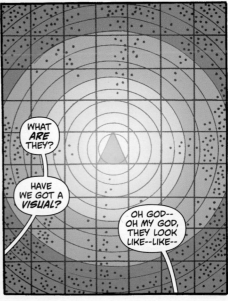

WHAT *ARE* THEY?

HAVE WE GOT A *VISUAL*?

OH GOD-- OH MY GOD, THEY LOOK LIKE--LIKE--

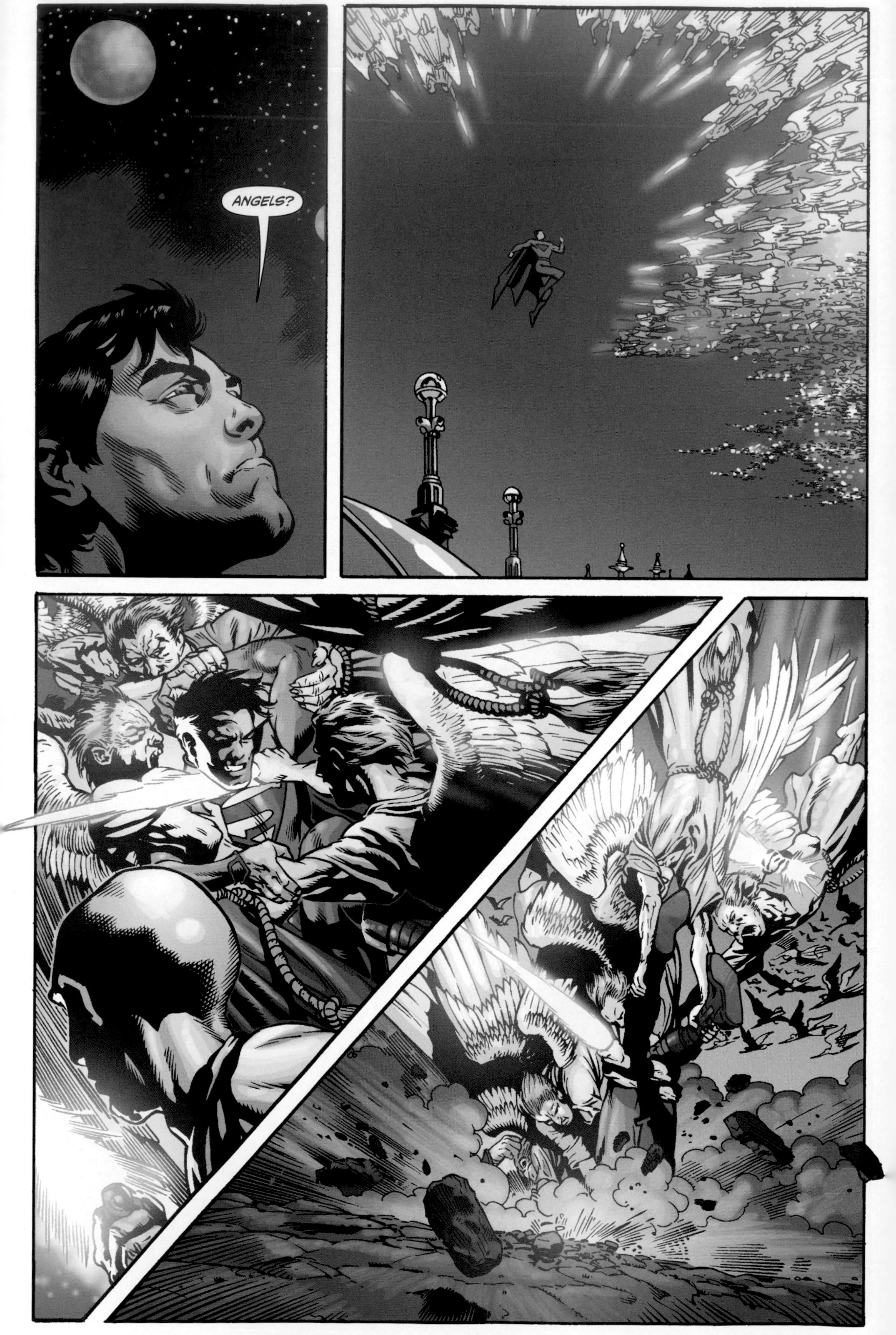
ANGELS?

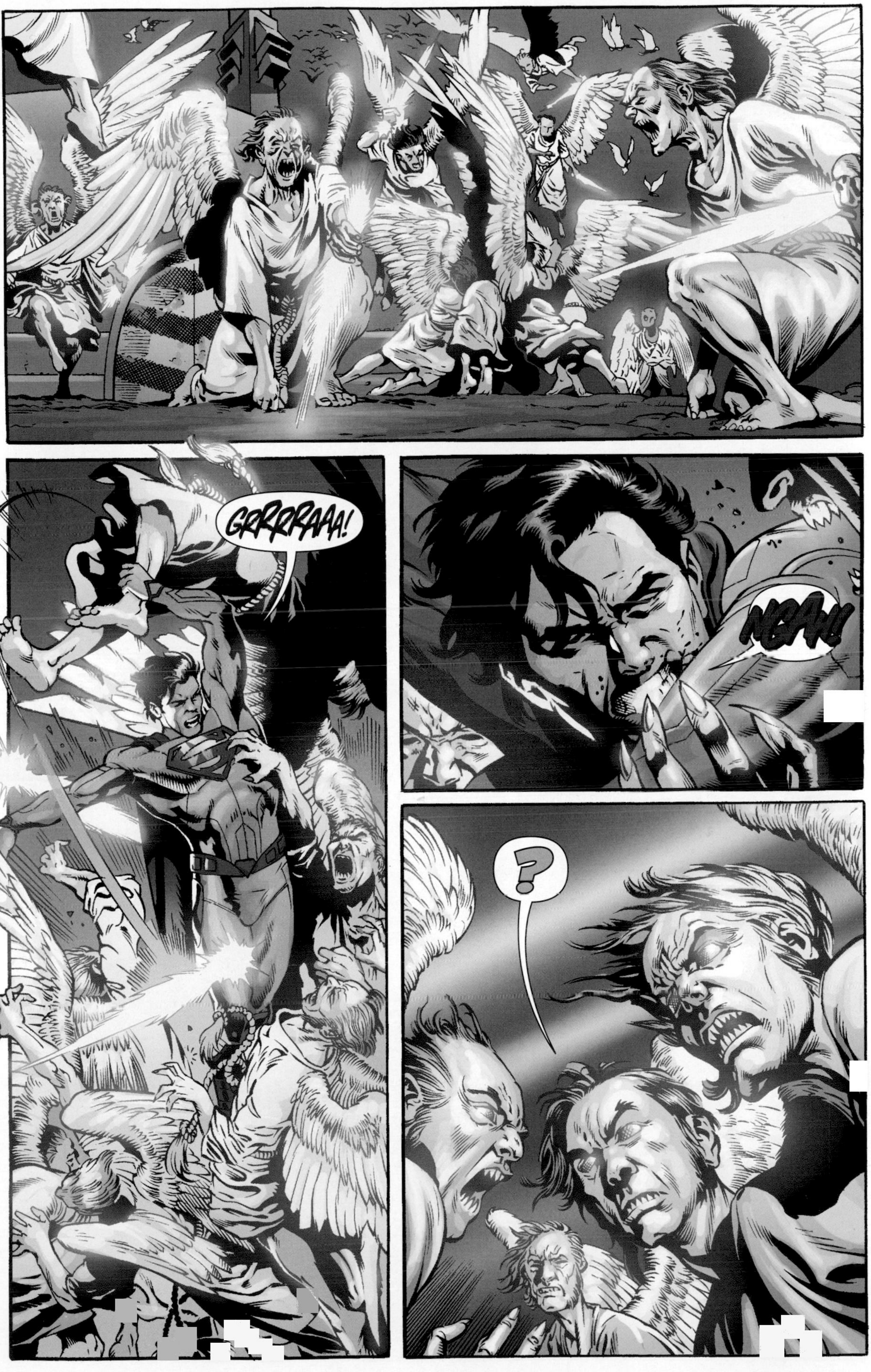
GRRRRAAA!
NGAH!
?

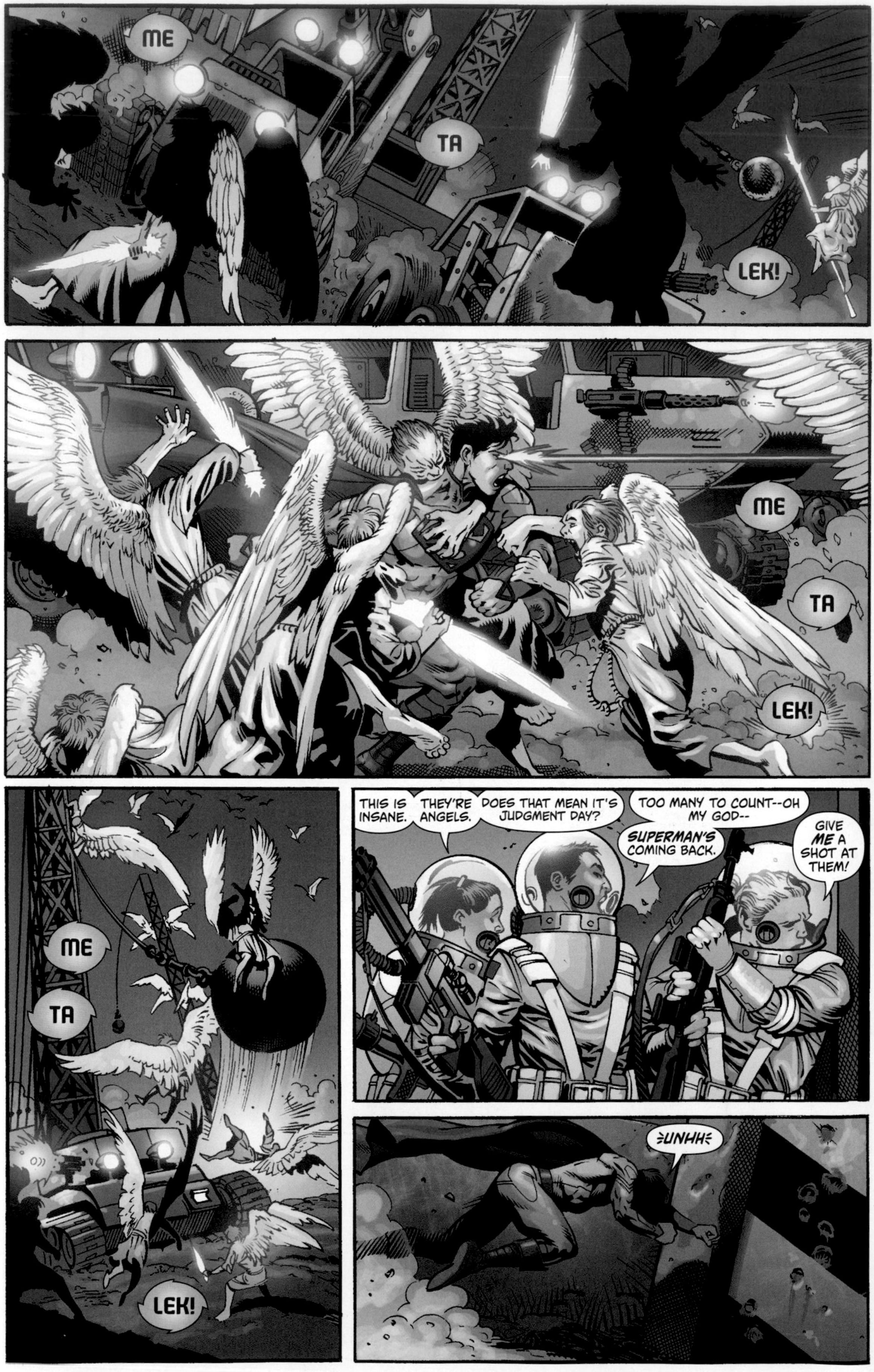

ME
TA
LEK!
ME
TA
LEK!
ME
TA
LEK!
THIS IS INSANE.
THEY'RE ANGELS.
DOES THAT MEAN IT'S JUDGMENT DAY?
TOO MANY TO COUNT--OH MY GOD--
SUPERMAN'S COMING BACK.
GIVE ME A SHOT AT THEM!
UNHH

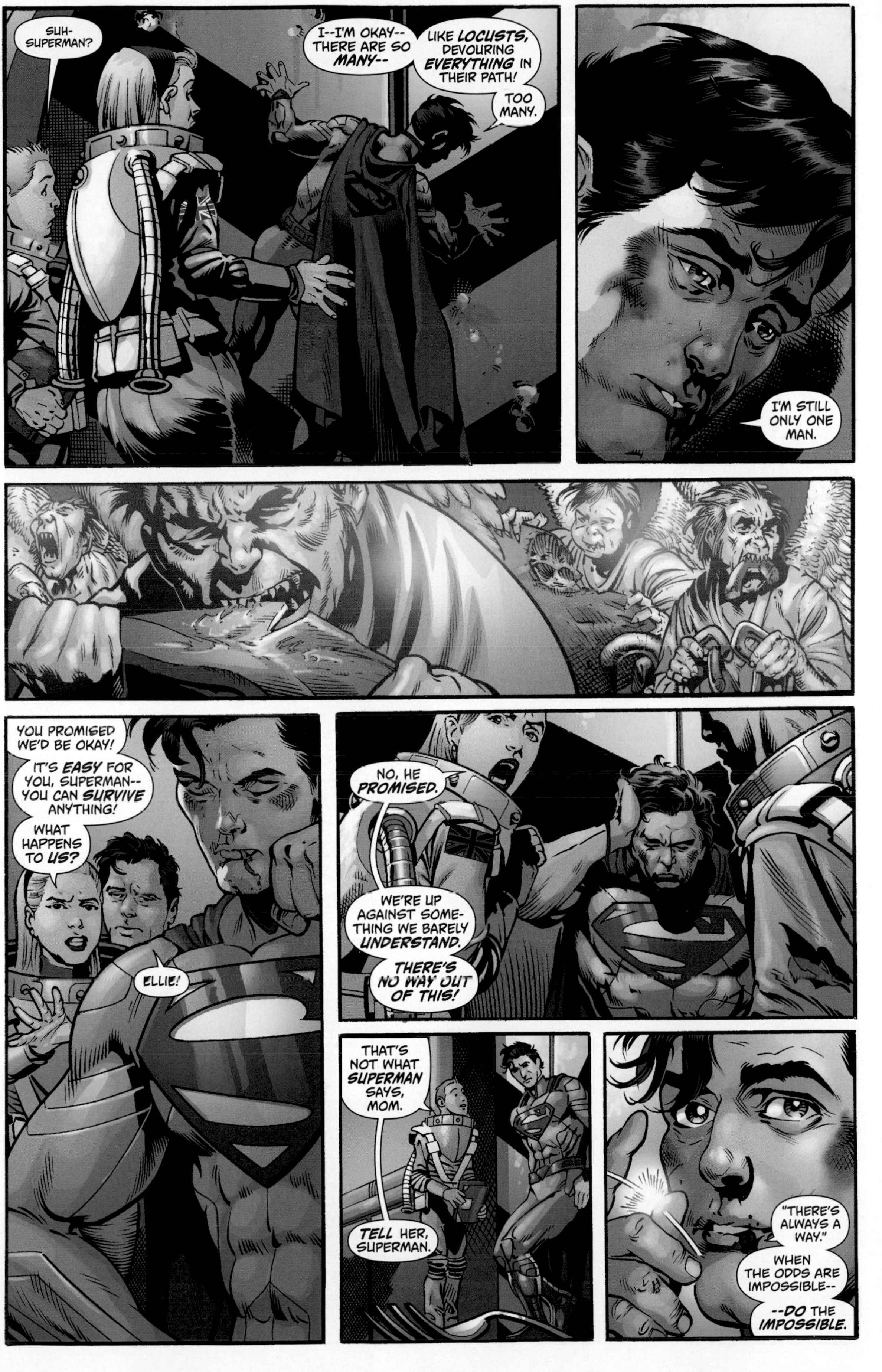
SUH-SUPERMAN?
I--I'M OKAY--THERE ARE SO MANY--
LIKE LOCUSTS, DEVOURING EVERYTHING IN THEIR PATH!
TOO MANY.
I'M STILL ONLY ONE MAN.
YOU PROMISED WE'D BE OKAY!
IT'S EASY FOR YOU, SUPERMAN--YOU CAN SURVIVE ANYTHING!
WHAT HAPPENS TO US?
ELLIE!
NO, HE PROMISED.
WE'RE UP AGAINST SOME-THING WE BARELY UNDERSTAND.
THERE'S NO WAY OUT OF THIS!
THAT'S NOT WHAT SUPERMAN SAYS, MOM.
TELL HER, SUPERMAN.
"THERE'S ALWAYS A WAY."
WHEN THE ODDS ARE IMPOSSIBLE--
--DO THE IMPOSSIBLE.

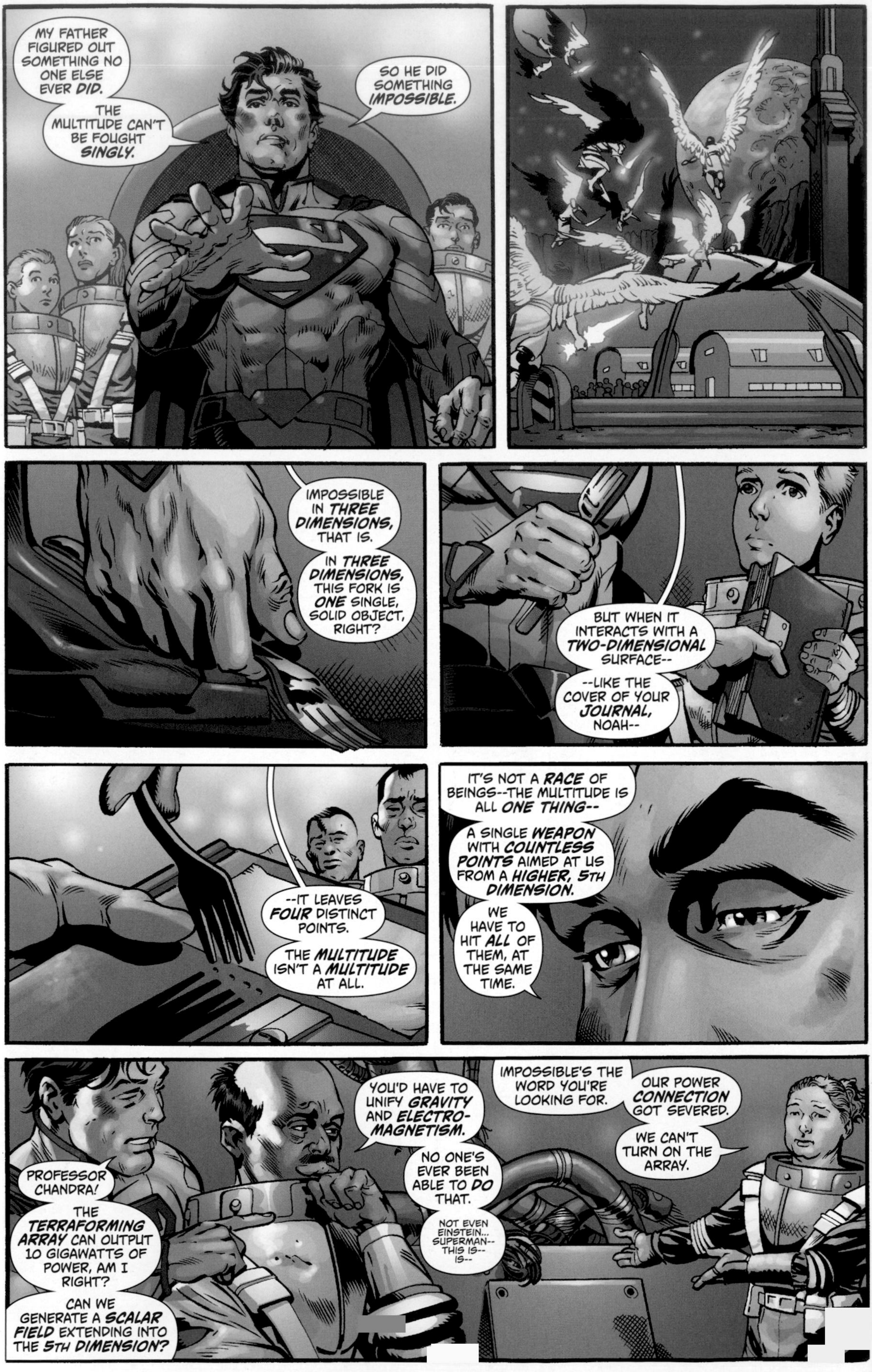
MY FATHER FIGURED OUT SOMETHING NO ONE ELSE EVER DID.
THE MULTITUDE CAN'T BE FOUGHT SINGLY.
SO HE DID SOMETHING IMPOSSIBLE.
IMPOSSIBLE IN THREE DIMENSIONS, THAT IS.
IN THREE DIMENSIONS, THIS FORK IS ONE SINGLE, SOLID OBJECT, RIGHT?
BUT WHEN IT INTERACTS WITH A TWO-DIMENSIONAL SURFACE--
--LIKE THE COVER OF YOUR JOURNAL, NOAH--
--IT LEAVES FOUR DISTINCT POINTS.
THE MULTITUDE ISN'T A MULTITUDE AT ALL.
IT'S NOT A RACE OF BEINGS--THE MULTITUDE IS ALL ONE THING--
A SINGLE WEAPON WITH COUNTLESS POINTS AIMED AT US FROM A HIGHER, 5TH DIMENSION.
WE HAVE TO HIT ALL OF THEM, AT THE SAME TIME.
PROFESSOR CHANDRA!
THE TERRAFORMING ARRAY CAN OUTPUT 10 GIGAWATTS OF POWER, AM I RIGHT?
CAN WE GENERATE A SCALAR FIELD EXTENDING INTO THE 5TH DIMENSION?
YOU'D HAVE TO UNIFY GRAVITY AND ELECTRO-MAGNETISM.
NO ONE'S EVER BEEN ABLE TO DO THAT.
NOT EVEN EINSTEIN... SUPERMAN-- THIS IS-- IS--
IMPOSSIBLE'S THE WORD YOU'RE LOOKING FOR.
OUR POWER CONNECTION GOT SEVERED.
WE CAN'T TURN ON THE ARRAY.

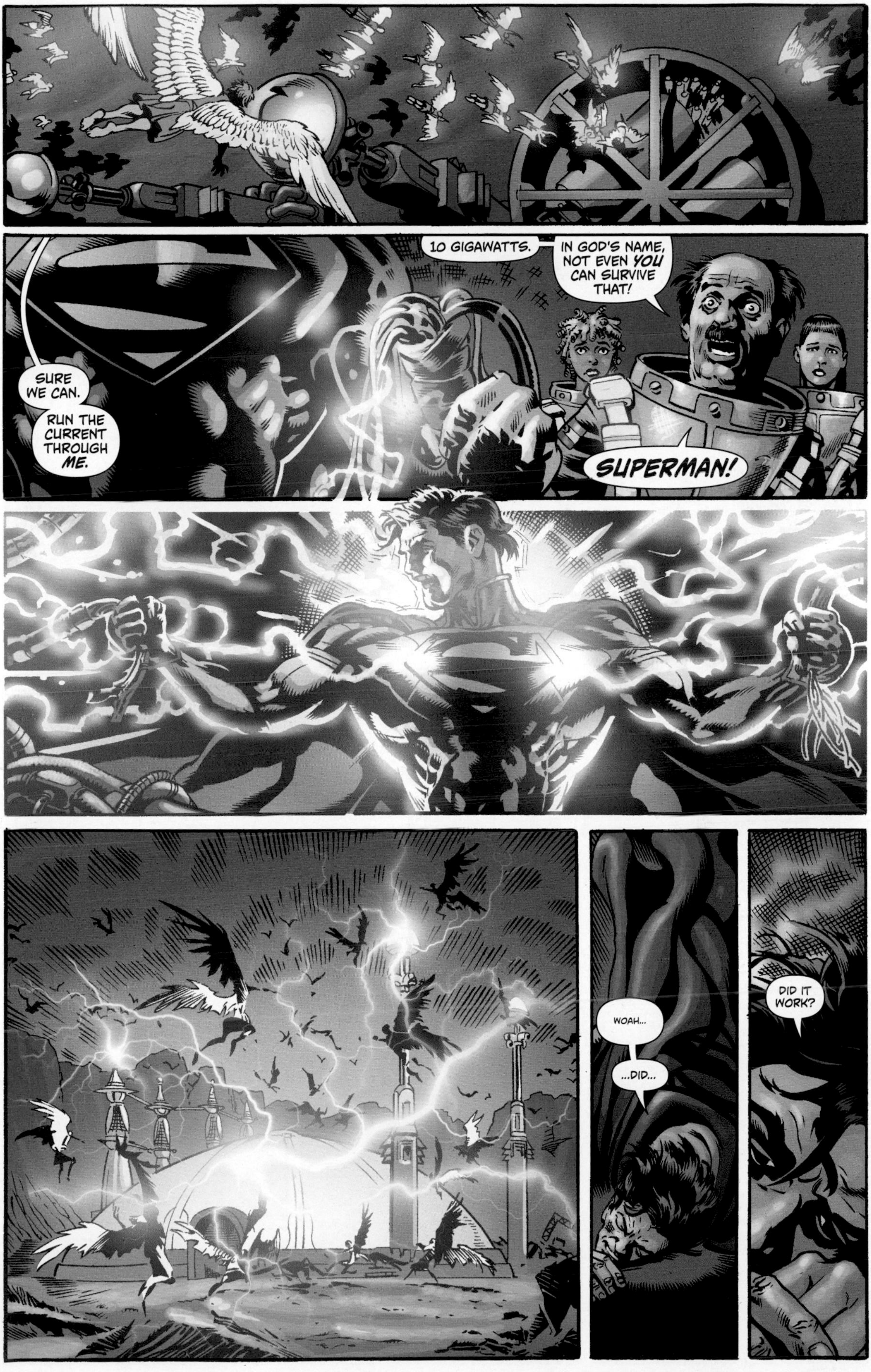
10 GIGAWATTS.
IN GOD'S NAME, NOT EVEN YOU CAN SURVIVE THAT!
SURE WE CAN.
RUN THE CURRENT THROUGH ME.
SUPERMAN!
WOAH...
...DID...
DID IT WORK?

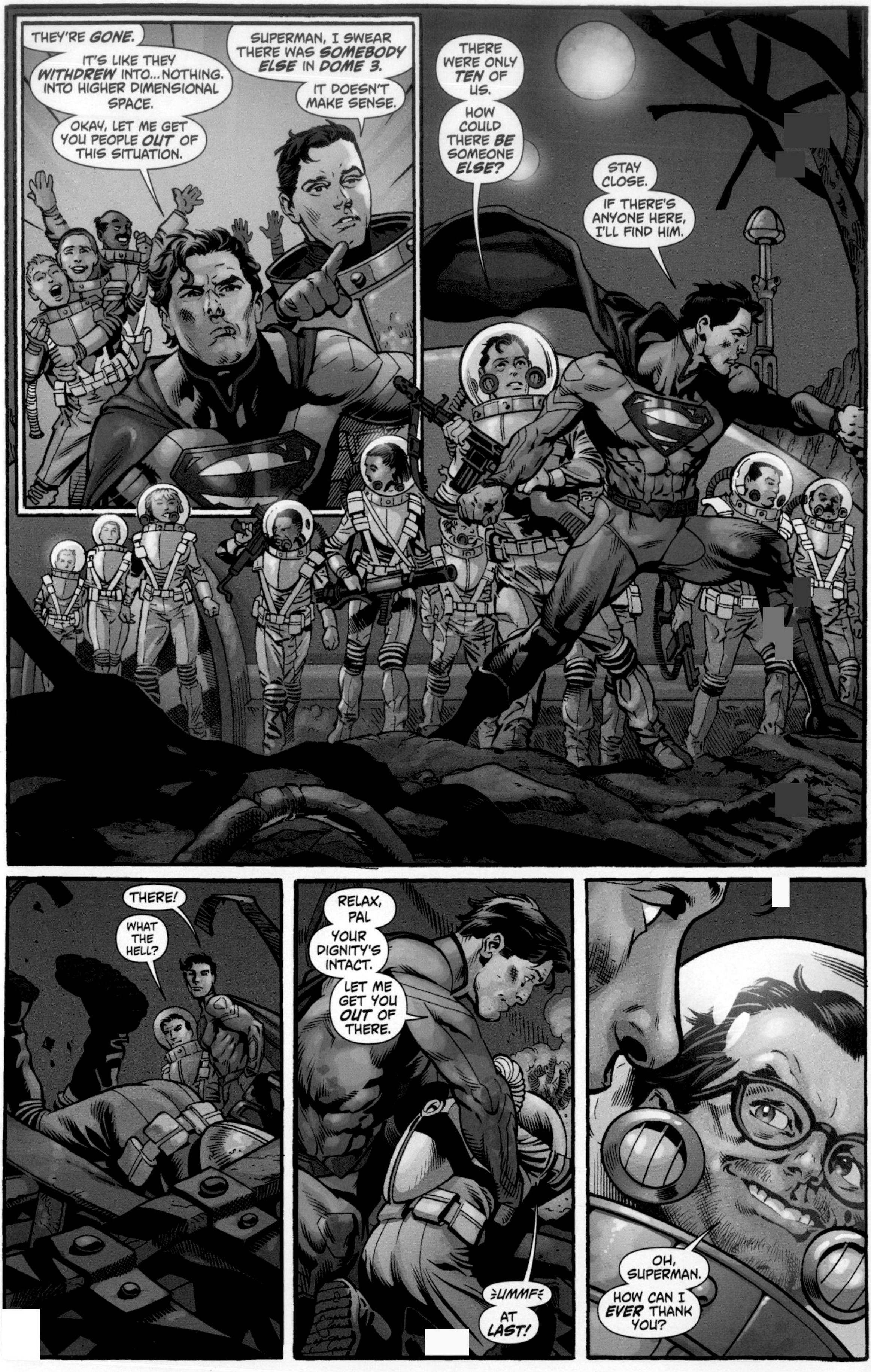
THEY'RE GONE.
IT'S LIKE THEY WITHDREW INTO...NOTHING. INTO HIGHER DIMENSIONAL SPACE.
OKAY, LET ME GET YOU PEOPLE OUT OF THIS SITUATION.
SUPERMAN, I SWEAR THERE WAS SOMEBODY ELSE IN DOME 3.
IT DOESN'T MAKE SENSE.
THERE WERE ONLY TEN OF US.
HOW COULD THERE BE SOMEONE ELSE?
STAY CLOSE.
IF THERE'S ANYONE HERE, I'LL FIND HIM.
THERE!
WHAT THE HELL?
RELAX, PAL
YOUR DIGNITY'S INTACT.
LET ME GET YOU OUT OF THERE.
UMMF
AT LAST!
OH, SUPERMAN.
HOW CAN I EVER THANK YOU?

NO...NO. VYNDKTVX. IT'S *YOU*, ISN'T IT?

YOU HURT MY *HAND*. YOU AND YOUR *SMART-ALECK* FATHER.

AAAAAAA!

HUNHUN HUNHUN

I'VE BEEN DIPPING INTO *YOUR* SMELLY LITTLE BARNYARD WORLD FOR A LONG, LONG TIME-- MAKING DEALS.

NOW I'M HERE TO *CONCLUDE* MY BUSINESS WITH *YOU*, BOY.

MOM?

UUHHHWHASSS HAPPENNNNNN

NOAH! SUPERMAN!

STOP IT! LEAVE THEM ALONE!

OR *WHAT?* HUNHUN HUNHUN

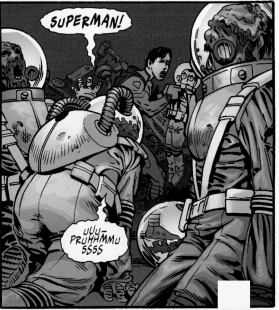

SUPERMAN!

UUU-PRUHHMMU SSSS

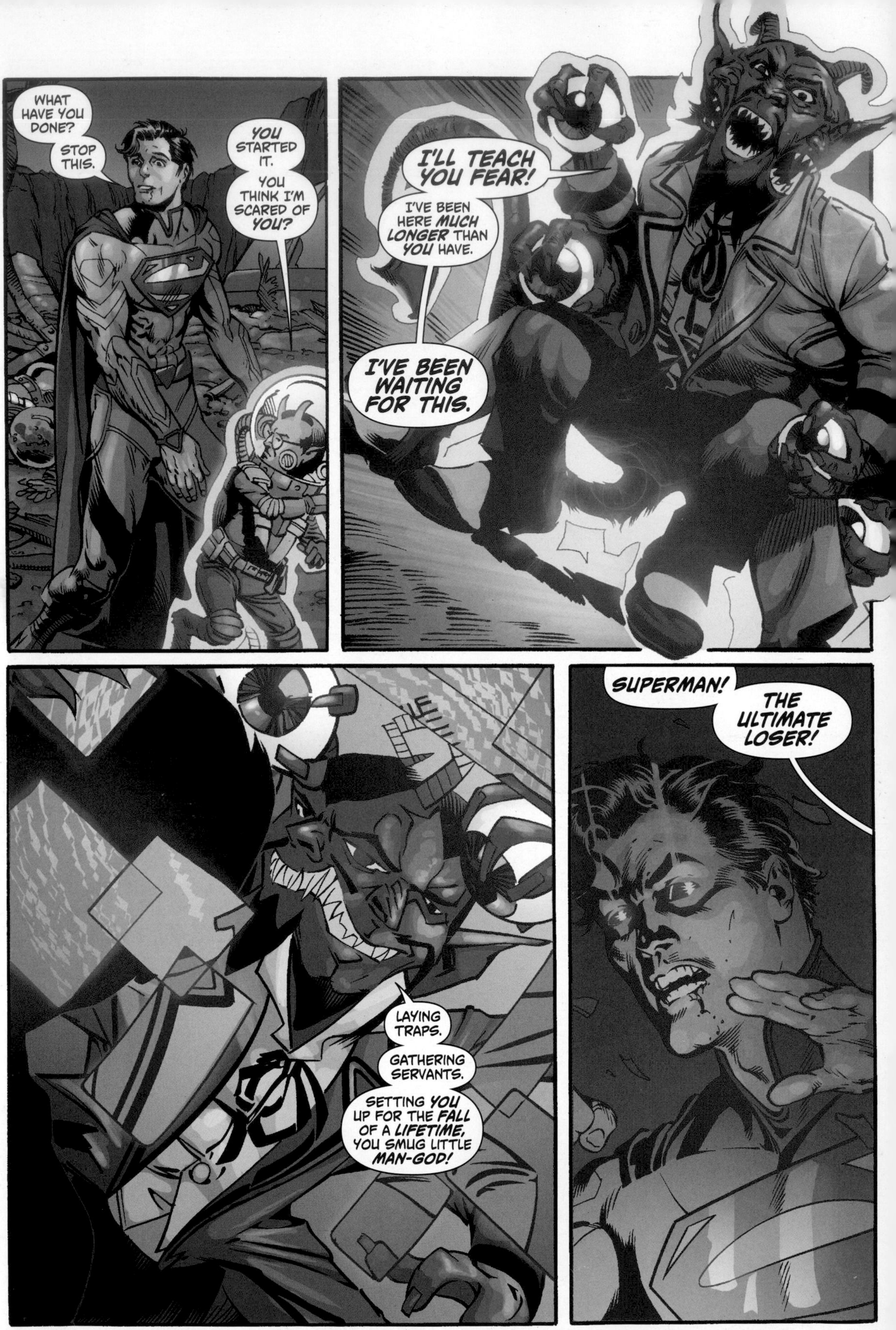
WHAT HAVE YOU DONE?
STOP THIS.
YOU STARTED IT.
YOU THINK I'M SCARED OF YOU?
I'LL TEACH YOU FEAR!
I'VE BEEN HERE MUCH LONGER THAN YOU HAVE.
I'VE BEEN WAITING FOR THIS.
LAYING TRAPS.
GATHERING SERVANTS.
SETTING YOU UP FOR THE FALL OF A LIFETIME, YOU SMUG LITTLE MAN-GOD!
SUPERMAN!
THE ULTIMATE LOSER!

NEXT: SUPERMAN AT THE END OF DAYS

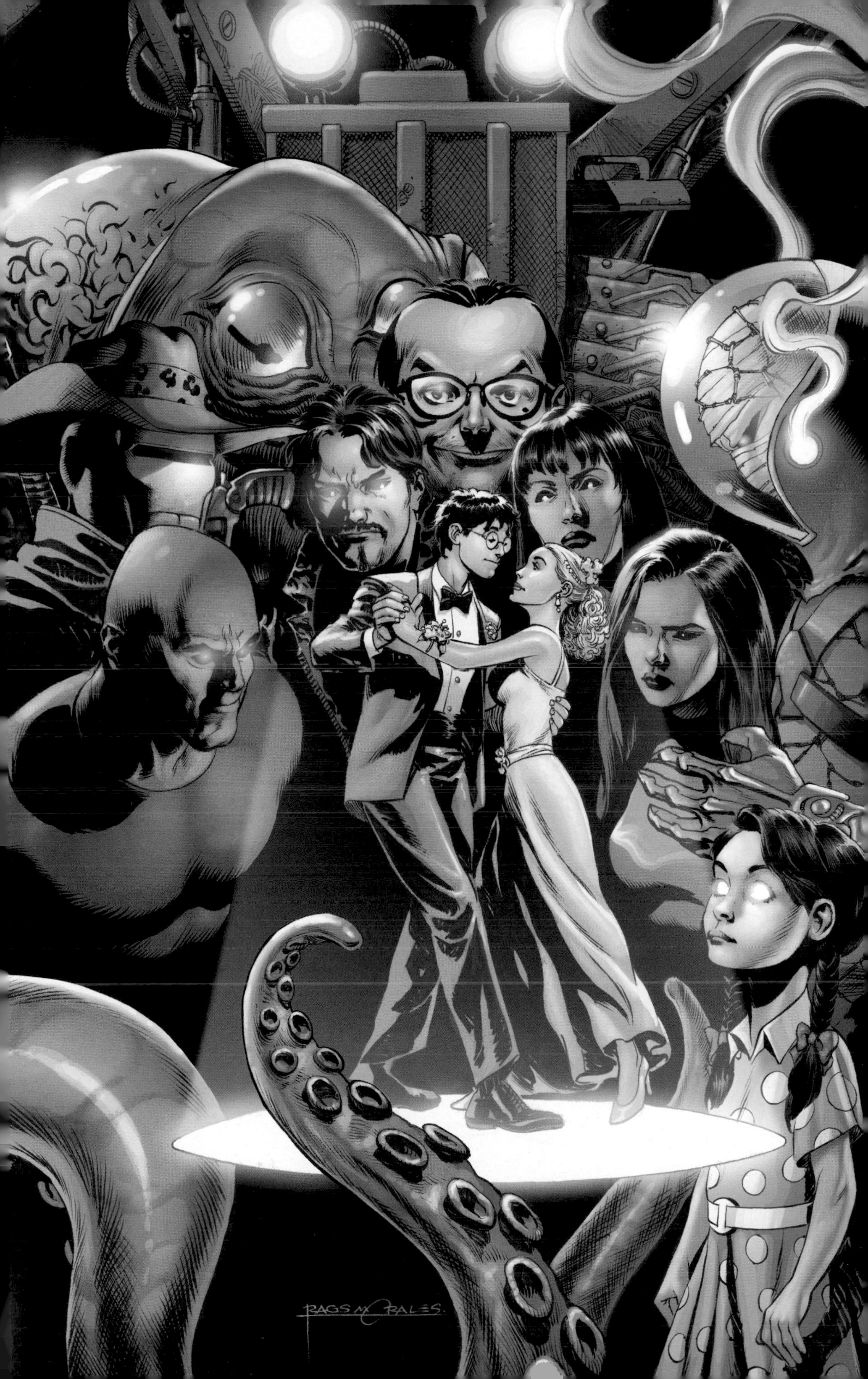
RAGS MORALES

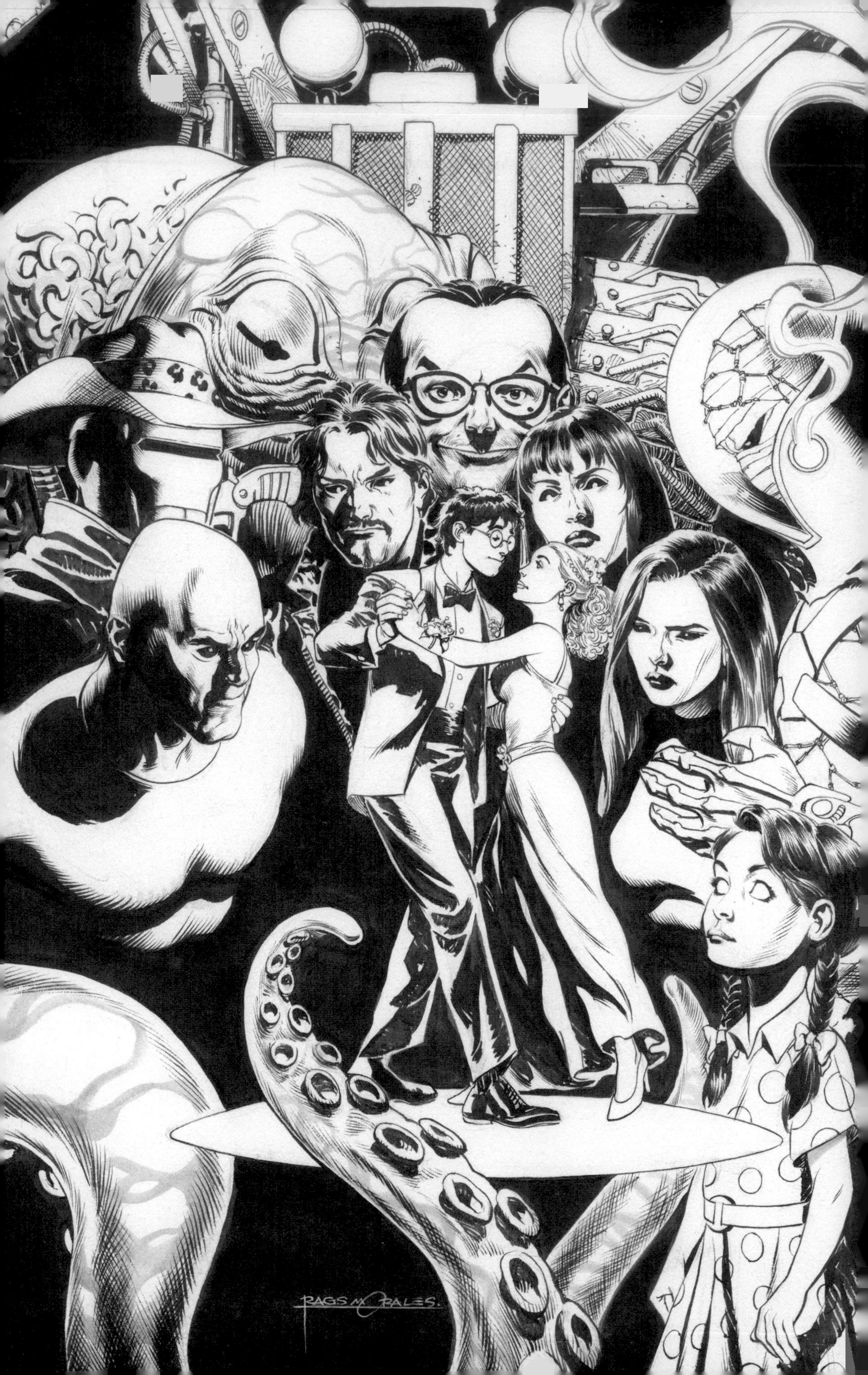

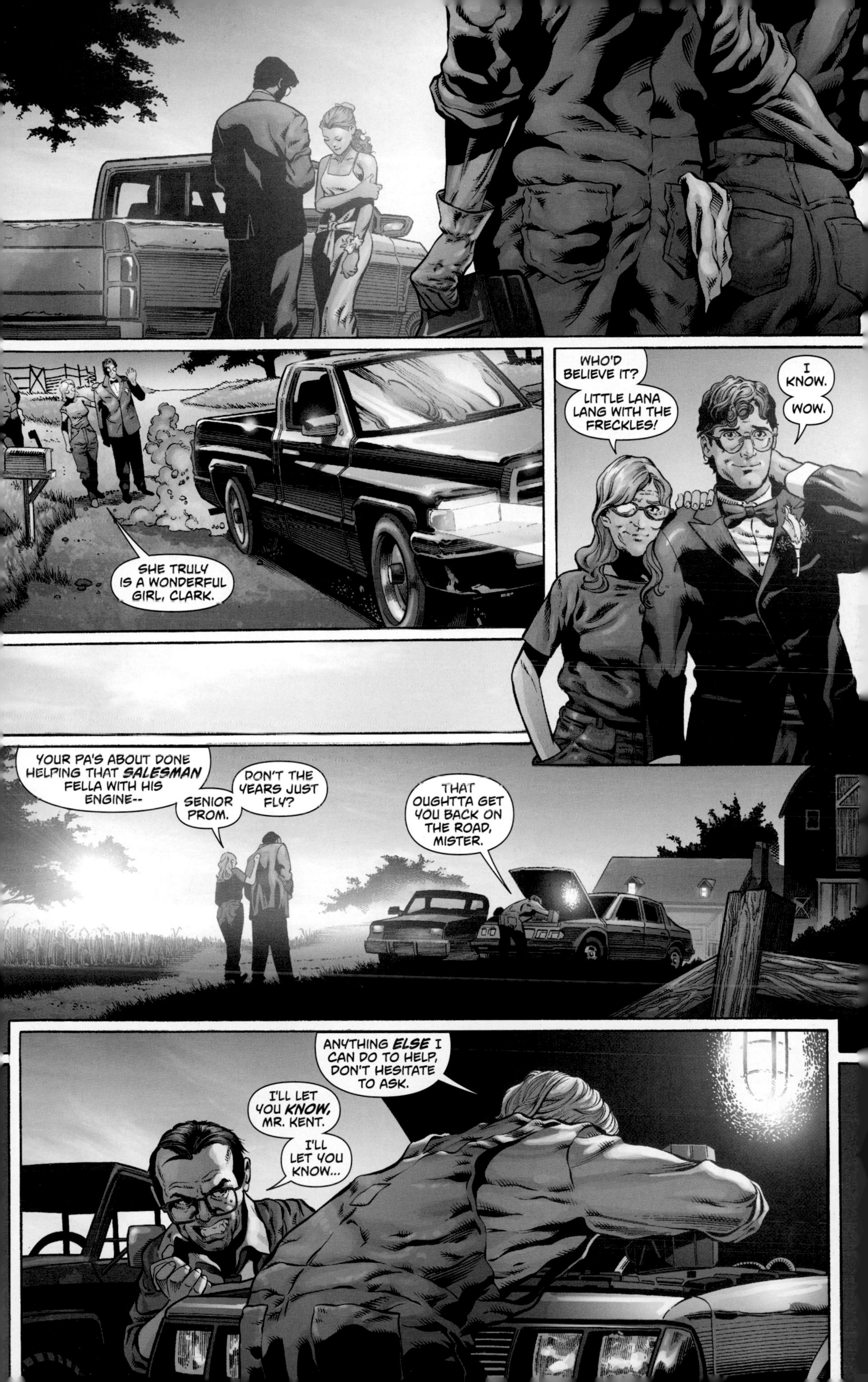

SHE TRULY IS A WONDERFUL GIRL, CLARK.
WHO'D BELIEVE IT?
LITTLE LANA LANG WITH THE FRECKLES!
I KNOW.
WOW.
YOUR PA'S ABOUT DONE HELPING THAT SALESMAN FELLA WITH HIS ENGINE--
SENIOR PROM.
DON'T THE YEARS JUST FLY?
THAT OUGHTTA GET YOU BACK ON THE ROAD, MISTER.
ANYTHING ELSE I CAN DO TO HELP, DON'T HESITATE TO ASK.
I'LL LET YOU KNOW, MR. KENT.
I'LL LET YOU KNOW...

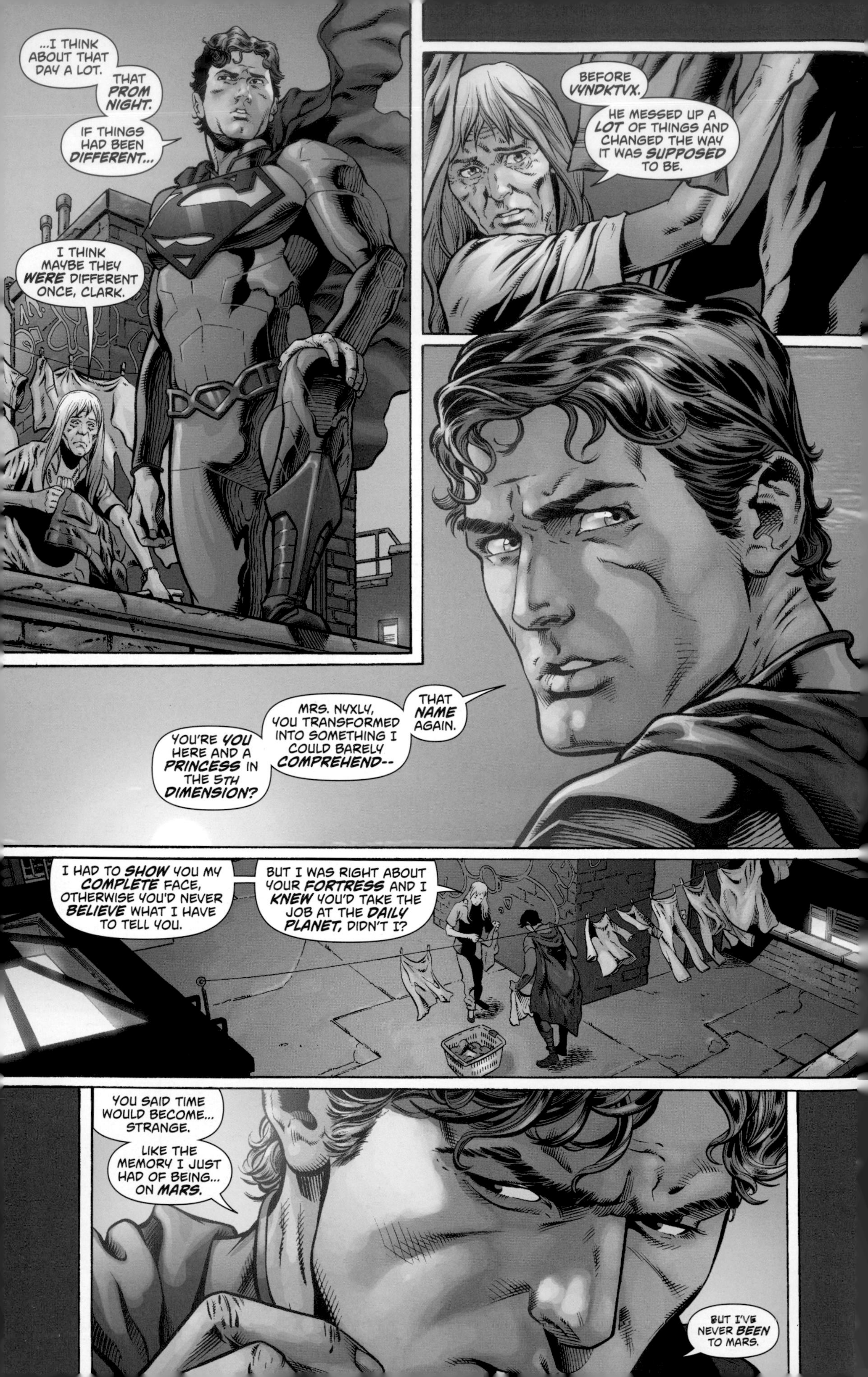
...I THINK ABOUT THAT DAY A LOT.
THAT PROM NIGHT.
IF THINGS HAD BEEN DIFFERENT...
I THINK MAYBE THEY WERE DIFFERENT ONCE, CLARK.
BEFORE VYNDKTVX.
HE MESSED UP A LOT OF THINGS AND CHANGED THE WAY IT WAS SUPPOSED TO BE.
THAT NAME AGAIN.
MRS. NYXLY, YOU TRANSFORMED INTO SOMETHING I COULD BARELY COMPREHEND--
YOU'RE YOU HERE AND A PRINCESS IN THE 5TH DIMENSION?
I HAD TO SHOW YOU MY COMPLETE FACE, OTHERWISE YOU'D NEVER BELIEVE WHAT I HAVE TO TELL YOU.
BUT I WAS RIGHT ABOUT YOUR FORTRESS AND I KNEW YOU'D TAKE THE JOB AT THE DAILY PLANET, DIDN'T I?
YOU SAID TIME WOULD BECOME... STRANGE.
LIKE THE MEMORY I JUST HAD OF BEING... ON MARS.
BUT I'VE NEVER BEEN TO MARS.

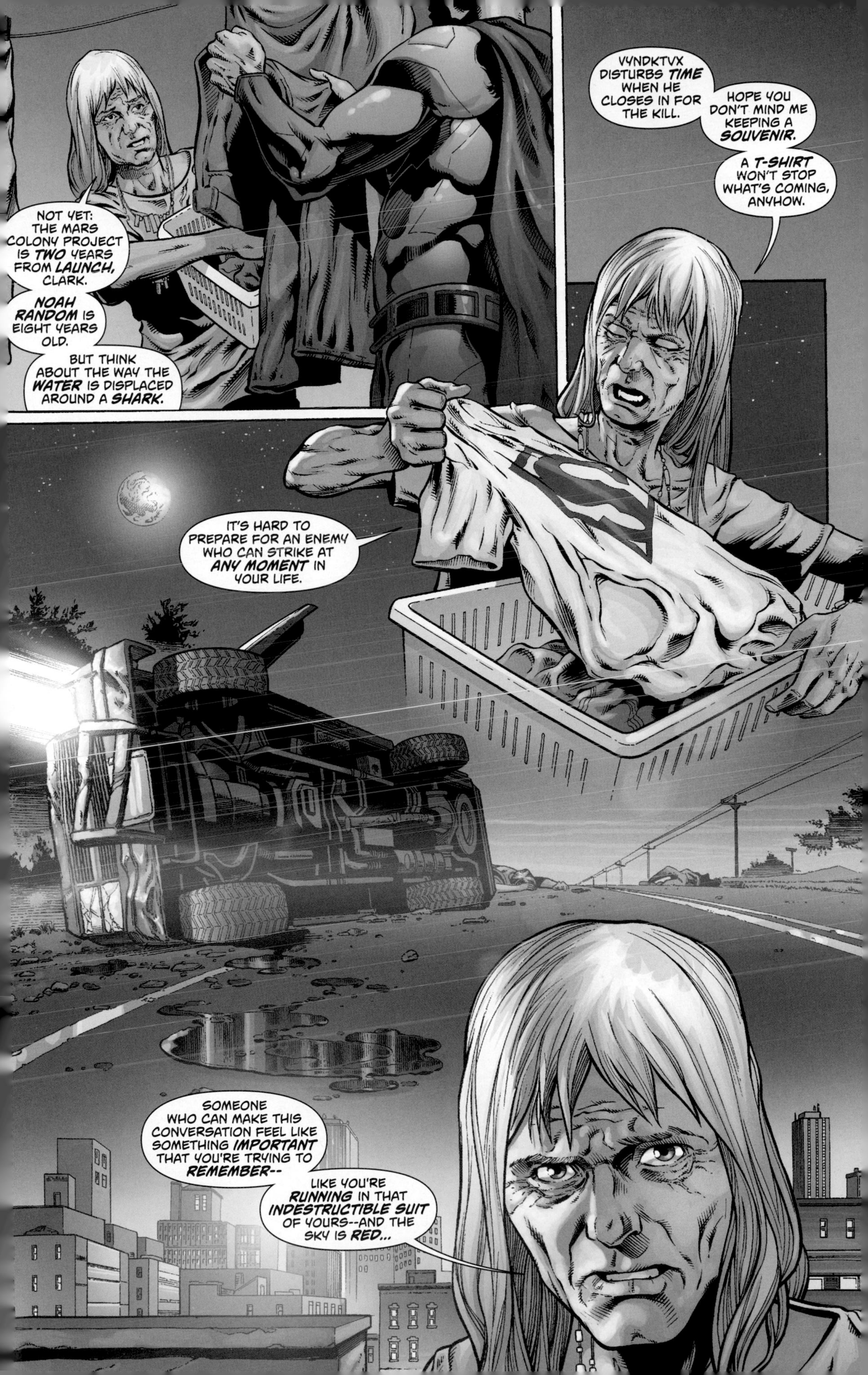
NOT YET: THE MARS COLONY PROJECT IS TWO YEARS FROM LAUNCH, CLARK.
NOAH RANDOM IS EIGHT YEARS OLD.
BUT THINK ABOUT THE WAY THE WATER IS DISPLACED AROUND A SHARK.
VYNDKTVX DISTURBS TIME WHEN HE CLOSES IN FOR THE KILL.
HOPE YOU DON'T MIND ME KEEPING A SOUVENIR.
A T-SHIRT WON'T STOP WHAT'S COMING, ANYHOW.
IT'S HARD TO PREPARE FOR AN ENEMY WHO CAN STRIKE AT ANY MOMENT IN YOUR LIFE.
SOMEONE WHO CAN MAKE THIS CONVERSATION FEEL LIKE SOMETHING IMPORTANT THAT YOU'RE TRYING TO REMEMBER--
LIKE YOU'RE RUNNING IN THAT INDESTRUCTIBLE SUIT OF YOURS--AND THE SKY IS RED...

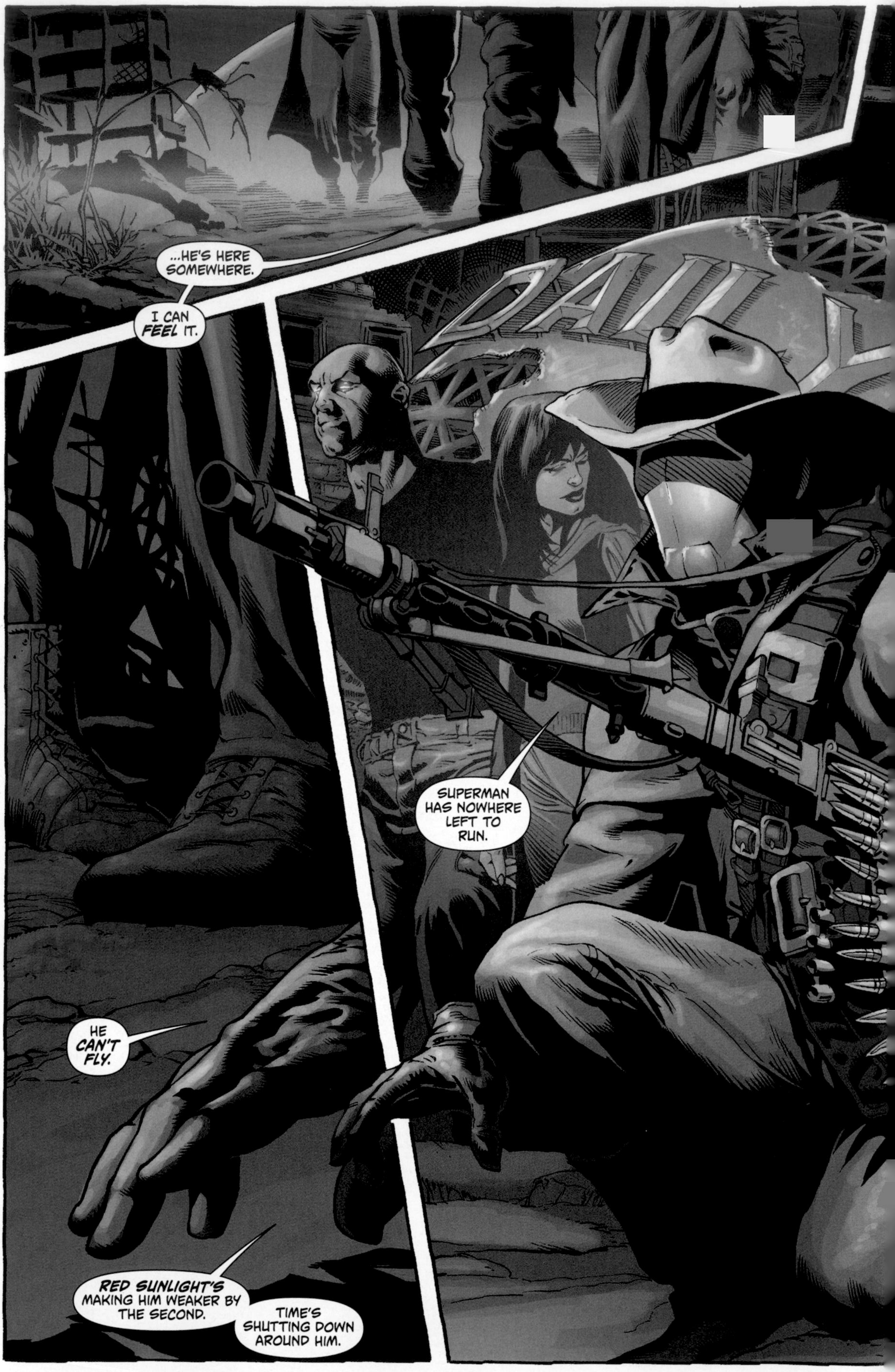
...HE'S HERE SOMEWHERE.
I CAN FEEL IT.
SUPERMAN HAS NOWHERE LEFT TO RUN.
HE CAN'T FLY.
RED SUNLIGHT'S MAKING HIM WEAKER BY THE SECOND.
TIME'S SHUTTING DOWN AROUND HIM.

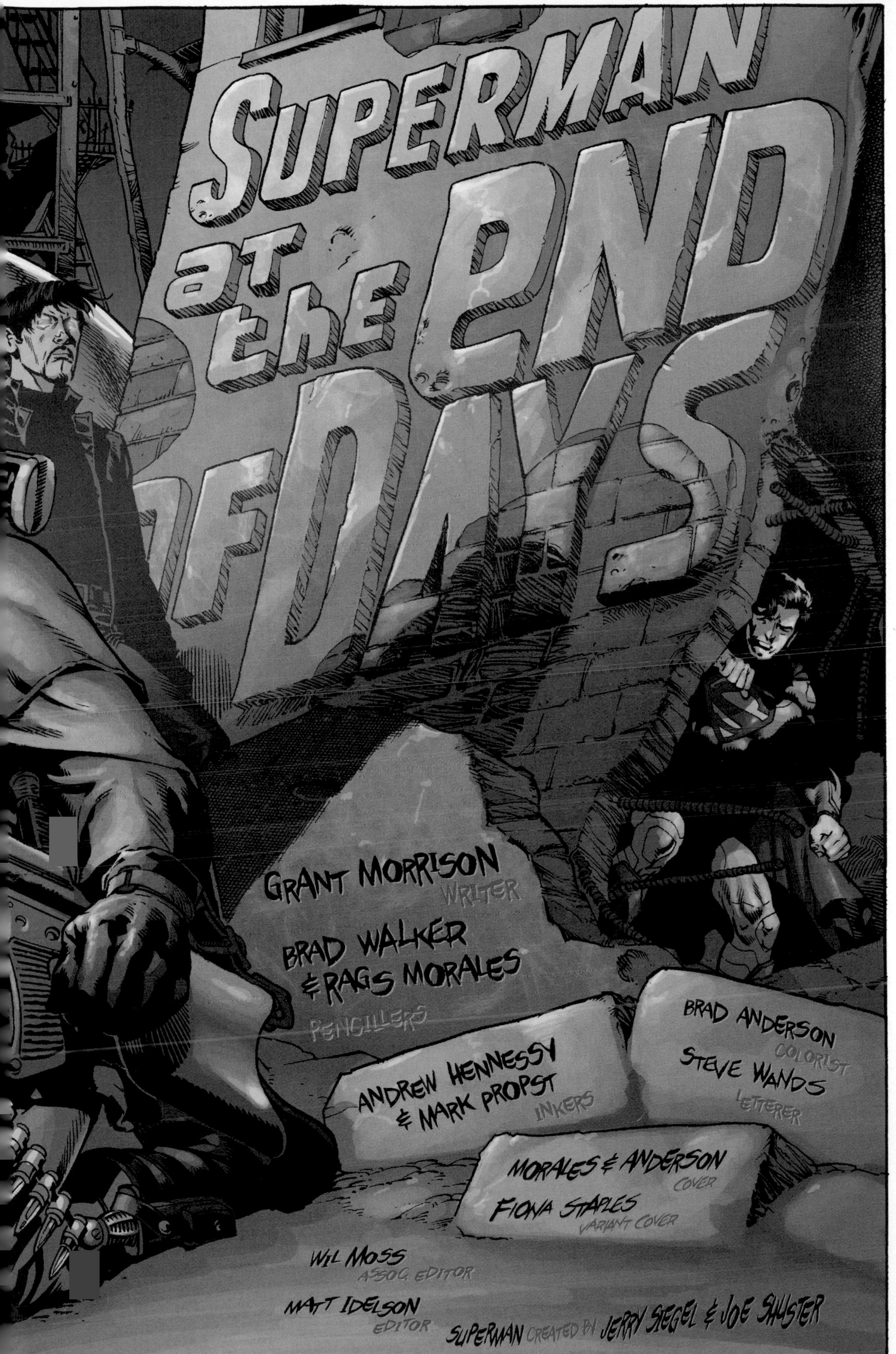
SUPERMAN at the END of DAYS
GRANT MORRISON
WRITER
BRAD WALKER & RAGS MORALES
PENCILLERS
ANDREW HENNESSY & MARK PROPST
INKERS
BRAD ANDERSON
COLORIST
STEVE WANDS
LETTERER
MORALES & ANDERSON
COVER
FIONA STAPLES
VARIANT COVER
WIL MOSS
ASSOC. EDITOR
MATT IDELSON
EDITOR
SUPERMAN CREATED BY JERRY SIEGEL & JOE SHUSTER

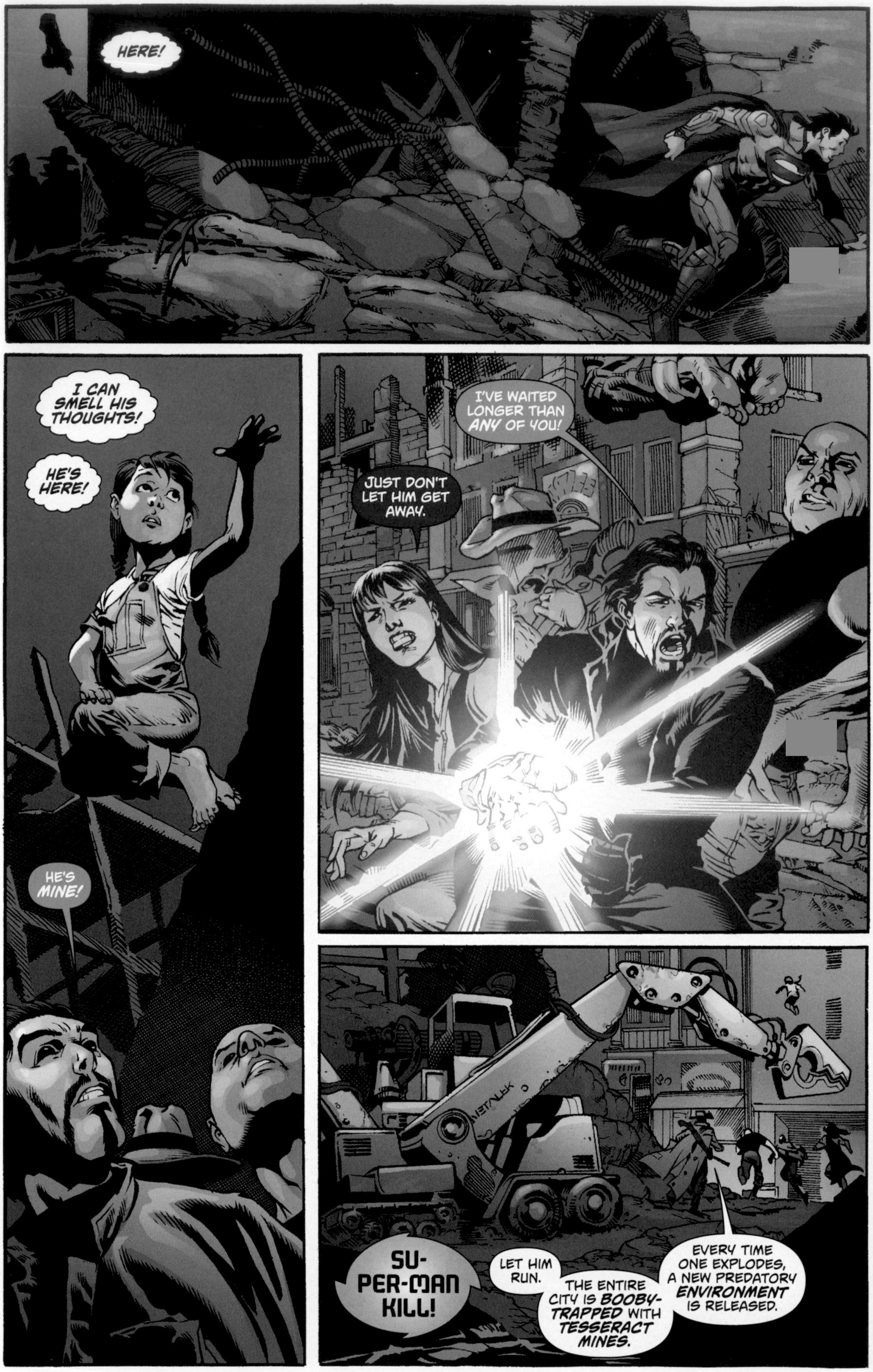
HERE!
I CAN SMELL HIS THOUGHTS!
HE'S HERE!
HE'S MINE!
I'VE WAITED LONGER THAN ANY OF YOU!
JUST DON'T LET HIM GET AWAY.
SU-PER-MAN KILL!
LET HIM RUN.
THE ENTIRE CITY IS BOOBY-TRAPPED WITH TESSERACT MINES.
EVERY TIME ONE EXPLODES, A NEW PREDATORY ENVIRONMENT IS RELEASED.

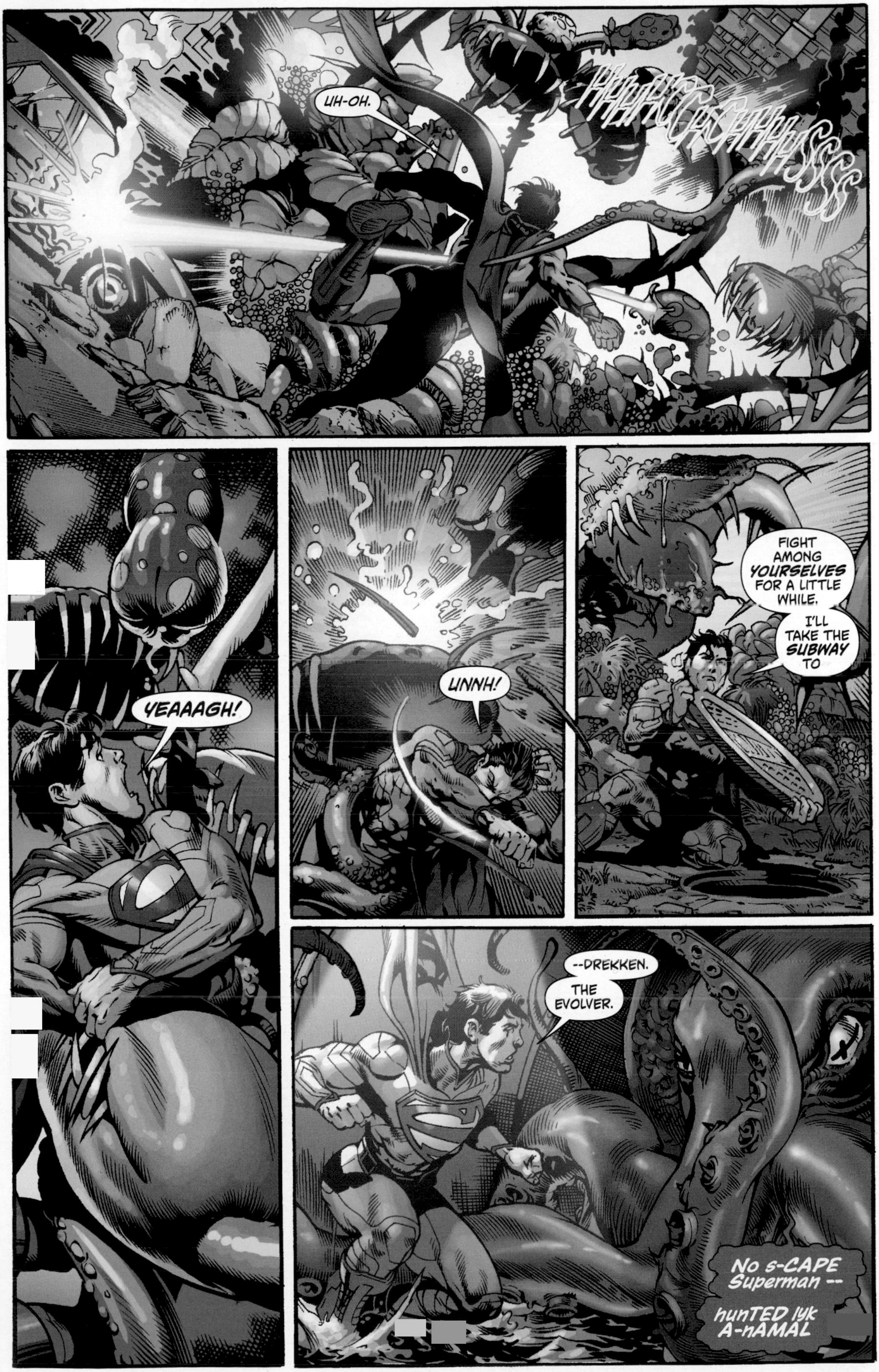
UH-OH.
YEAAAGH!
UNNH!
FIGHT AMONG YOURSELVES FOR A LITTLE WHILE.
I'LL TAKE THE SUBWAY TO
--DREKKEN.
THE EVOLVER.
No s-CAPE Superman --
hunTED lyk A-nAMAL

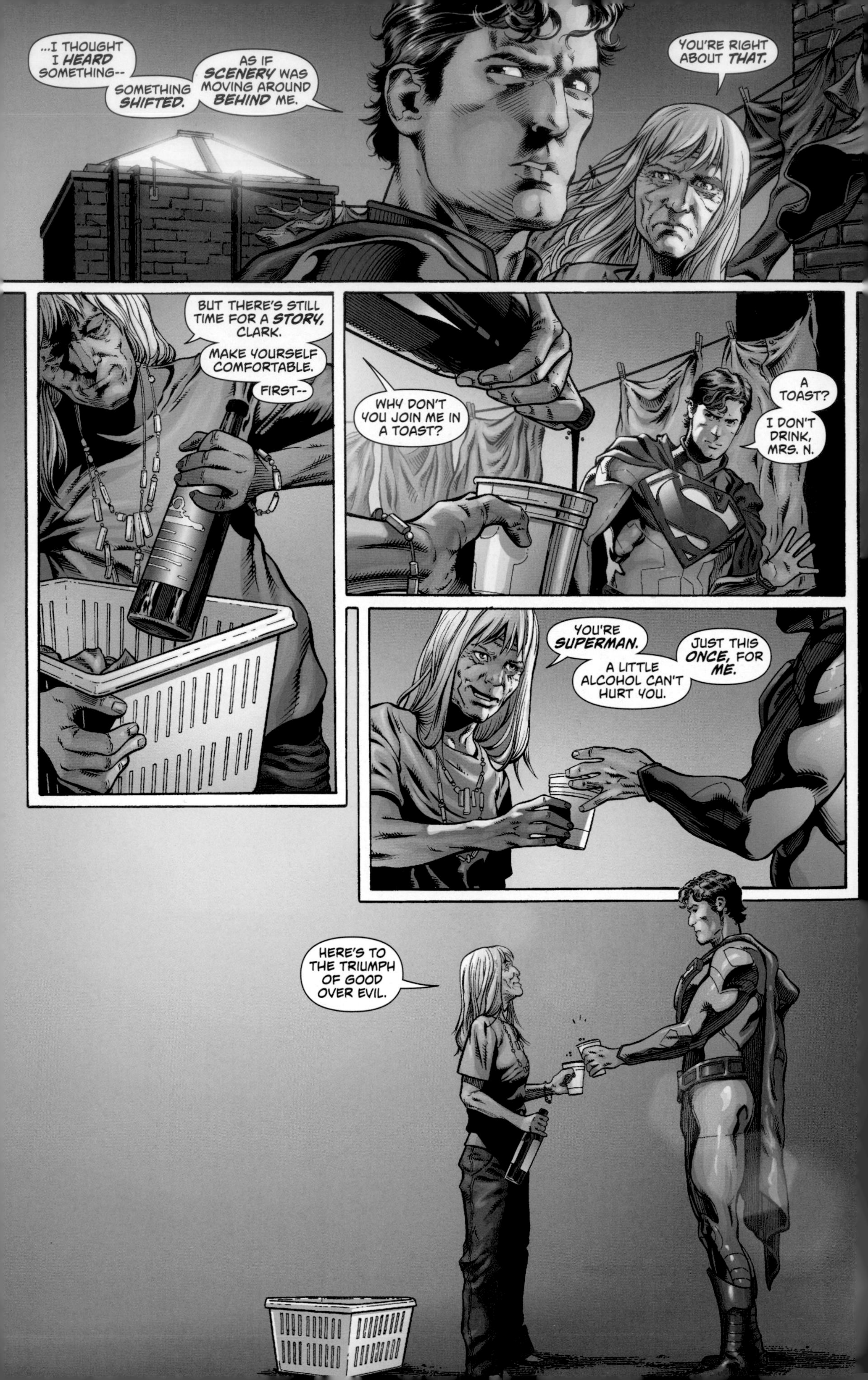

...I THOUGHT I HEARD SOMETHING--
SOMETHING SHIFTED.
AS IF SCENERY WAS MOVING AROUND BEHIND ME.
YOU'RE RIGHT ABOUT THAT.
BUT THERE'S STILL TIME FOR A STORY, CLARK.
MAKE YOURSELF COMFORTABLE.
FIRST--
WHY DON'T YOU JOIN ME IN A TOAST?
A TOAST?
I DON'T DRINK, MRS. N.
YOU'RE SUPERMAN.
A LITTLE ALCOHOL CAN'T HURT YOU.
JUST THIS ONCE, FOR ME.
HERE'S TO THE TRIUMPH OF GOOD OVER EVIL.

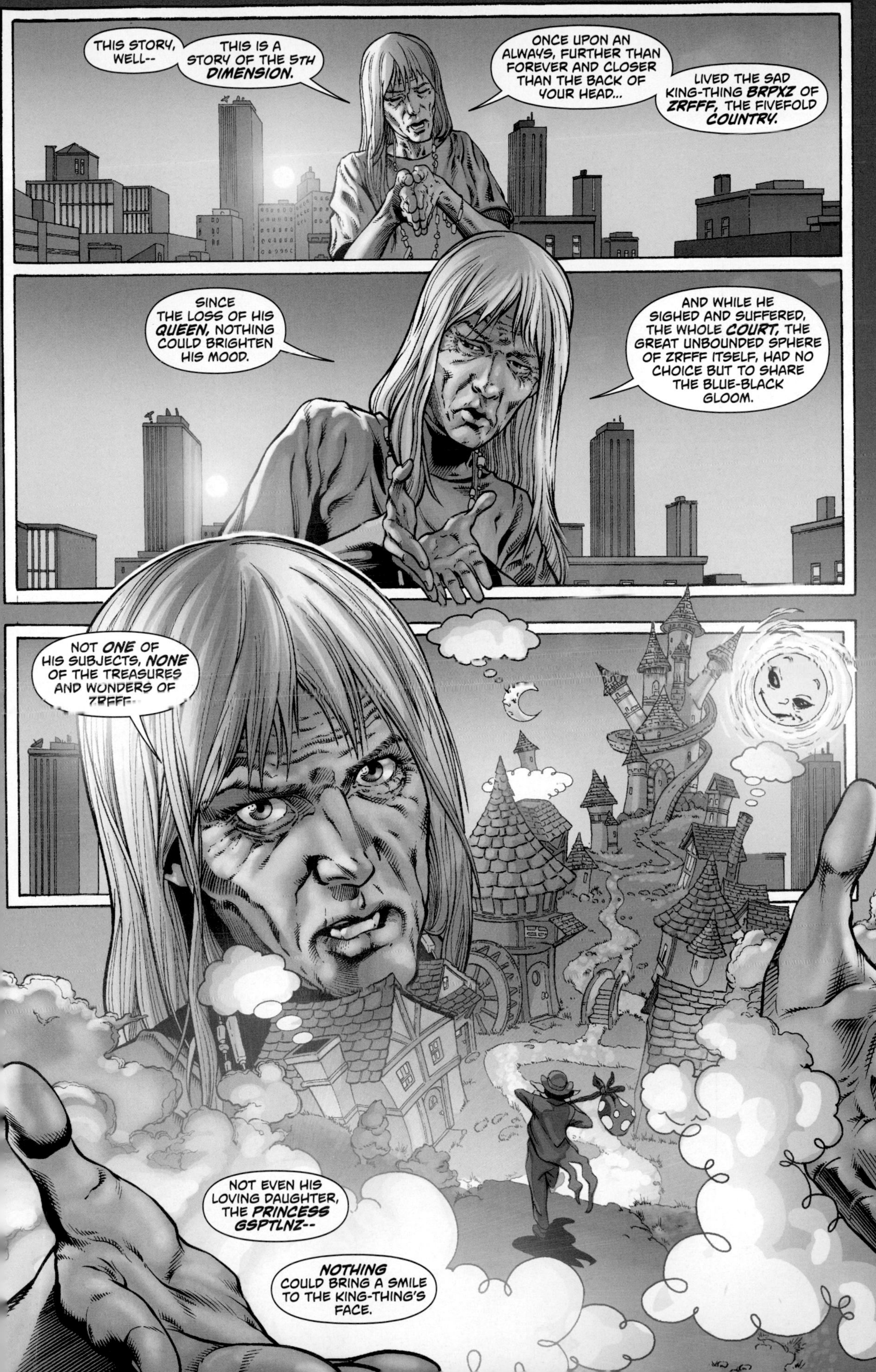
THIS STORY, WELL--
THIS IS A STORY OF THE 5TH DIMENSION.
ONCE UPON AN ALWAYS, FURTHER THAN FOREVER AND CLOSER THAN THE BACK OF YOUR HEAD...
LIVED THE SAD KING-THING BRPXZ OF ZRFFF, THE FIVEFOLD COUNTRY.
SINCE THE LOSS OF HIS QUEEN, NOTHING COULD BRIGHTEN HIS MOOD.
AND WHILE HE SIGHED AND SUFFERED, THE WHOLE COURT, THE GREAT UNBOUNDED SPHERE OF ZRFFF ITSELF, HAD NO CHOICE BUT TO SHARE THE BLUE-BLACK GLOOM.
NOT ONE OF HIS SUBJECTS, NONE OF THE TREASURES AND WONDERS OF ZRFFF--
NOT EVEN HIS LOVING DAUGHTER, THE PRINCESS GSPTLNZ--
NOTHING COULD BRING A SMILE TO THE KING-THING'S FACE.

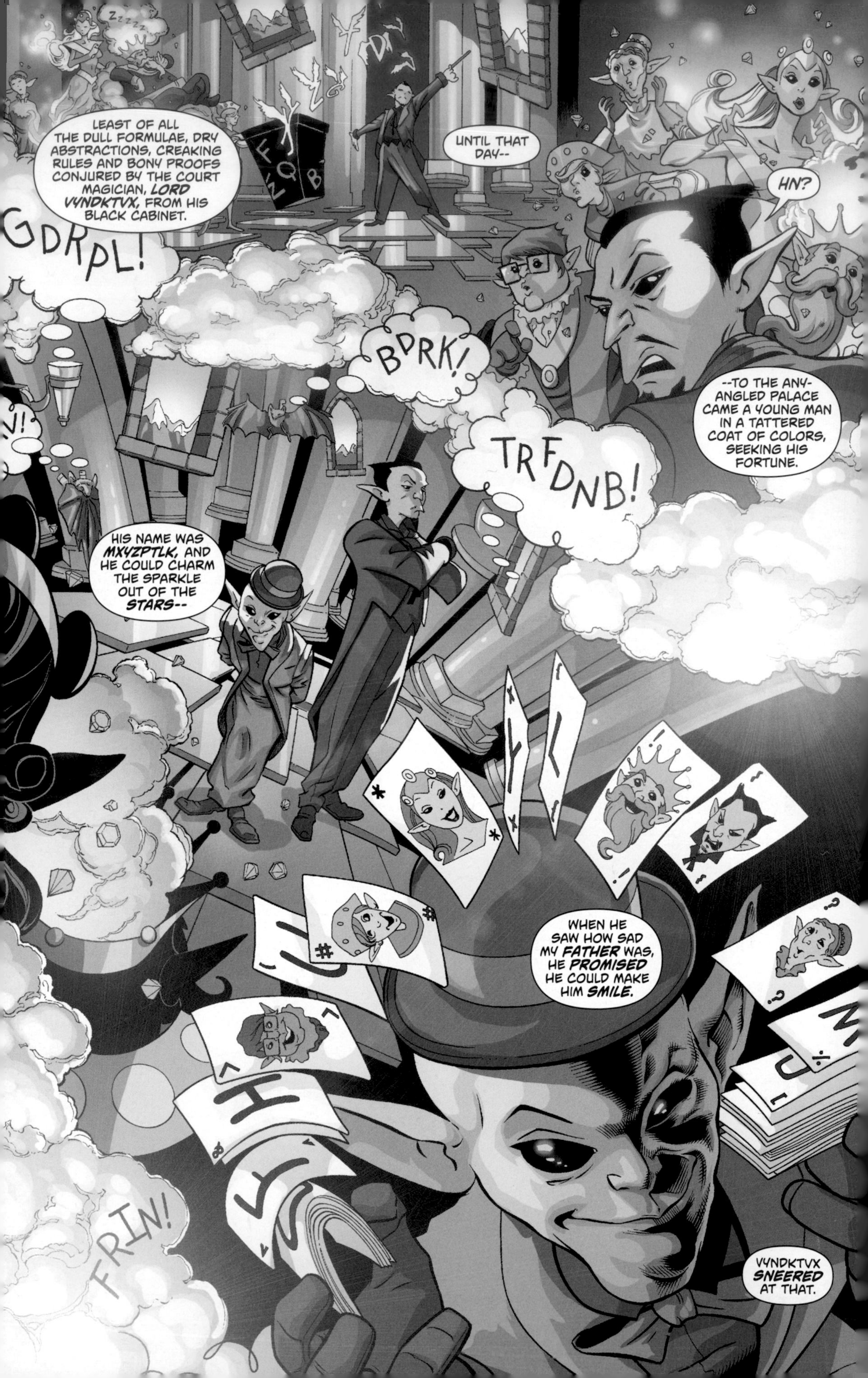
LEAST OF ALL THE DULL FORMULAE, DRY ABSTRACTIONS, CREAKING RULES AND BONY PROOFS CONJURED BY THE COURT MAGICIAN, LORD VYNDKTVX, FROM HIS BLACK CABINET.
UNTIL THAT DAY--
HN?
GDRPL!
BDRK!
TRFDNB!
--TO THE ANY-ANGLED PALACE CAME A YOUNG MAN IN A TATTERED COAT OF COLORS, SEEKING HIS FORTUNE.
HIS NAME WAS MXYZPTLK, AND HE COULD CHARM THE SPARKLE OUT OF THE STARS--
WHEN HE SAW HOW SAD MY FATHER WAS, HE PROMISED HE COULD MAKE HIM SMILE.
FRIN!
VYNDKTVX SNEERED AT THAT.

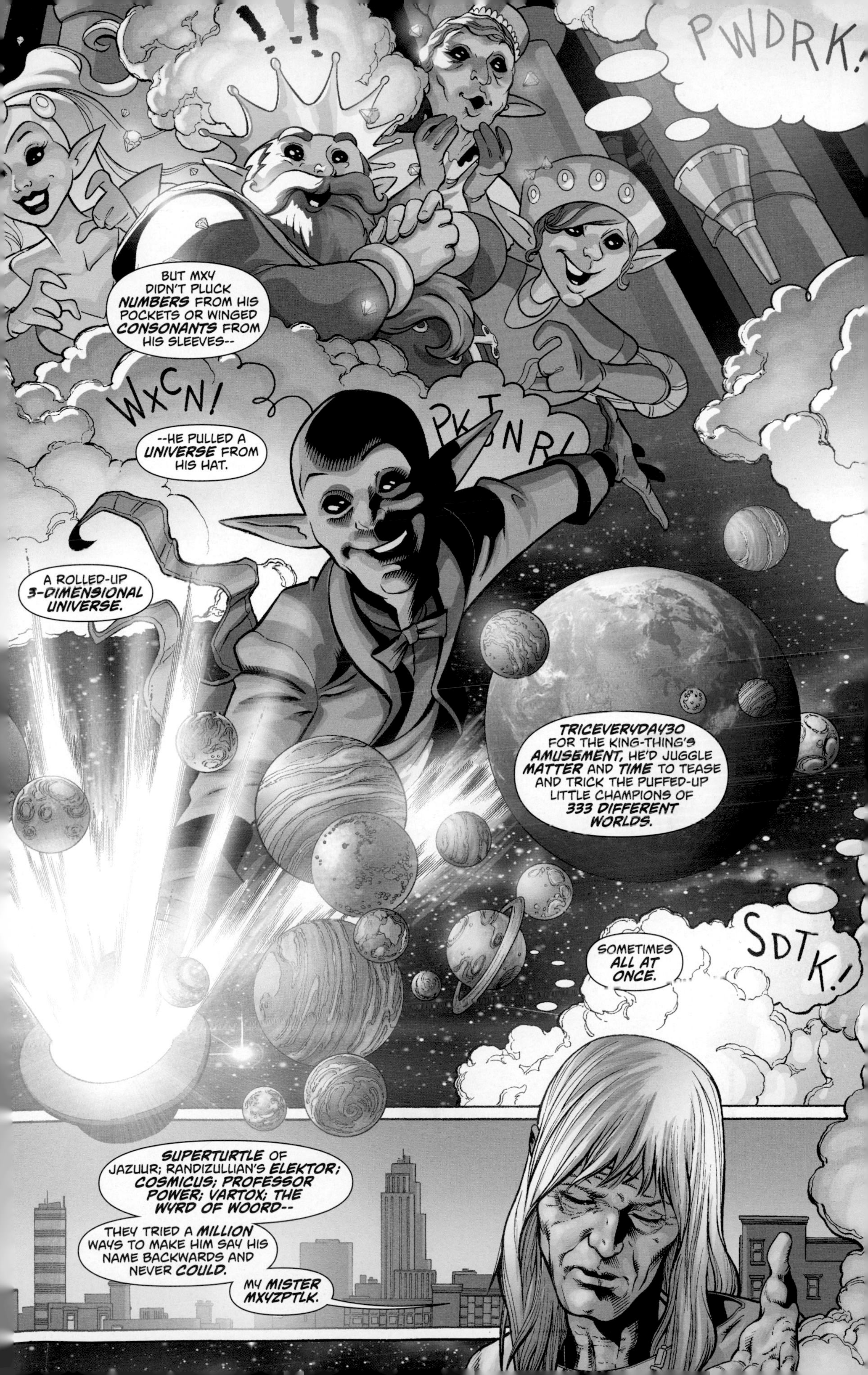
!!!
PWDRK!
BUT MXY DIDN'T PLUCK NUMBERS FROM HIS POCKETS OR WINGED CONSONANTS FROM HIS SLEEVES--
WXCN!
PKTNR!
--HE PULLED A UNIVERSE FROM HIS HAT.
A ROLLED-UP 3-DIMENSIONAL UNIVERSE.
TRICEVERYDAY30 FOR THE KING-THING'S AMUSEMENT, HE'D JUGGLE MATTER AND TIME TO TEASE AND TRICK THE PUFFED-UP LITTLE CHAMPIONS OF 333 DIFFERENT WORLDS.
SOMETIMES ALL AT ONCE.
SDTK!
SUPERTURTLE OF JAZUUR; RANDIZULLIAN'S ELEKTOR; COSMICUS; PROFESSOR POWER; VARTOX; THE WYRD OF WOORD--
THEY TRIED A MILLION WAYS TO MAKE HIM SAY HIS NAME BACKWARDS AND NEVER COULD.
MY MISTER MXYZPTLK.

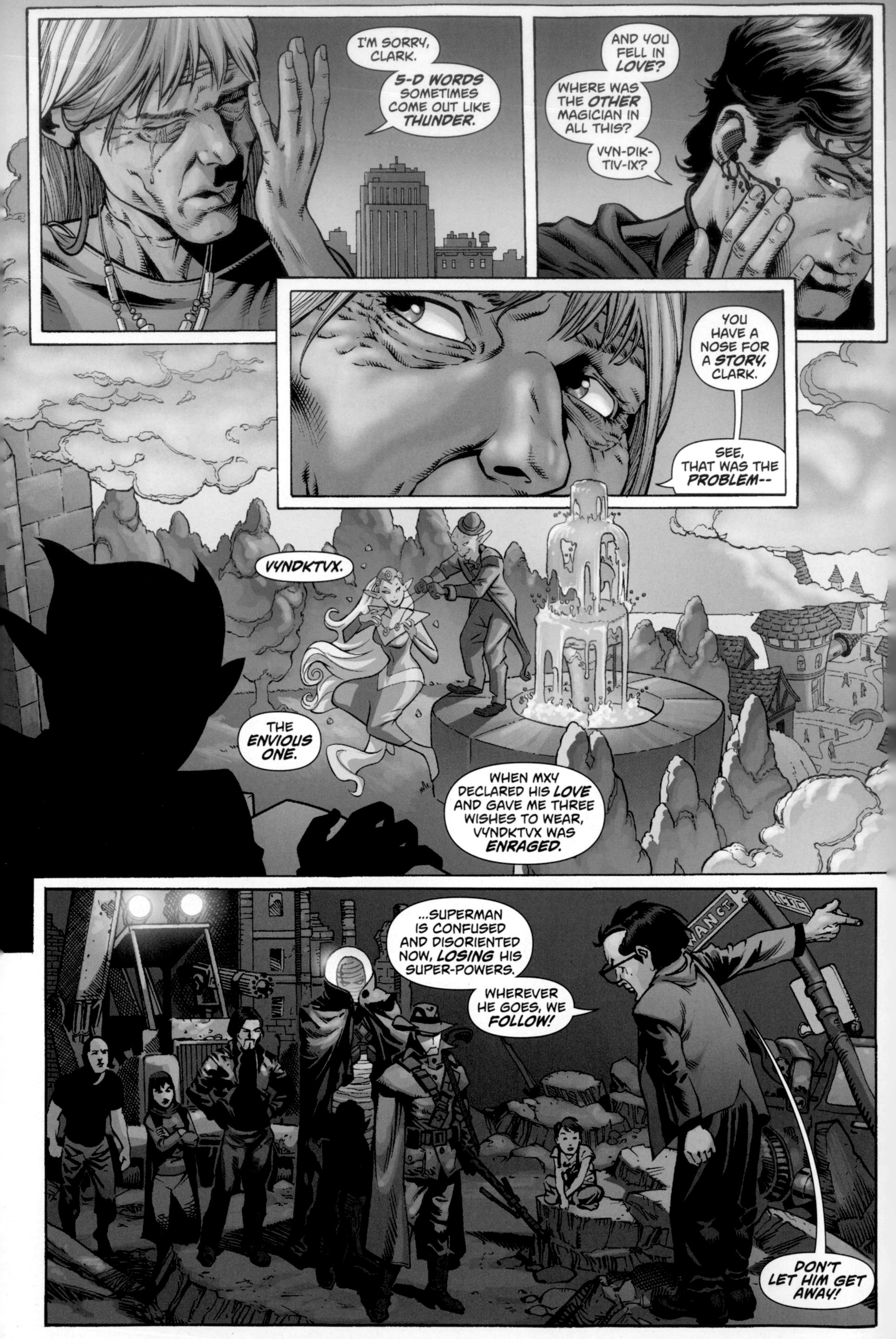

I'M SORRY, CLARK.
5-D WORDS SOMETIMES COME OUT LIKE THUNDER.
AND YOU FELL IN LOVE?
WHERE WAS THE OTHER MAGICIAN IN ALL THIS?
VYN-DIK-TIV-IX?
YOU HAVE A NOSE FOR A STORY, CLARK.
SEE, THAT WAS THE PROBLEM--
VYNDKTVX.
THE ENVIOUS ONE.
WHEN MXY DECLARED HIS LOVE AND GAVE ME THREE WISHES TO WEAR, VYNDKTVX WAS ENRAGED.
...SUPERMAN IS CONFUSED AND DISORIENTED NOW, LOSING HIS SUPER-POWERS.
WHEREVER HE GOES, WE FOLLOW!
DON'T LET HIM GET AWAY!

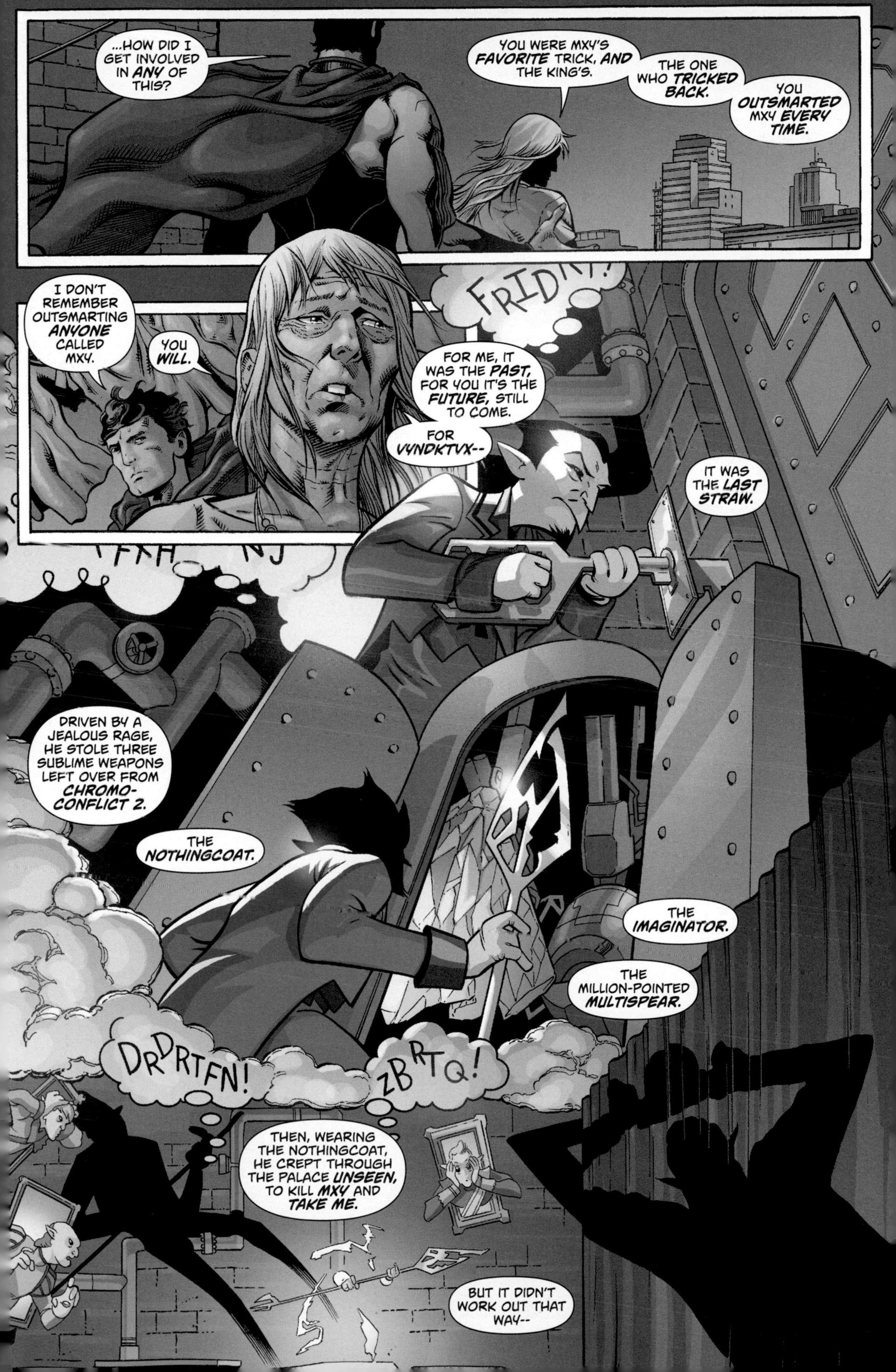
...HOW DID I GET INVOLVED IN *ANY* OF THIS?
YOU WERE MXY'S *FAVORITE* TRICK, *AND* THE KING'S.
THE ONE WHO *TRICKED BACK.*
YOU *OUTSMARTED* MXY *EVERY TIME.*
I DON'T REMEMBER OUTSMARTING *ANYONE* CALLED MXY.
YOU *WILL.*
FRIDK!
FOR ME, IT WAS THE *PAST,* FOR YOU IT'S THE *FUTURE,* STILL TO COME.
FOR *VYNDKTVX--*
IT WAS THE *LAST STRAW.*
DRIVEN BY A JEALOUS RAGE, HE STOLE THREE SUBLIME WEAPONS LEFT OVER FROM *CHROMO-CONFLICT 2.*
THE *NOTHINGCOAT.*
THE *IMAGINATOR.*
THE MILLION-POINTED *MULTISPEAR.*
DRDRTFN!
ZBRTQ!
THEN, WEARING THE NOTHINGCOAT, HE CREPT THROUGH THE PALACE *UNSEEN,* TO KILL *MXY* AND *TAKE ME.*
BUT IT DIDN'T WORK OUT THAT WAY--

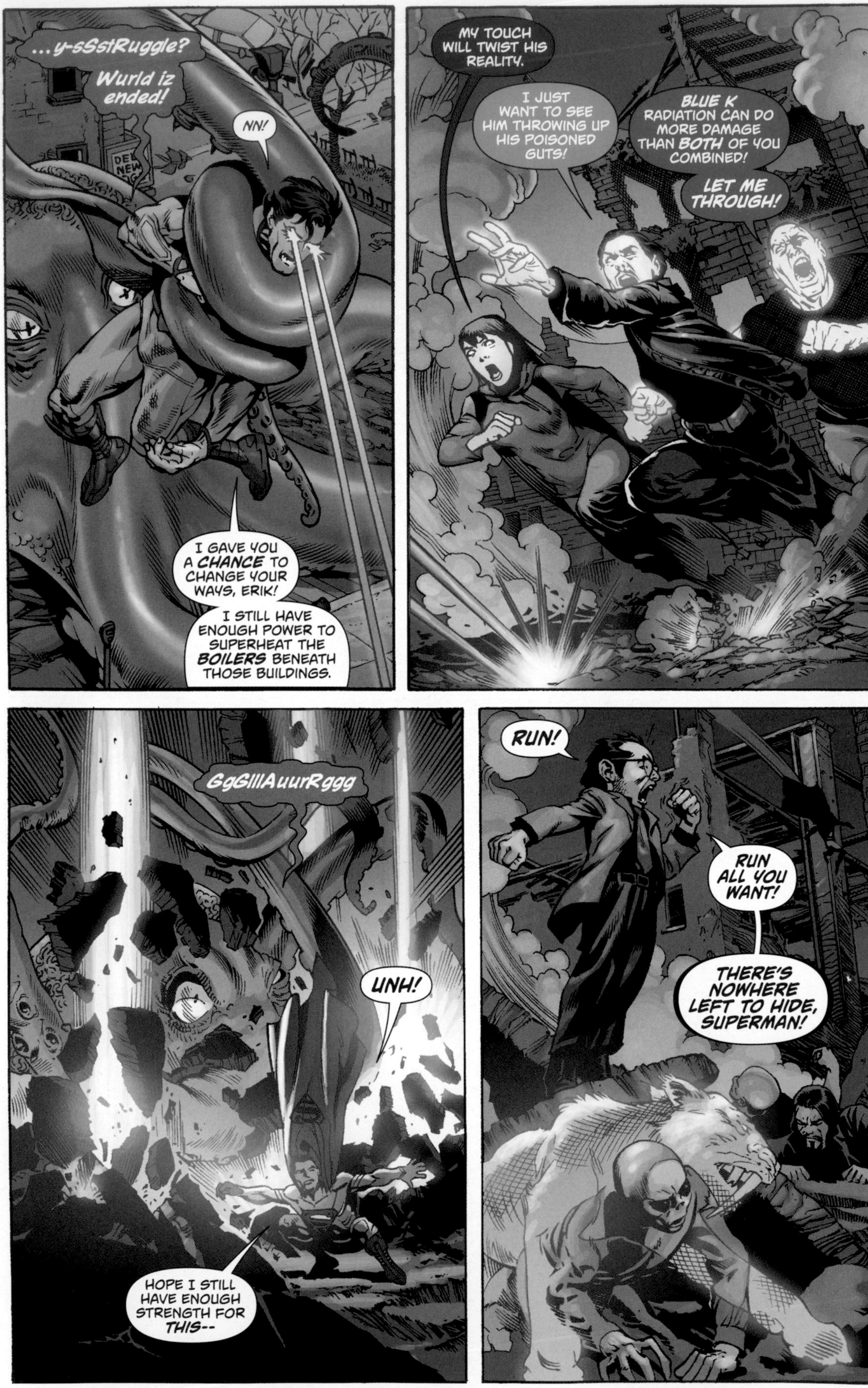
...y-sSstRuggle?
Wurld iz ended!
NN!
I GAVE YOU A CHANCE TO CHANGE YOUR WAYS, ERIK!
I STILL HAVE ENOUGH POWER TO SUPERHEAT THE BOILERS BENEATH THOSE BUILDINGS.
MY TOUCH WILL TWIST HIS REALITY.
I JUST WANT TO SEE HIM THROWING UP HIS POISONED GUTS!
BLUE K RADIATION CAN DO MORE DAMAGE THAN BOTH OF YOU COMBINED!
LET ME THROUGH!
GgGlllAuurRggg
UNH!
HOPE I STILL HAVE ENOUGH STRENGTH FOR THIS--
RUN!
RUN ALL YOU WANT!
THERE'S NOWHERE LEFT TO HIDE, SUPERMAN!

...I HOPE YOU CAN *HEAR* ME.

THEY *GUTTED* THE *ARCTIC* FORTRESS, BUT MY *YUCATAN BASE* IS STILL HERE.

THE *SECOND* OF THREE 5-D WEAPONS WAS THE *MULTITUDE.*

THE *THIRD* IS SOME KIND OF *DEMON* IN A *BOX.*

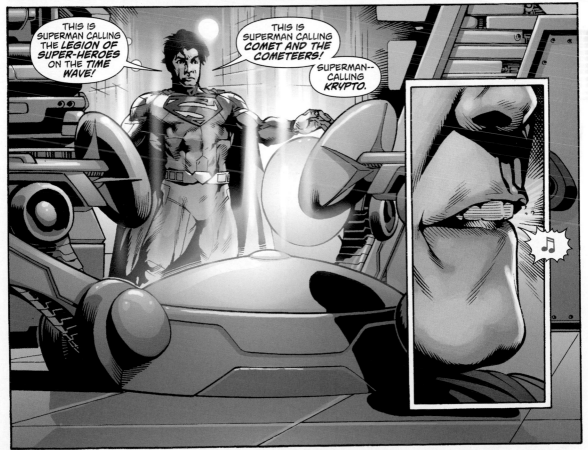

THIS IS SUPERMAN CALLING THE *LEGION OF SUPER-HEROES* ON THE *TIME WAVE!*

THIS IS SUPERMAN CALLING *COMET* AND THE *COMETEERS!*

SUPERMAN-- CALLING *KRYPTO.*

♪

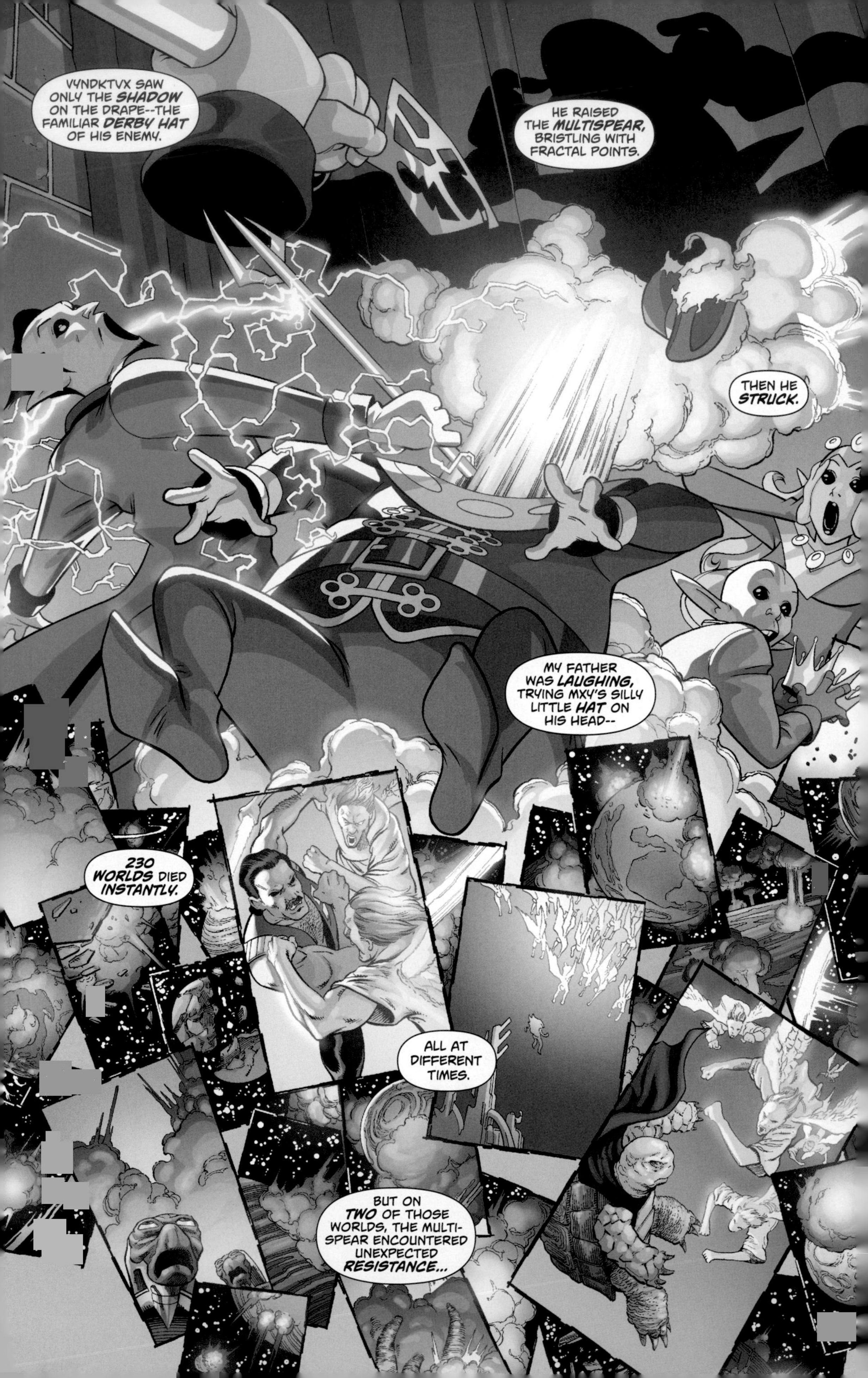
VYNDKTVX SAW ONLY THE SHADOW ON THE DRAPE--THE FAMILIAR DERBY HAT OF HIS ENEMY.
HE RAISED THE MULTISPEAR, BRISTLING WITH FRACTAL POINTS.
THEN HE STRUCK.
MY FATHER WAS LAUGHING, TRYING MXY'S SILLY LITTLE HAT ON HIS HEAD--
230 WORLDS DIED INSTANTLY.
ALL AT DIFFERENT TIMES.
BUT ON TWO OF THOSE WORLDS, THE MULTI-SPEAR ENCOUNTERED UNEXPECTED RESISTANCE...

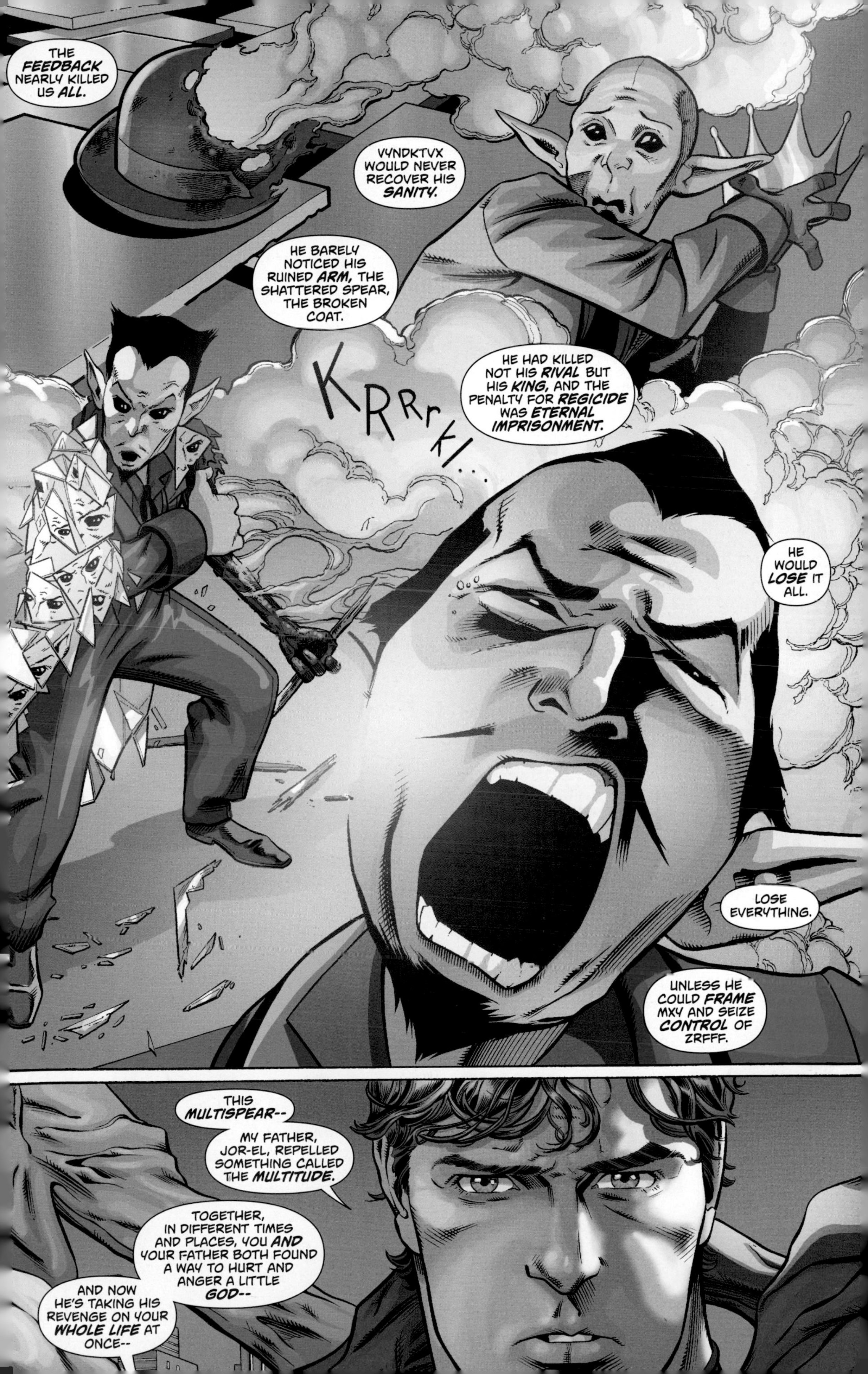
THE FEEDBACK NEARLY KILLED US ALL.
VYNDKTVX WOULD NEVER RECOVER HIS SANITY.
HE BARELY NOTICED HIS RUINED ARM, THE SHATTERED SPEAR, THE BROKEN COAT.
KRRrKl...
HE HAD KILLED NOT HIS RIVAL BUT HIS KING, AND THE PENALTY FOR REGICIDE WAS ETERNAL IMPRISONMENT.
HE WOULD LOSE IT ALL.
LOSE EVERYTHING.
UNLESS HE COULD FRAME MXY AND SEIZE CONTROL OF ZRFFF.
THIS MULTISPEAR--
MY FATHER, JOR-EL, REPELLED SOMETHING CALLED THE MULTITUDE.
TOGETHER, IN DIFFERENT TIMES AND PLACES, YOU AND YOUR FATHER BOTH FOUND A WAY TO HURT AND ANGER A LITTLE GOD--
AND NOW HE'S TAKING HIS REVENGE ON YOUR WHOLE LIFE AT ONCE--

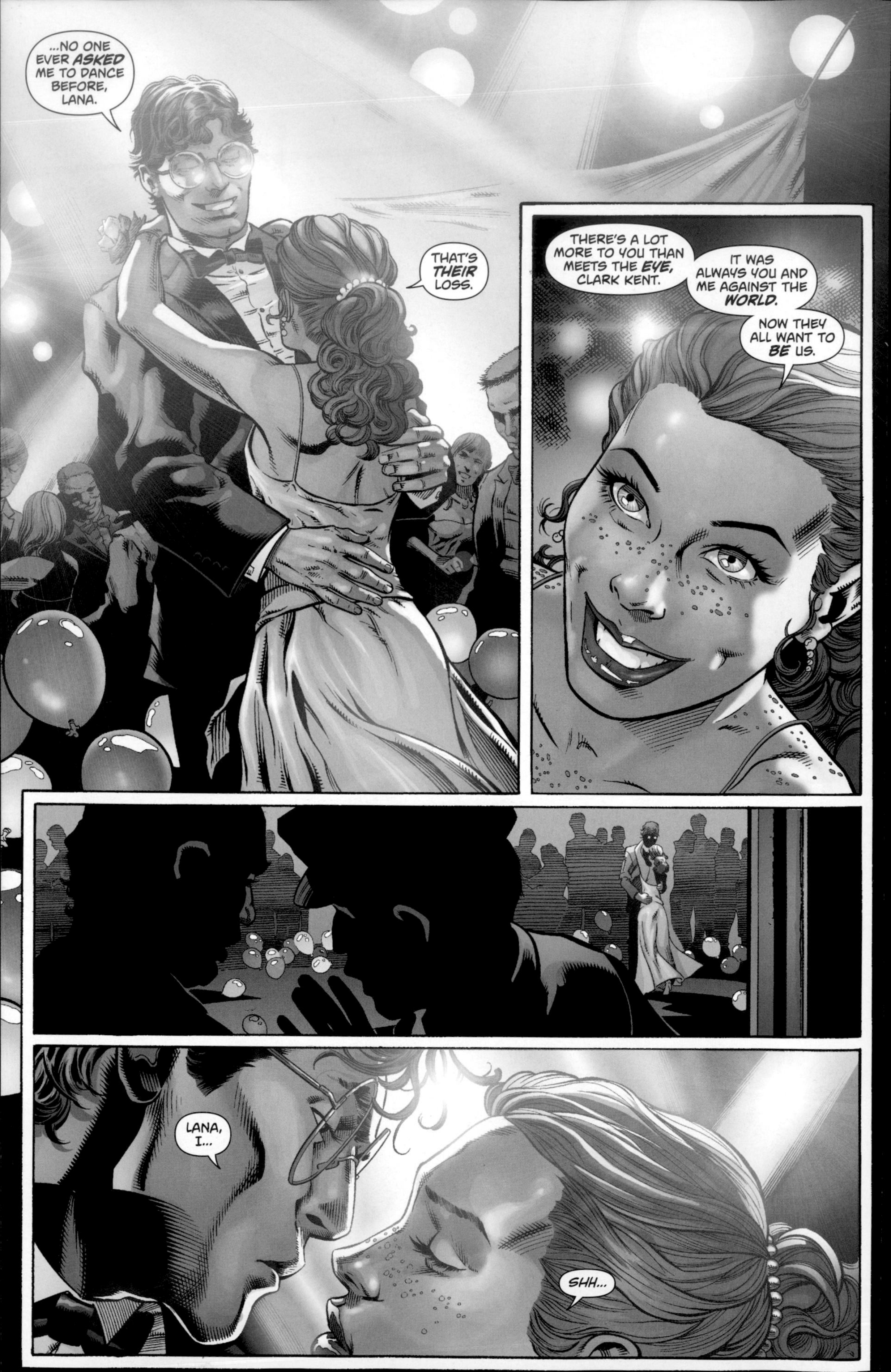
...NO ONE EVER ASKED ME TO DANCE BEFORE, LANA.
THAT'S THEIR LOSS.
THERE'S A LOT MORE TO YOU THAN MEETS THE EYE, CLARK KENT.
IT WAS ALWAYS YOU AND ME AGAINST THE WORLD.
NOW THEY ALL WANT TO BE US.
LANA, I...
SHH...

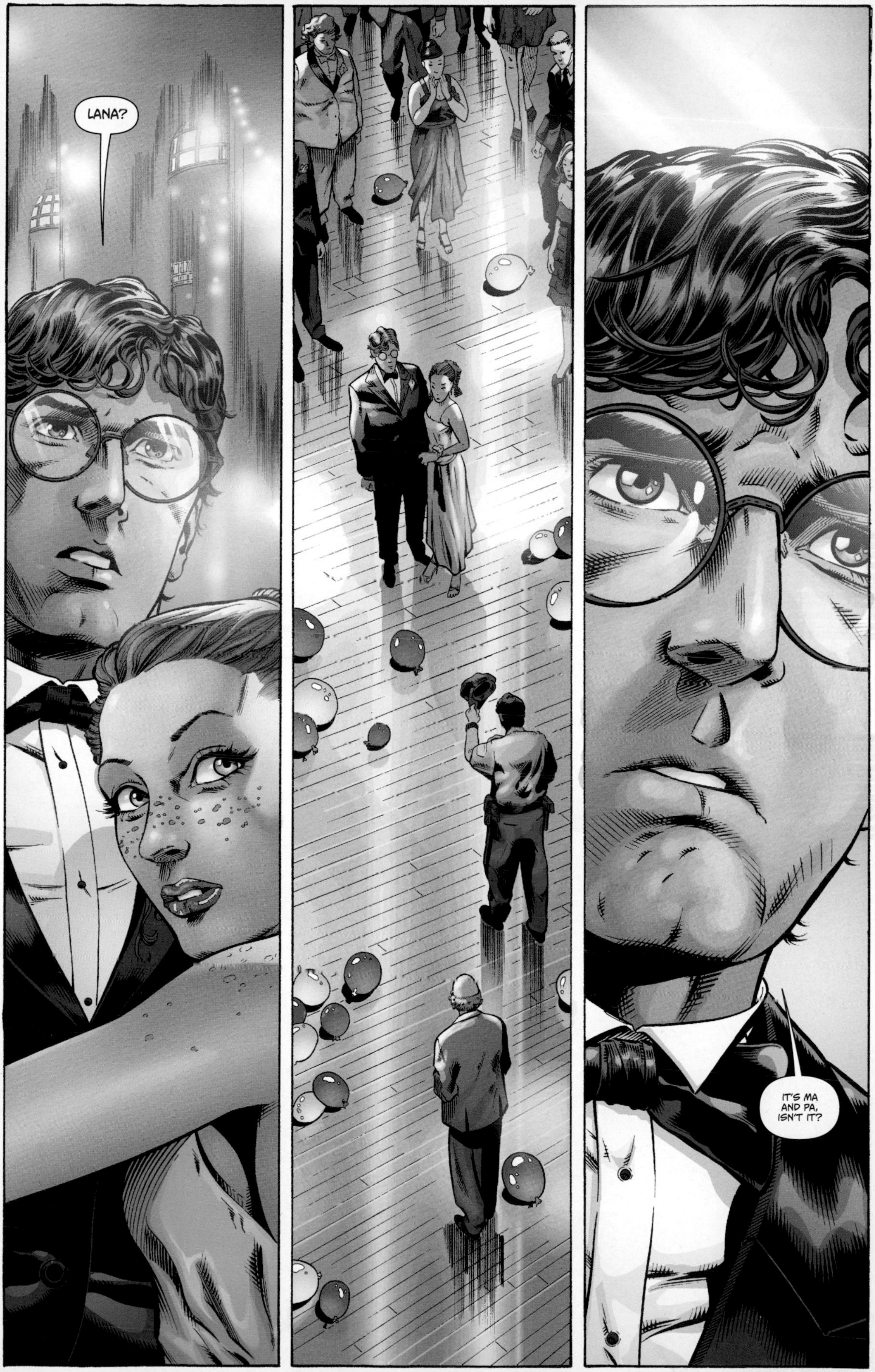
LANA?
IT'S MA AND PA, ISN'T IT?

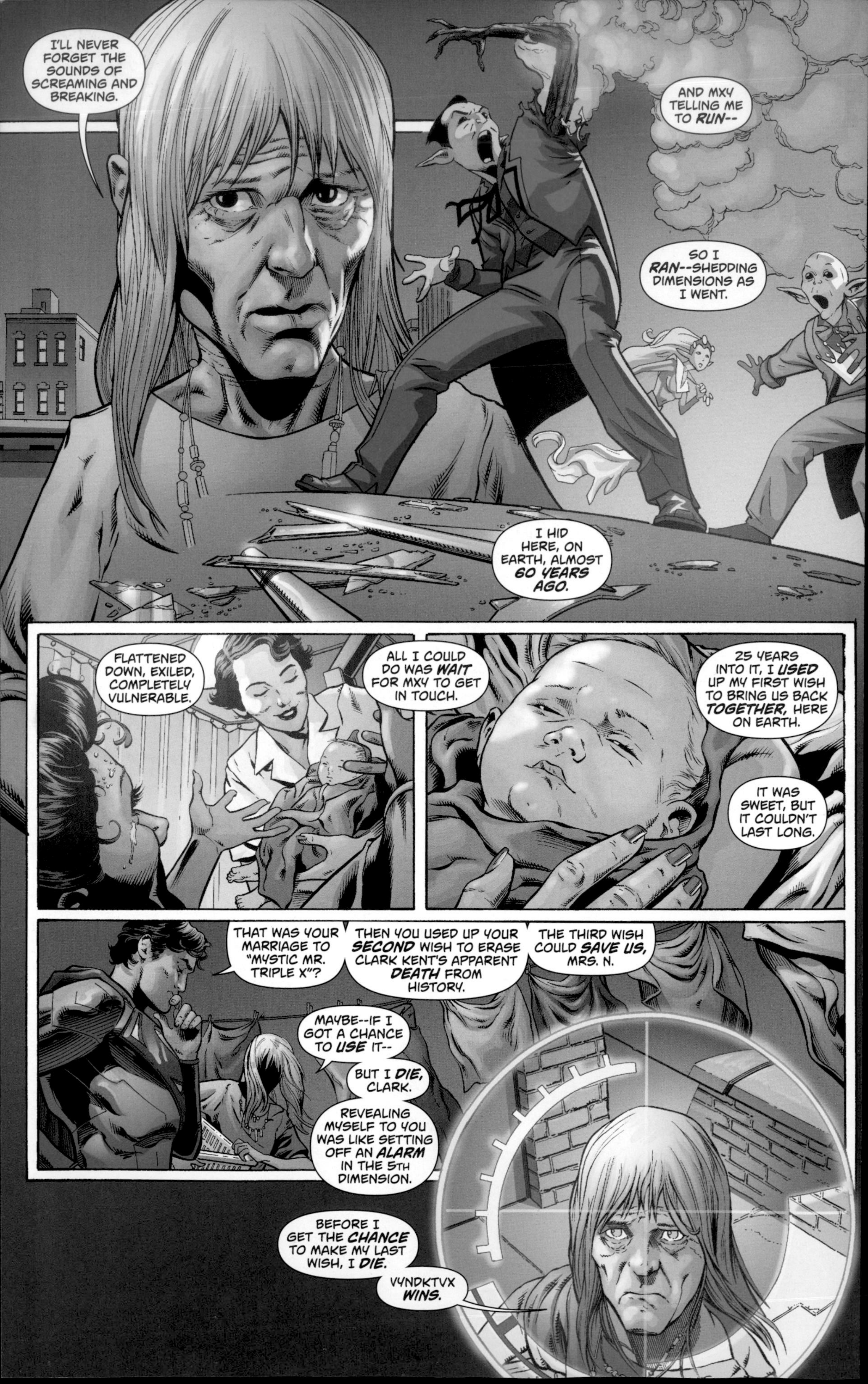
I'LL NEVER FORGET THE SOUNDS OF SCREAMING AND BREAKING.
AND MXY TELLING ME TO RUN--
SO I RAN--SHEDDING DIMENSIONS AS I WENT.
I HID HERE, ON EARTH, ALMOST 60 YEARS AGO.
FLATTENED DOWN, EXILED, COMPLETELY VULNERABLE.
ALL I COULD DO WAS WAIT FOR MXY TO GET IN TOUCH.
25 YEARS INTO IT, I USED UP MY FIRST WISH TO BRING US BACK TOGETHER, HERE ON EARTH.
IT WAS SWEET, BUT IT COULDN'T LAST LONG.
THAT WAS YOUR MARRIAGE TO "MYSTIC MR. TRIPLE X"?
THEN YOU USED UP YOUR SECOND WISH TO ERASE CLARK KENT'S APPARENT DEATH FROM HISTORY.
THE THIRD WISH COULD SAVE US, MRS. N.
MAYBE--IF I GOT A CHANCE TO USE IT--
BUT I DIE, CLARK.
REVEALING MYSELF TO YOU WAS LIKE SETTING OFF AN ALARM IN THE 5TH DIMENSION.
BEFORE I GET THE CHANCE TO MAKE MY LAST WISH, I DIE.
VYNDKTVX WINS.

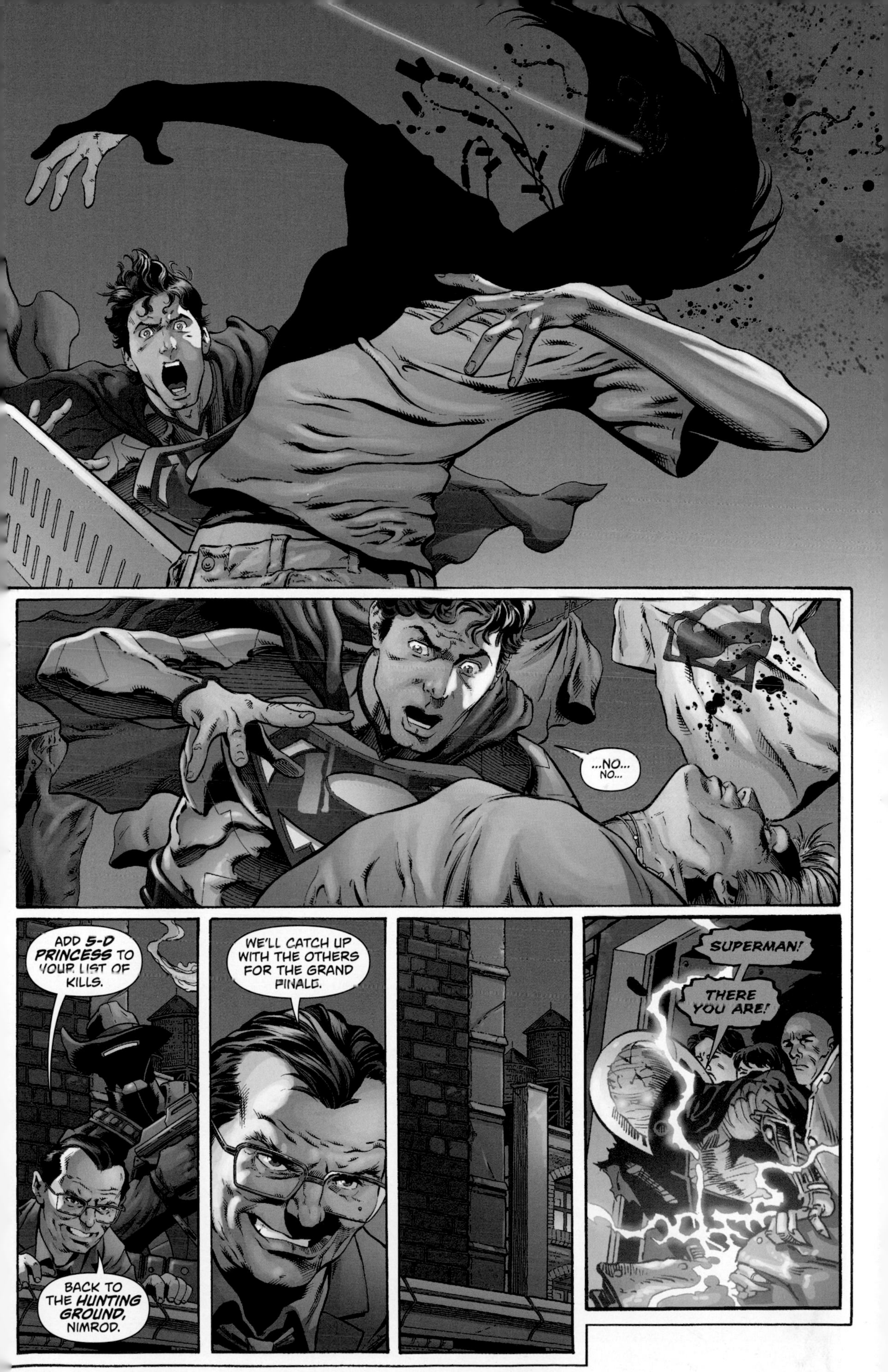
...NO...
NO...
ADD 5-D PRINCESS TO YOUR LIST OF KILLS.
BACK TO THE HUNTING GROUND, NIMROD.
WE'LL CATCH UP WITH THE OTHERS FOR THE GRAND FINALE.
SUPERMAN!
THERE YOU ARE!

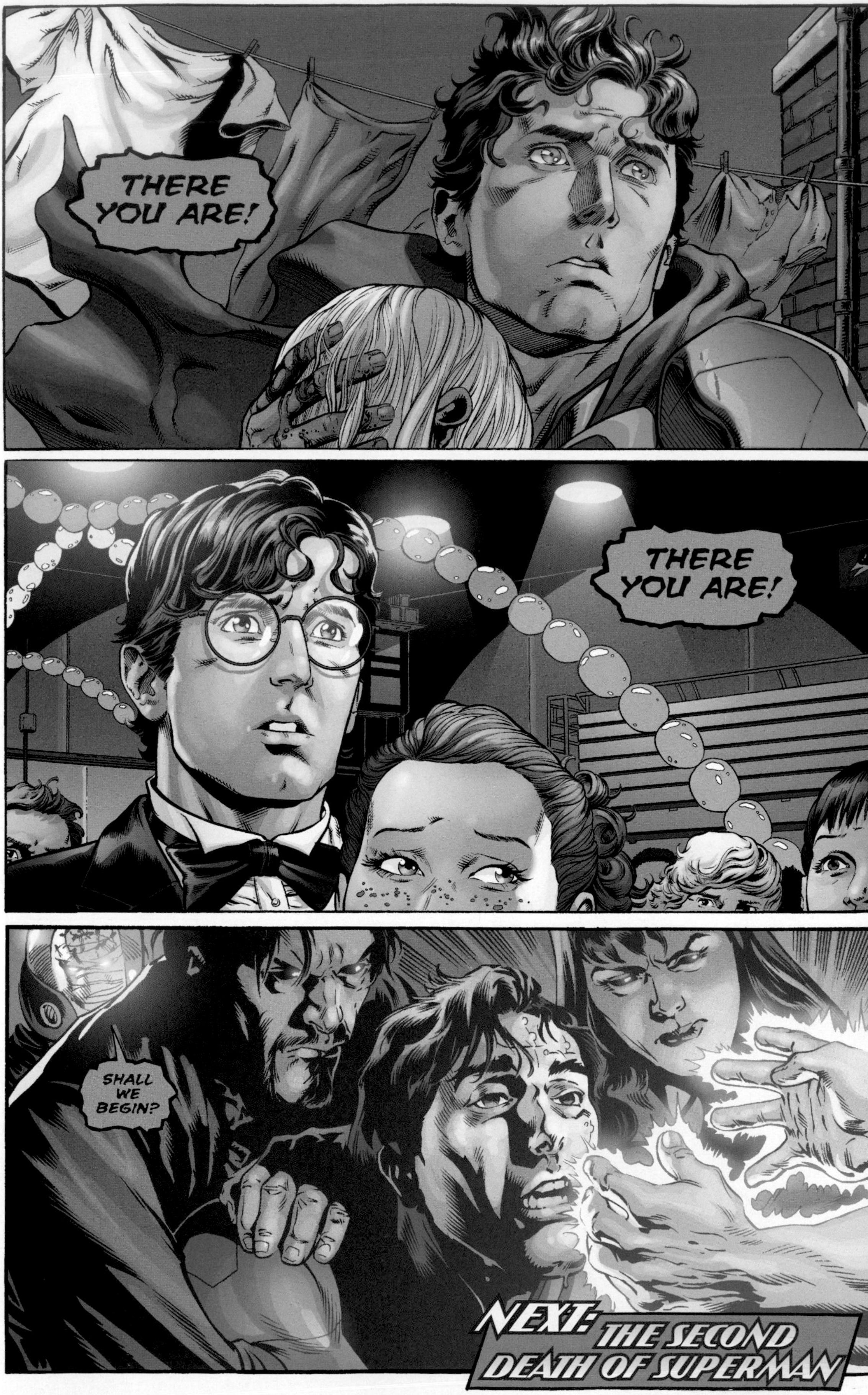
THERE YOU ARE!
THERE YOU ARE!
SHALL WE BEGIN?
NEXT: THE SECOND DEATH OF SUPERMAN

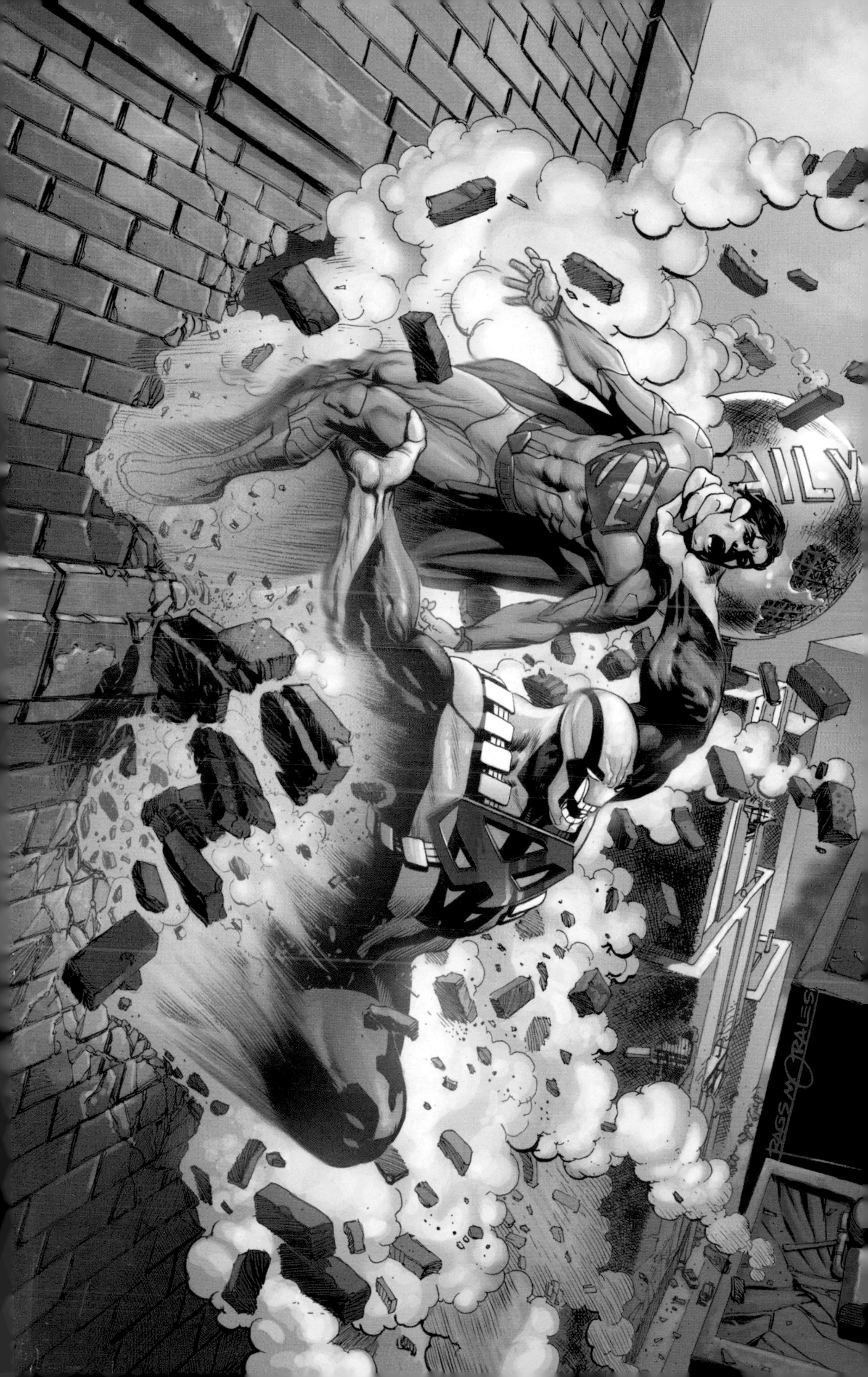

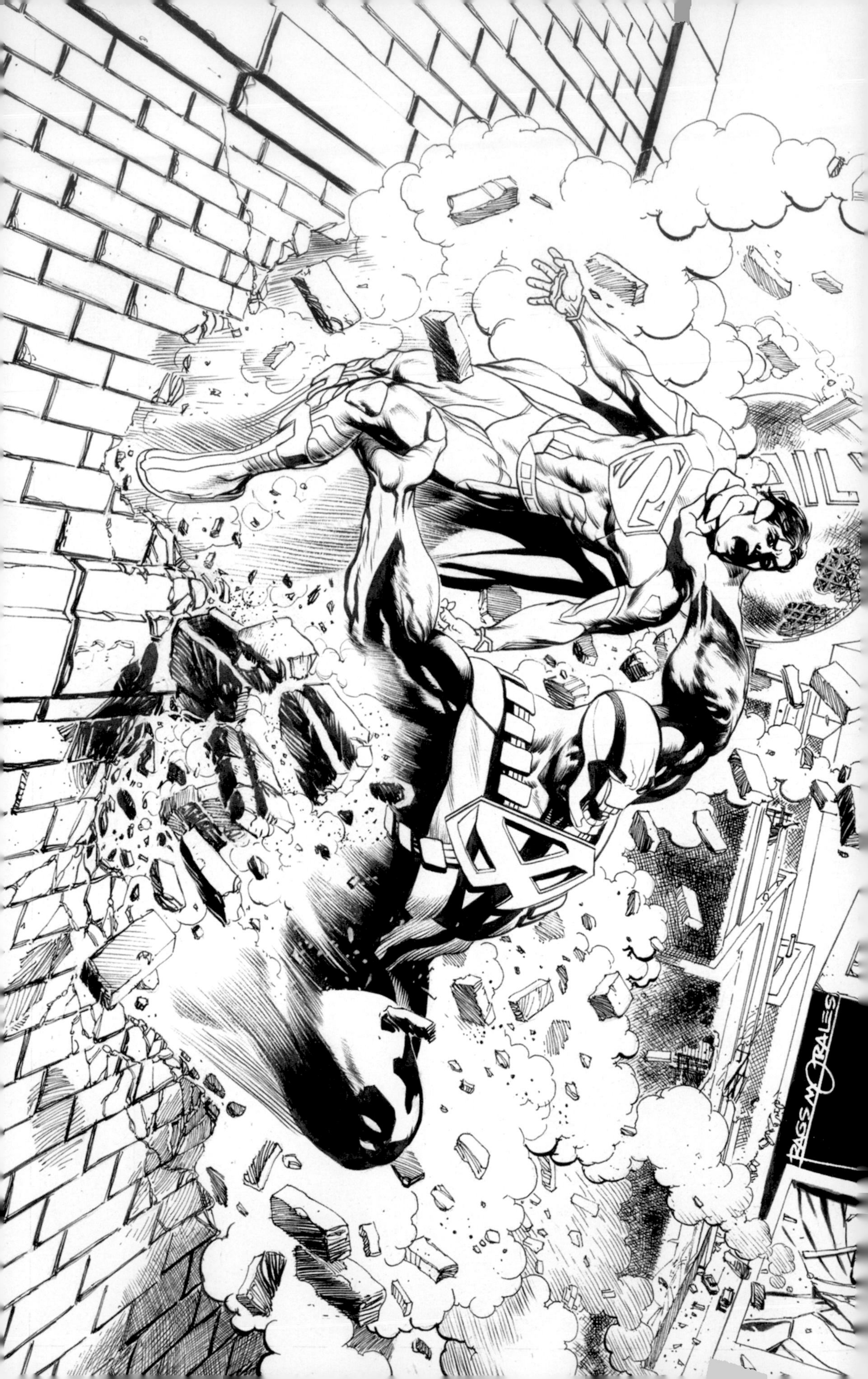
RAGS MORALES

A.D. 3030.

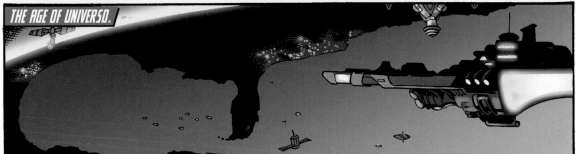

THE AGE OF UNIVERSO.

NUGOTHOTROPOLIS MEGURB.

THEY'RE WEARING *PSI-BAFFLES*, SO THEY CAN'T HEAR ME THINK.

BUT *YOU* CAN...

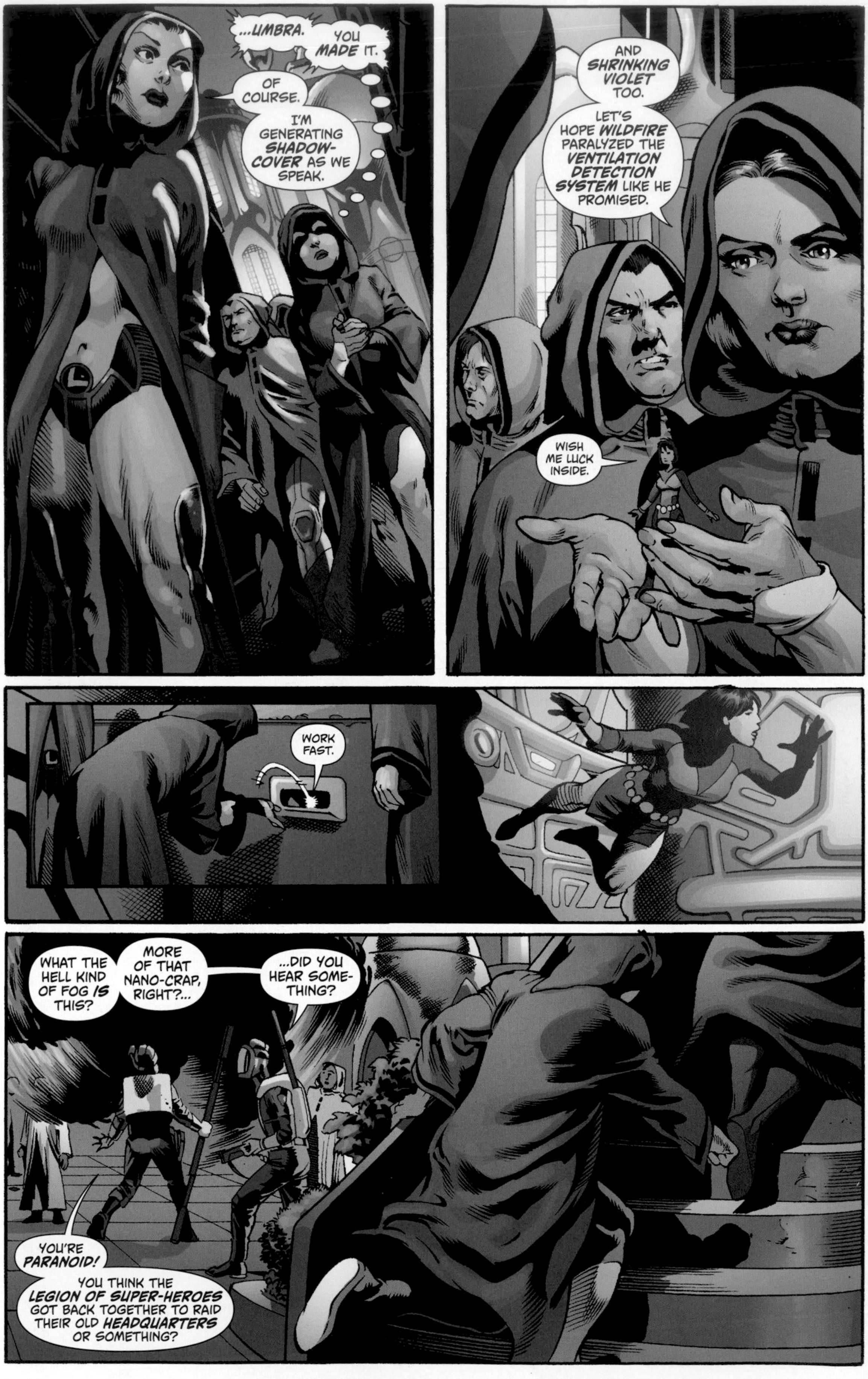
...UMBRA.
YOU MADE IT.
OF COURSE.
I'M GENERATING SHADOW-COVER AS WE SPEAK.
AND SHRINKING VIOLET TOO.
LET'S HOPE WILDFIRE PARALYZED THE VENTILATION DETECTION SYSTEM LIKE HE PROMISED.
WISH ME LUCK INSIDE.
WORK FAST.
WHAT THE HELL KIND OF FOG IS THIS?
MORE OF THAT NANO-CRAP, RIGHT?...
...DID YOU HEAR SOME-THING?
YOU'RE PARANOID!
YOU THINK THE LEGION OF SUPER-HEROES GOT BACK TOGETHER TO RAID THEIR OLD HEADQUARTERS OR SOMETHING?

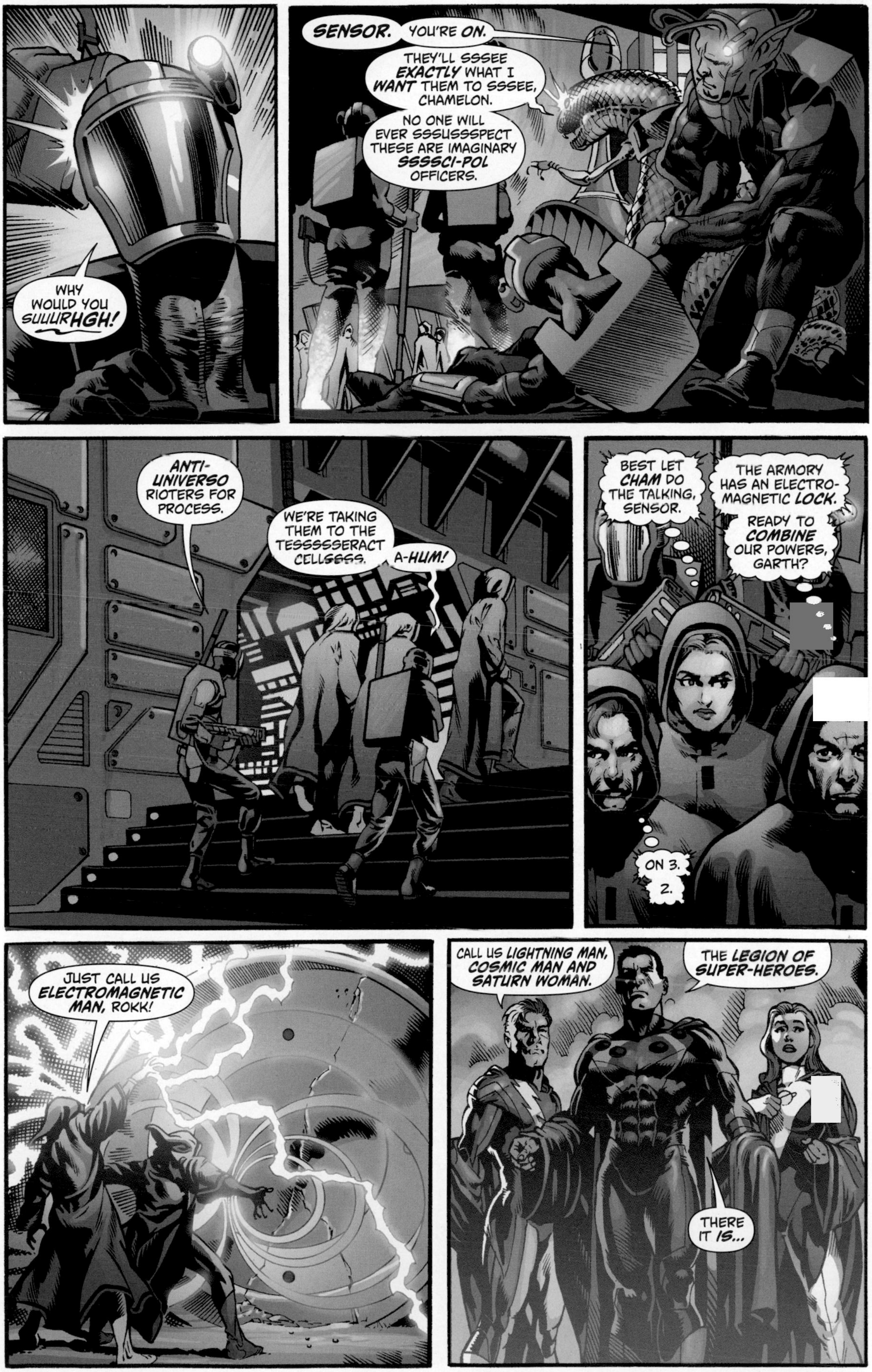
WHY WOULD YOU SUUURHGH!
SENSOR. YOU'RE ON.
THEY'LL SSSEE EXACTLY WHAT I WANT THEM TO SSSEE, CHAMELON.
NO ONE WILL EVER SSSUSSSPECT THESE ARE IMAGINARY SSSSCI-POL OFFICERS.
ANTI-UNIVERSO RIOTERS FOR PROCESS.
WE'RE TAKING THEM TO THE TESSSSSERACT CELLSSSS.
A-HUM!
BEST LET CHAM DO THE TALKING, SENSOR.
THE ARMORY HAS AN ELECTRO-MAGNETIC LOCK.
READY TO COMBINE OUR POWERS, GARTH?
ON 3.
2.
JUST CALL US ELECTROMAGNETIC MAN, ROKK!
CALL US LIGHTNING MAN, COSMIC MAN AND SATURN WOMAN.
THE LEGION OF SUPER-HEROES.
THERE IT IS...

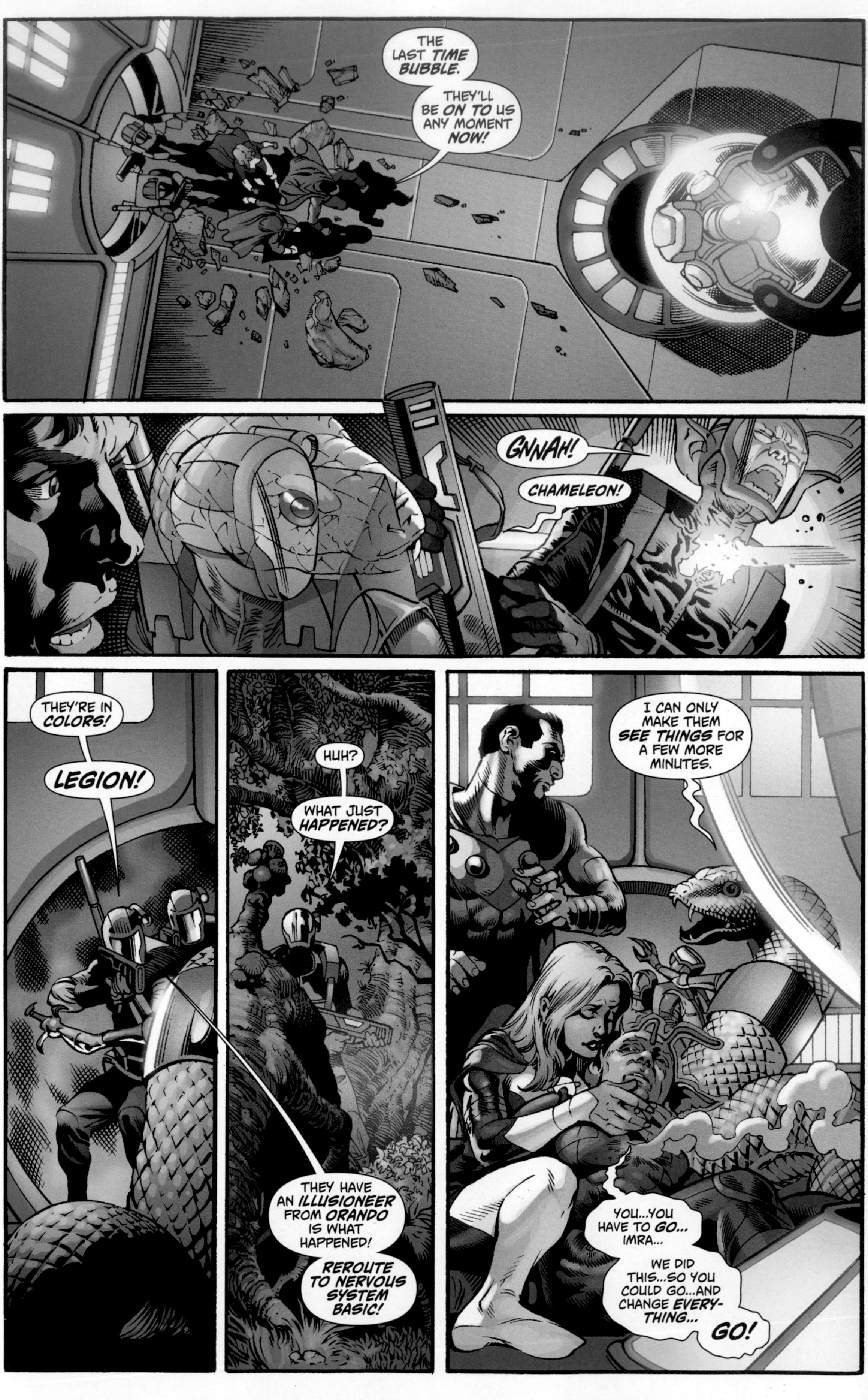
THE LAST TIME BUBBLE.
THEY'LL BE ON TO US ANY MOMENT NOW!
GNNAH!
CHAMELEON!
THEY'RE IN COLORS!
LEGION!
HUH?
WHAT JUST HAPPENED?
THEY HAVE AN ILLUSIONEER FROM ORANDO IS WHAT HAPPENED!
REROUTE TO NERVOUS SYSTEM BASIC!
I CAN ONLY MAKE THEM SEE THINGS FOR A FEW MORE MINUTES.
YOU...YOU HAVE TO GO... IMRA...
WE DID THIS...SO YOU COULD GO...AND CHANGE EVERY-THING...
GO!

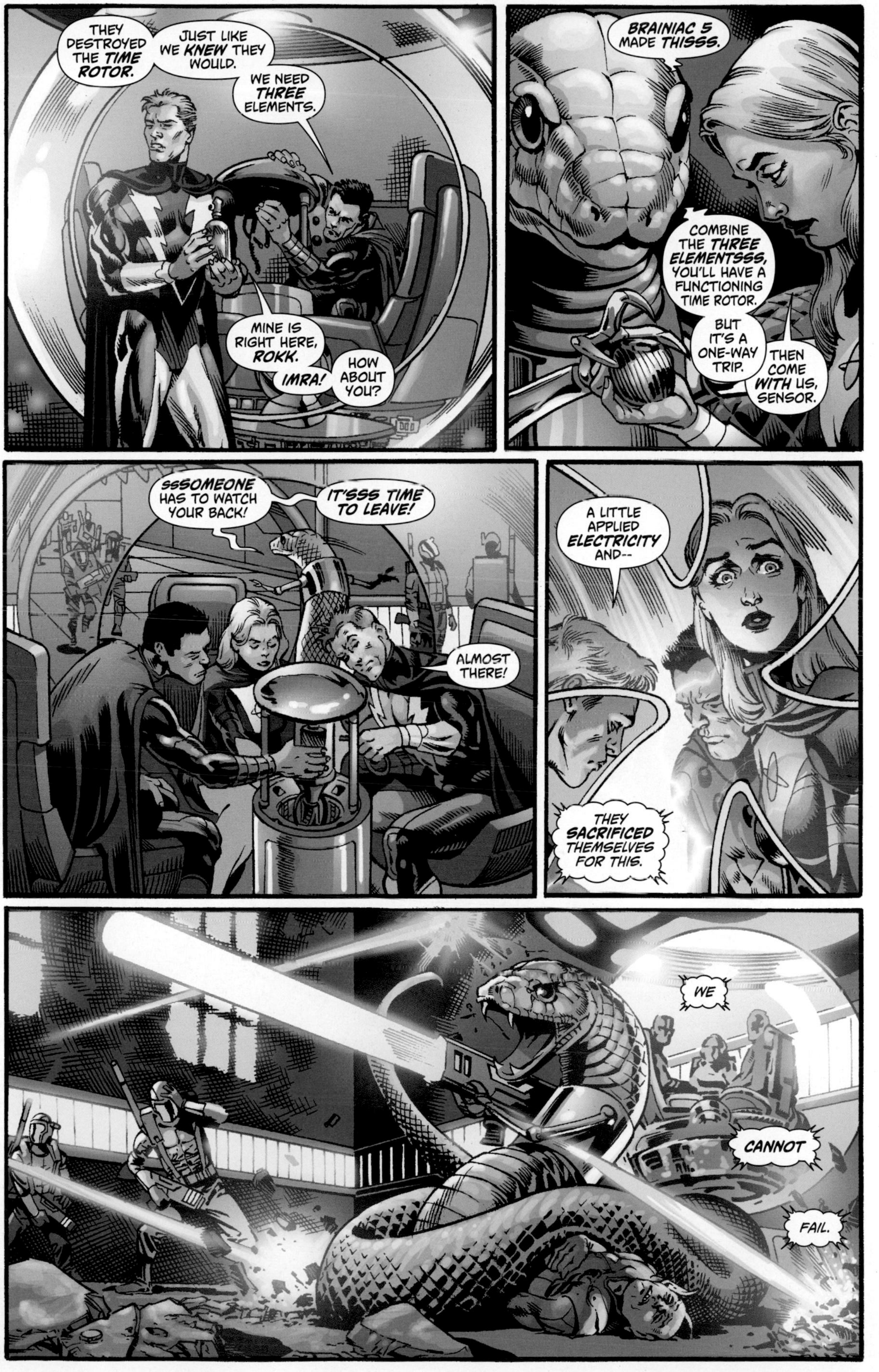

THEY DESTROYED THE TIME ROTOR.
JUST LIKE WE KNEW THEY WOULD.
WE NEED THREE ELEMENTS.
MINE IS RIGHT HERE, ROKK.
IMRA!
HOW ABOUT YOU?
BRAINIAC 5 MADE THISSS.
COMBINE THE THREE ELEMENTSSS, YOU'LL HAVE A FUNCTIONING TIME ROTOR.
BUT IT'S A ONE-WAY TRIP.
THEN COME WITH US, SENSOR.
ssSOMEONE HAS TO WATCH YOUR BACK!
IT'SSS TIME TO LEAVE!
ALMOST THERE!
A LITTLE APPLIED ELECTRICITY AND--
THEY SACRIFICED THEMSELVES FOR THIS.
WE
CANNOT
FAIL.

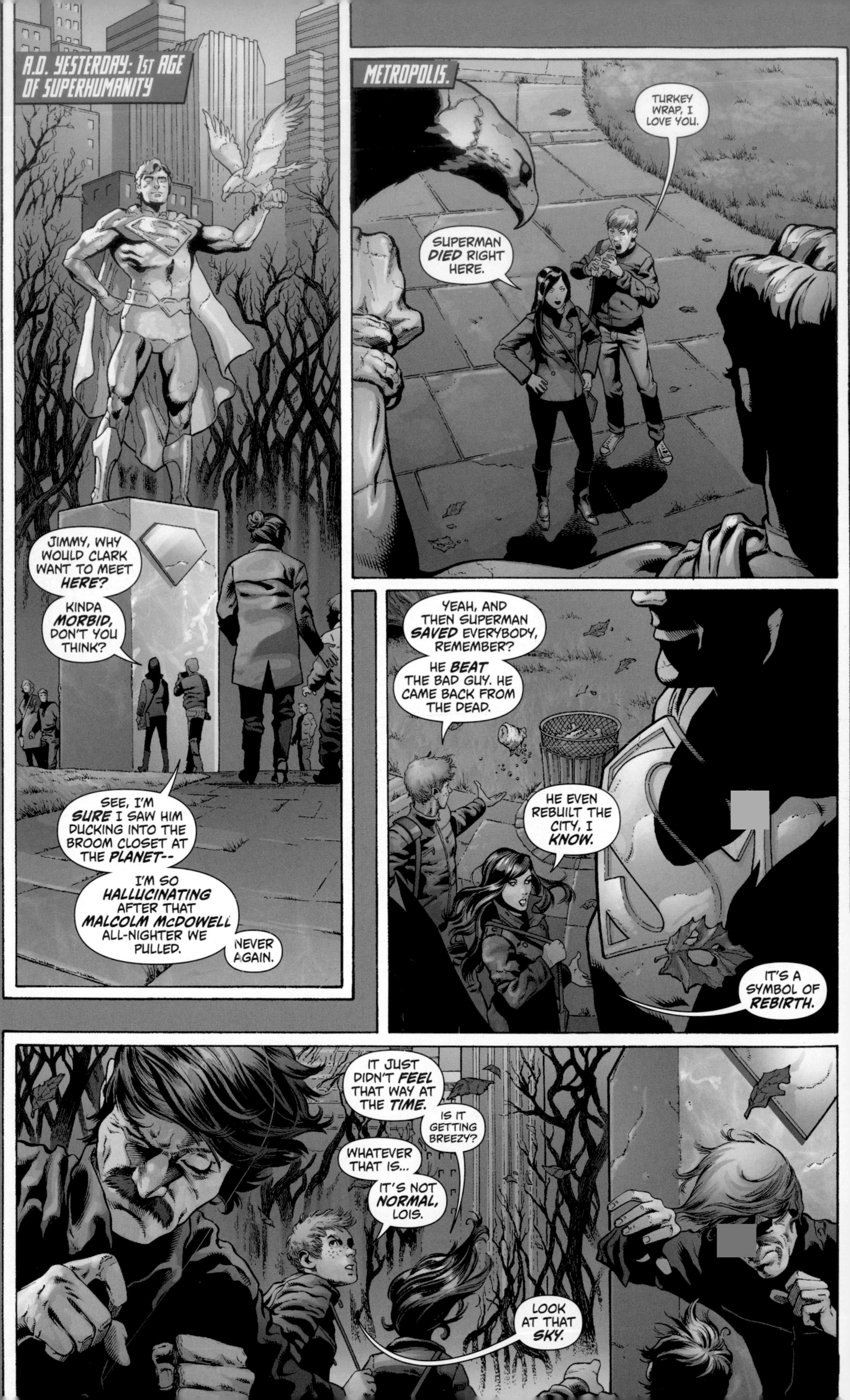
A.D. YESTERDAY: 1ST AGE OF SUPERHUMANITY
JIMMY, WHY WOULD CLARK WANT TO MEET HERE?
KINDA MORBID, DON'T YOU THINK?
SEE, I'M SURE I SAW HIM DUCKING INTO THE BROOM CLOSET AT THE PLANET--
I'M SO HALLUCINATING AFTER THAT MALCOLM McDOWELL ALL-NIGHTER WE PULLED.
NEVER AGAIN.
METROPOLIS.
TURKEY WRAP, I LOVE YOU.
SUPERMAN DIED RIGHT HERE.
YEAH, AND THEN SUPERMAN SAVED EVERYBODY, REMEMBER?
HE BEAT THE BAD GUY. HE CAME BACK FROM THE DEAD.
HE EVEN REBUILT THE CITY, I KNOW.
IT'S A SYMBOL OF REBIRTH.
IT JUST DIDN'T FEEL THAT WAY AT THE TIME.
IS IT GETTING BREEZY?
WHATEVER THAT IS...
IT'S NOT NORMAL, LOIS.
LOOK AT THAT SKY.

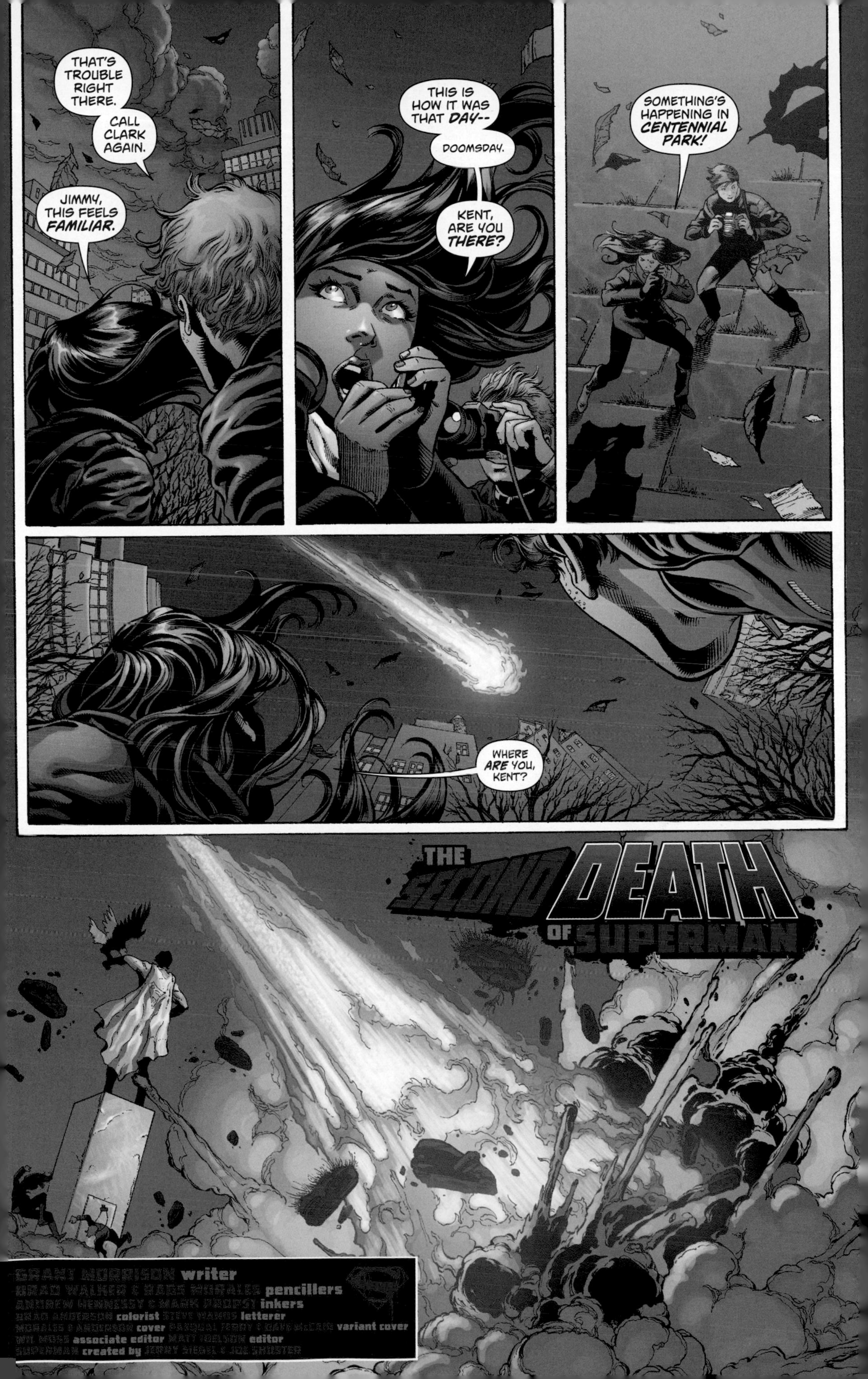
THAT'S TROUBLE RIGHT THERE.
CALL CLARK AGAIN.
JIMMY, THIS FEELS FAMILIAR.
THIS IS HOW IT WAS THAT DAY--
DOOMSDAY.
KENT, ARE YOU THERE?
SOMETHING'S HAPPENING IN CENTENNIAL PARK!
WHERE ARE YOU, KENT?
THE SECOND DEATH OF SUPERMAN
GRANT MORRISON writer
BRAD WALKER & RAGS MORALES pencillers
ANDREW HENNESSY & MARK PROPST inkers
BRAD ANDERSON colorist STEVE WANDS letterer
MORALES & ANDERSON cover PASQUAL FERRY & DAVE McCAIG variant cover
WIL MOSS associate editor MATT IDELSON editor
SUPERMAN created by JERRY SIEGEL & JOE SHUSTER

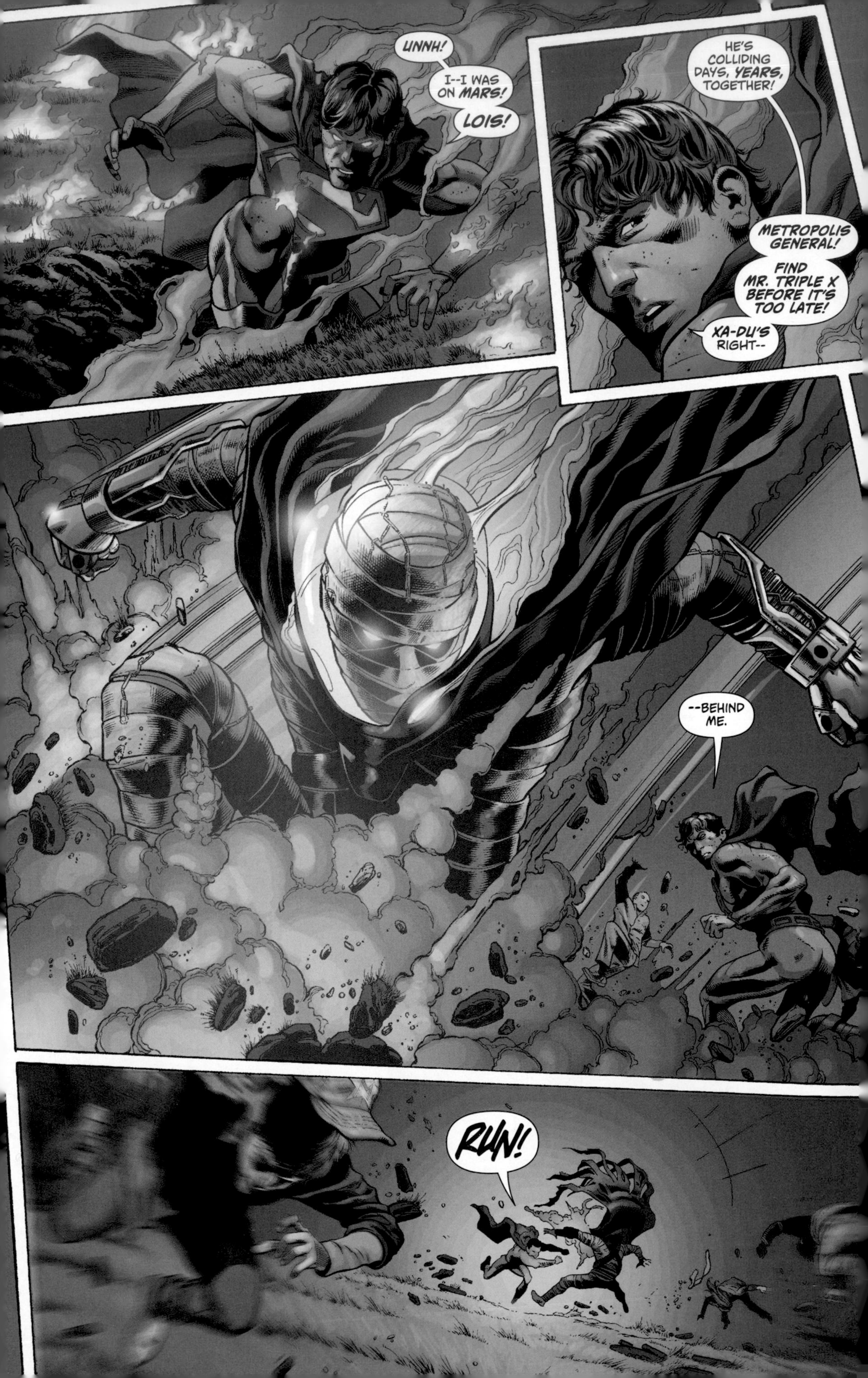
UNNH!
I--I WAS ON MARS!
LOIS!
HE'S COLLIDING DAYS, YEARS, TOGETHER!
METROPOLIS GENERAL!
FIND MR. TRIPLE X BEFORE IT'S TOO LATE!
XA-DU'S RIGHT--
--BEHIND ME.
RUN!

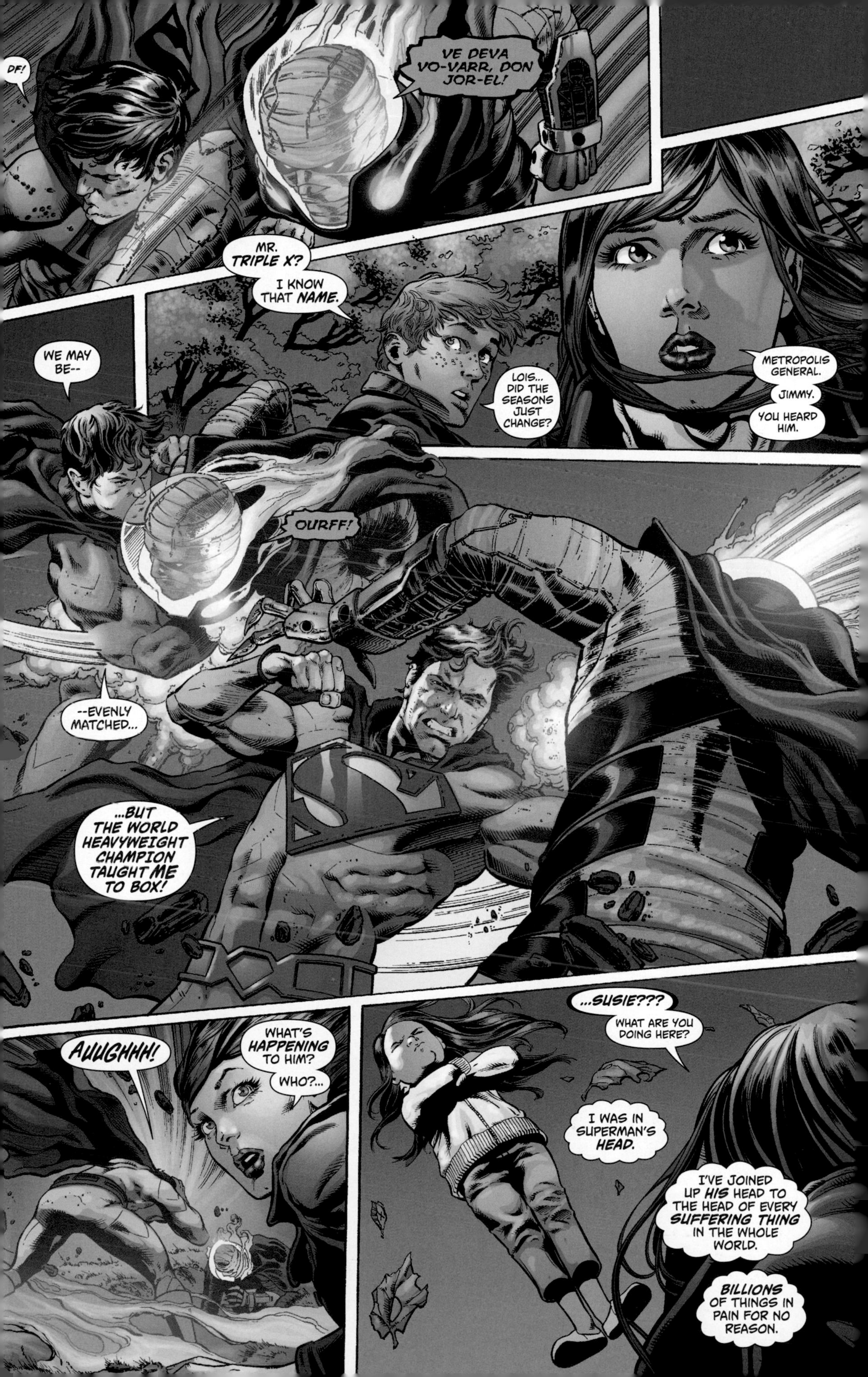
DF!
VE DEVA VO-VARR, DON JOR-EL!
MR. TRIPLE X?
I KNOW THAT NAME.
LOIS... DID THE SEASONS JUST CHANGE?
METROPOLIS GENERAL.
JIMMY.
YOU HEARD HIM.
WE MAY BE--
OURFF!
--EVENLY MATCHED...
...BUT THE WORLD HEAVYWEIGHT CHAMPION TAUGHT ME TO BOX!
AUUGHHH!
WHAT'S HAPPENING TO HIM?
WHO?...
...SUSIE???
WHAT ARE YOU DOING HERE?
I WAS IN SUPERMAN'S HEAD.
I'VE JOINED UP HIS HEAD TO THE HEAD OF EVERY SUFFERING THING IN THE WHOLE WORLD.
BILLIONS OF THINGS IN PAIN FOR NO REASON.

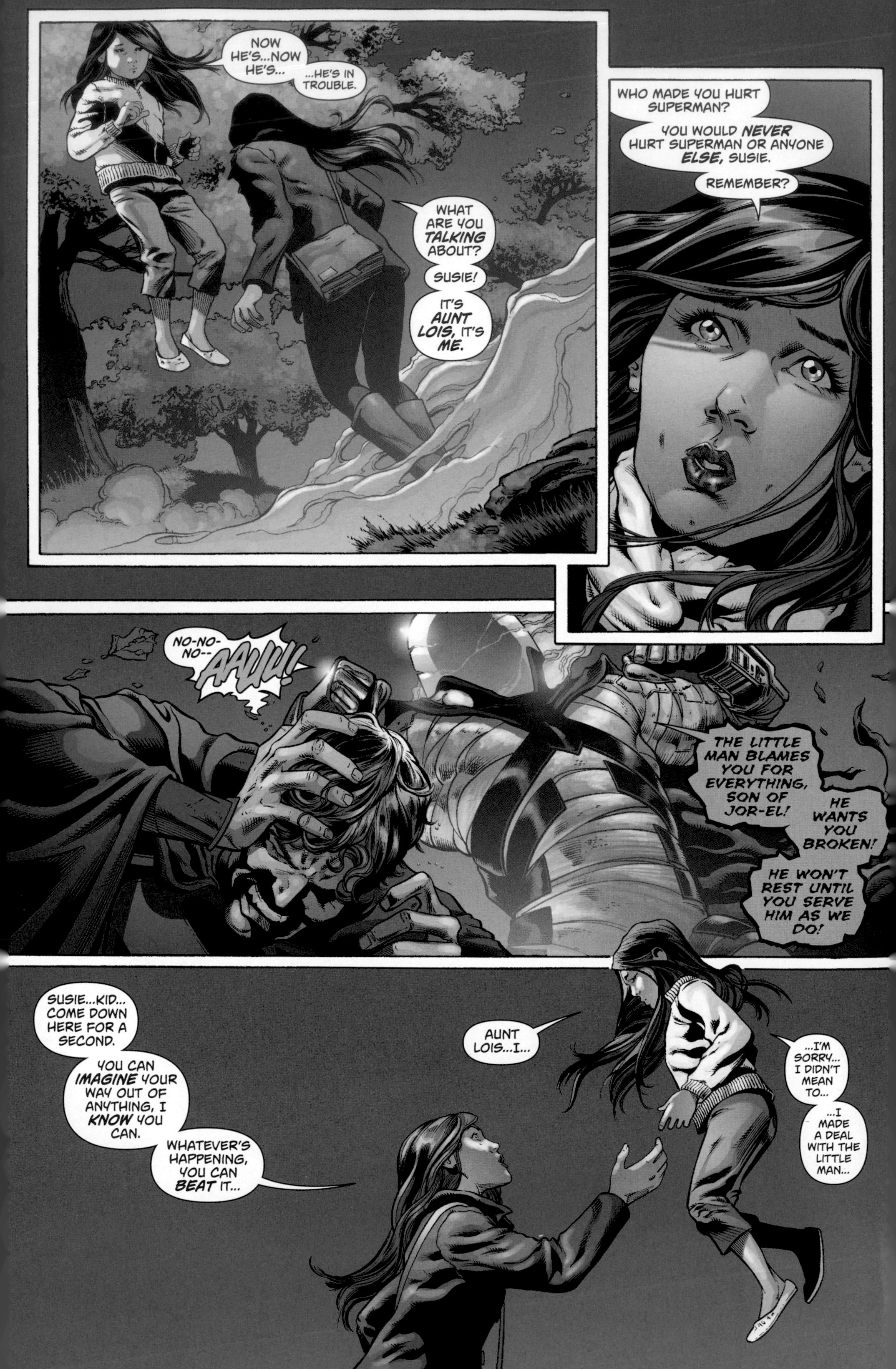
NOW HE'S...NOW HE'S...
...HE'S IN TROUBLE.
WHAT ARE YOU TALKING ABOUT?
SUSIE!
IT'S AUNT LOIS, IT'S ME.
WHO MADE YOU HURT SUPERMAN?
YOU WOULD NEVER HURT SUPERMAN OR ANYONE ELSE, SUSIE.
REMEMBER?
NO-NO-NO--AAUU!
THE LITTLE MAN BLAMES YOU FOR EVERYTHING, SON OF JOR-EL!
HE WANTS YOU BROKEN!
HE WON'T REST UNTIL YOU SERVE HIM AS WE DO!
SUSIE...KID... COME DOWN HERE FOR A SECOND.
YOU CAN IMAGINE YOUR WAY OUT OF ANYTHING, I KNOW YOU CAN.
WHATEVER'S HAPPENING, YOU CAN BEAT IT...
AUNT LOIS...I...
...I'M SORRY... I DIDN'T MEAN TO...
...I MADE A DEAL WITH THE LITTLE MAN...

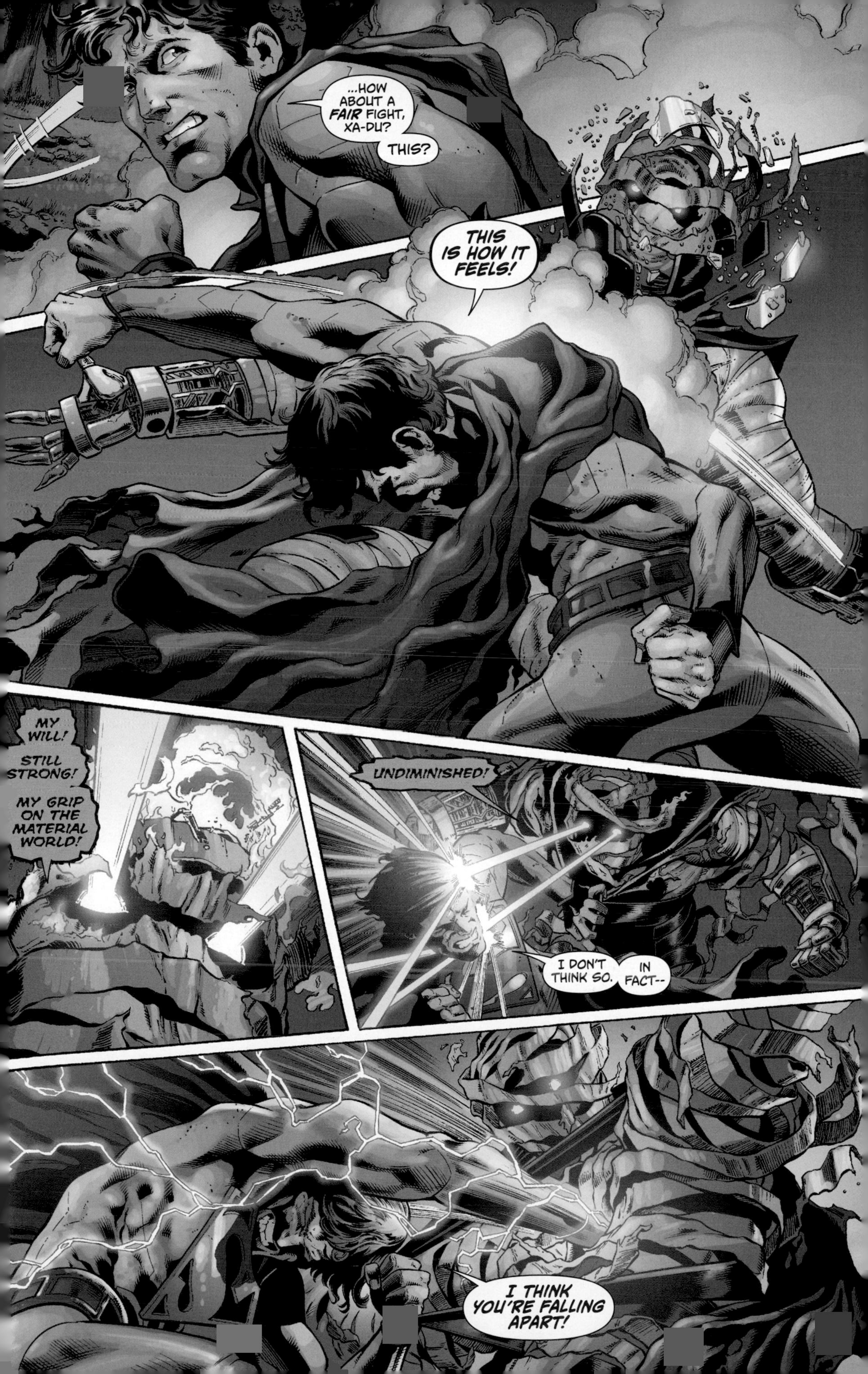
...HOW ABOUT A FAIR FIGHT, XA-DU?
THIS?
THIS IS HOW IT FEELS!
MY WILL!
STILL STRONG!
MY GRIP ON THE MATERIAL WORLD!
UNDIMINISHED!
I DON'T THINK SO.
IN FACT--
I THINK YOU'RE FALLING APART!

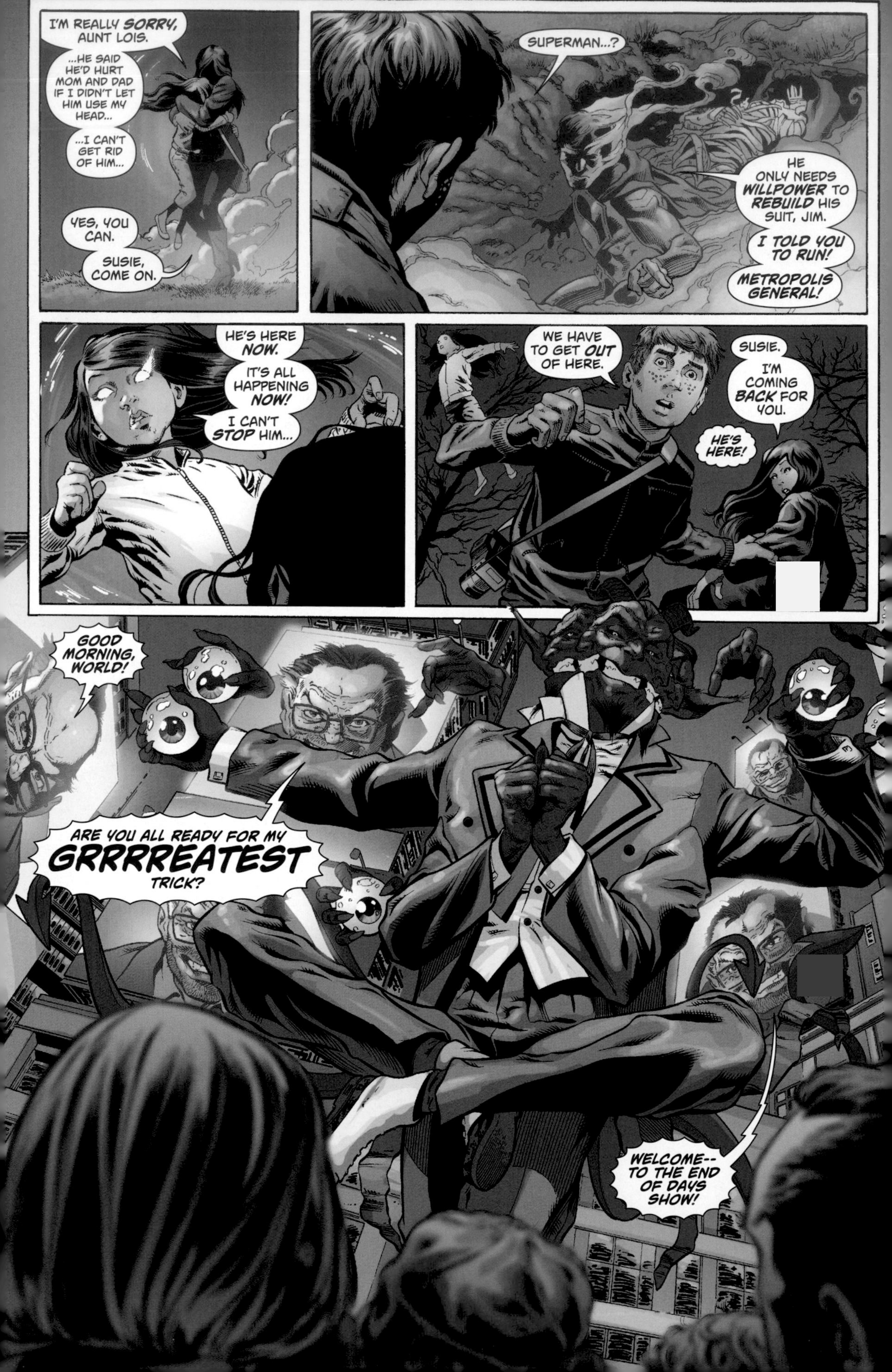
I'M REALLY SORRY, AUNT LOIS.
...HE SAID HE'D HURT MOM AND DAD IF I DIDN'T LET HIM USE MY HEAD...
...I CAN'T GET RID OF HIM...
YES, YOU CAN.
SUSIE, COME ON.
SUPERMAN...?
HE ONLY NEEDS WILLPOWER TO REBUILD HIS SUIT, JIM.
I TOLD YOU TO RUN!
METROPOLIS GENERAL!
HE'S HERE NOW.
IT'S ALL HAPPENING NOW!
I CAN'T STOP HIM...
WE HAVE TO GET OUT OF HERE.
SUSIE.
I'M COMING BACK FOR YOU.
HE'S HERE!
GOOD MORNING, WORLD!
ARE YOU ALL READY FOR MY GRRRREATEST TRICK?
WELCOME-- TO THE END OF DAYS SHOW!

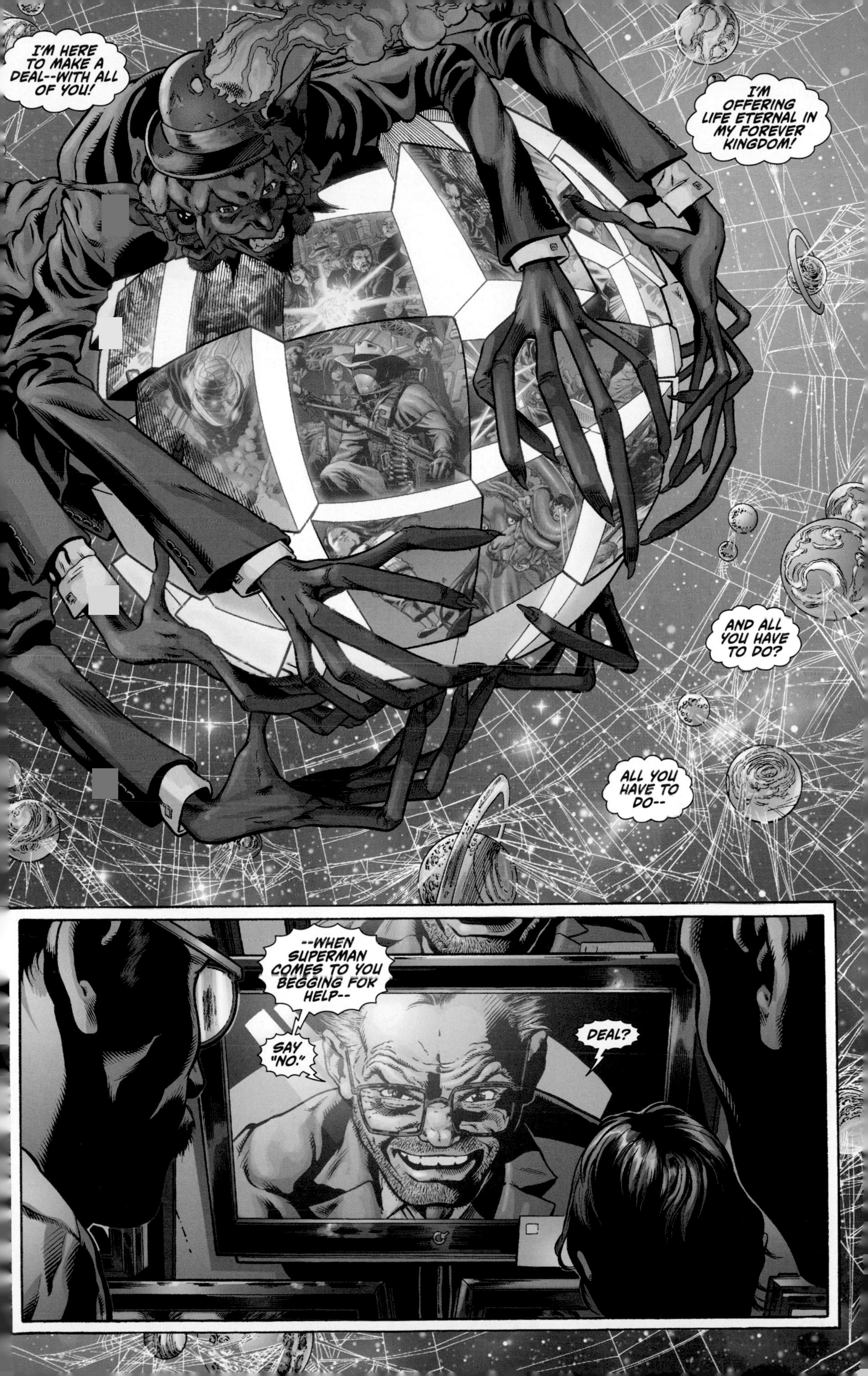
I'M HERE TO MAKE A DEAL--WITH ALL OF YOU!
I'M OFFERING LIFE ETERNAL IN MY FOREVER KINGDOM!
AND ALL YOU HAVE TO DO?
ALL YOU HAVE TO DO--
--WHEN SUPERMAN COMES TO YOU BEGGING FOR HELP--
SAY "NO."
DEAL?

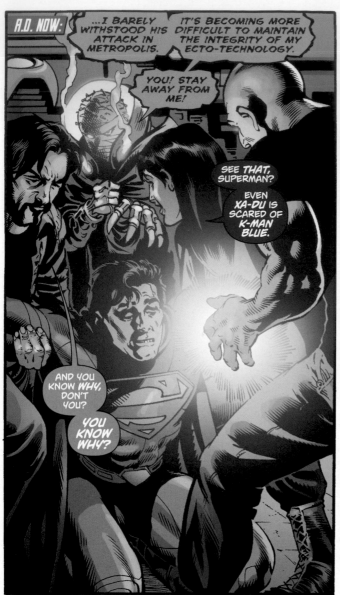

....I BARELY WITHSTOOD HIS ATTACK IN METROPOLIS.

IT'S BECOMING MORE DIFFICULT TO MAINTAIN THE INTEGRITY OF MY ECTO-TECHNOLOGY.

YOU! STAY AWAY FROM ME!

SEE *THAT*, SUPERMAN? EVEN *XA-DU* IS SCARED OF K-MAN BLUE.

AND YOU KNOW *WHY*, DON'T YOU? *YOU KNOW WHY*?

MY *BLUE K* TOUCH CAN *KILL* XA-DU'S *PHANTOM* FORM.

MY K-WAVELENGTH HAS *SPECIAL* PROPERTIES.

RED RADIATION RADICALLY ALTERS YOUR *PERCEPTIONS*.

GREEN CAUSES FATAL *BLOOD POISONING*.

BUT *BLUE KRYPTONITE*...

BLUE KRYPTONITE KILLS YOUR *SPIRIT*.

OH, HOW I *HATE* YOU.

YOU *REJECTED* ME.

UH? WHAT THE HELL'S *THAT* TERRIBLE...

...NOISE...

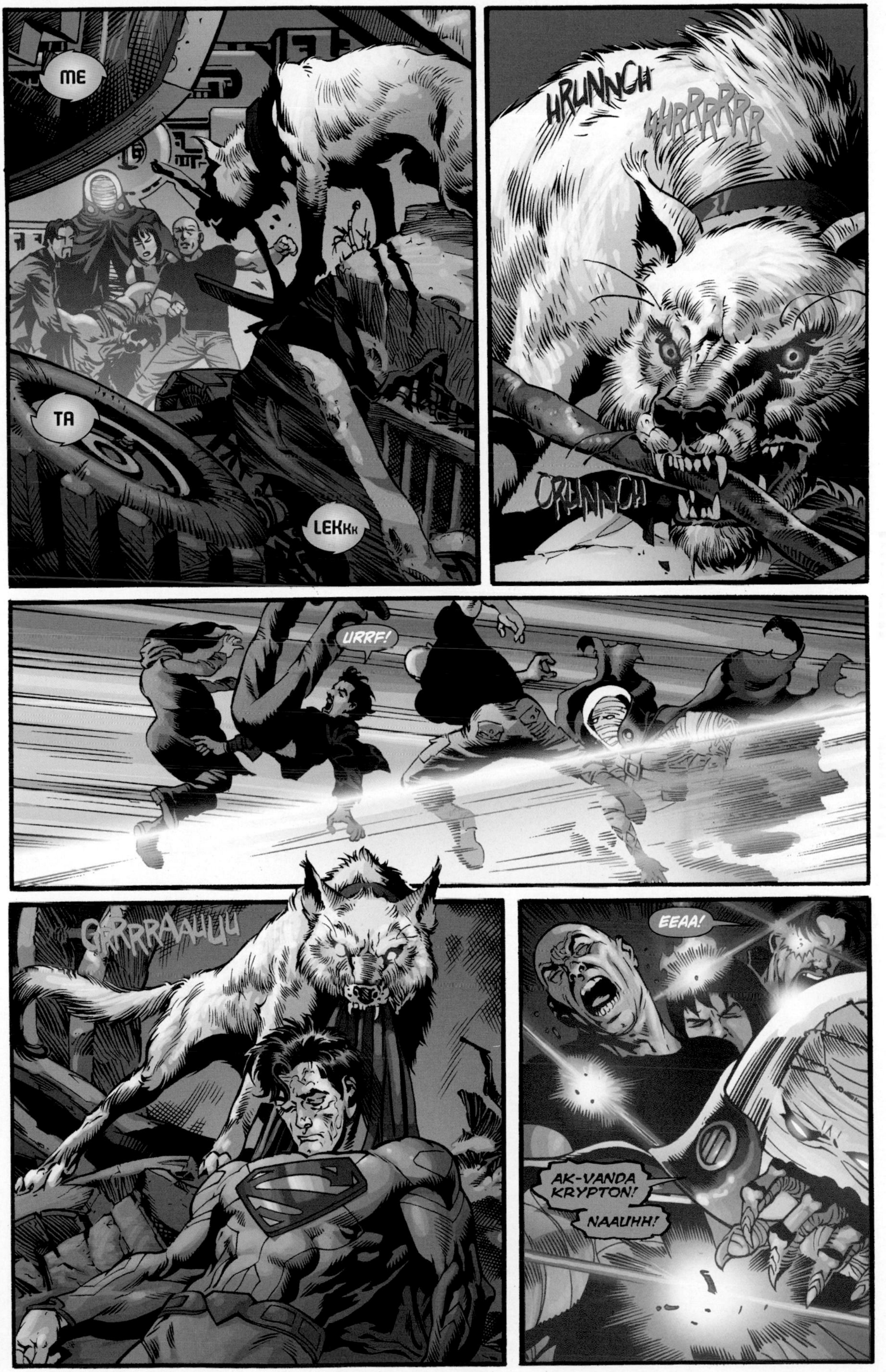
ME
TA
LEKkk
HRUNNCH
GHRRRRRR
CRUNNCH
URRF!
GRRRRAAHUU
EEAA!
AK-VANDA KRYPTON!
NAAUHH!

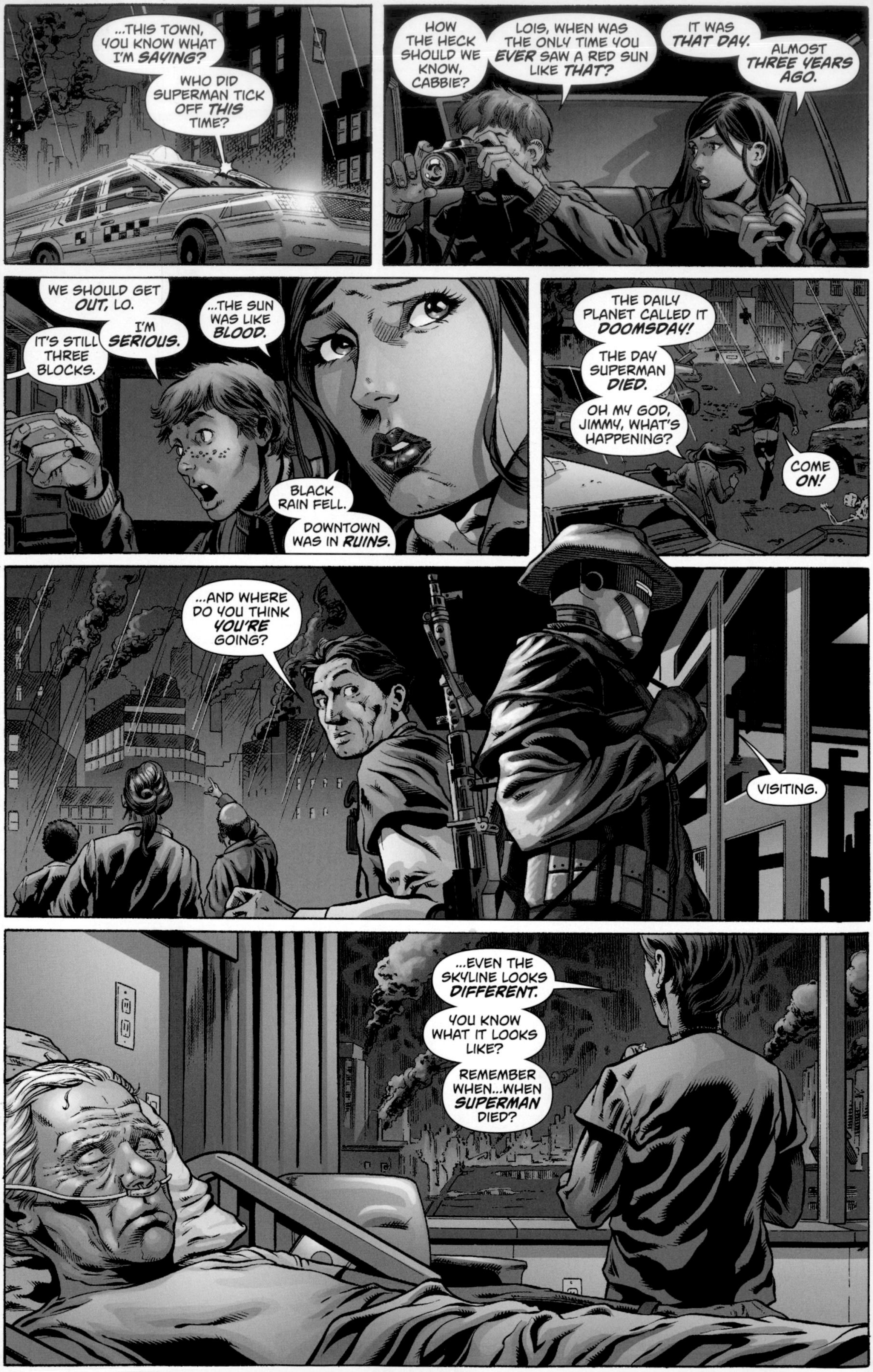
...THIS TOWN, YOU KNOW WHAT I'M SAYING?
WHO DID SUPERMAN TICK OFF THIS TIME?
HOW THE HECK SHOULD WE KNOW, CABBIE?
LOIS, WHEN WAS THE ONLY TIME YOU EVER SAW A RED SUN LIKE THAT?
IT WAS THAT DAY.
ALMOST THREE YEARS AGO.
WE SHOULD GET OUT, LO.
I'M SERIOUS.
IT'S STILL THREE BLOCKS.
...THE SUN WAS LIKE BLOOD.
BLACK RAIN FELL.
DOWNTOWN WAS IN RUINS.
THE DAILY PLANET CALLED IT DOOMSDAY!
THE DAY SUPERMAN DIED.
OH MY GOD, JIMMY, WHAT'S HAPPENING?
COME ON!
...AND WHERE DO YOU THINK YOU'RE GOING?
VISITING.
...EVEN THE SKYLINE LOOKS DIFFERENT.
YOU KNOW WHAT IT LOOKS LIKE?
REMEMBER WHEN...WHEN SUPERMAN DIED?

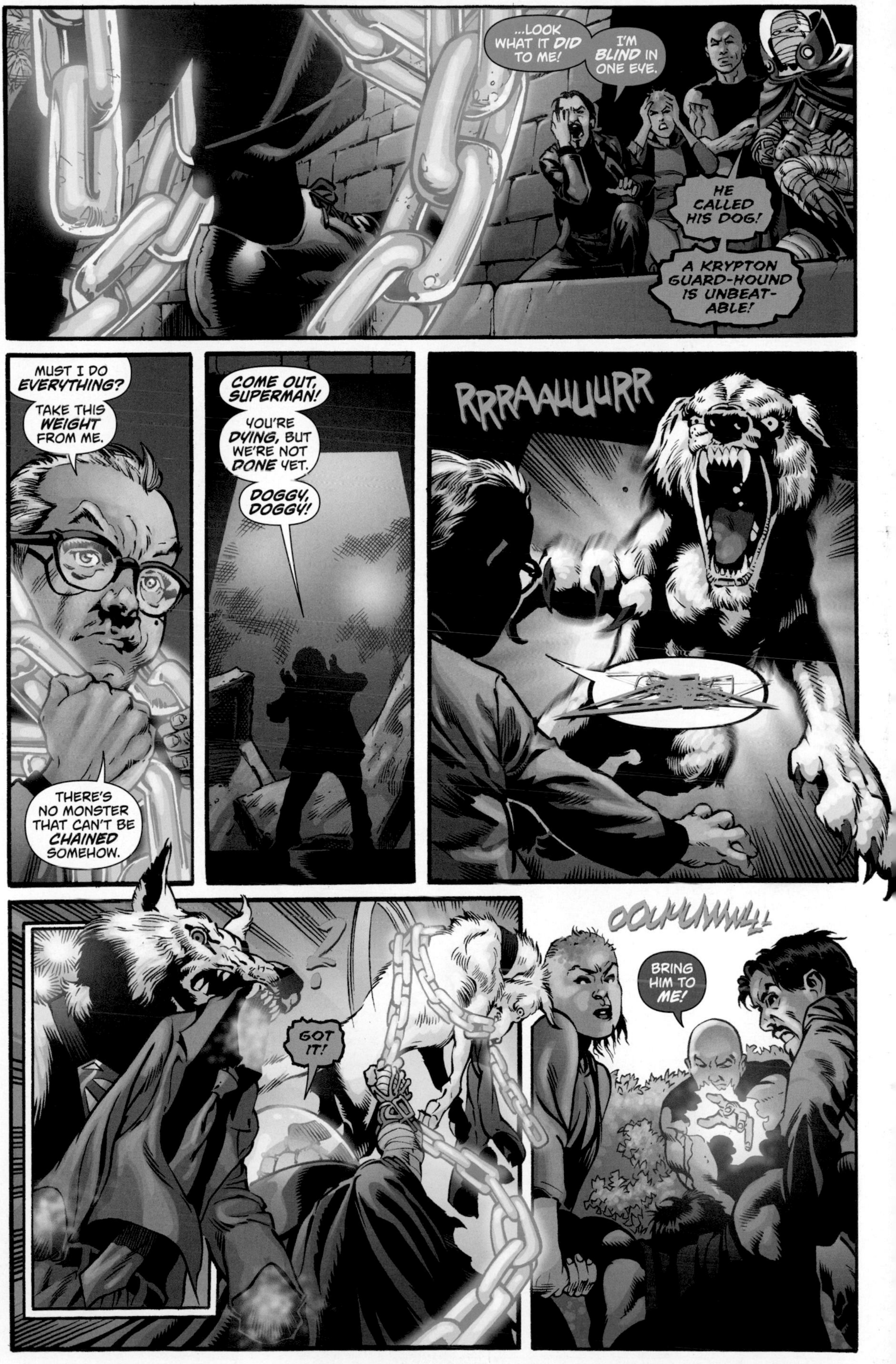

...LOOK WHAT IT DID TO ME!
I'M BLIND IN ONE EYE.
HE CALLED HIS DOG!
A KRYPTON GUARD-HOUND IS UNBEAT-ABLE!
MUST I DO EVERYTHING?
TAKE THIS WEIGHT FROM ME.
THERE'S NO MONSTER THAT CAN'T BE CHAINED SOMEHOW.
COME OUT, SUPERMAN!
YOU'RE DYING, BUT WE'RE NOT DONE YET.
DOGGY, DOGGY!
RRRAAUUURR
GOT IT!
BRING HIM TO ME!

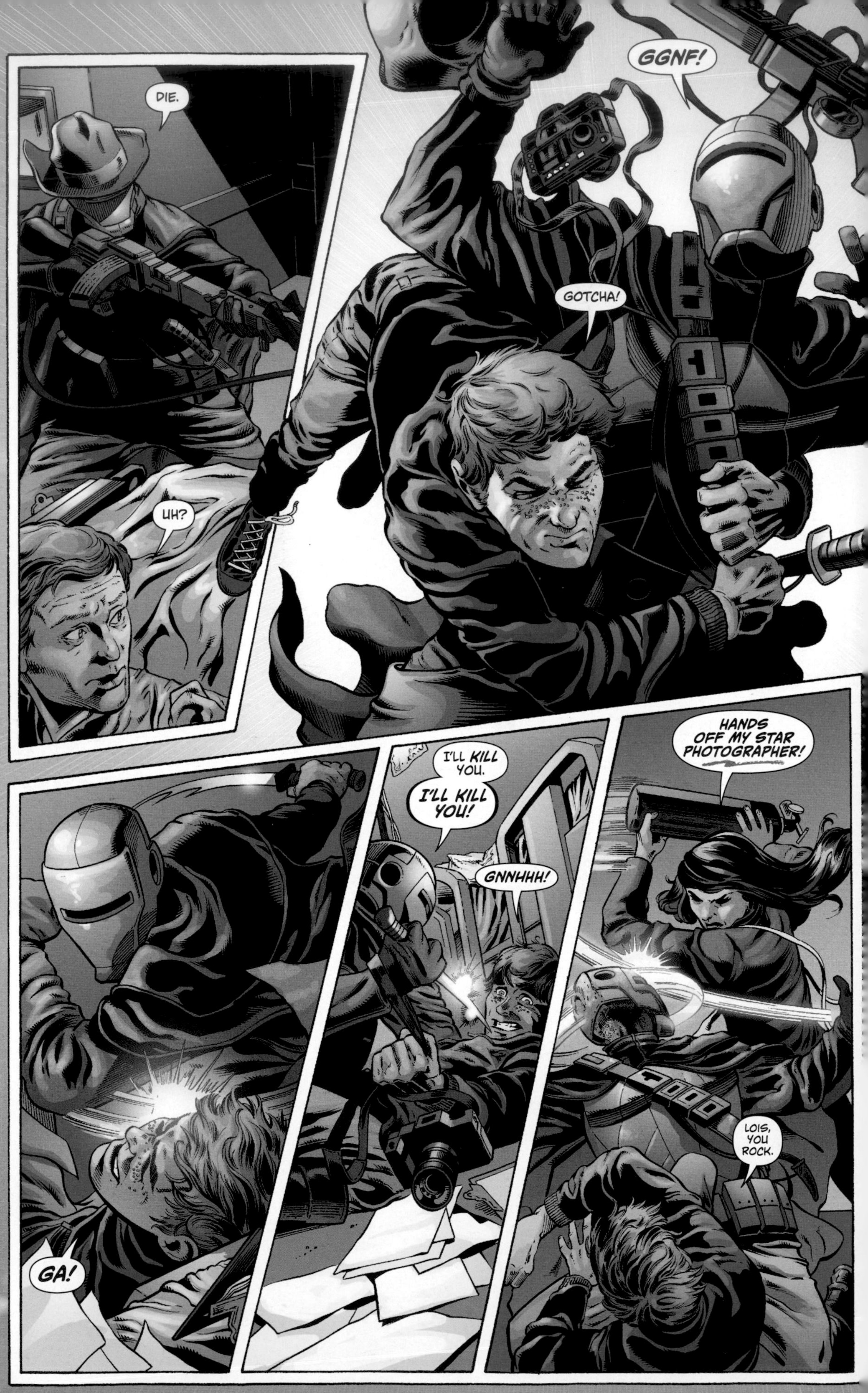
DIE.
UH?
GGNF!
GOTCHA!
GA!
I'LL KILL YOU.
I'LL KILL YOU!
GNNHHH!
HANDS OFF MY STAR PHOTOGRAPHER!
LOIS, YOU ROCK.

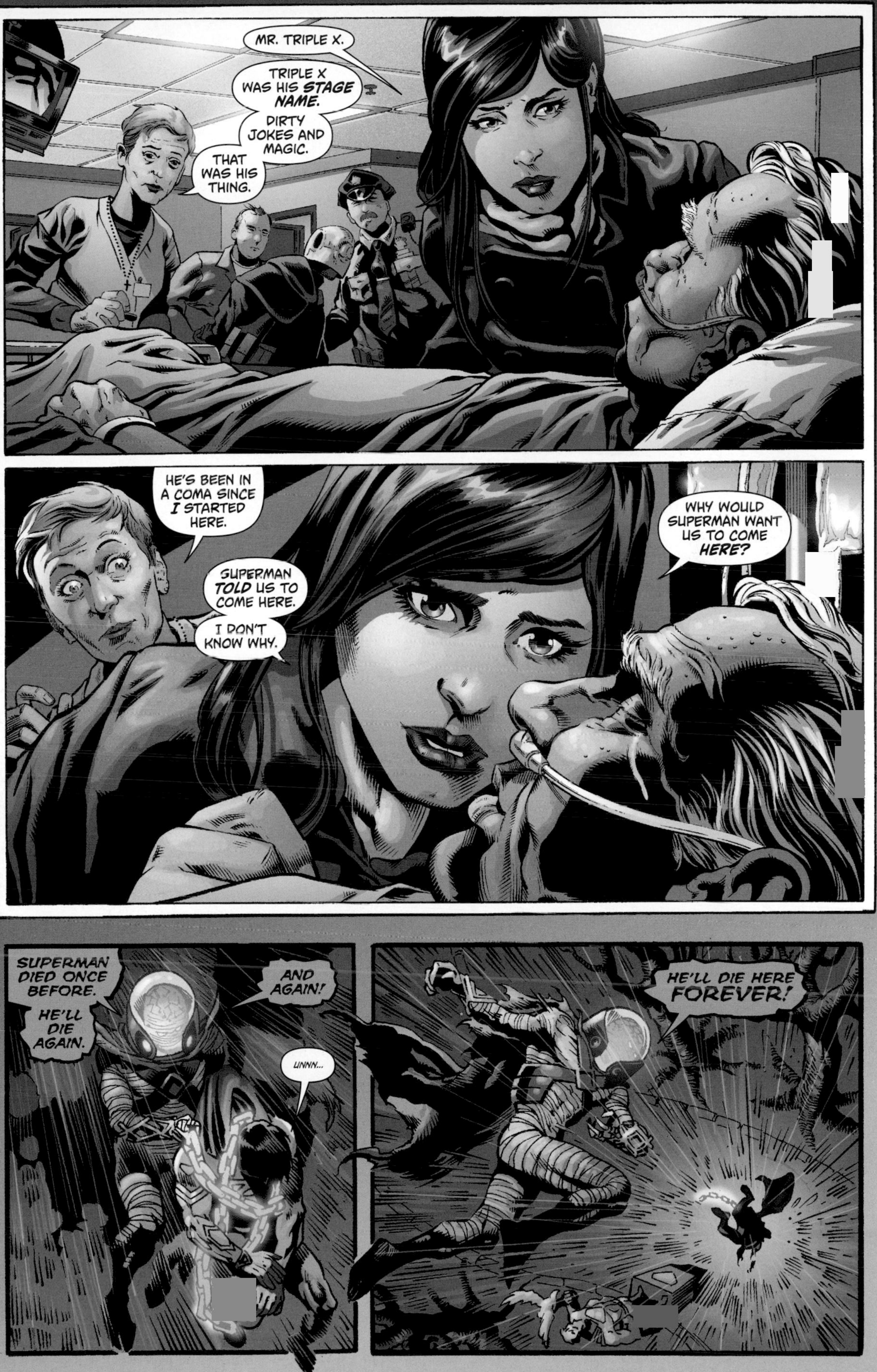
MR. TRIPLE X.
TRIPLE X WAS HIS STAGE NAME.
DIRTY JOKES AND MAGIC.
THAT WAS HIS THING.
HE'S BEEN IN A COMA SINCE I STARTED HERE.
SUPERMAN TOLD US TO COME HERE.
I DON'T KNOW WHY.
WHY WOULD SUPERMAN WANT US TO COME HERE?
SUPERMAN DIED ONCE BEFORE.
HE'LL DIE AGAIN.
AND AGAIN!
UNNN...
HE'LL DIE HERE FOREVER!

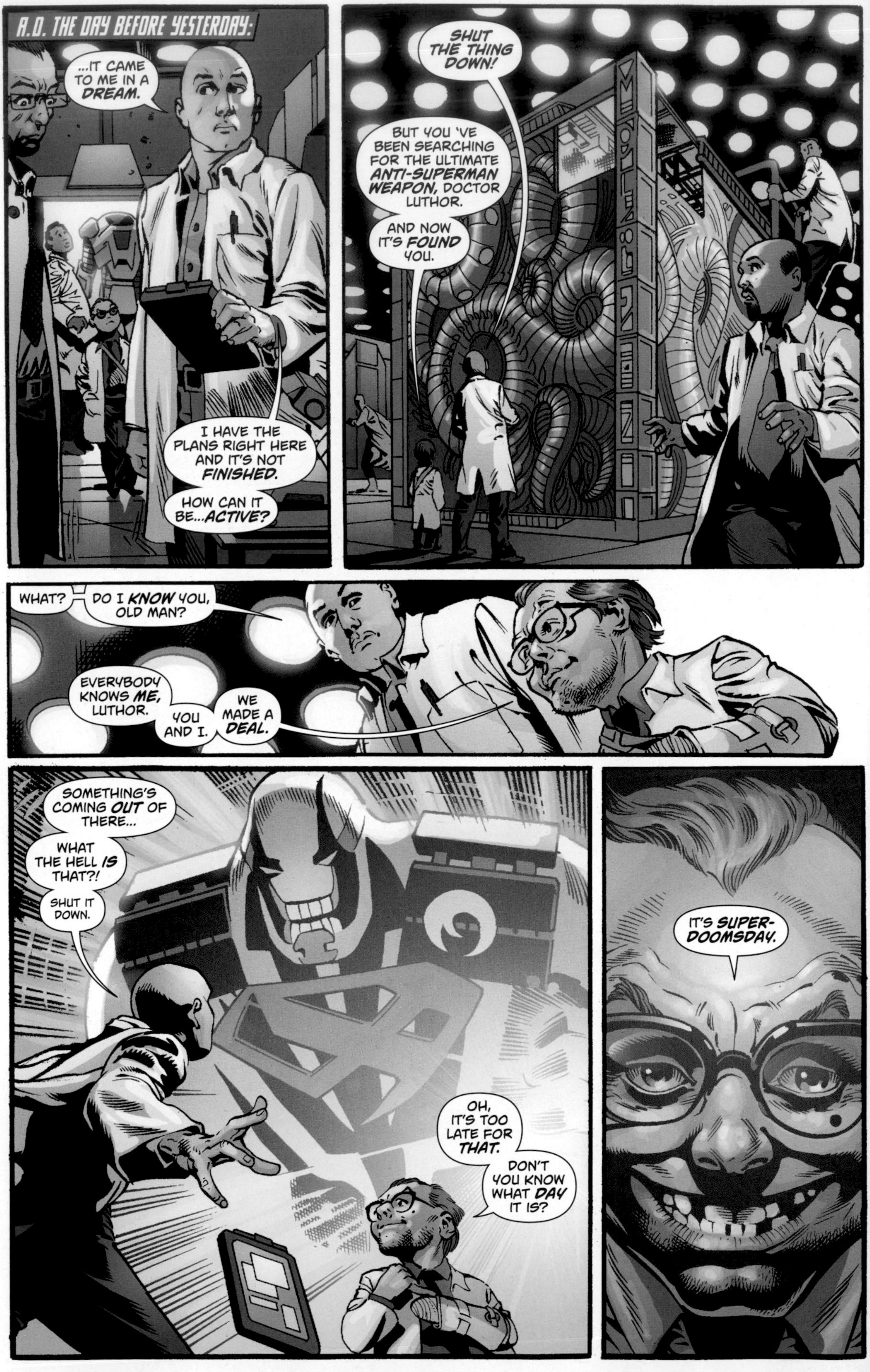
A.D. THE DAY BEFORE YESTERDAY:
...IT CAME TO ME IN A DREAM.
I HAVE THE PLANS RIGHT HERE AND IT'S NOT FINISHED.
HOW CAN IT BE...ACTIVE?
SHUT THE THING DOWN!
BUT YOU 'VE BEEN SEARCHING FOR THE ULTIMATE ANTI-SUPERMAN WEAPON, DOCTOR LUTHOR.
AND NOW IT'S FOUND YOU.
WHAT?
DO I KNOW YOU, OLD MAN?
EVERYBODY KNOWS ME, LUTHOR.
YOU AND I.
WE MADE A DEAL.
SOMETHING'S COMING OUT OF THERE...
WHAT THE HELL IS THAT?!
SHUT IT DOWN.
OH, IT'S TOO LATE FOR THAT.
DON'T YOU KNOW WHAT DAY IT IS?
IT'S SUPER-DOOMSDAY.

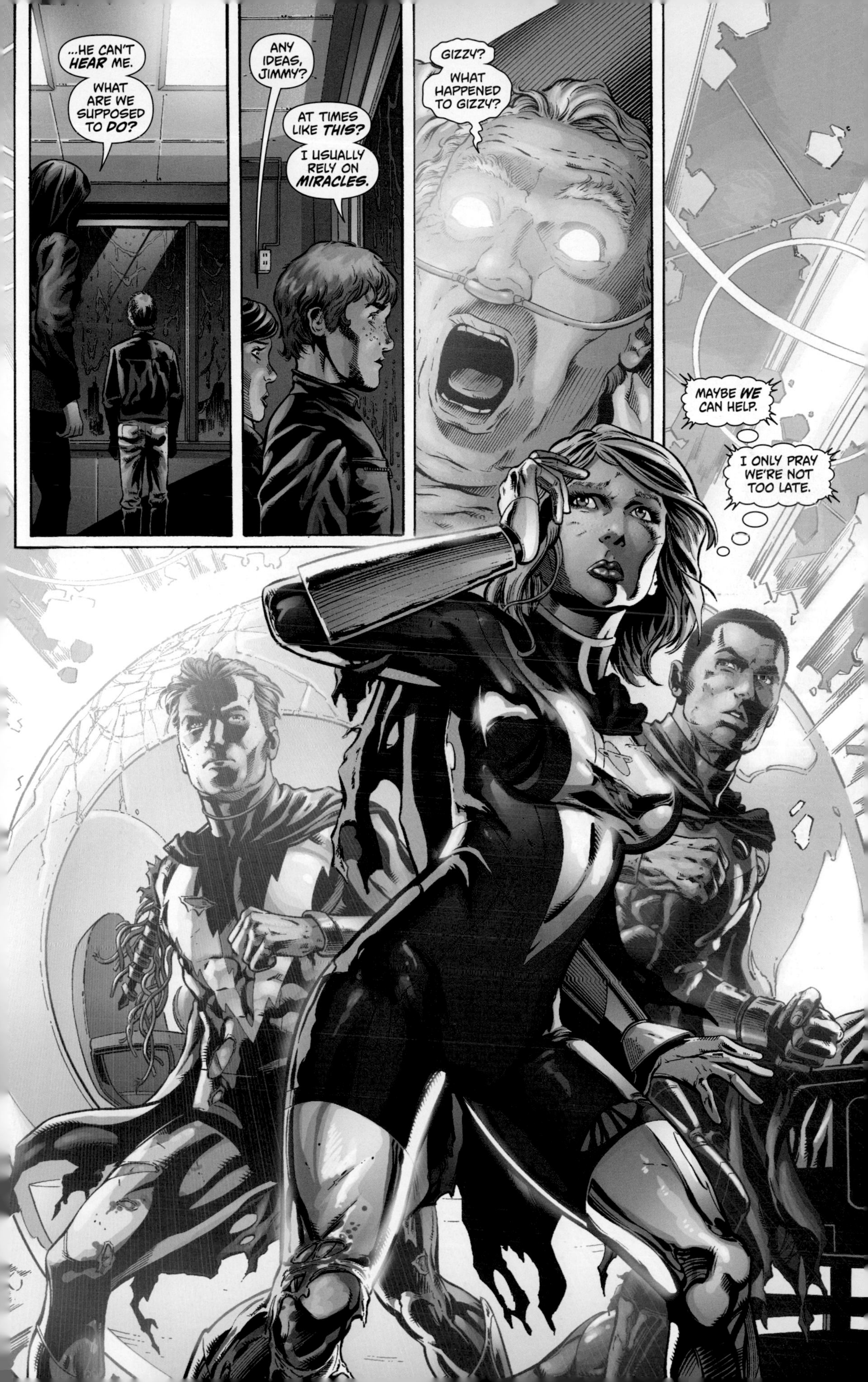
...HE CAN'T HEAR ME.
WHAT ARE WE SUPPOSED TO DO?
ANY IDEAS, JIMMY?
AT TIMES LIKE THIS?
I USUALLY RELY ON MIRACLES.
GIZZY?
WHAT HAPPENED TO GIZZY?
MAYBE WE CAN HELP.
I ONLY PRAY WE'RE NOT TOO LATE.

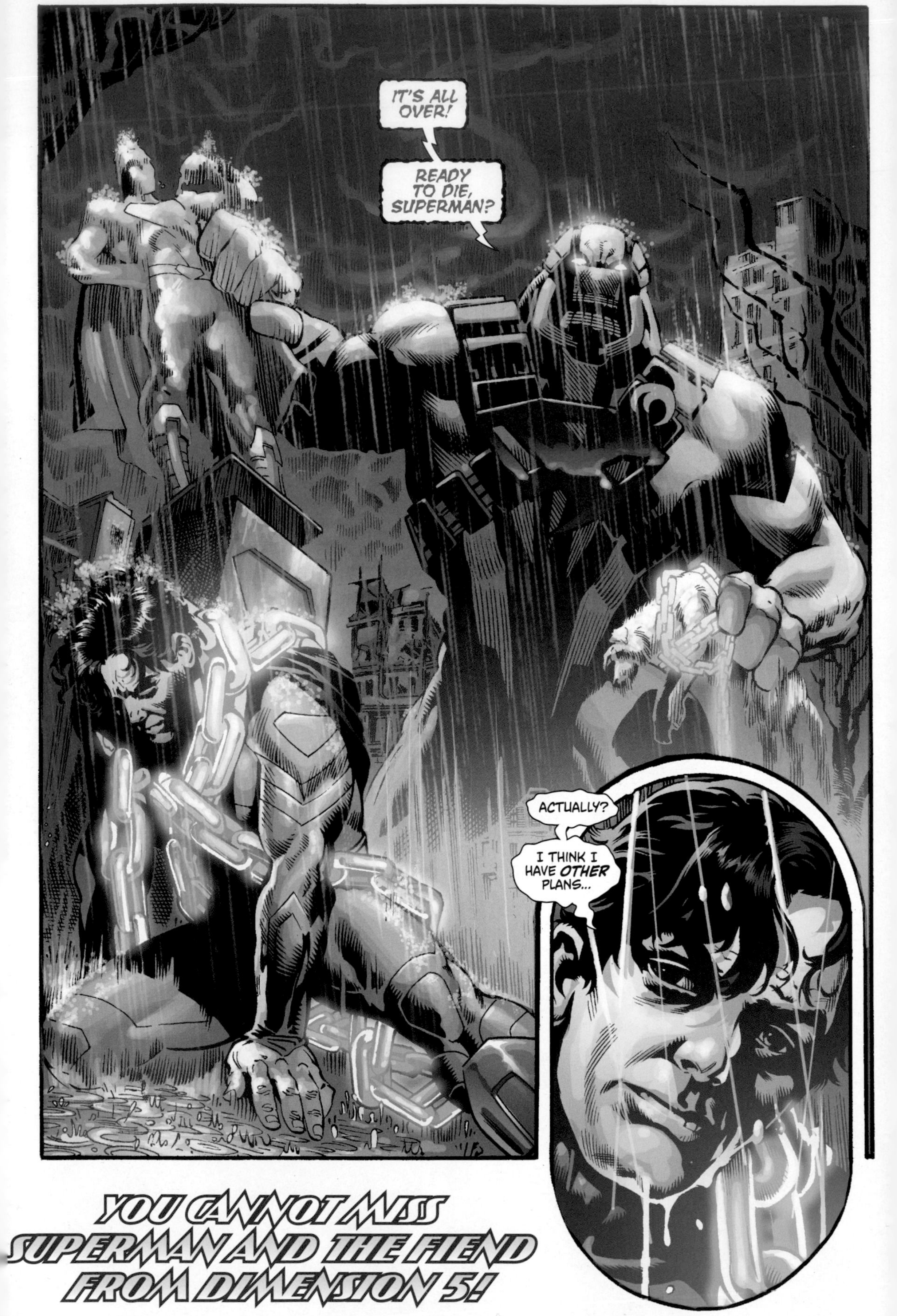
IT'S ALL OVER!
READY TO DIE, SUPERMAN?
ACTUALLY?
I THINK I HAVE OTHER PLANS...
YOU CANNOT MISS SUPERMAN AND THE FIEND FROM DIMENSION 5!

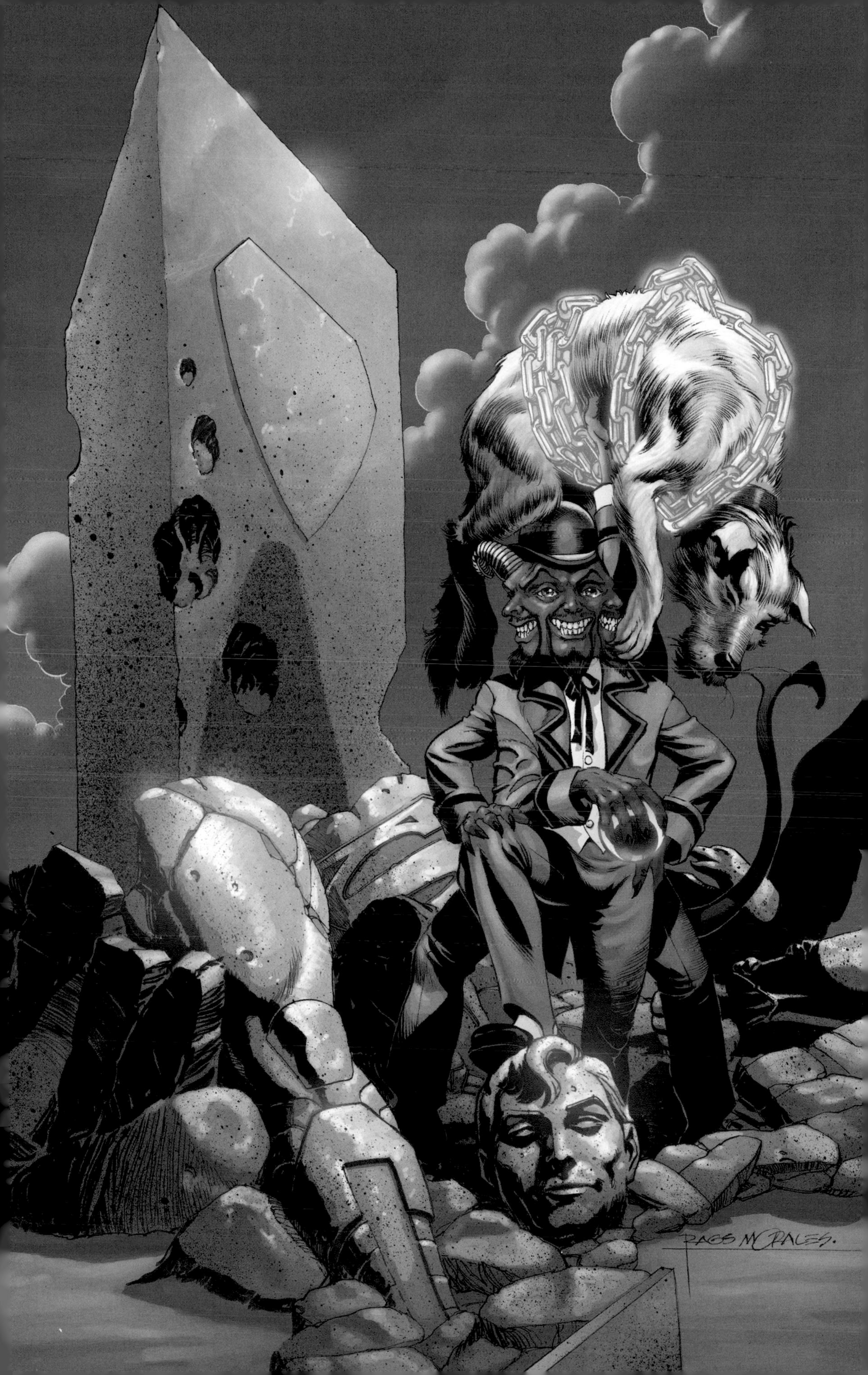
RAGS MORALES.

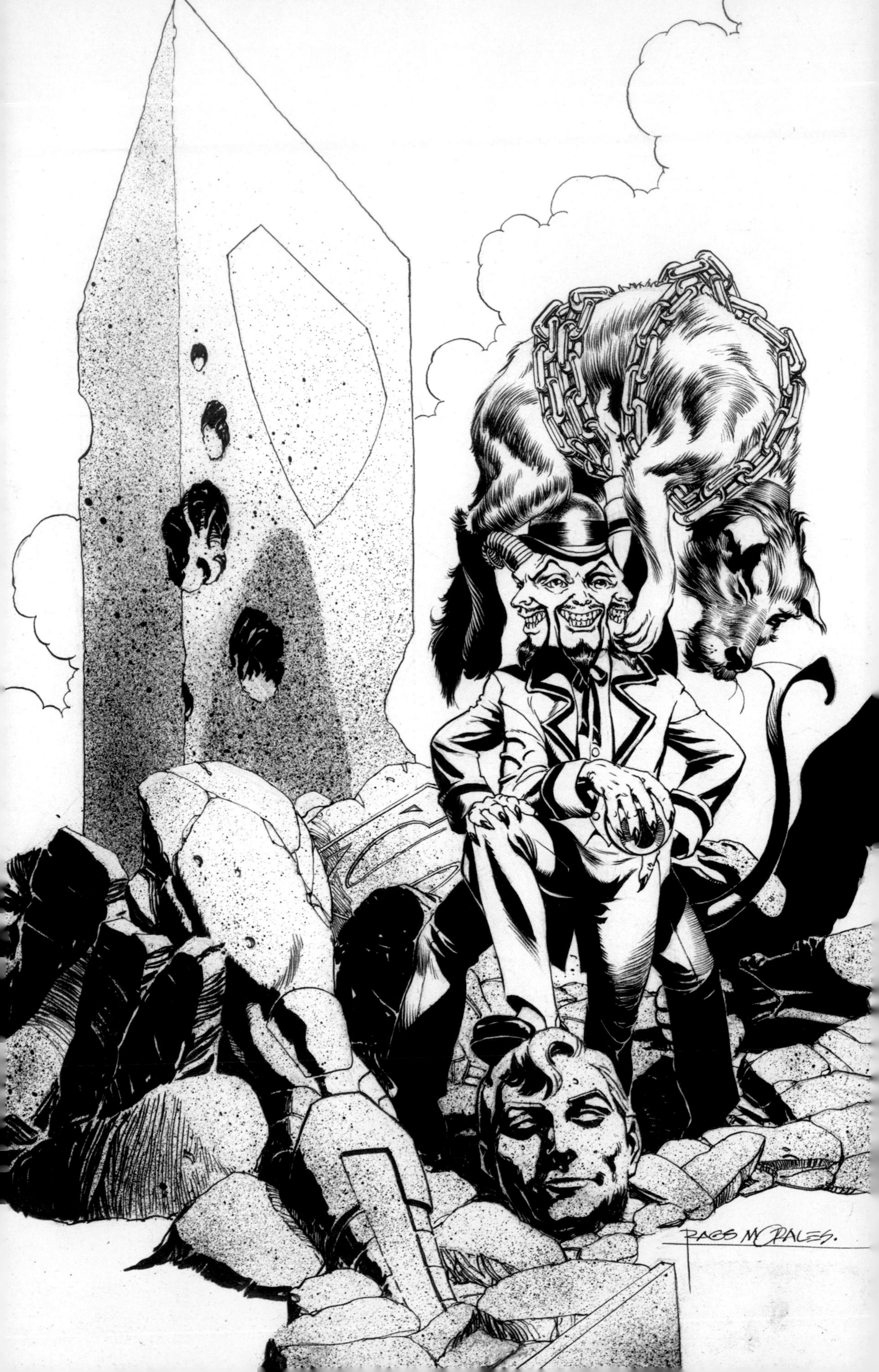
RAGS MORALES.

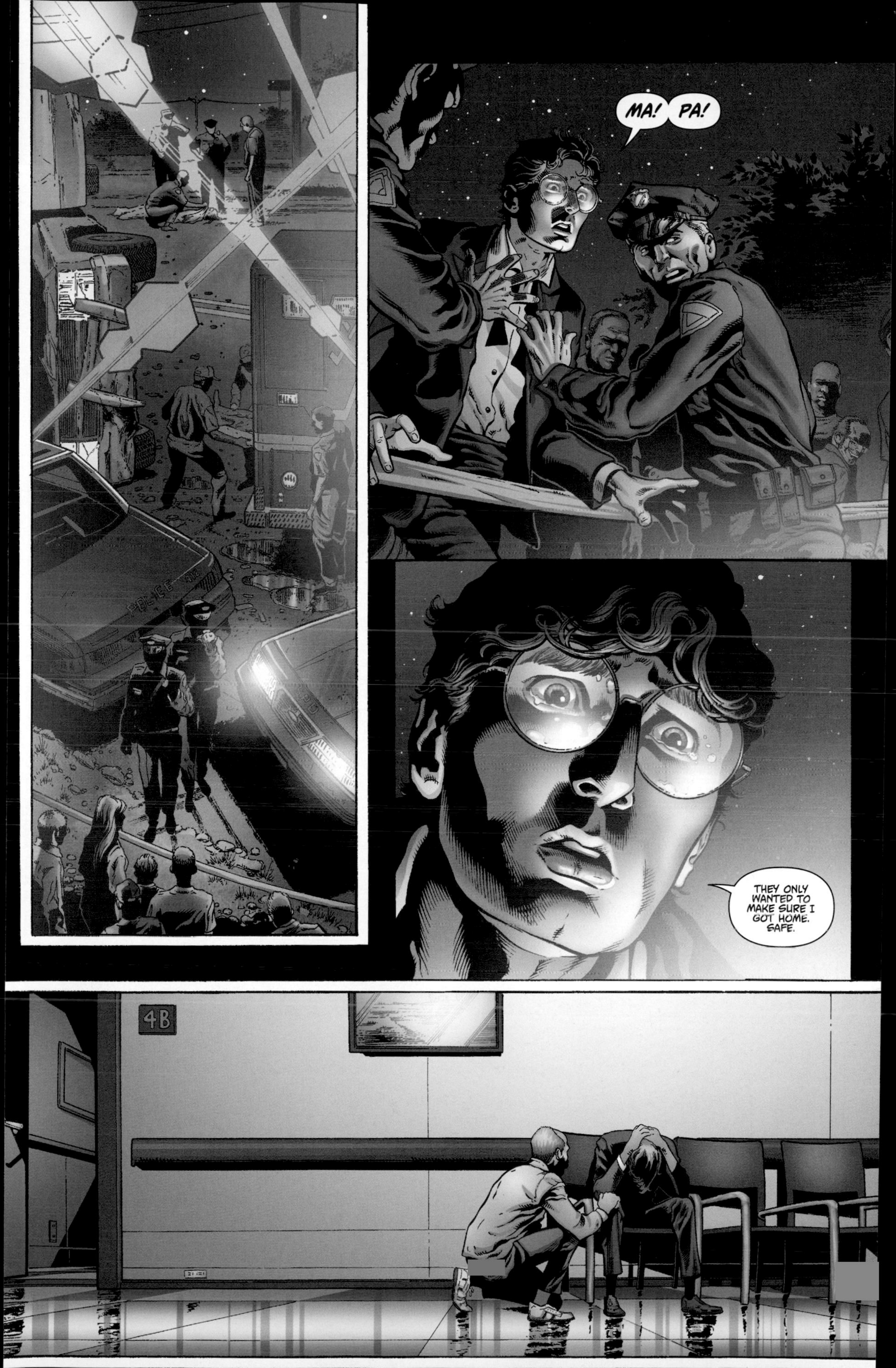
MA! PA!
THEY ONLY WANTED TO MAKE SURE I GOT HOME. SAFE.
4B

BUT I SAW ANGELS, CLARK--AND THEY GATHERED HER UP.

I'M GOING TO *DIE*, I KNOW THAT.

I WANT TO DIE AT HOME.

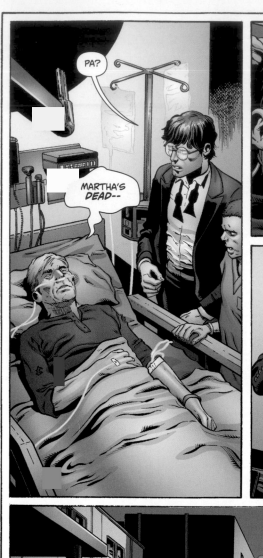

PA?

MARTHA'S DEAD--

MR. KENT, YOU CAN'T...!

YOU CAN DO WHAT YOU WANT, PA.

I'LL MAKE SURE OF THAT.

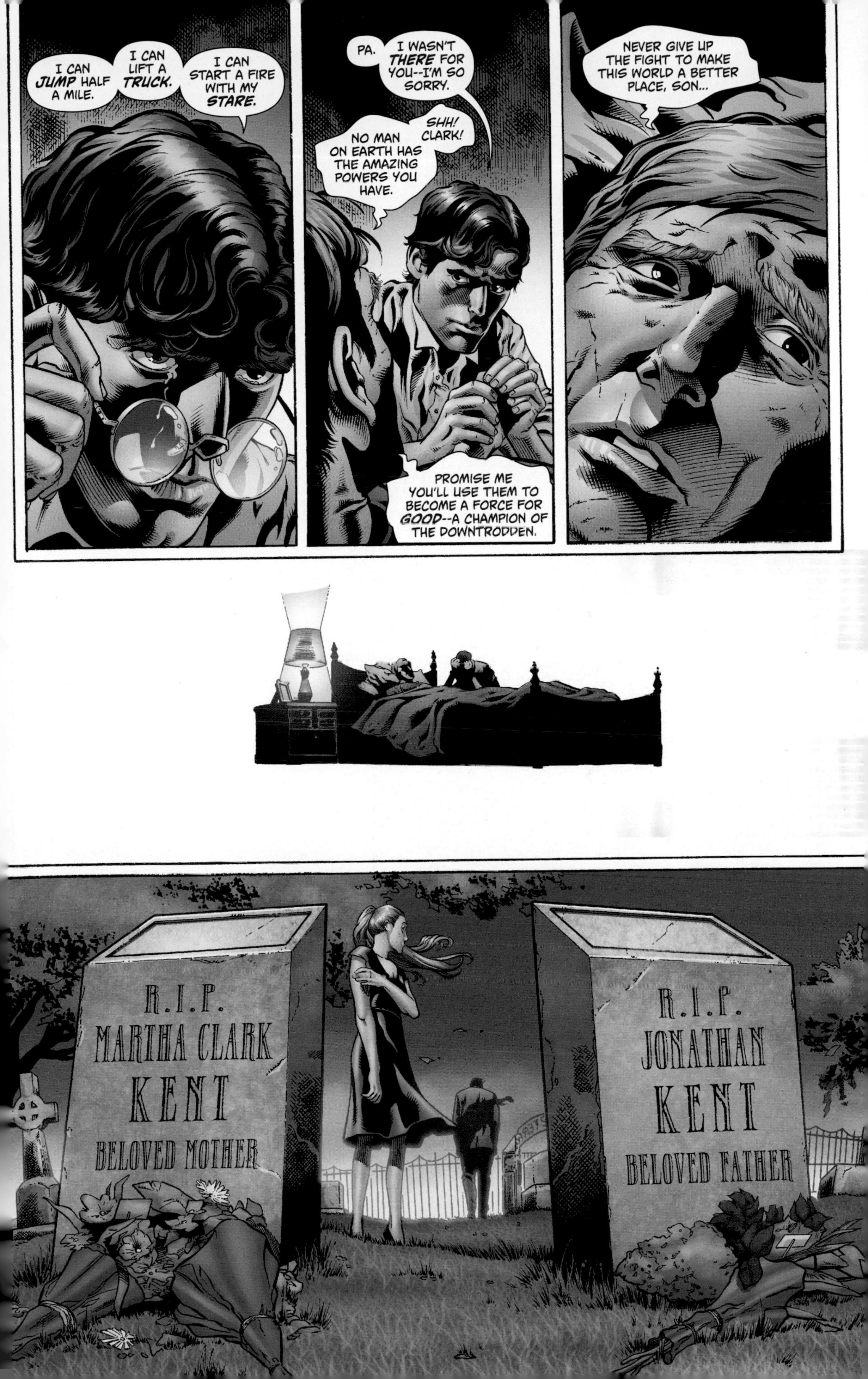
I CAN JUMP HALF A MILE.
I CAN LIFT A TRUCK.
I CAN START A FIRE WITH MY STARE.
PA.
I WASN'T THERE FOR YOU--I'M SO SORRY.
SHH! CLARK!
NO MAN ON EARTH HAS THE AMAZING POWERS YOU HAVE.
PROMISE ME YOU'LL USE THEM TO BECOME A FORCE FOR GOOD--A CHAMPION OF THE DOWNTRODDEN.
NEVER GIVE UP THE FIGHT TO MAKE THIS WORLD A BETTER PLACE, SON...
R.I.P. MARTHA CLARK KENT BELOVED MOTHER
R.I.P. JONATHAN KENT BELOVED FATHER

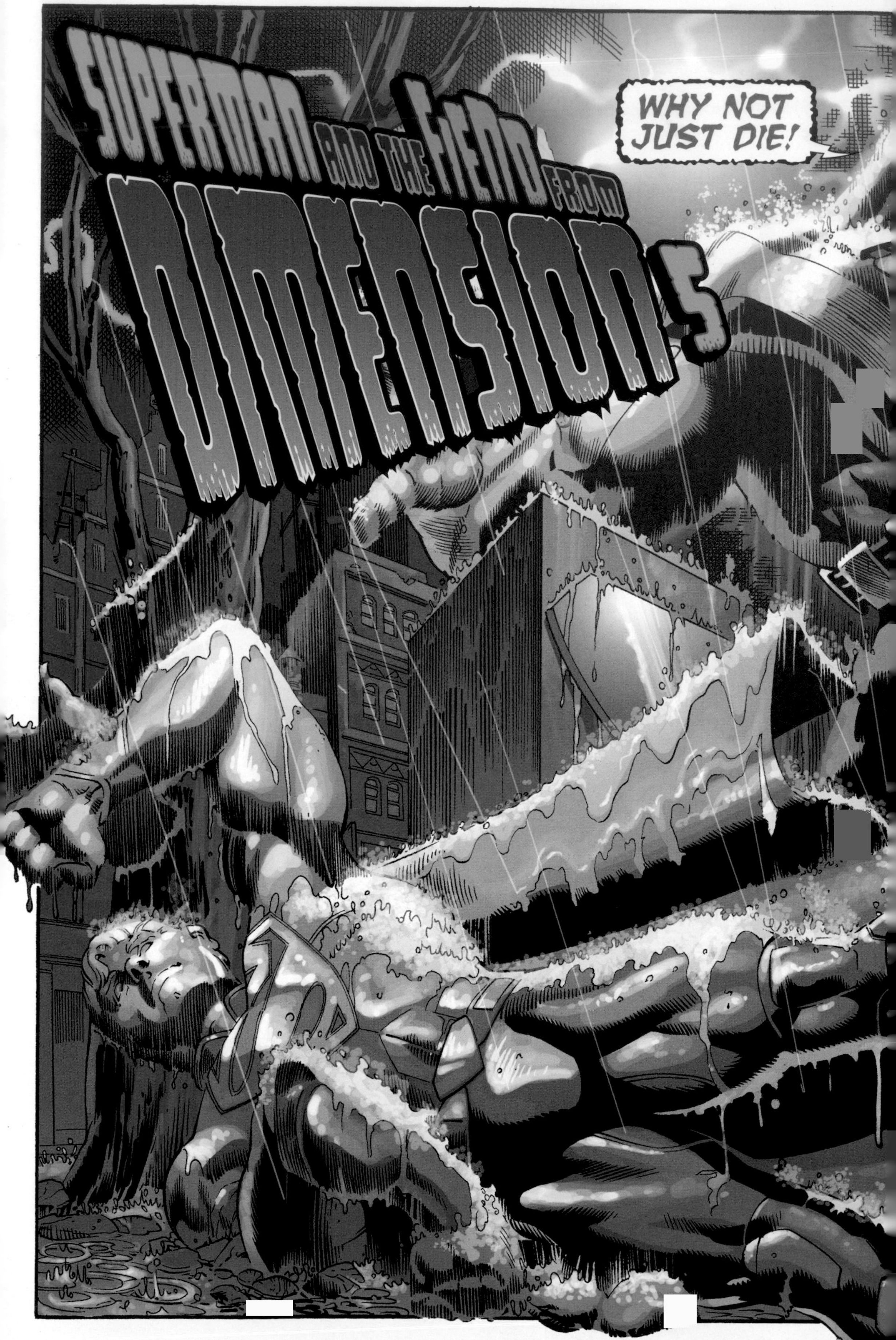
SUPERMAN AND THE FIEND FROM DIMENSION 5
WHY NOT JUST DIE!

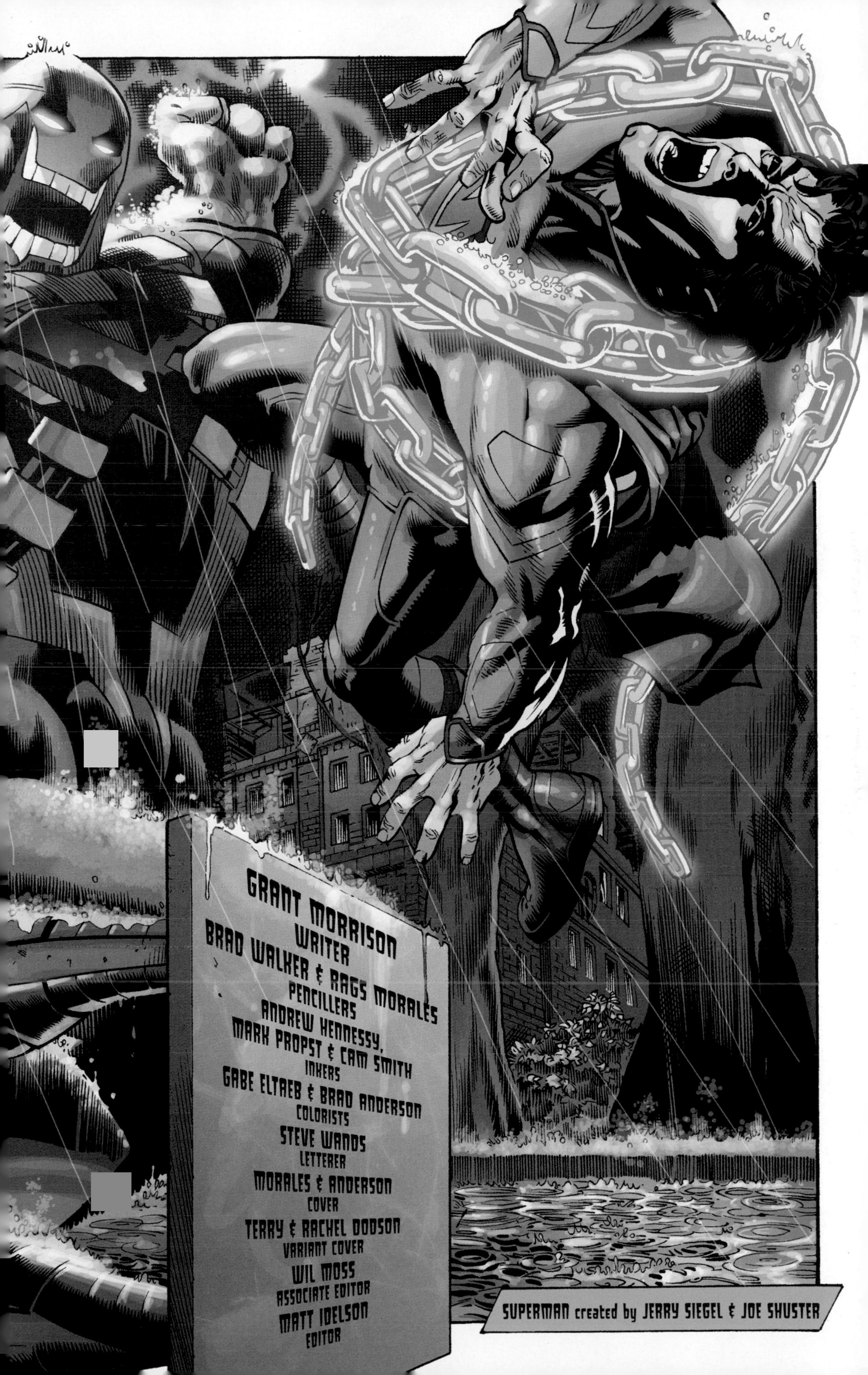
GRANT MORRISON
WRITER
BRAD WALKER & RAGS MORALES
PENCILLERS
ANDREW HENNESSY,
MARK PROPST & CAM SMITH
INKERS
GABE ELTAEB & BRAD ANDERSON
COLORISTS
STEVE WANDS
LETTERER
MORALES & ANDERSON
COVER
TERRY & RACHEL DODSON
VARIANT COVER
WIL MOSS
ASSOCIATE EDITOR
MATT IDELSON
EDITOR
SUPERMAN created by JERRY SIEGEL & JOE SHUSTER

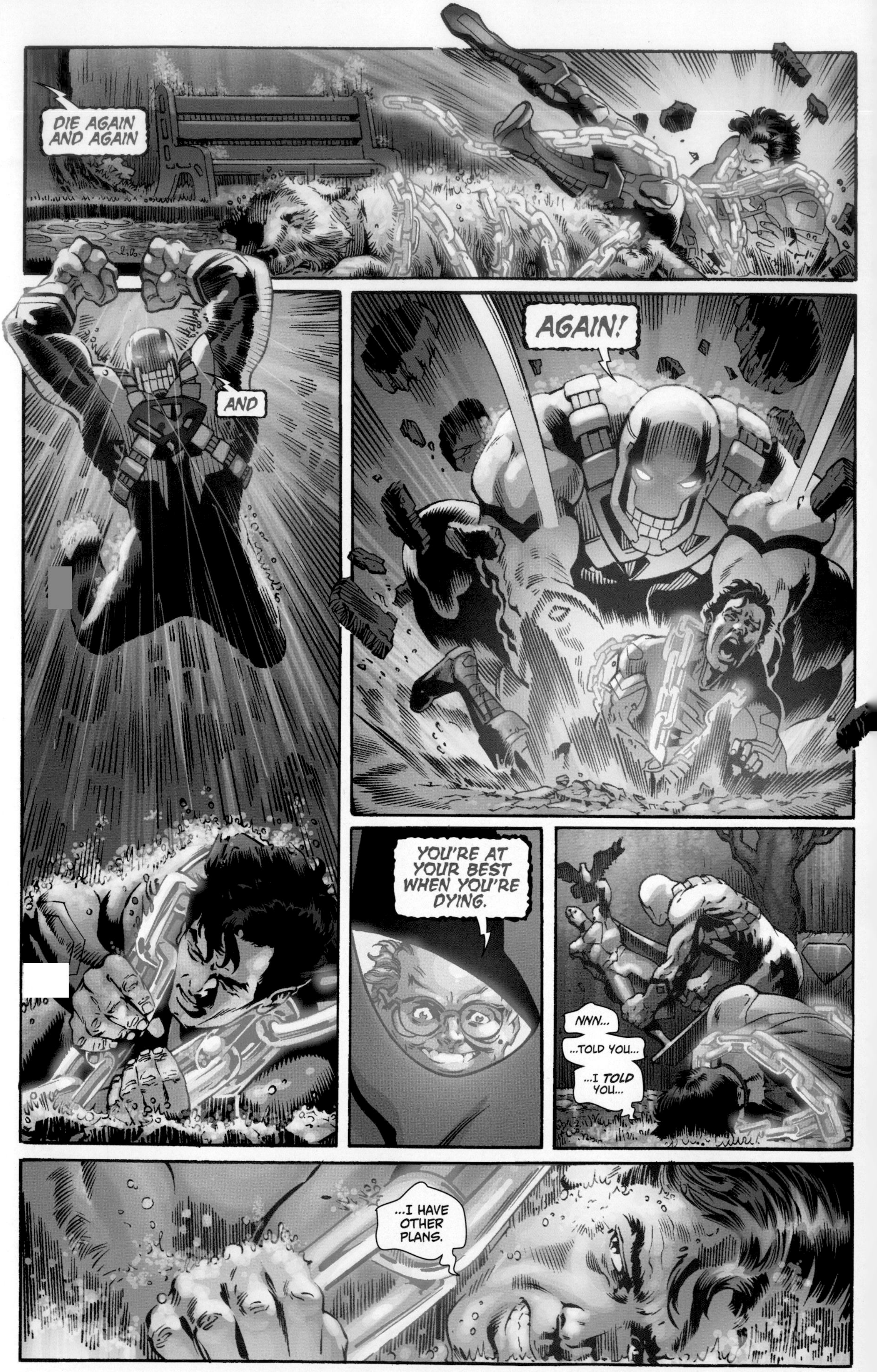
DIE AGAIN AND AGAIN
AND
AGAIN!
YOU'RE AT YOUR BEST WHEN YOU'RE DYING.
NNN...
...TOLD YOU...
...I TOLD YOU...
...I HAVE OTHER PLANS.

PLANS?

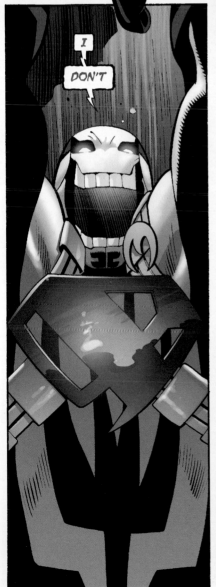

I DON'T

CARE!

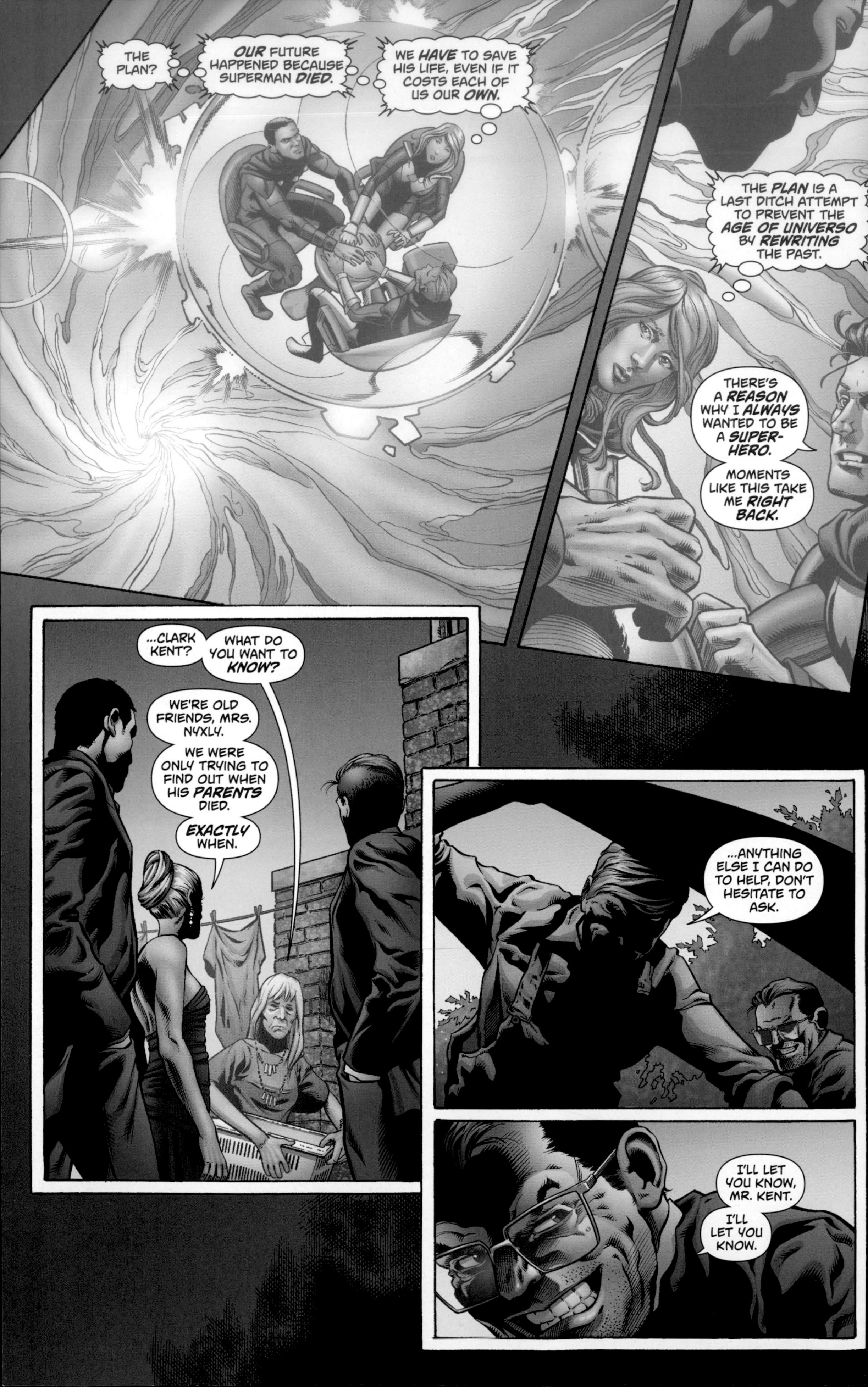
THE PLAN?
OUR FUTURE HAPPENED BECAUSE SUPERMAN DIED.
WE HAVE TO SAVE HIS LIFE, EVEN IF IT COSTS EACH OF US OUR OWN.
THE PLAN IS A LAST DITCH ATTEMPT TO PREVENT THE AGE OF UNIVERSO BY REWRITING THE PAST.
THERE'S A REASON WHY I ALWAYS WANTED TO BE A SUPER-HERO.
MOMENTS LIKE THIS TAKE ME RIGHT BACK.
...CLARK KENT?
WHAT DO YOU WANT TO KNOW?
WE'RE OLD FRIENDS, MRS. NYXLY.
WE WERE ONLY TRYING TO FIND OUT WHEN HIS PARENTS DIED.
EXACTLY WHEN.
...ANYTHING ELSE I CAN DO TO HELP, DON'T HESITATE TO ASK.
I'LL LET YOU KNOW, MR. KENT.
I'LL LET YOU KNOW.

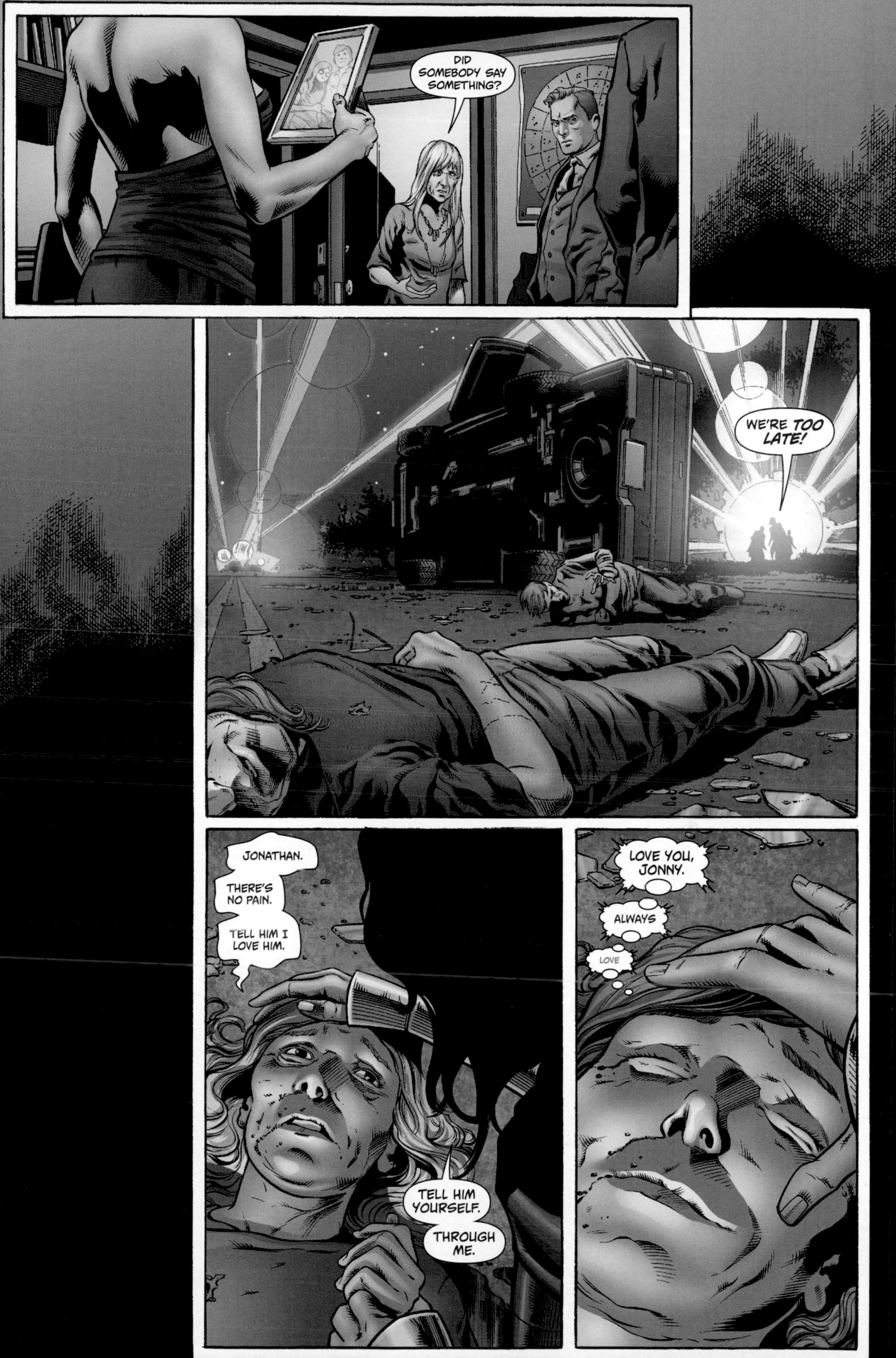
DID SOMEBODY SAY SOMETHING?
WE'RE TOO LATE!
JONATHAN.
THERE'S NO PAIN.
TELL HIM I LOVE HIM.
TELL HIM YOURSELF.
THROUGH ME.
LOVE YOU, JONNY.
ALWAYS
LOVE

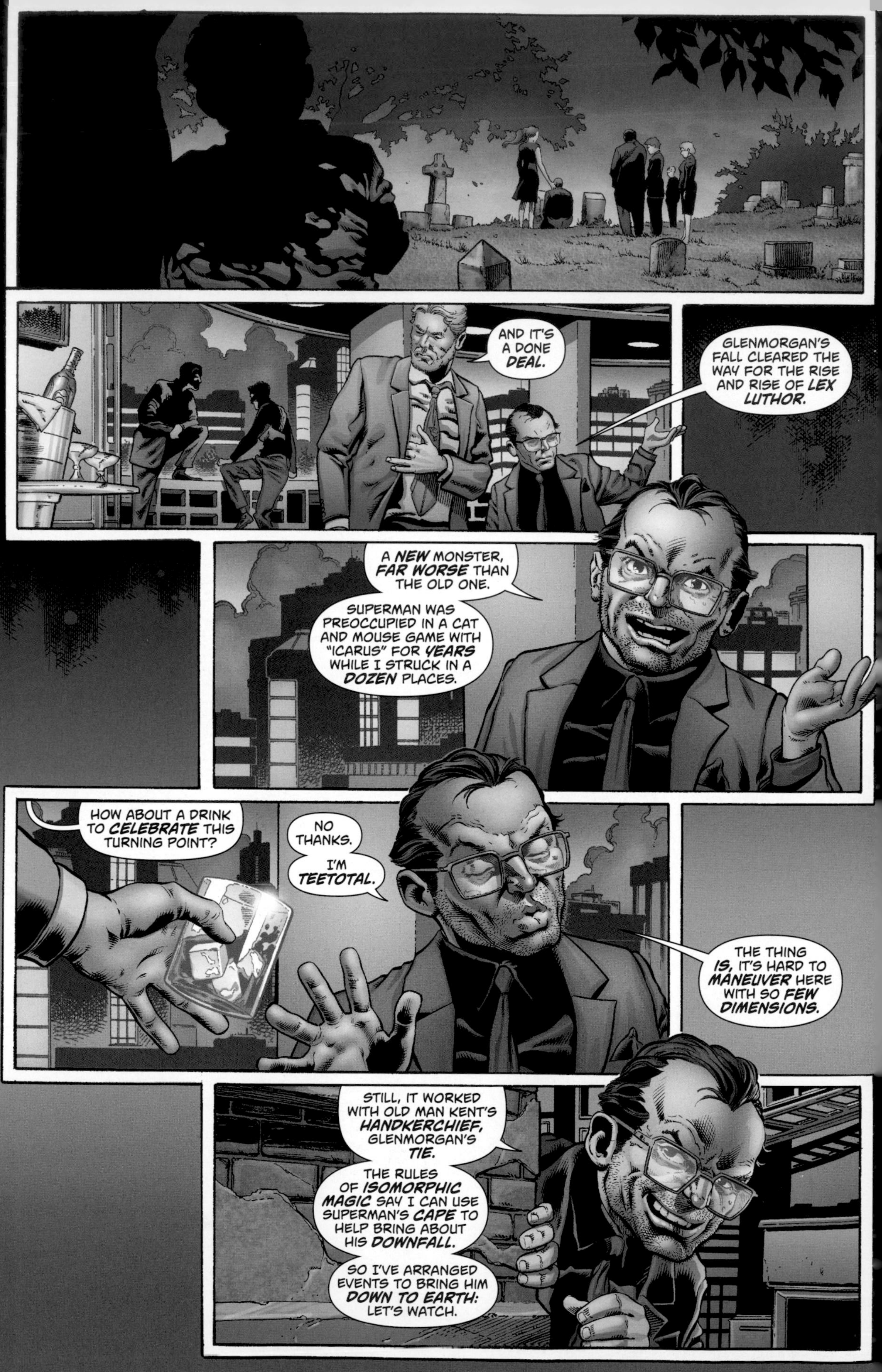

AND IT'S A DONE DEAL.
GLENMORGAN'S FALL CLEARED THE WAY FOR THE RISE AND RISE OF LEX LUTHOR.
A NEW MONSTER, FAR WORSE THAN THE OLD ONE.
SUPERMAN WAS PREOCCUPIED IN A CAT AND MOUSE GAME WITH "ICARUS" FOR YEARS WHILE I STRUCK IN A DOZEN PLACES.
HOW ABOUT A DRINK TO CELEBRATE THIS TURNING POINT?
NO THANKS.
I'M TEETOTAL.
THE THING IS, IT'S HARD TO MANEUVER HERE WITH SO FEW DIMENSIONS.
STILL, IT WORKED WITH OLD MAN KENT'S HANDKERCHIEF, GLENMORGAN'S TIE.
THE RULES OF ISOMORPHIC MAGIC SAY I CAN USE SUPERMAN'S CAPE TO HELP BRING ABOUT HIS DOWNFALL.
SO I'VE ARRANGED EVENTS TO BRING HIM DOWN TO EARTH: LET'S WATCH.

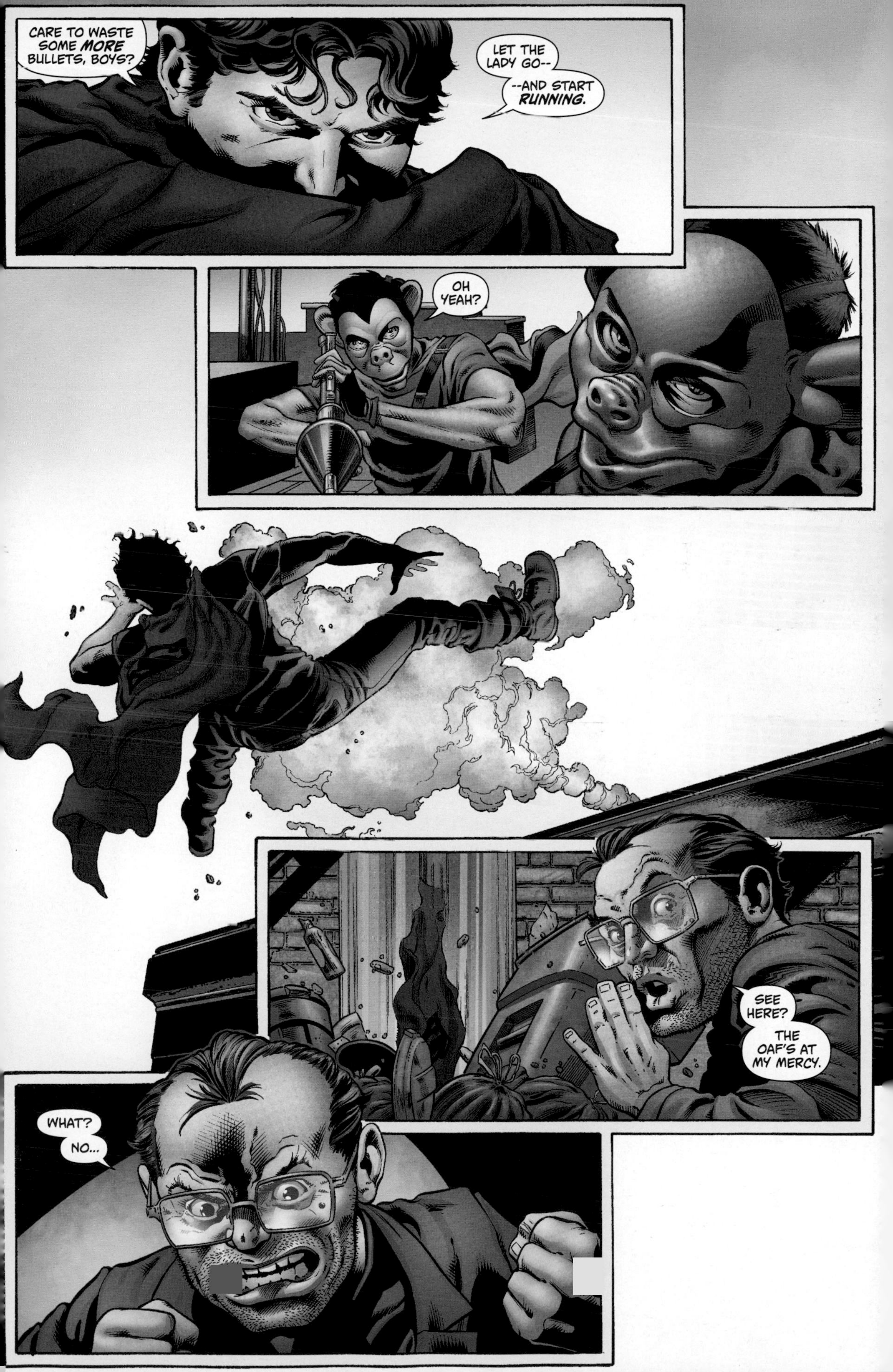
CARE TO WASTE SOME MORE BULLETS, BOYS?
LET THE LADY GO--
--AND START RUNNING.
OH YEAH?
SEE HERE?
THE OAF'S AT MY MERCY.
WHAT?
NO...

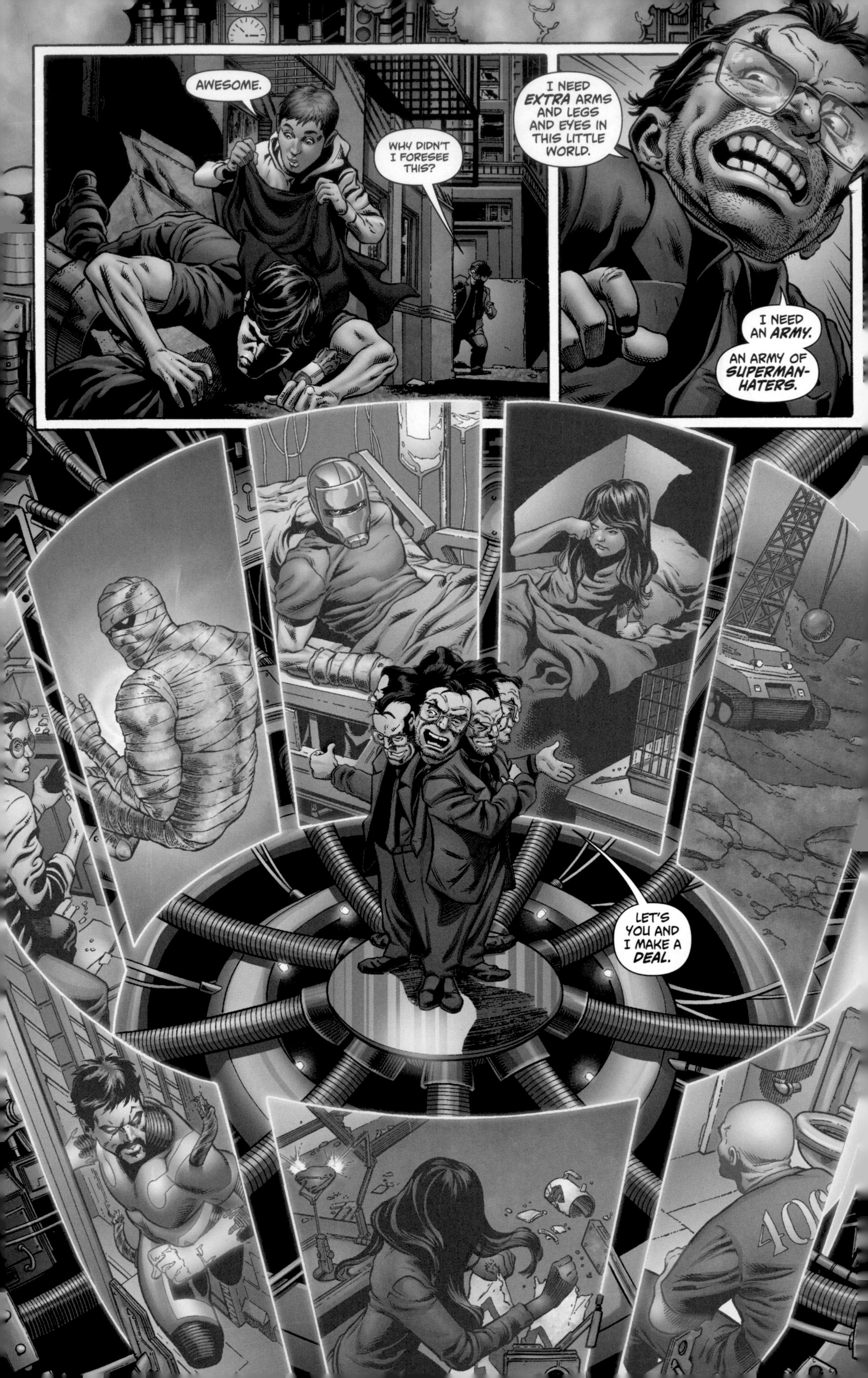
AWESOME.
WHY DIDN'T I FORESEE THIS?
I NEED EXTRA ARMS AND LEGS AND EYES IN THIS LITTLE WORLD.
I NEED AN ARMY.
AN ARMY OF SUPERMAN-HATERS.
LET'S YOU AND I MAKE A DEAL.
406

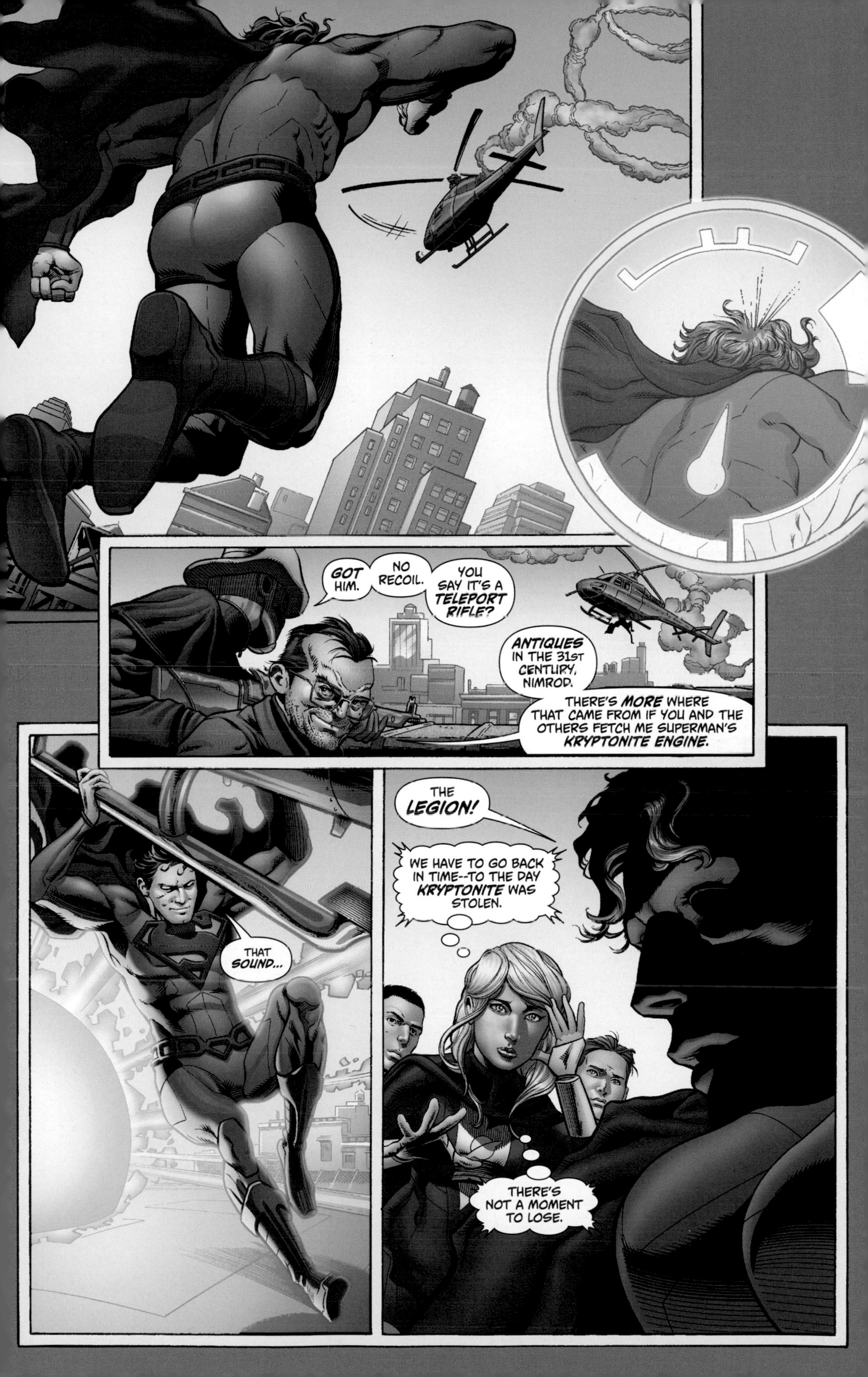
GOT HIM.
NO RECOIL.
YOU SAY IT'S A TELEPORT RIFLE?
ANTIQUES IN THE 31ST CENTURY, NIMROD.
THERE'S MORE WHERE THAT CAME FROM IF YOU AND THE OTHERS FETCH ME SUPERMAN'S KRYPTONITE ENGINE.
THAT SOUND...
THE LEGION!
WE HAVE TO GO BACK IN TIME--TO THE DAY KRYPTONITE WAS STOLEN.
THERE'S NOT A MOMENT TO LOSE.

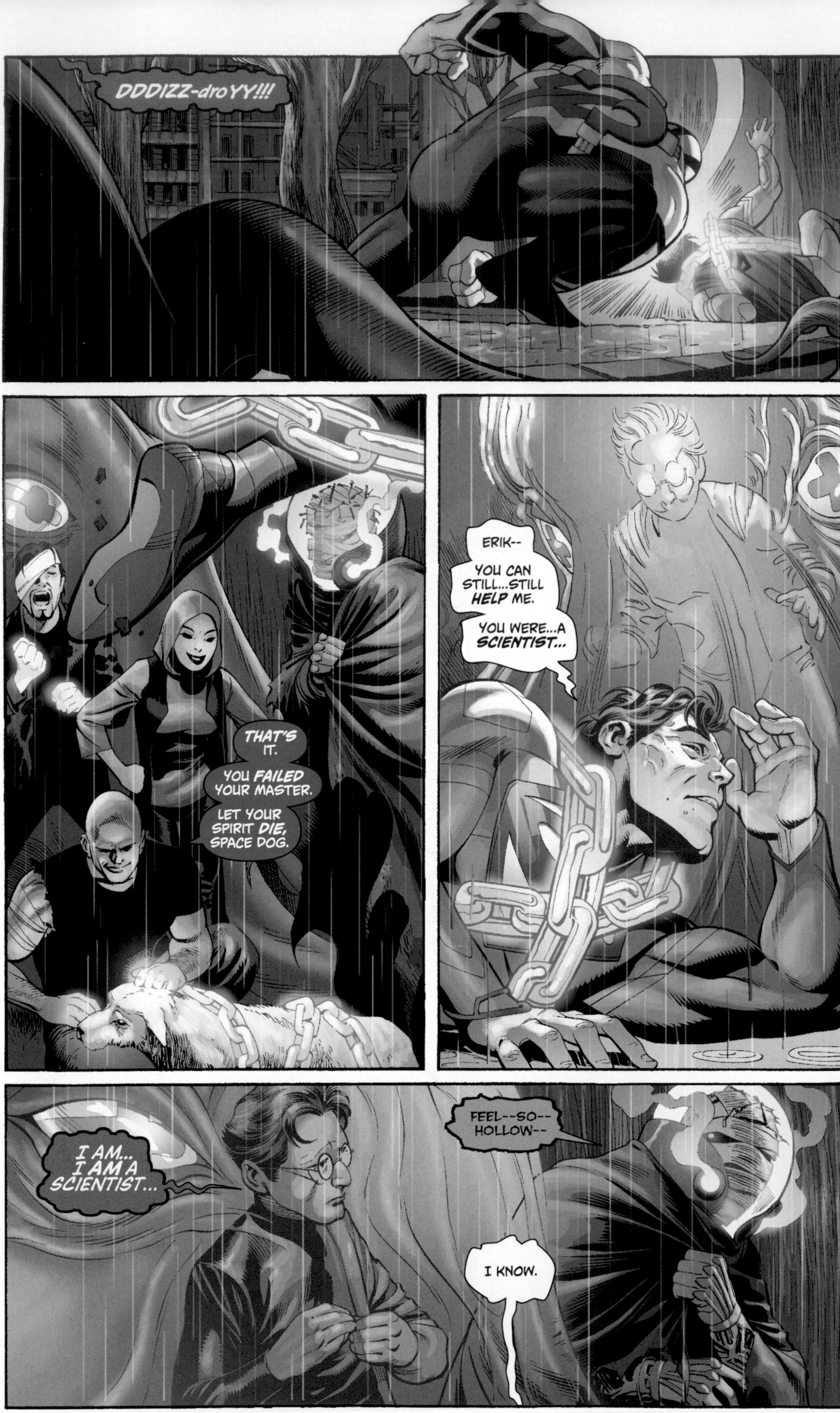
DDDIZZ-droYY!!!
THAT'S IT.
YOU FAILED YOUR MASTER.
LET YOUR SPIRIT DIE, SPACE DOG.
ERIK--
YOU CAN STILL...STILL HELP ME.
YOU WERE...A SCIENTIST...
I AM... I AM A SCIENTIST...
FEEL--SO--HOLLOW--
I KNOW.

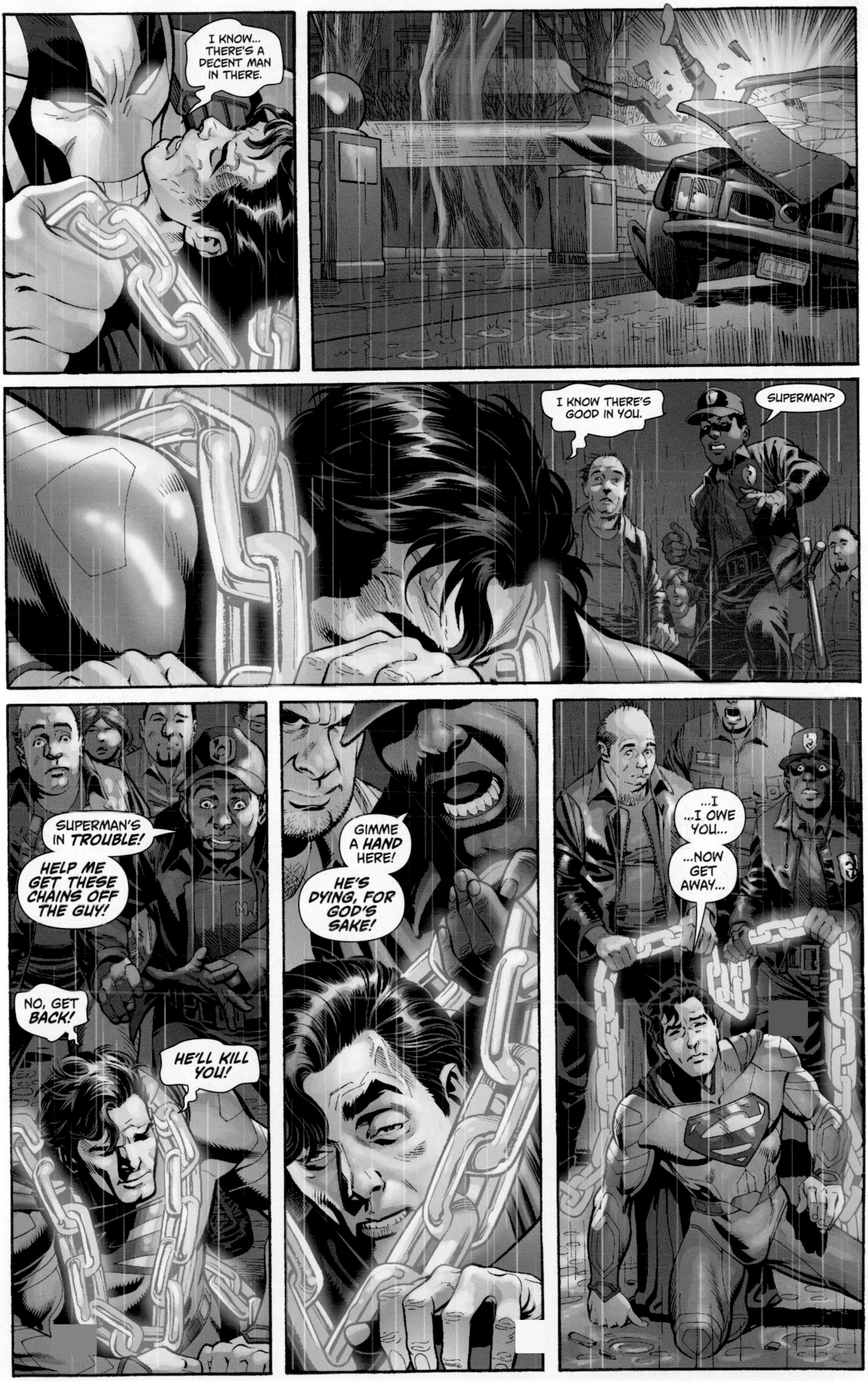
I KNOW... THERE'S A DECENT MAN IN THERE.
I KNOW THERE'S GOOD IN YOU.
SUPERMAN?
SUPERMAN'S IN TROUBLE!
HELP ME GET THESE CHAINS OFF THE GUY!
NO, GET BACK!
HE'LL KILL YOU!
GIMME A HAND HERE!
HE'S DYING, FOR GOD'S SAKE!
...I ...I OWE YOU...
...NOW GET AWAY...

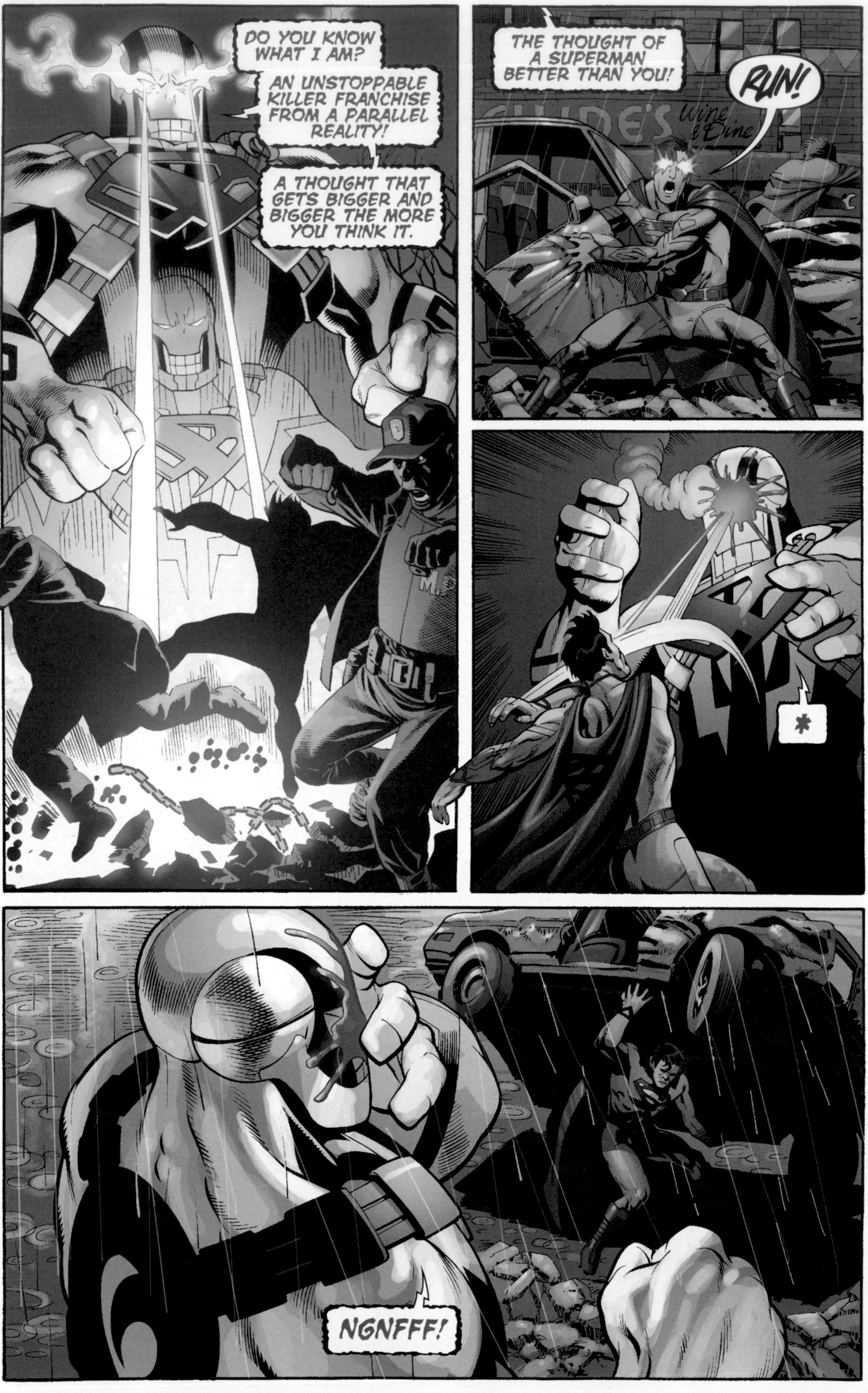
DO YOU KNOW WHAT I AM?
AN UNSTOPPABLE KILLER FRANCHISE FROM A PARALLEL REALITY!
A THOUGHT THAT GETS BIGGER AND BIGGER THE MORE YOU THINK IT.
THE THOUGHT OF A SUPERMAN BETTER THAN YOU!
RUN!
*
NGNFFF!

WHAT *HAPPENED* TO YOU? YOU'RE *HURT.*

IT'S BEEN *MONTHS* SINCE I LAST SAW YOU...

WHAT HAPPENED TO *YOU?*

XA-DU GOT LOOSE.

THIS IS *IT,* ISN'T IT? *VYNDKTVX* IS ABOUT TO ATTACK FROM THE *5TH* DIMENSION.

HE'S *ALWAYS* ATTACKING--

THIS IS JUST WHERE YOU REALLY START TO *FEEL* IT.

YOU ALL KNOW THE *FUTURE,* SATURN WOMAN.

DO I *WIN?*

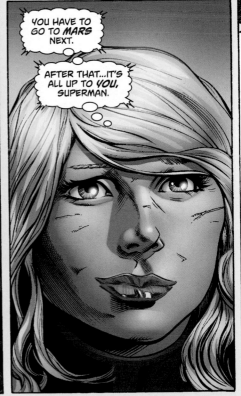

YOU HAVE TO GO TO *MARS* NEXT.

AFTER THAT...IT'S ALL UP TO *YOU,* SUPERMAN.

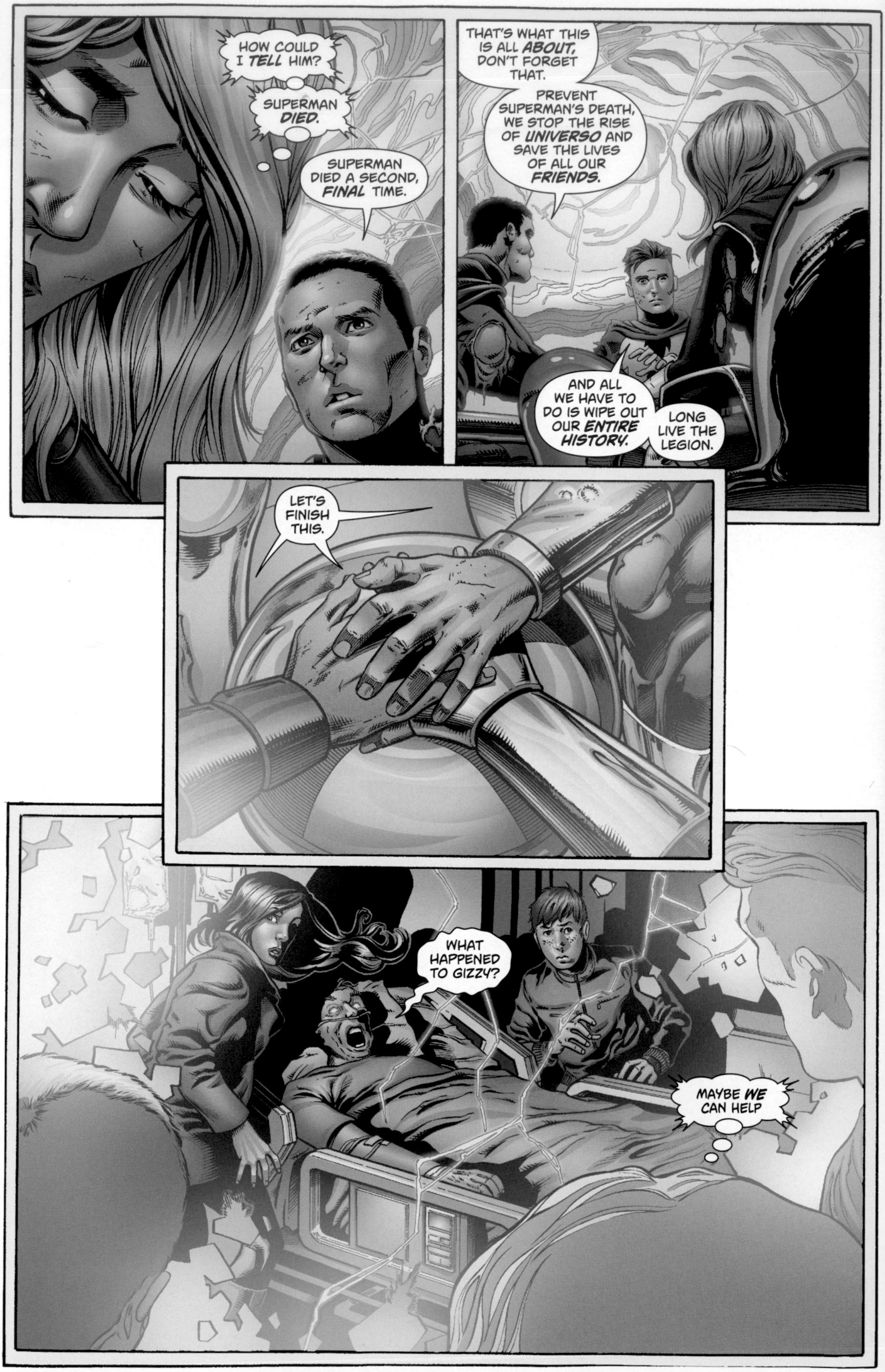
HOW COULD I TELL HIM?
SUPERMAN DIED.
SUPERMAN DIED A SECOND, FINAL TIME.
THAT'S WHAT THIS IS ALL ABOUT, DON'T FORGET THAT.
PREVENT SUPERMAN'S DEATH, WE STOP THE RISE OF UNIVERSO AND SAVE THE LIVES OF ALL OUR FRIENDS.
AND ALL WE HAVE TO DO IS WIPE OUT OUR ENTIRE HISTORY.
LONG LIVE THE LEGION.
LET'S FINISH THIS.
WHAT HAPPENED TO GIZZY?
MAYBE WE CAN HELP

I'M THE THOUGHT OF A BIGGER SUPERMAN.

A STRONGER, MORE RUTHLESS SUPERMAN!

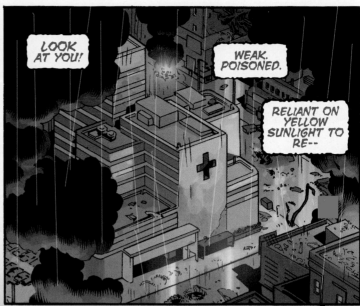

LOOK AT YOU!

WEAK. POISONED.

RELIANT ON YELLOW SUNLIGHT TO RE--

...I'M POWERED BY A SIMPLE CORPORATE DIRECTIVE: ANNIHILATE THE COMPETITION!

LOOK AT ME!

YOUR REPLACEMENT.

THE LAST KNIGHT OF TOMORROW!

STEP ASIDE!

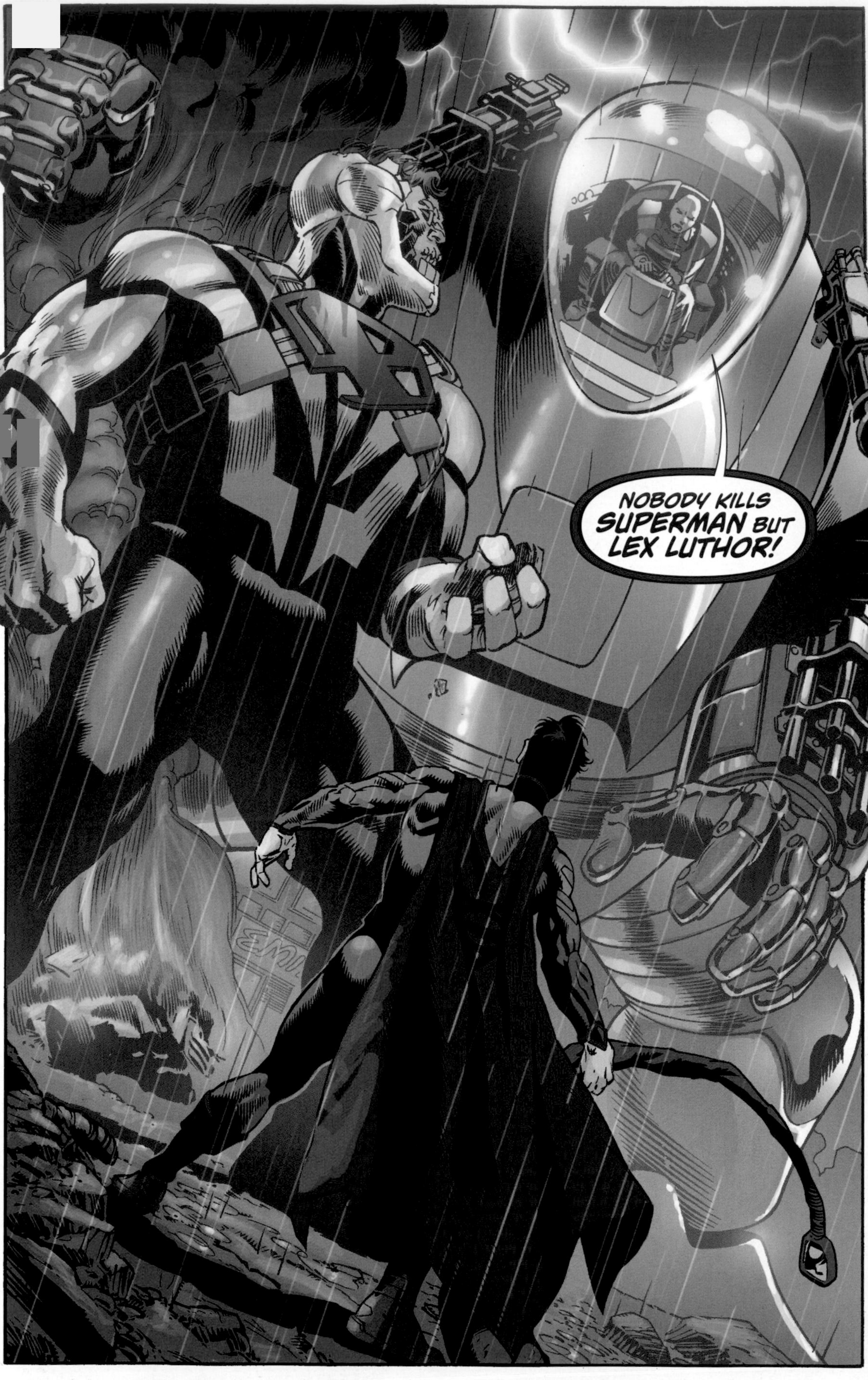
NOBODY KILLS SUPERMAN BUT LEX LUTHOR!

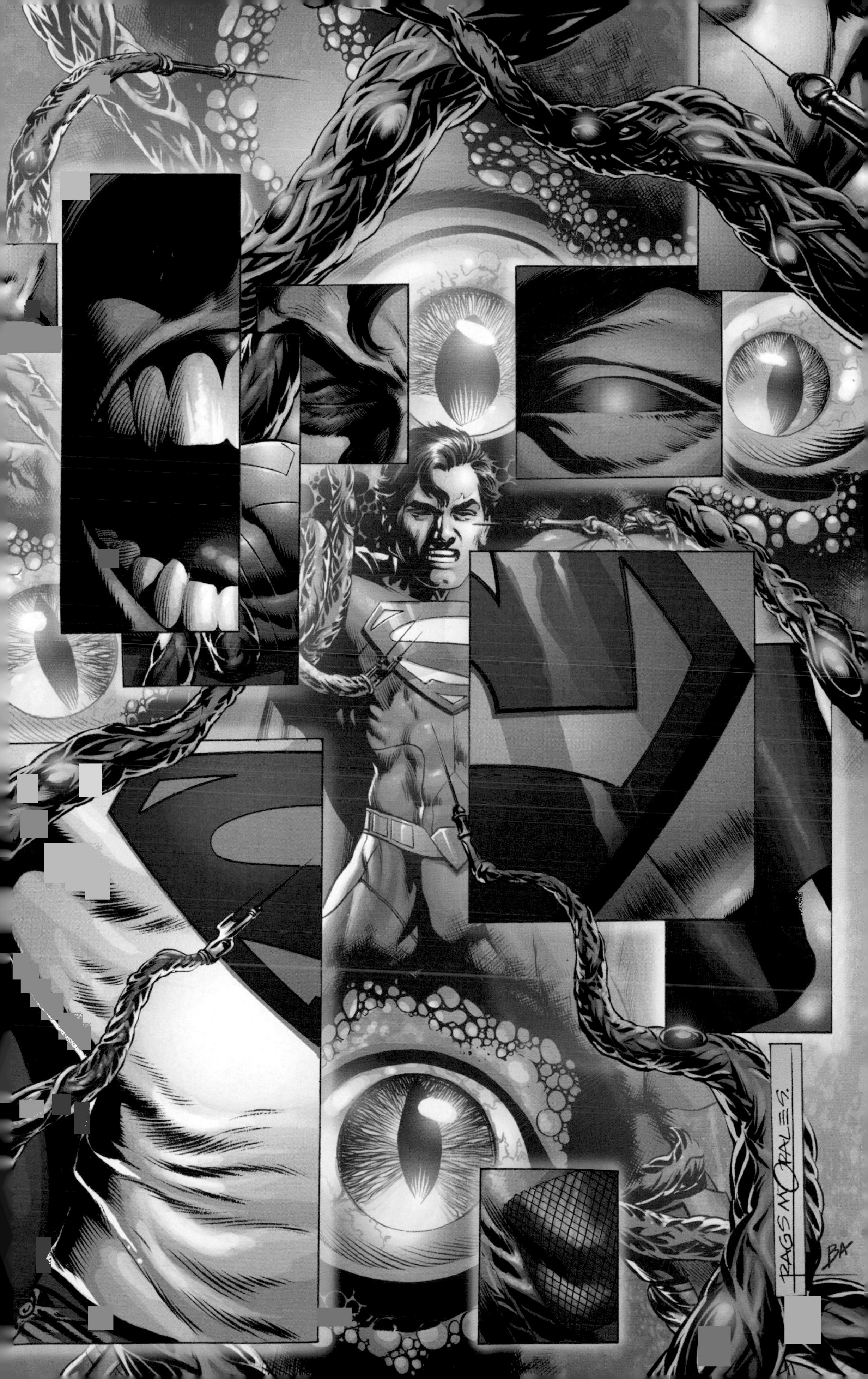
RAGS MORALES.
BA

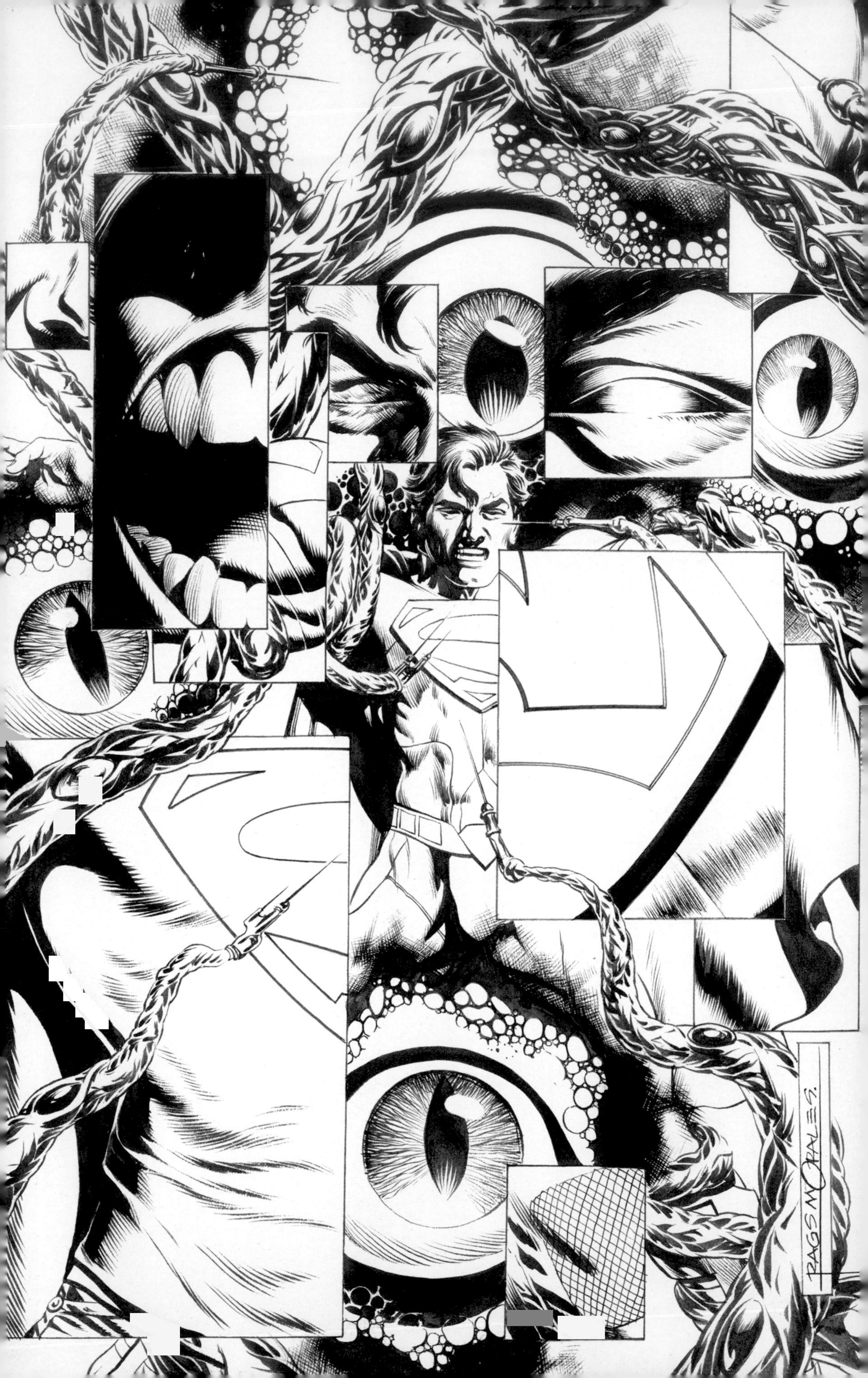
RAGS MORALES

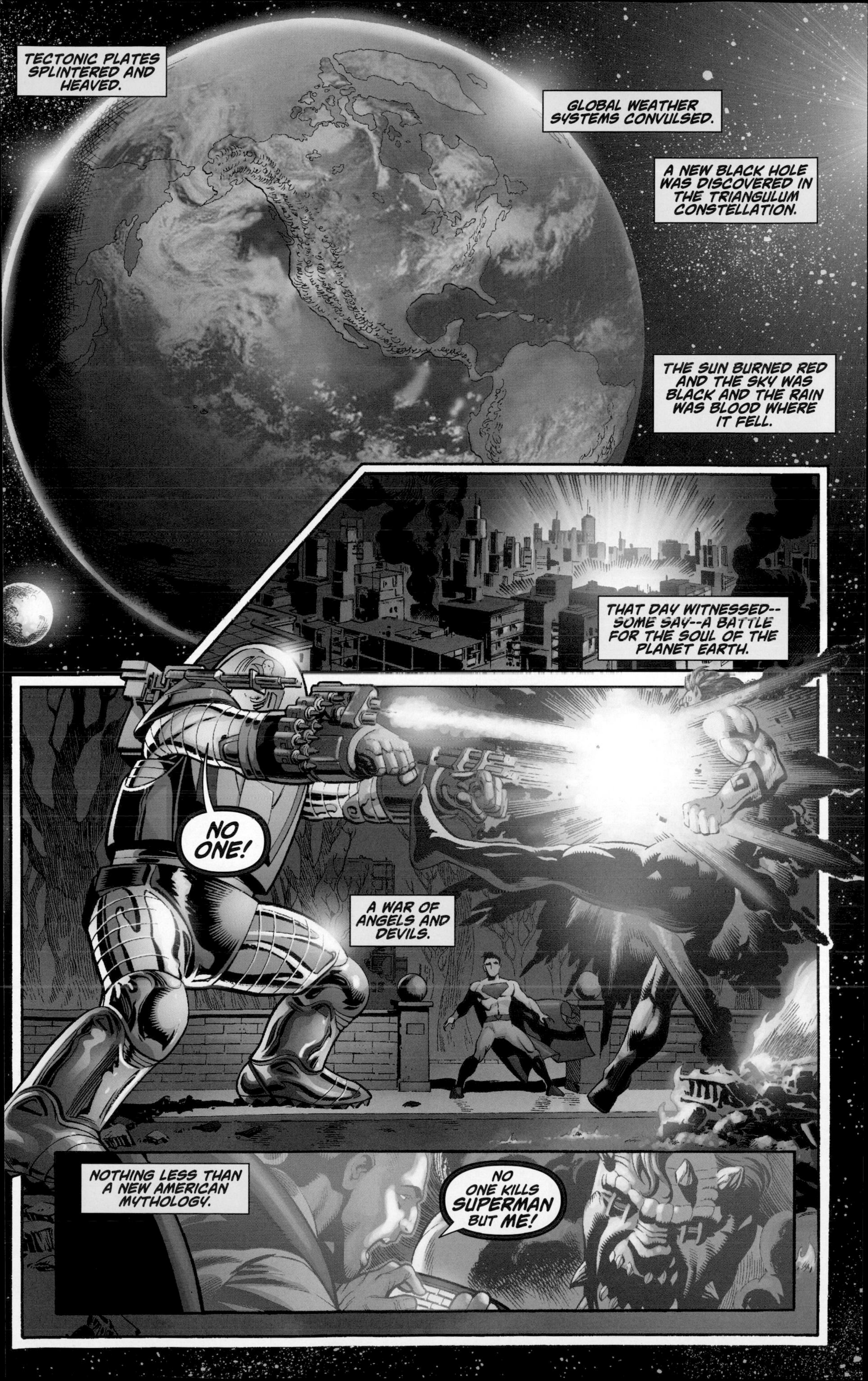
TECTONIC PLATES SPLINTERED AND HEAVED.
GLOBAL WEATHER SYSTEMS CONVULSED.
A NEW BLACK HOLE WAS DISCOVERED IN THE TRIANGULUM CONSTELLATION.
THE SUN BURNED RED AND THE SKY WAS BLACK AND THE RAIN WAS BLOOD WHERE IT FELL.
THAT DAY WITNESSED--SOME SAY--A BATTLE FOR THE SOUL OF THE PLANET EARTH.
NO ONE!
A WAR OF ANGELS AND DEVILS.
NOTHING LESS THAN A NEW AMERICAN MYTHOLOGY.
NO ONE KILLS SUPERMAN BUT ME!

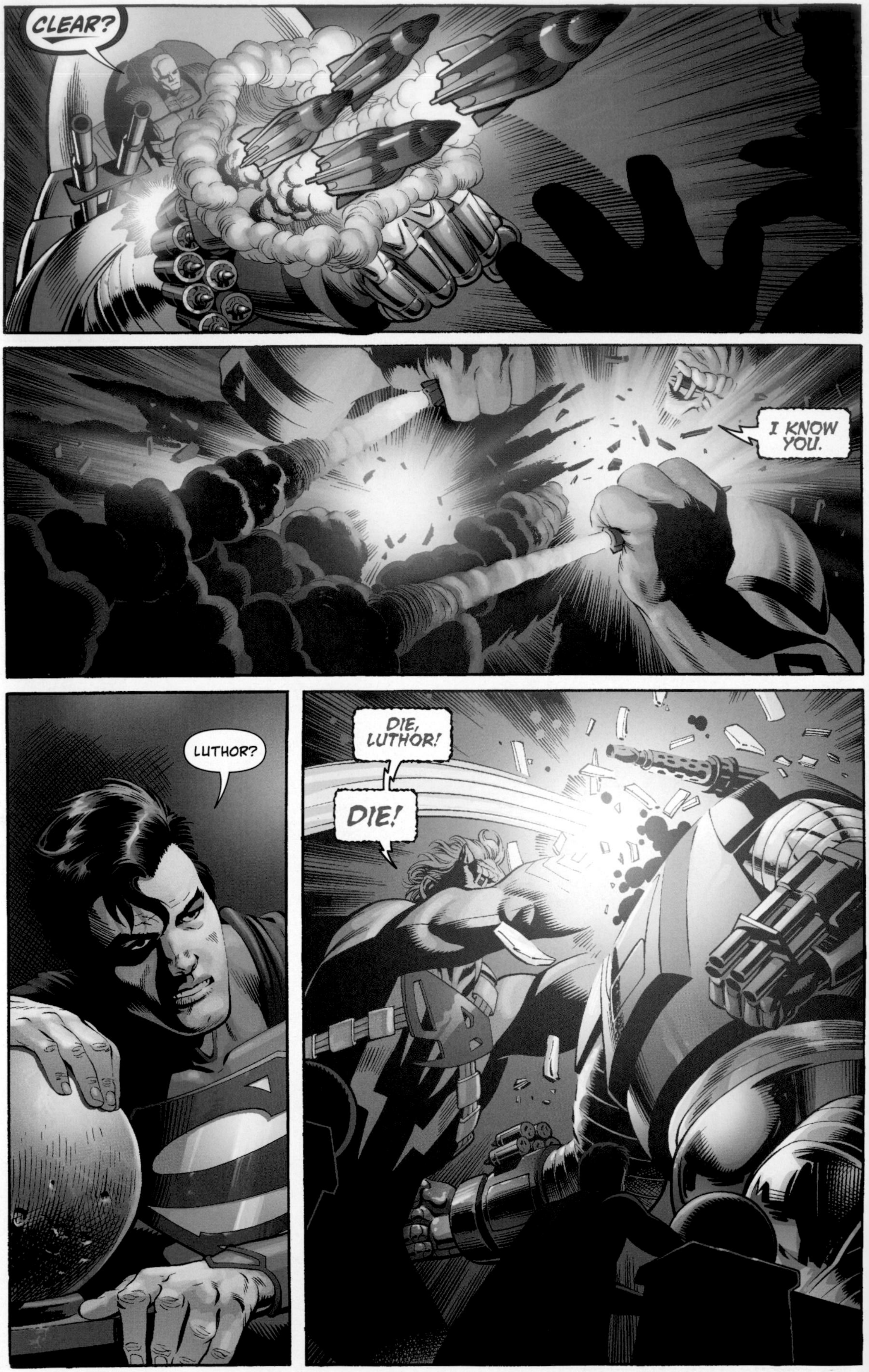
CLEAR?
I KNOW YOU.
LUTHOR?
DIE, LUTHOR!
DIE!

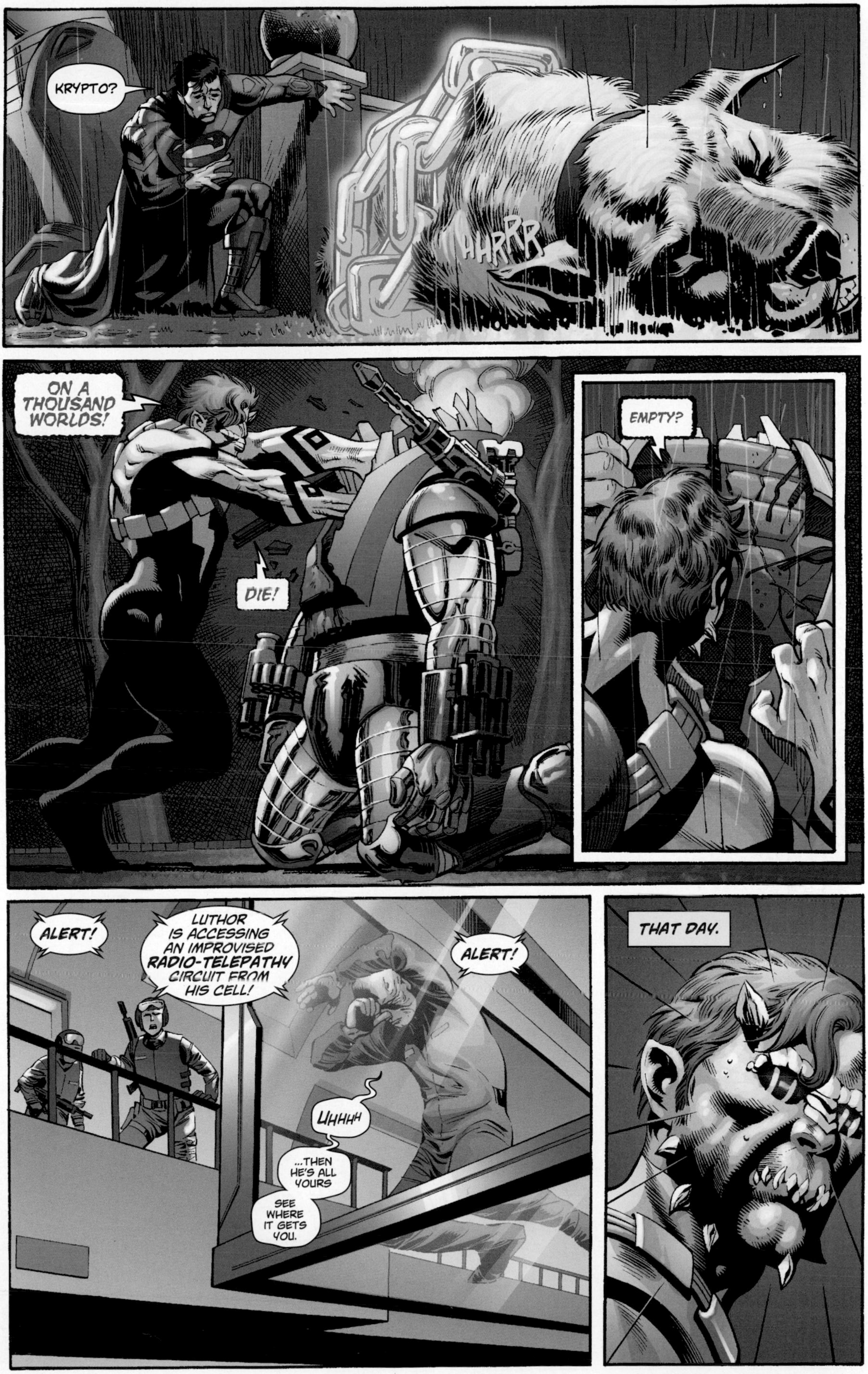
KRYPTO?
HHRRR
ON A THOUSAND WORLDS!
DIE!
EMPTY?
ALERT!
LUTHOR IS ACCESSING AN IMPROVISED RADIO-TELEPATHY CIRCUIT FROM HIS CELL!
ALERT!
UHHHH
...THEN HE'S ALL YOURS
SEE WHERE IT GETS YOU.
THAT DAY.

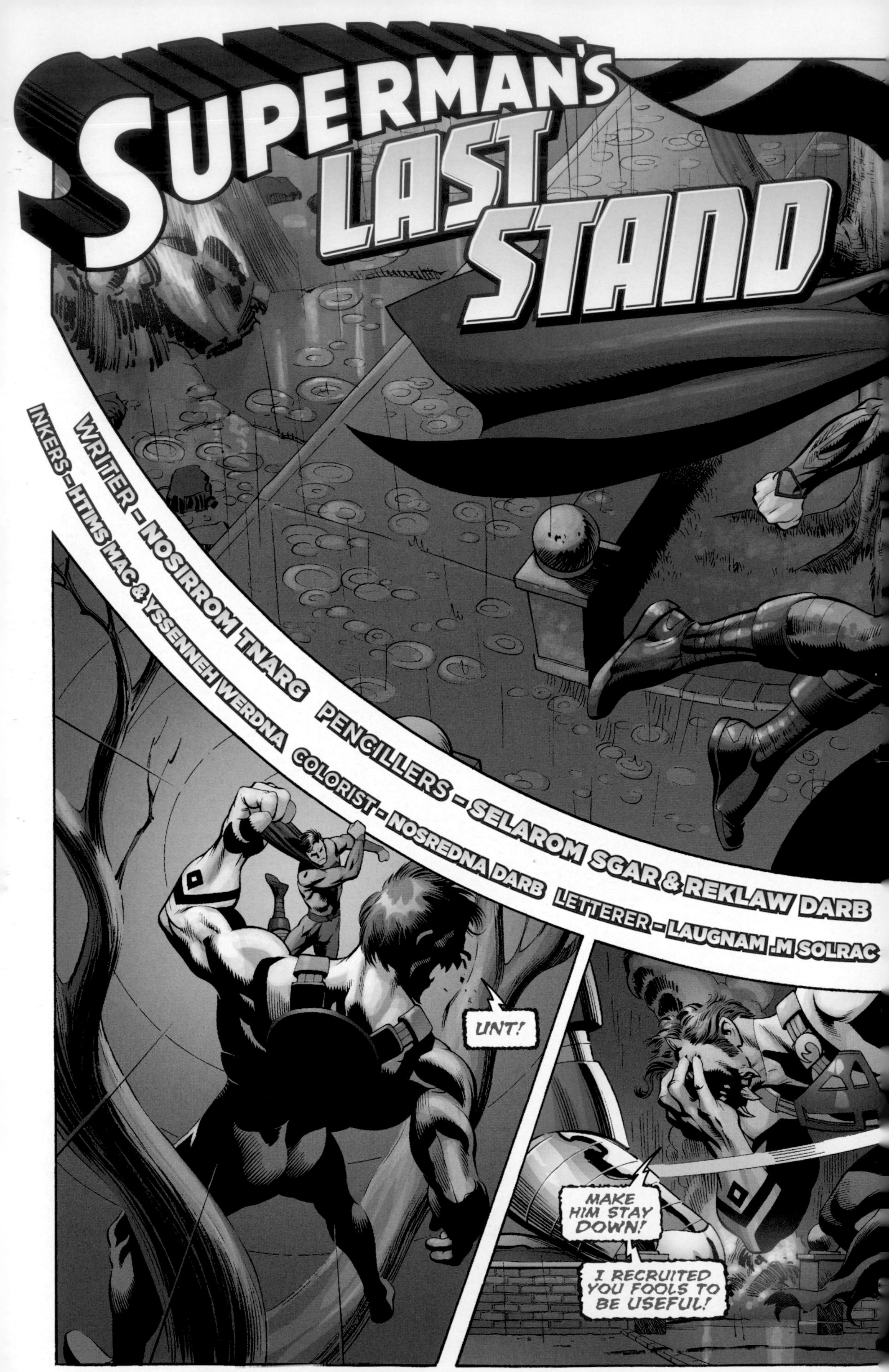
SUPERMAN'S LAST STAND
WRITER - NOSIRROM TNARG PENCILLERS - SELAROM SGAR & REKLAW DARB
INKERS - HTIMS MAC & YSSENNEH WERDNA COLORIST - NOSREDNA DARB LETTERER - LAUGNAM .M SOLRAC
UNT!
MAKE HIM STAY DOWN!
I RECRUITED YOU FOOLS TO BE USEFUL!

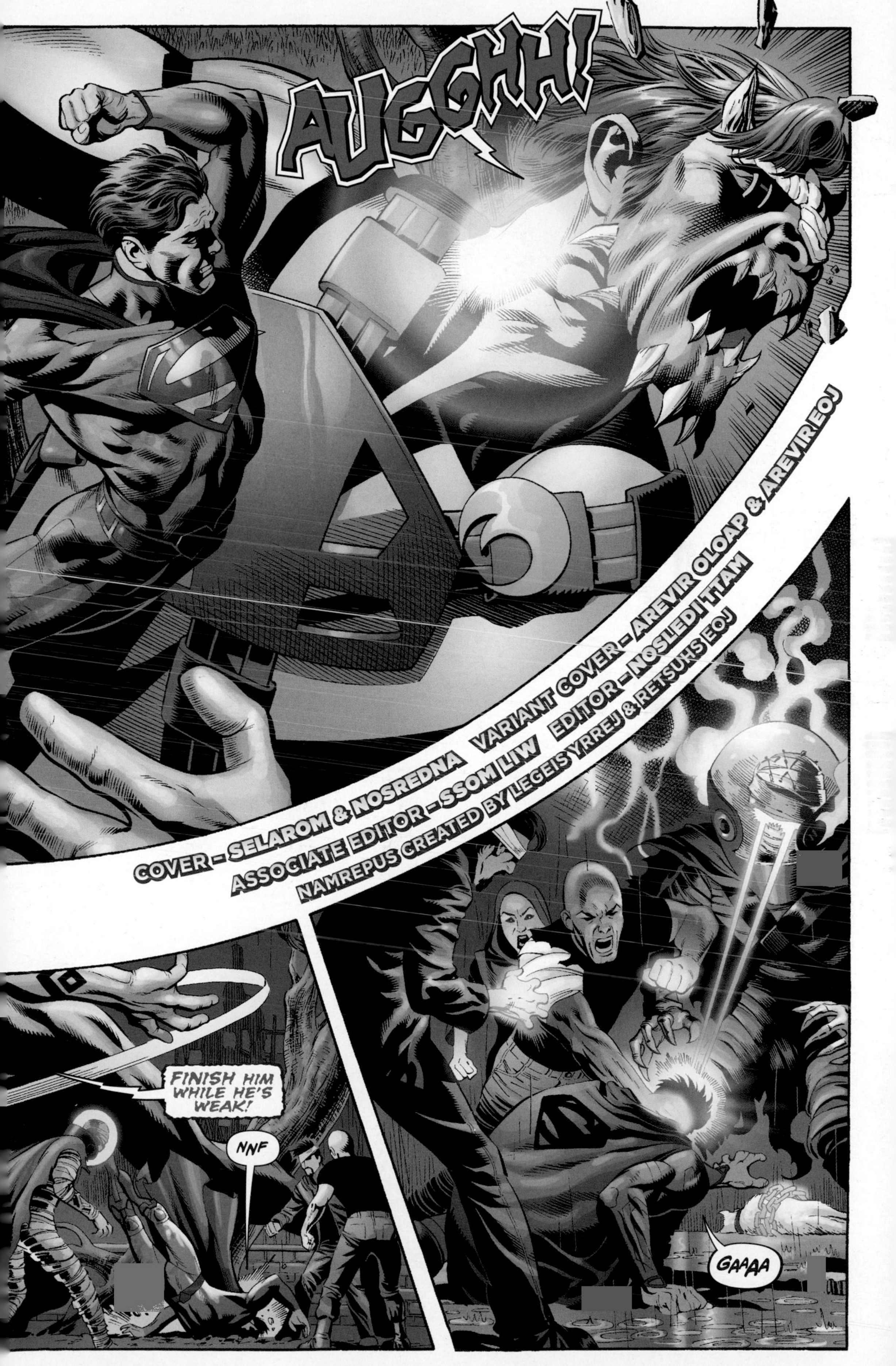
AUGGHH!
COVER - SELAROM & NOSREDNA VARIANT COVER - AREVIR OLOAP & AREVIR EOJ
ASSOCIATE EDITOR - SSOM LIW EDITOR - NOSLEDI TTAM
NAMREPUS CREATED BY LEGEIS YRREJ & RETSUHS EOJ
FINISH HIM WHILE HE'S WEAK!
NNF
GAAAA

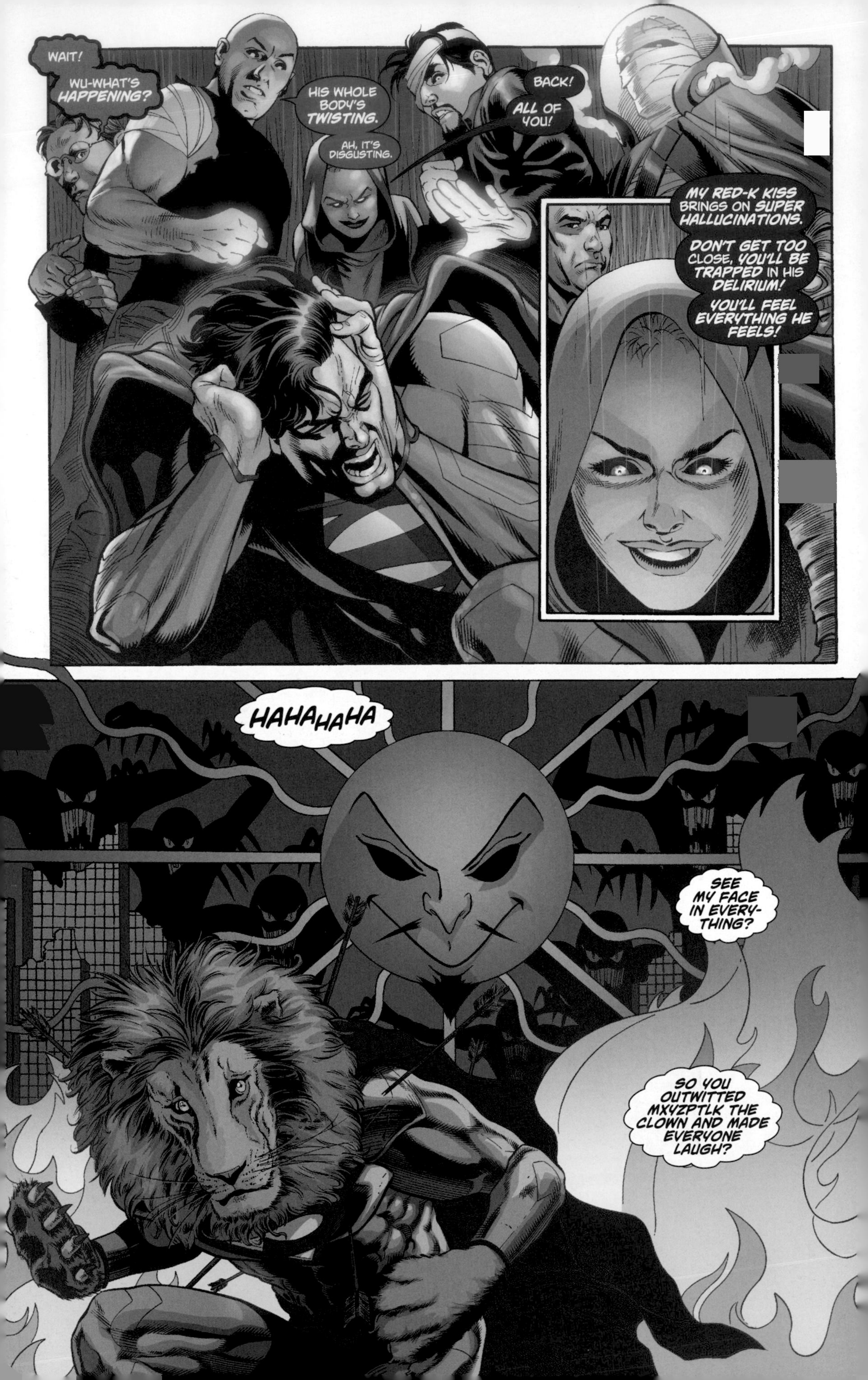
WAIT!
WU-WHAT'S HAPPENING?
HIS WHOLE BODY'S TWISTING.
AH, IT'S DISGUSTING.
BACK!
ALL OF YOU!
MY RED-K KISS BRINGS ON SUPER HALLUCINATIONS.
DON'T GET TOO CLOSE, YOU'LL BE TRAPPED IN HIS DELIRIUM!
YOU'LL FEEL EVERYTHING HE FEELS!
HAHAHAHA
SEE MY FACE IN EVERY-THING?
SO YOU OUTWITTED MXYZPTLK THE CLOWN AND MADE EVERYONE LAUGH?

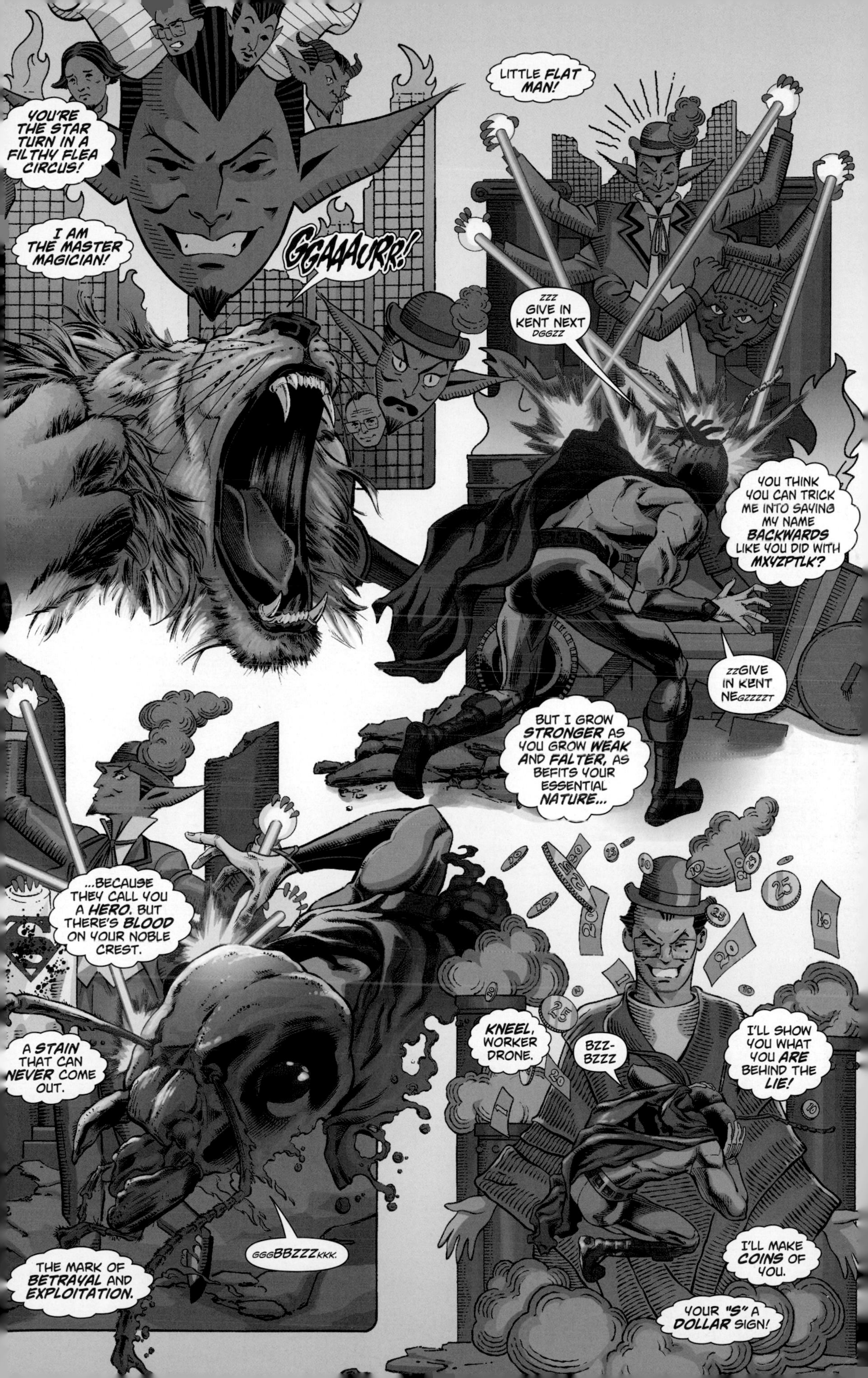
YOU'RE THE STAR TURN IN A FILTHY FLEA CIRCUS!
I AM THE MASTER MAGICIAN!
GGAAAAURR!
LITTLE FLAT MAN!
ZZZ GIVE IN KENT NEXT DGGZZ
YOU THINK YOU CAN TRICK ME INTO SAYING MY NAME BACKWARDS LIKE YOU DID WITH MXYZPTLK?
ZZGIVE IN KENT NEGZZZZT
BUT I GROW STRONGER AS YOU GROW WEAK AND FALTER, AS BEFITS YOUR ESSENTIAL NATURE...
...BECAUSE THEY CALL YOU A HERO. BUT THERE'S BLOOD ON YOUR NOBLE CREST.
A STAIN THAT CAN NEVER COME OUT.
THE MARK OF BETRAYAL AND EXPLOITATION.
GGGBBZZZKKK.
KNEEL, WORKER DRONE.
BZZ-BZZZ
I'LL SHOW YOU WHAT YOU ARE BEHIND THE LIE!
I'LL MAKE COINS OF YOU.
YOUR "S" A DOLLAR SIGN!

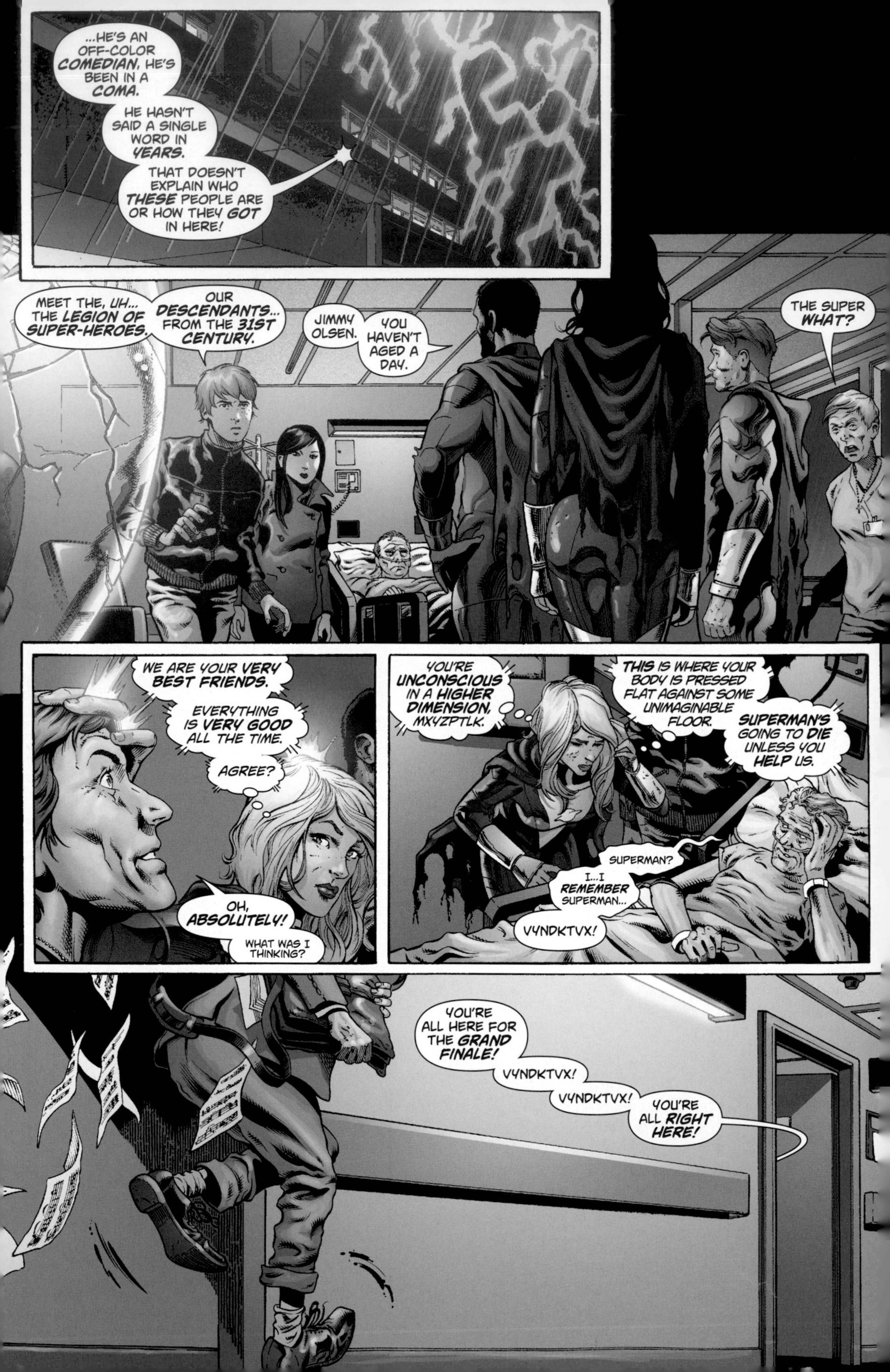

...HE'S AN OFF-COLOR COMEDIAN, HE'S BEEN IN A COMA.
HE HASN'T SAID A SINGLE WORD IN YEARS.
THAT DOESN'T EXPLAIN WHO THESE PEOPLE ARE OR HOW THEY GOT IN HERE!
MEET THE, UH... THE LEGION OF SUPER-HEROES.
OUR DESCENDANTS... FROM THE 31ST CENTURY.
JIMMY OLSEN.
YOU HAVEN'T AGED A DAY.
THE SUPER WHAT?
WE ARE YOUR VERY BEST FRIENDS.
EVERYTHING IS VERY GOOD ALL THE TIME.
AGREE?
OH, ABSOLUTELY!
WHAT WAS I THINKING?
YOU'RE UNCONSCIOUS IN A HIGHER DIMENSION, MXYZPTLK.
THIS IS WHERE YOUR BODY IS PRESSED FLAT AGAINST SOME UNIMAGINABLE FLOOR.
SUPERMAN'S GOING TO DIE UNLESS YOU HELP US.
SUPERMAN?
I...I REMEMBER SUPERMAN...
VYNDKTVX!
YOU'RE ALL HERE FOR THE GRAND FINALE!
VYNDKTVX!
VYNDKTVX!
YOU'RE ALL RIGHT HERE!

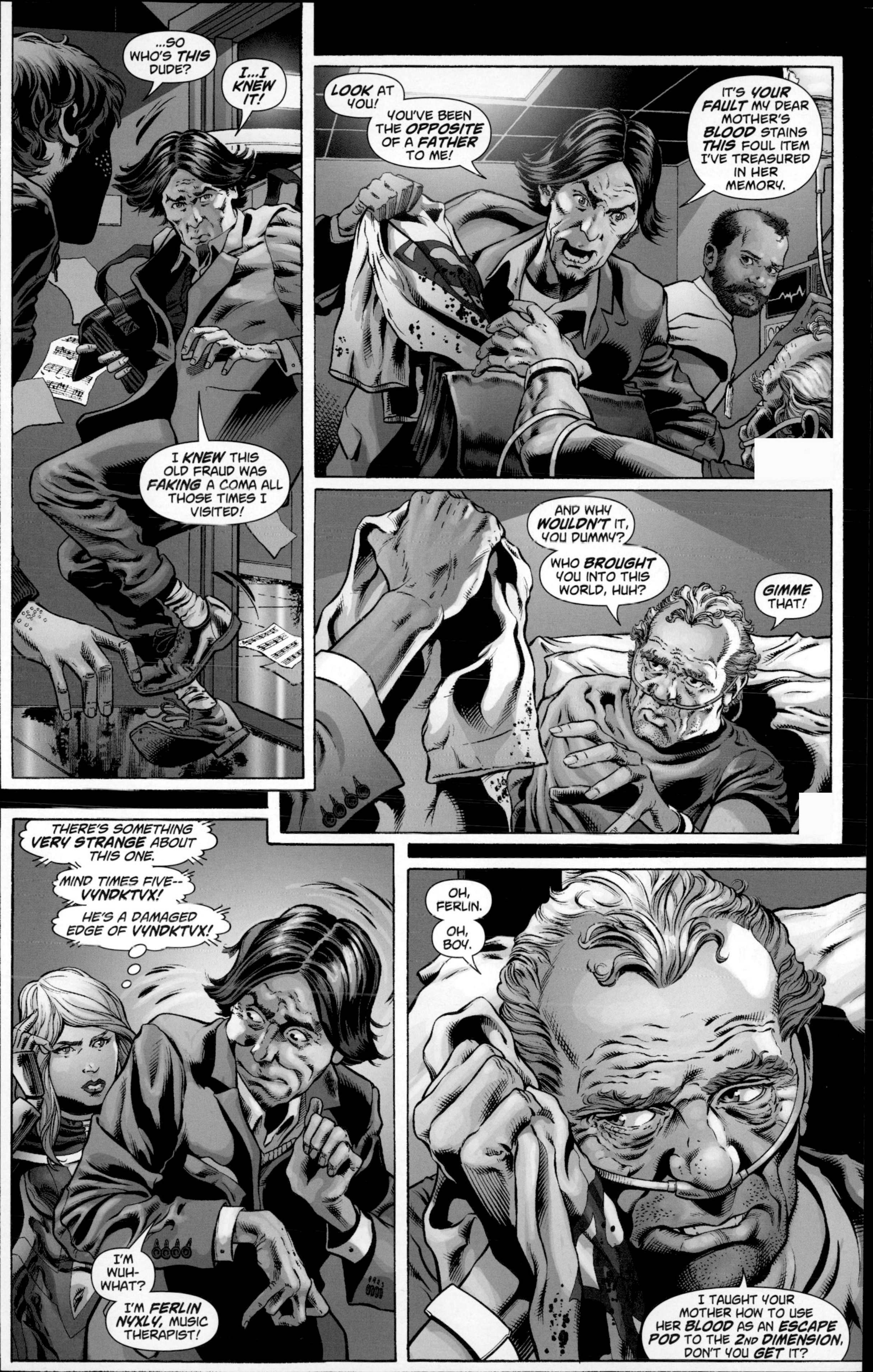
...SO WHO'S THIS DUDE?
I...I KNEW IT!
I KNEW THIS OLD FRAUD WAS FAKING A COMA ALL THOSE TIMES I VISITED!
LOOK AT YOU!
YOU'VE BEEN THE OPPOSITE OF A FATHER TO ME!
IT'S YOUR FAULT MY DEAR MOTHER'S BLOOD STAINS THIS FOUL ITEM I'VE TREASURED IN HER MEMORY.
AND WHY WOULDN'T IT, YOU DUMMY?
WHO BROUGHT YOU INTO THIS WORLD, HUH?
GIMME THAT!
THERE'S SOMETHING VERY STRANGE ABOUT THIS ONE.
MIND TIMES FIVE-- VYNDKTVX!
HE'S A DAMAGED EDGE OF VYNDKTVX!
I'M WUH-WHAT?
I'M FERLIN NYXLY, MUSIC THERAPIST!
OH, FERLIN.
OH, BOY.
I TAUGHT YOUR MOTHER HOW TO USE HER BLOOD AS AN ESCAPE POD TO THE 2ND DIMENSION, DON'T YOU GET IT?

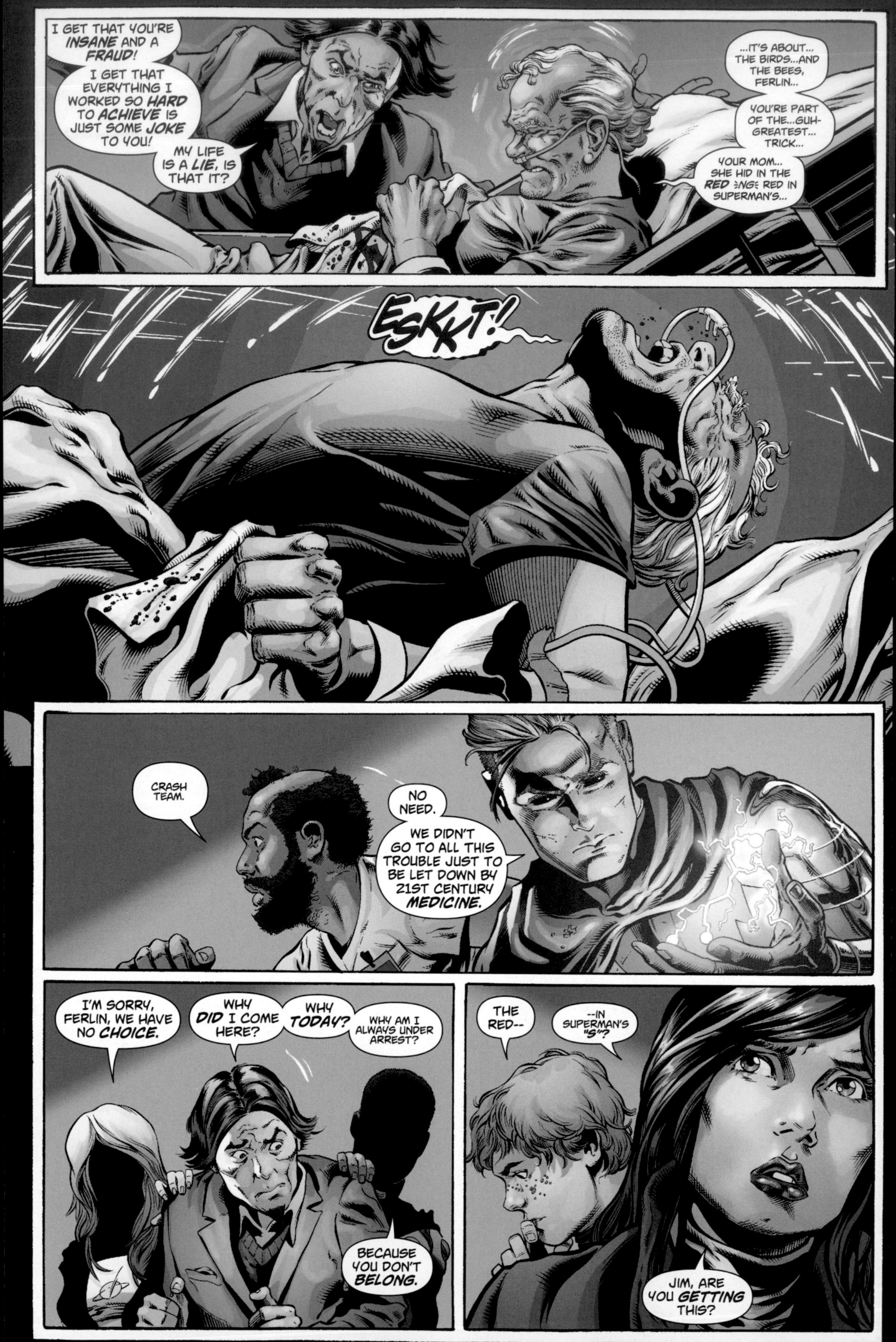

I GET THAT YOU'RE INSANE AND A FRAUD!
I GET THAT EVERYTHING I WORKED SO HARD TO ACHIEVE IS JUST SOME JOKE TO YOU!
MY LIFE IS A LIE, IS THAT IT?
...IT'S ABOUT... THE BIRDS...AND THE BEES, FERLIN...
YOU'RE PART OF THE...GUH- GREATEST... TRICK...
YOUR MOM... SHE HID IN THE RED ≤NG≤ RED IN SUPERMAN'S...
ESKKT!
CRASH TEAM.
NO NEED.
WE DIDN'T GO TO ALL THIS TROUBLE JUST TO BE LET DOWN BY 21ST CENTURY MEDICINE.
I'M SORRY, FERLIN, WE HAVE NO CHOICE.
WHY DID I COME HERE?
WHY TODAY?
WHY AM I ALWAYS UNDER ARREST?
BECAUSE YOU DON'T BELONG.
THE RED--
--IN SUPERMAN'S "S"?
JIM, ARE YOU GETTING THIS?

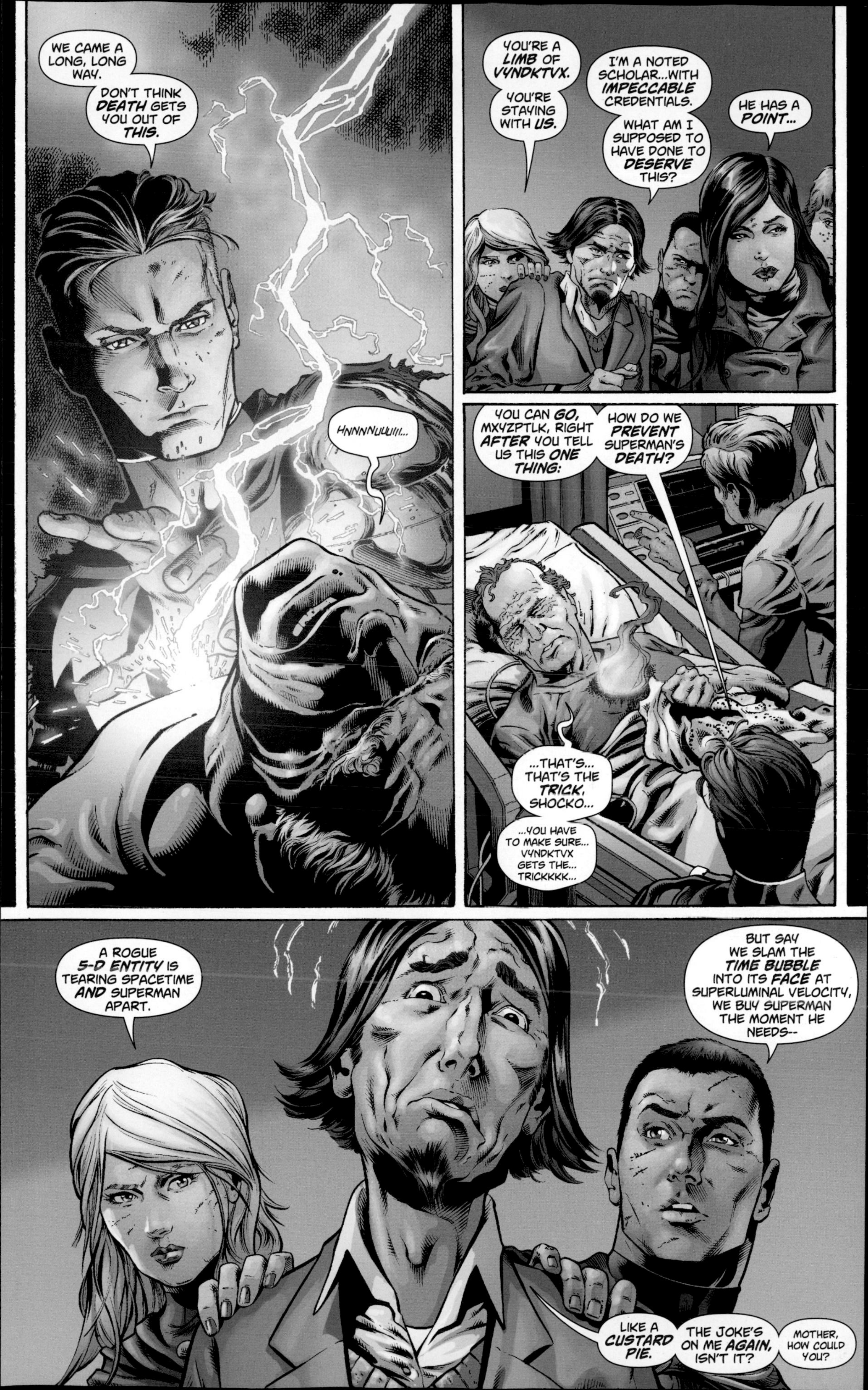
WE CAME A LONG, LONG WAY.
DON'T THINK DEATH GETS YOU OUT OF THIS.
HNNNNUUIII...
YOU'RE A LIMB OF VYNDKTVX.
YOU'RE STAYING WITH US.
I'M A NOTED SCHOLAR...WITH IMPECCABLE CREDENTIALS.
WHAT AM I SUPPOSED TO HAVE DONE TO DESERVE THIS?
HE HAS A POINT...
YOU CAN GO, MXYZPTLK, RIGHT AFTER YOU TELL US THIS ONE THING:
HOW DO WE PREVENT SUPERMAN'S DEATH?
...THAT'S... THAT'S THE TRICK, SHOCKO...
...YOU HAVE TO MAKE SURE... VYNDKTVX GETS THE... TRICKKKK...
A ROGUE 5-D ENTITY IS TEARING SPACETIME AND SUPERMAN APART.
BUT SAY WE SLAM THE TIME BUBBLE INTO ITS FACE AT SUPERLUMINAL VELOCITY, WE BUY SUPERMAN THE MOMENT HE NEEDS--
LIKE A CUSTARD PIE.
THE JOKE'S ON ME AGAIN, ISN'T IT?
MOTHER, HOW COULD YOU?

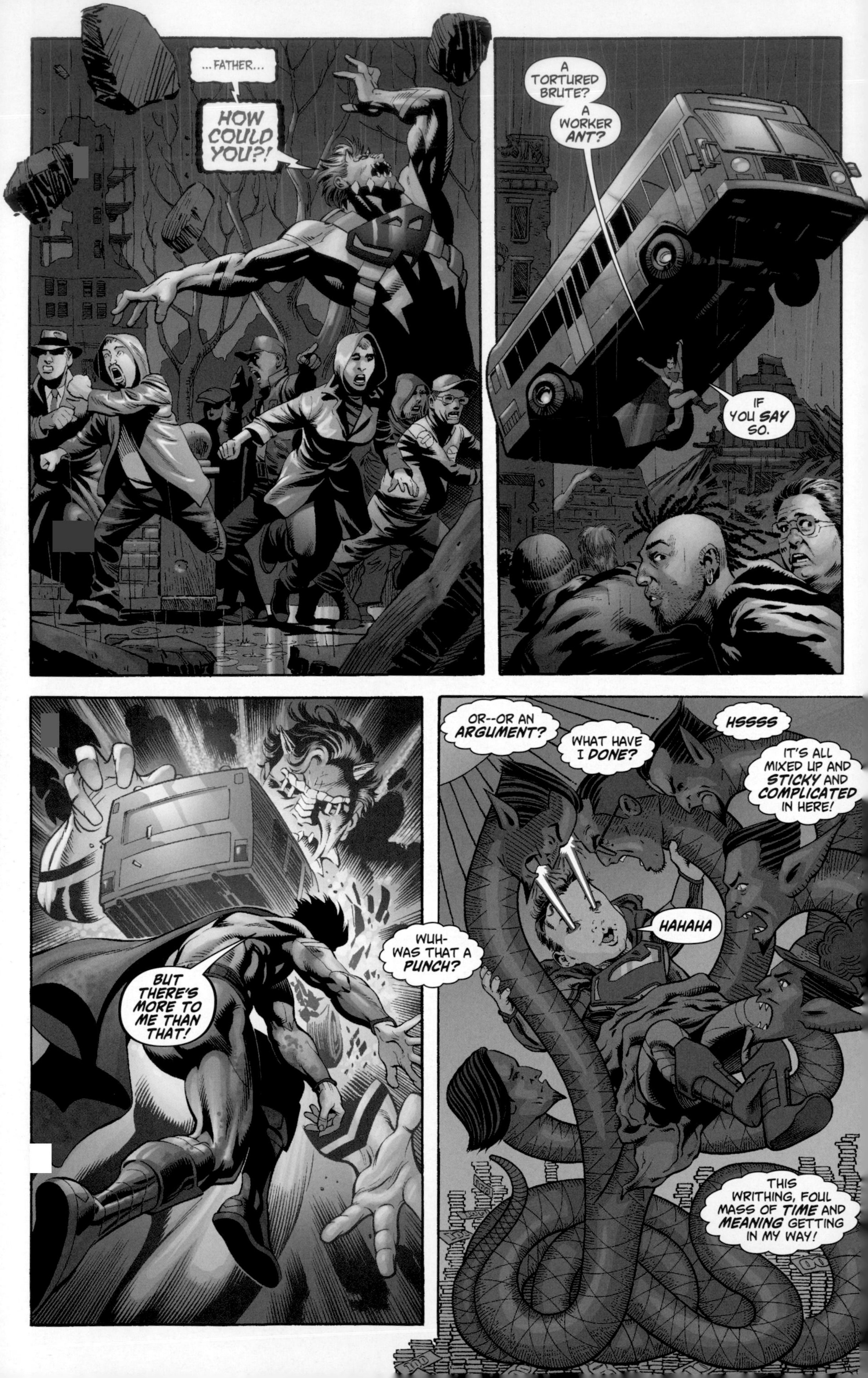
...FATHER...
HOW COULD YOU?!
A TORTURED BRUTE?
A WORKER ANT?
IF YOU SAY SO.
BUT THERE'S MORE TO ME THAN THAT!
WUH- WAS THAT A PUNCH?
OR--OR AN ARGUMENT?
WHAT HAVE I DONE?
HSSSS
IT'S ALL MIXED UP AND STICKY AND COMPLICATED IN HERE!
HAHAHA
THIS WRITHING, FOUL MASS OF TIME AND MEANING GETTING IN MY WAY!

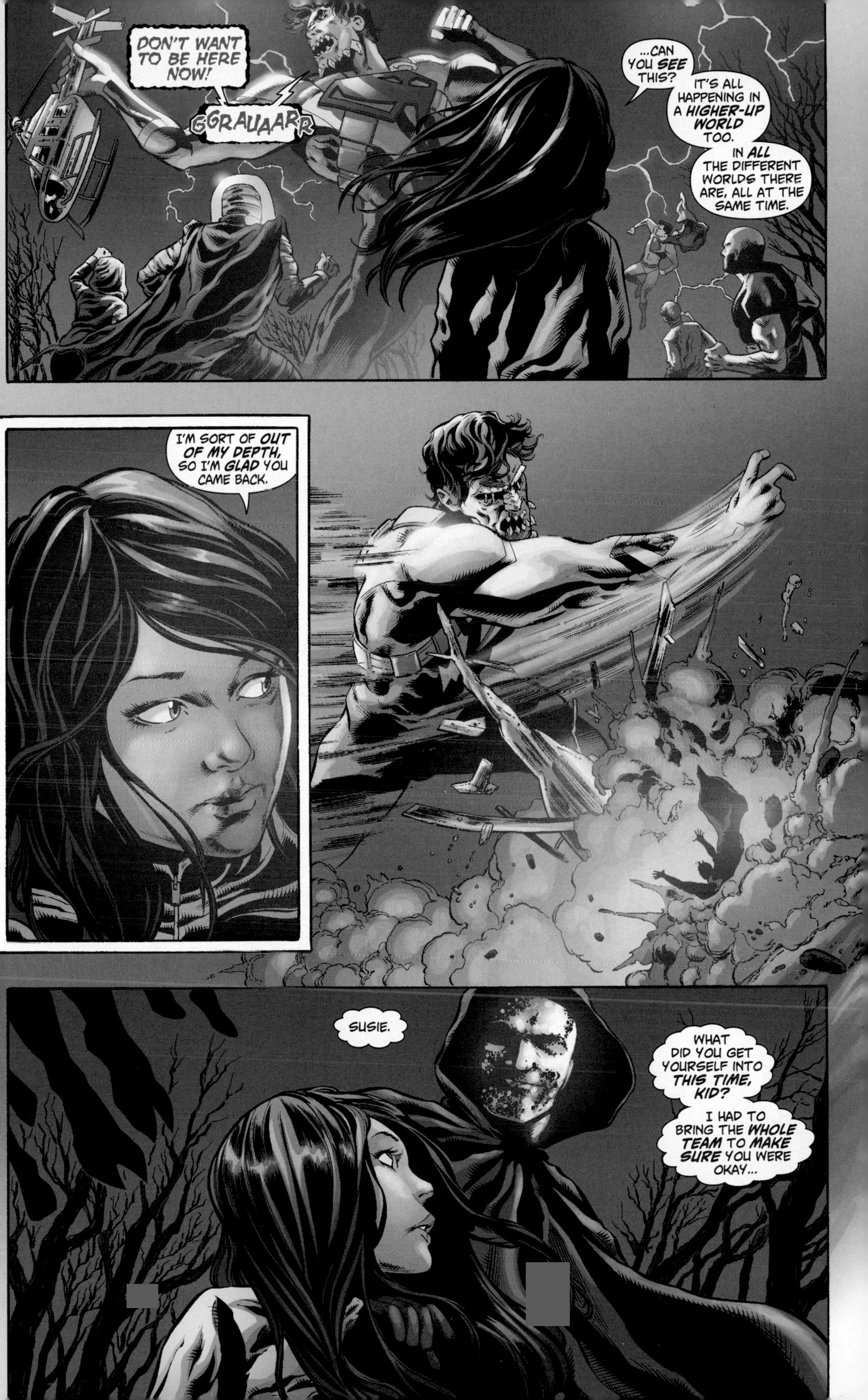
DON'T WANT TO BE HERE NOW!
GGRAUAARR
...CAN YOU SEE THIS?
IT'S ALL HAPPENING IN A HIGHER-UP WORLD TOO.
IN ALL THE DIFFERENT WORLDS THERE ARE, ALL AT THE SAME TIME.
I'M SORT OF OUT OF MY DEPTH, SO I'M GLAD YOU CAME BACK.
SUSIE.
WHAT DID YOU GET YOURSELF INTO THIS TIME, KID?
I HAD TO BRING THE WHOLE TEAM TO MAKE SURE YOU WERE OKAY...

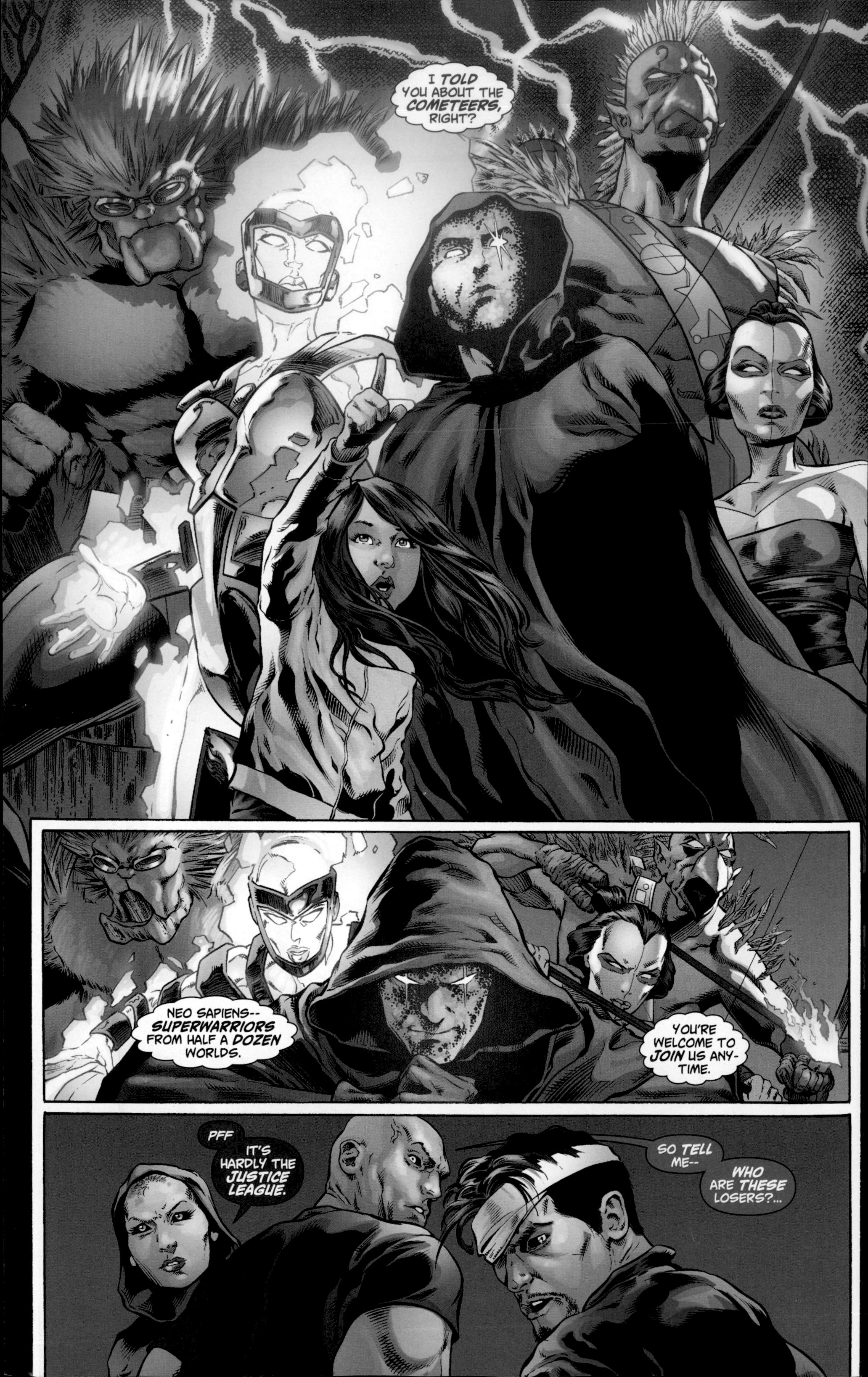
I TOLD YOU ABOUT THE COMETEERS, RIGHT?
NEO SAPIENS-- SUPERWARRIORS FROM HALF A DOZEN WORLDS.
YOU'RE WELCOME TO JOIN US ANY-TIME.
PFF
IT'S HARDLY THE JUSTICE LEAGUE.
SO TELL ME--
WHO ARE THESE LOSERS?...

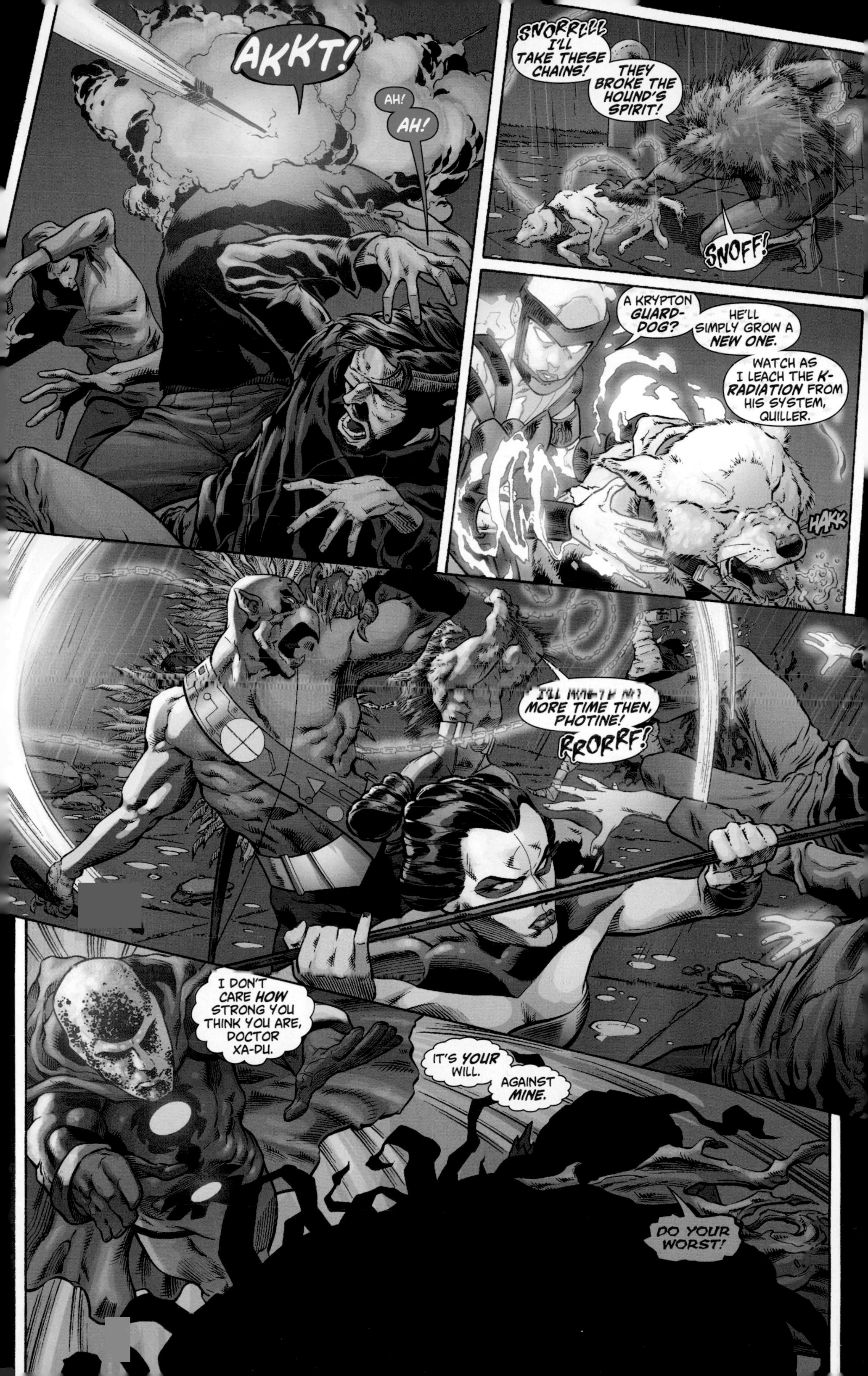
AKKT!
AH!
AH!
SNORRLLL
I'LL TAKE THESE CHAINS!
THEY BROKE THE HOUND'S SPIRIT!
SNOFF!
A KRYPTON GUARD-DOG?
HE'LL SIMPLY GROW A NEW ONE.
WATCH AS I LEACH THE K-RADIATION FROM HIS SYSTEM, QUILLER.
HAKK
MORE TIME THEN, PHOTINE!
RRORRF!
I DON'T CARE HOW STRONG YOU THINK YOU ARE, DOCTOR XA-DU.
IT'S YOUR WILL.
AGAINST MINE.
DO YOUR WORST!

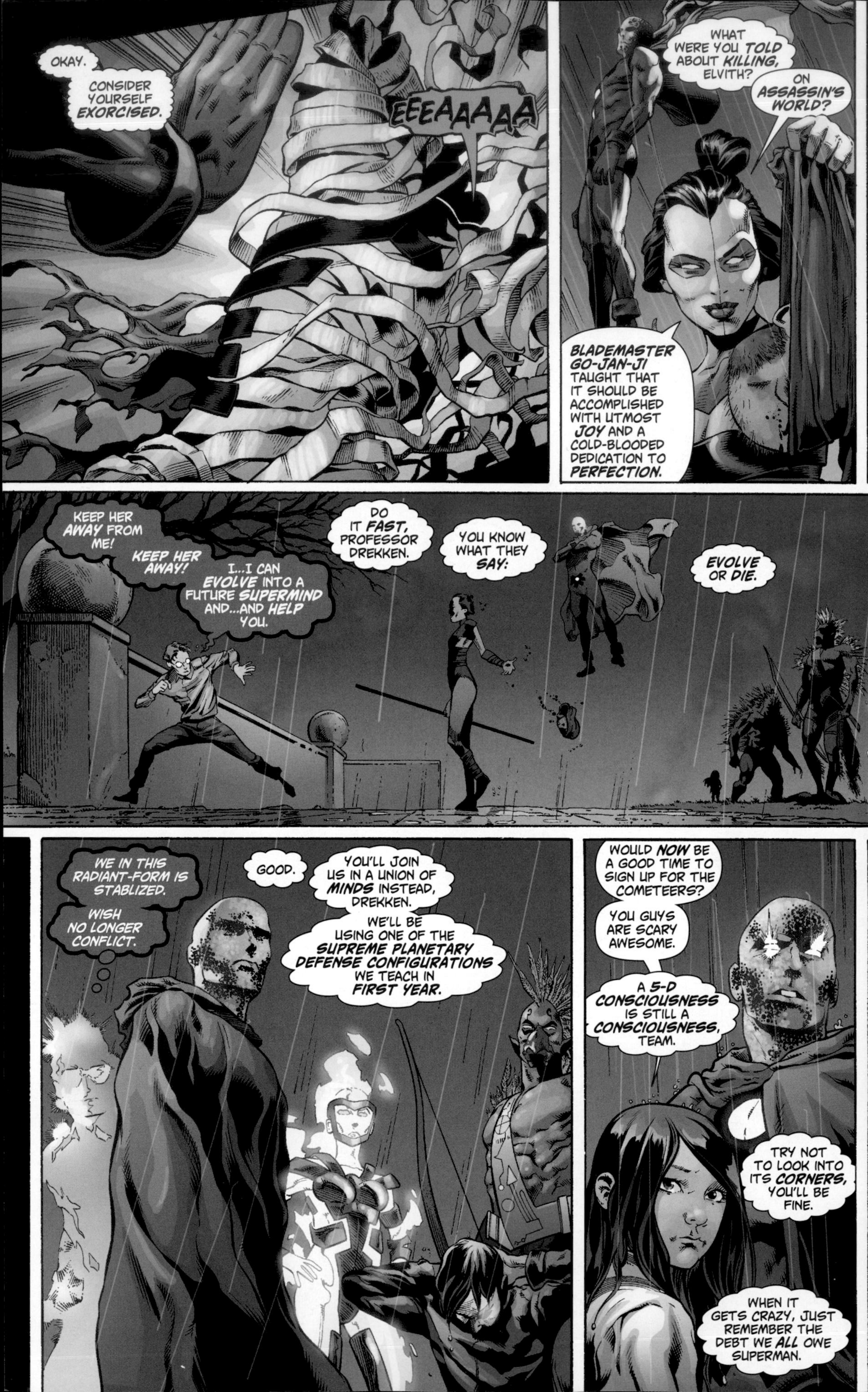
OKAY.
CONSIDER YOURSELF EXORCISED.
EEEAAAAA
WHAT WERE YOU TOLD ABOUT KILLING, ELVITH?
ON ASSASSIN'S WORLD?
BLADEMASTER GO-JAN-JI TAUGHT THAT IT SHOULD BE ACCOMPLISHED WITH UTMOST JOY AND A COLD-BLOODED DEDICATION TO PERFECTION.
KEEP HER AWAY FROM ME!
KEEP HER AWAY!
I...I CAN EVOLVE INTO A FUTURE SUPERMIND AND...AND HELP YOU.
DO IT FAST, PROFESSOR DREKKEN.
YOU KNOW WHAT THEY SAY:
EVOLVE OR DIE.
WE IN THIS RADIANT-FORM IS STABLIZED.
WISH NO LONGER CONFLICT.
GOOD.
YOU'LL JOIN US IN A UNION OF MINDS INSTEAD, DREKKEN.
WE'LL BE USING ONE OF THE SUPREME PLANETARY DEFENSE CONFIGURATIONS WE TEACH IN FIRST YEAR.
WOULD NOW BE A GOOD TIME TO SIGN UP FOR THE COMETEERS?
YOU GUYS ARE SCARY AWESOME.
A 5-D CONSCIOUSNESS IS STILL A CONSCIOUSNESS, TEAM.
TRY NOT TO LOOK INTO ITS CORNERS, YOU'LL BE FINE.
WHEN IT GETS CRAZY, JUST REMEMBER THE DEBT WE ALL OWE SUPERMAN.

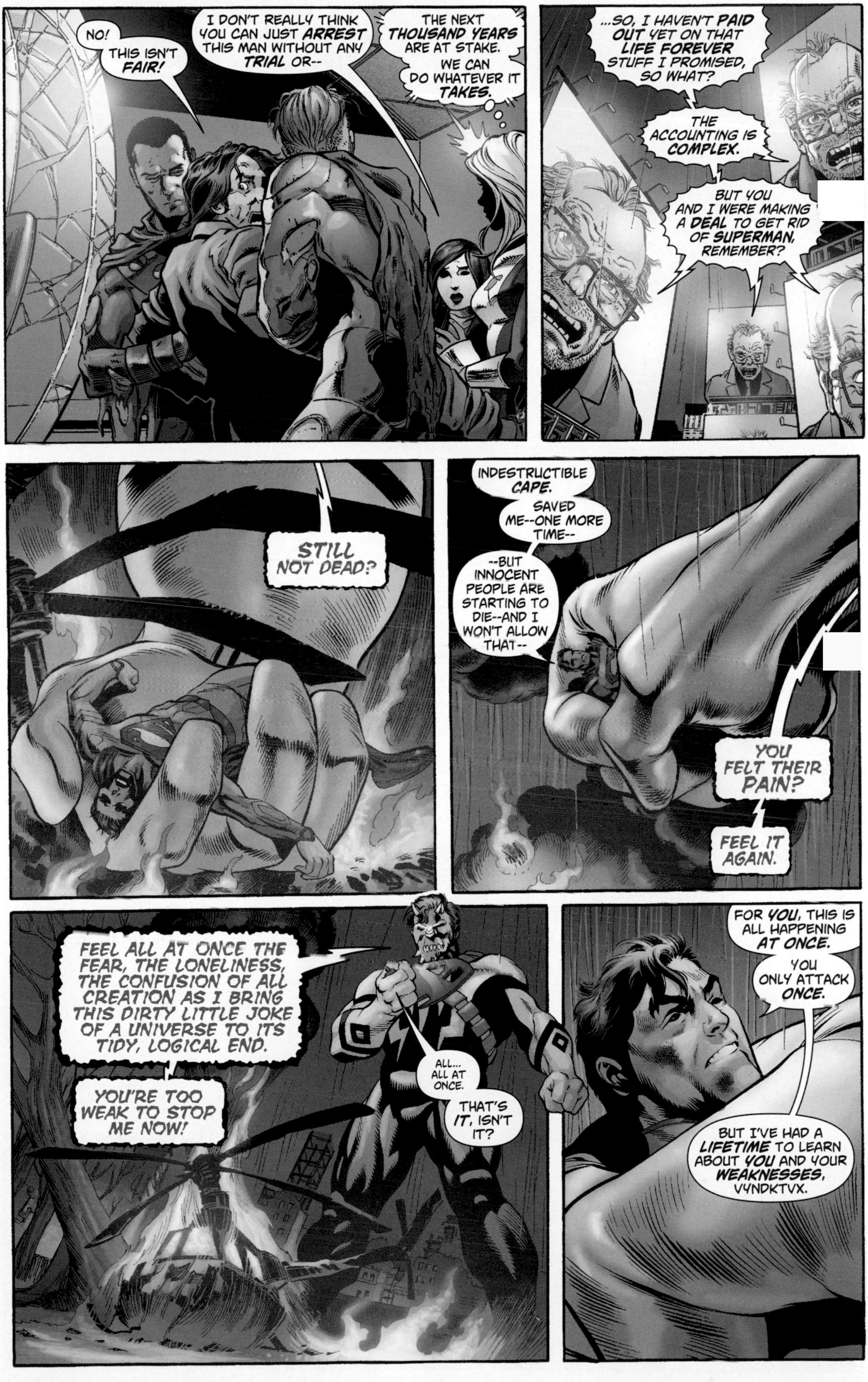
NO! THIS ISN'T FAIR!
I DON'T REALLY THINK YOU CAN JUST ARREST THIS MAN WITHOUT ANY TRIAL OR--
THE NEXT THOUSAND YEARS ARE AT STAKE. WE CAN DO WHATEVER IT TAKES.
...SO, I HAVEN'T PAID OUT YET ON THAT LIFE FOREVER STUFF I PROMISED, SO WHAT?
THE ACCOUNTING IS COMPLEX.
BUT YOU AND I WERE MAKING A DEAL TO GET RID OF SUPERMAN, REMEMBER?
STILL NOT DEAD?
INDESTRUCTIBLE CAPE.
SAVED ME--ONE MORE TIME--
--BUT INNOCENT PEOPLE ARE STARTING TO DIE--AND I WON'T ALLOW THAT--
YOU FELT THEIR PAIN?
FEEL IT AGAIN.
FEEL ALL AT ONCE THE FEAR, THE LONELINESS, THE CONFUSION OF ALL CREATION AS I BRING THIS DIRTY LITTLE JOKE OF A UNIVERSE TO ITS TIDY, LOGICAL END.
YOU'RE TOO WEAK TO STOP ME NOW!
ALL... ALL AT ONCE.
THAT'S IT, ISN'T IT?
FOR YOU, THIS IS ALL HAPPENING AT ONCE.
YOU ONLY ATTACK ONCE.
BUT I'VE HAD A LIFETIME TO LEARN ABOUT YOU AND YOUR WEAKNESSES, VYNDKTVX.

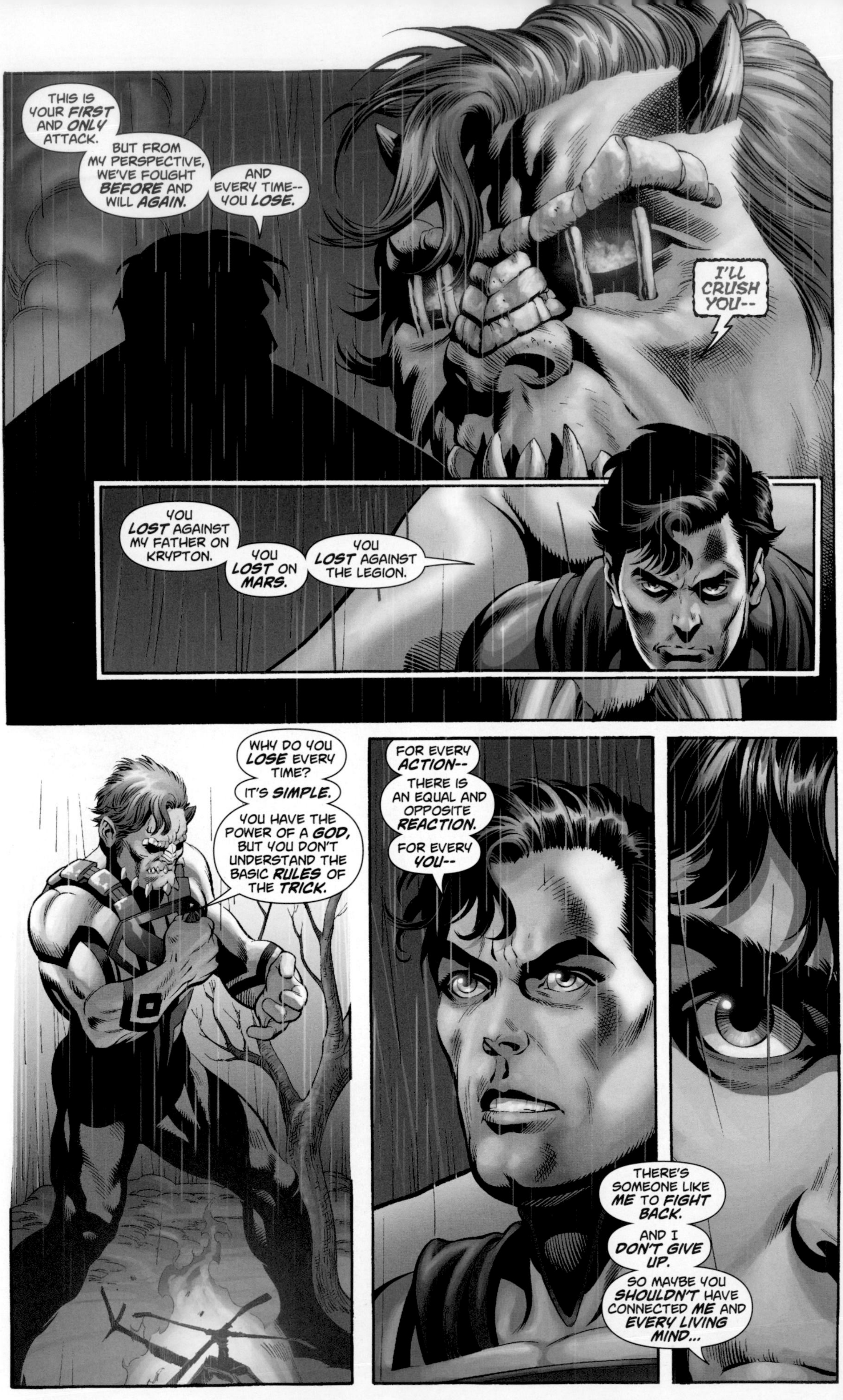
THIS IS YOUR FIRST AND ONLY ATTACK.
BUT FROM MY PERSPECTIVE, WE'VE FOUGHT BEFORE AND WILL AGAIN.
AND EVERY TIME-- YOU LOSE.
I'LL CRUSH YOU--
YOU LOST AGAINST MY FATHER ON KRYPTON.
YOU LOST ON MARS.
YOU LOST AGAINST THE LEGION.
WHY DO YOU LOSE EVERY TIME?
IT'S SIMPLE.
YOU HAVE THE POWER OF A GOD, BUT YOU DON'T UNDERSTAND THE BASIC RULES OF THE TRICK.
FOR EVERY ACTION--
THERE IS AN EQUAL AND OPPOSITE REACTION.
FOR EVERY YOU--
THERE'S SOMEONE LIKE ME TO FIGHT BACK.
AND I DON'T GIVE UP.
SO MAYBE YOU SHOULDN'T HAVE CONNECTED ME AND EVERY LIVING MIND...

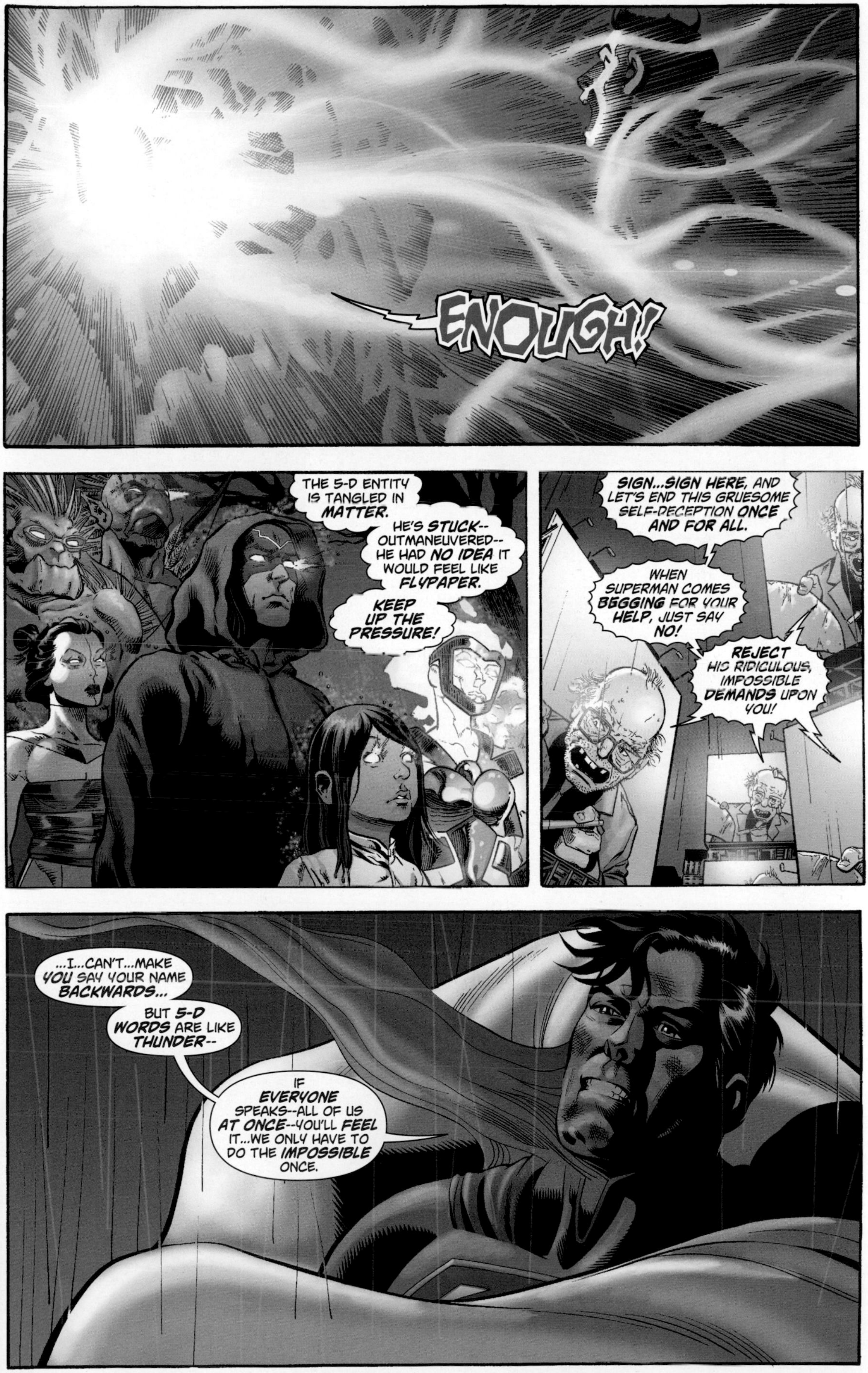
ENOUGH!
THE 5-D ENTITY IS TANGLED IN MATTER.
HE'S STUCK-- OUTMANEUVERED-- HE HAD NO IDEA IT WOULD FEEL LIKE FLYPAPER.
KEEP UP THE PRESSURE!
SIGN...SIGN HERE, AND LET'S END THIS GRUESOME SELF-DECEPTION ONCE AND FOR ALL.
WHEN SUPERMAN COMES BEGGING FOR YOUR HELP, JUST SAY NO!
REJECT HIS RIDICULOUS, IMPOSSIBLE DEMANDS UPON YOU!
...I...CAN'T...MAKE YOU SAY YOUR NAME BACKWARDS...
BUT 5-D WORDS ARE LIKE THUNDER--
IF EVERYONE SPEAKS--ALL OF US AT ONCE--YOU'LL FEEL IT...WE ONLY HAVE TO DO THE IMPOSSIBLE ONCE.

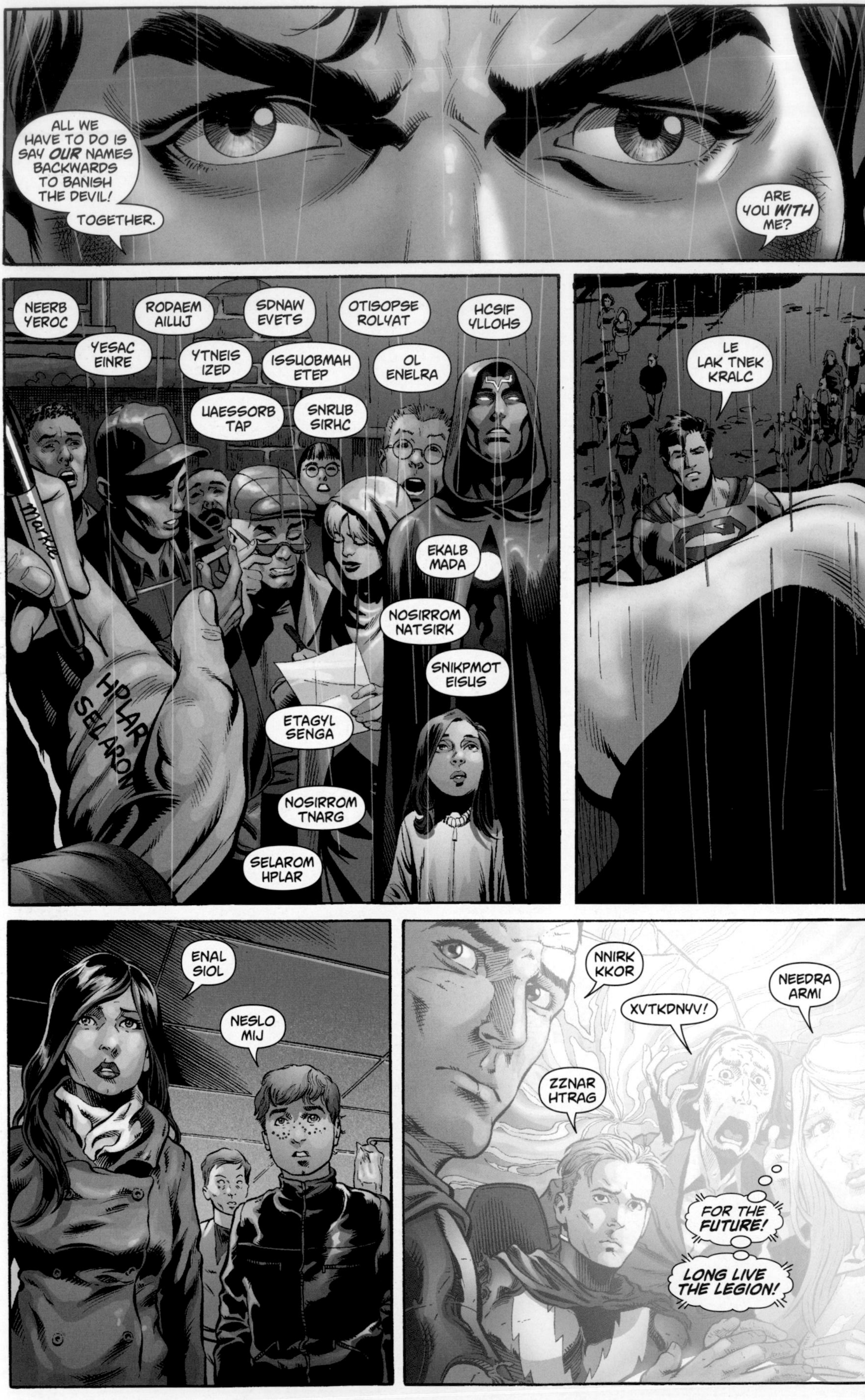

ALL WE HAVE TO DO IS SAY OUR NAMES BACKWARDS TO BANISH THE DEVIL!
TOGETHER.
ARE YOU WITH ME?
NEERB YEROC
RODAEM AILUJ
SDNAW EVETS
OTISOPSE ROLYAT
HCSIF YLLOHS
YESAC EINRE
YTNEIS IZED
ISSUOBMAH ETEP
OL ENELRA
UAESSORB TAP
SNRUB SIRHC
HPLAR
EKALB MADA
NOSIRROM NATSIRK
SNIKPMOT EISUS
ETAGYL SENGA
NOSIRROM TNARG
SELAROM HPLAR
LE LAK TNEK KRALC
ENAL SIOL
NESLO MIJ
NNIRK KKOR
XVTKDNYV!
NEEDRA ARMI
ZZNAR HTRAG
FOR THE FUTURE!
LONG LIVE THE LEGION!

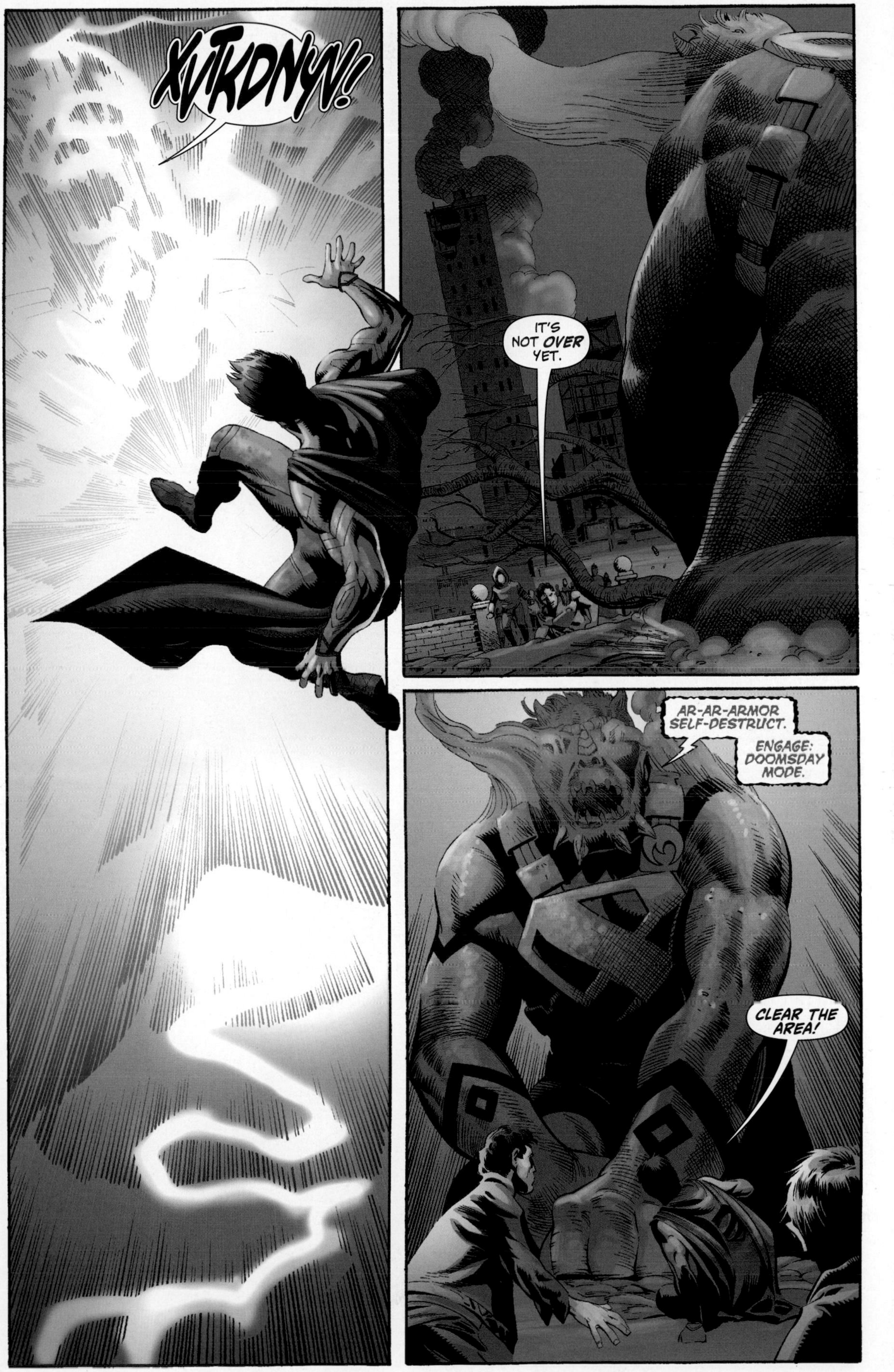
XVTKDNYN!
IT'S NOT OVER YET.
AR-AR-ARMOR SELF-DESTRUCT.
ENGAGE: DOOMSDAY MODE.
CLEAR THE AREA!

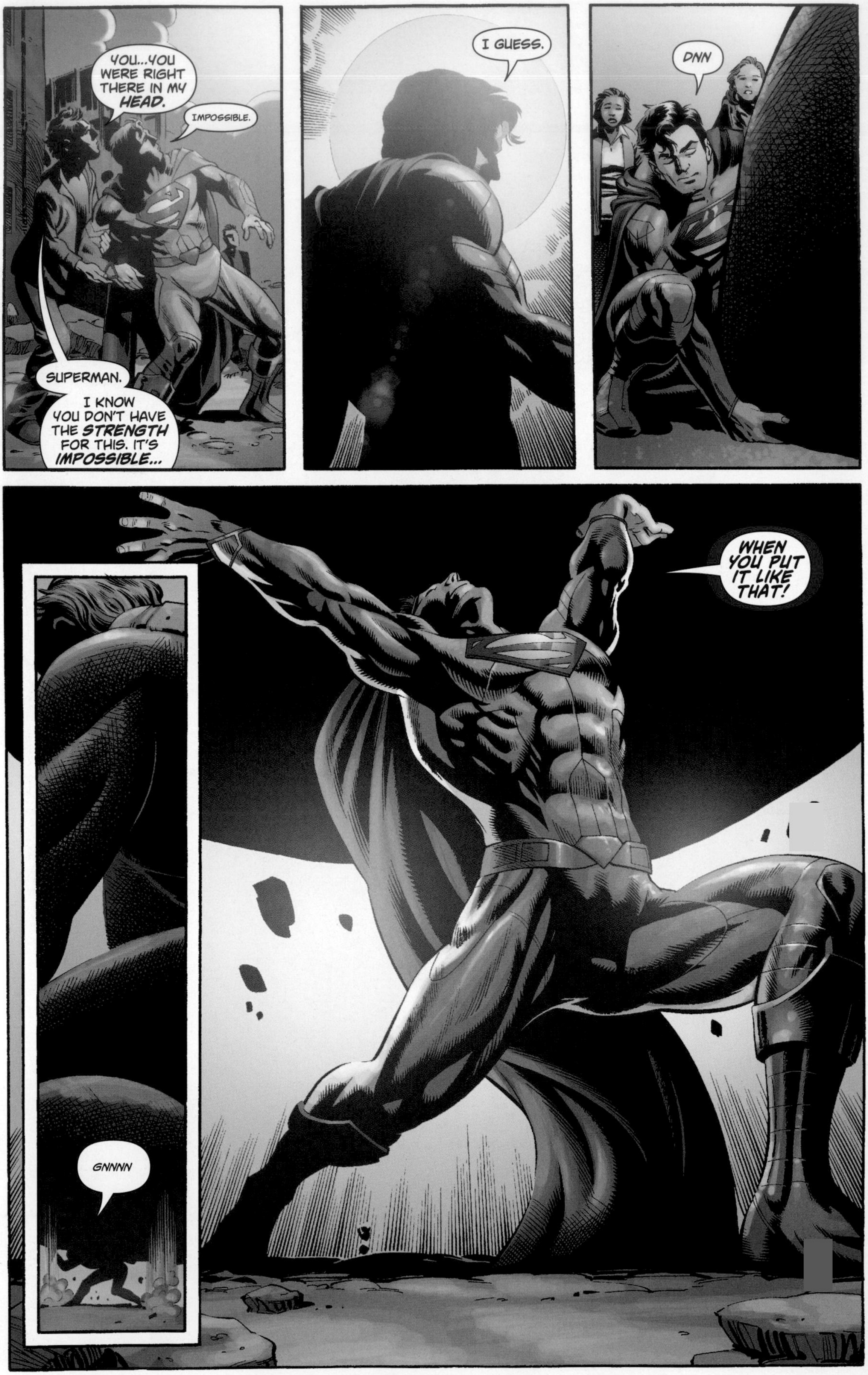
YOU...YOU WERE RIGHT THERE IN MY HEAD.
IMPOSSIBLE.
SUPERMAN.
I KNOW YOU DON'T HAVE THE STRENGTH FOR THIS. IT'S IMPOSSIBLE...
I GUESS.
DNN
GNNNN
WHEN YOU PUT IT LIKE THAT!

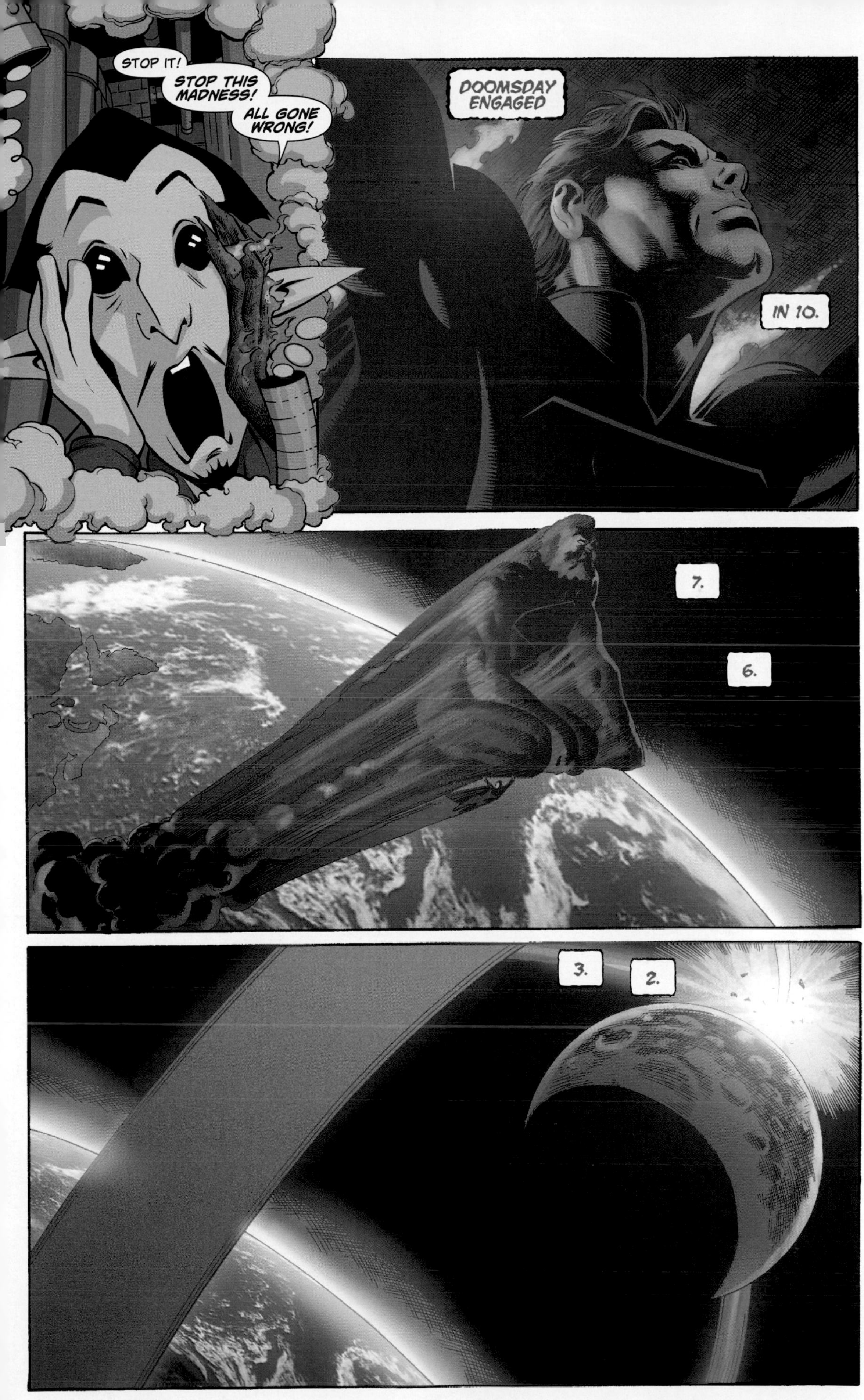
STOP IT!
STOP THIS MADNESS!
ALL GONE WRONG!
DOOMSDAY ENGAGED
IN 10.
7.
6.
3.
2.

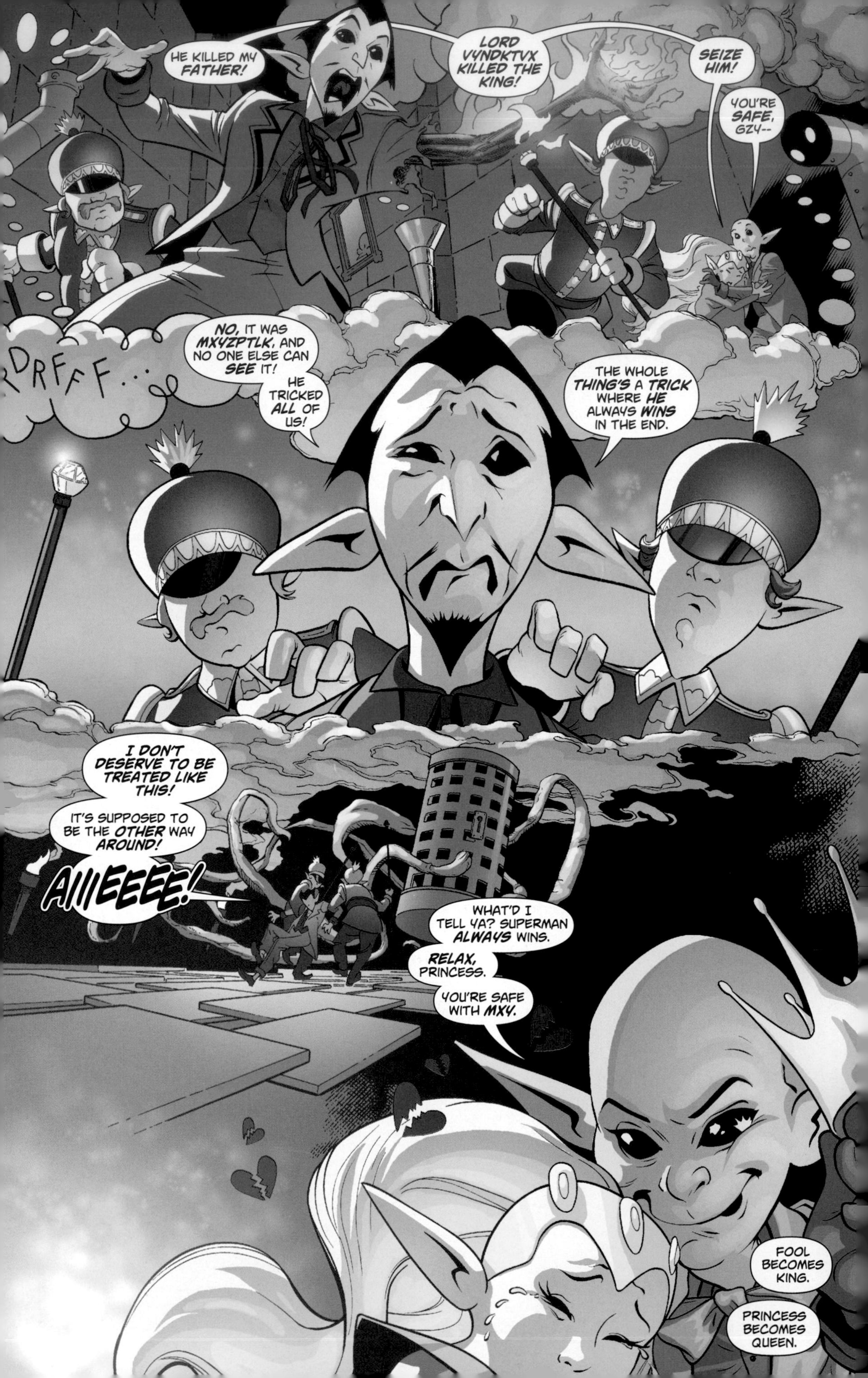
HE KILLED MY FATHER!
LORD VYNDKTVX KILLED THE KING!
SEIZE HIM!
YOU'RE SAFE, GZY--
DRFFF...
NO, IT WAS MXYZPTLK, AND NO ONE ELSE CAN SEE IT!
HE TRICKED ALL OF US!
THE WHOLE THING'S A TRICK WHERE HE ALWAYS WINS IN THE END.
I DON'T DESERVE TO BE TREATED LIKE THIS!
IT'S SUPPOSED TO BE THE OTHER WAY AROUND!
AIIIEEEE!
WHAT'D I TELL YA? SUPERMAN ALWAYS WINS.
RELAX, PRINCESS.
YOU'RE SAFE WITH MXY.
FOOL BECOMES KING.
PRINCESS BECOMES QUEEN.

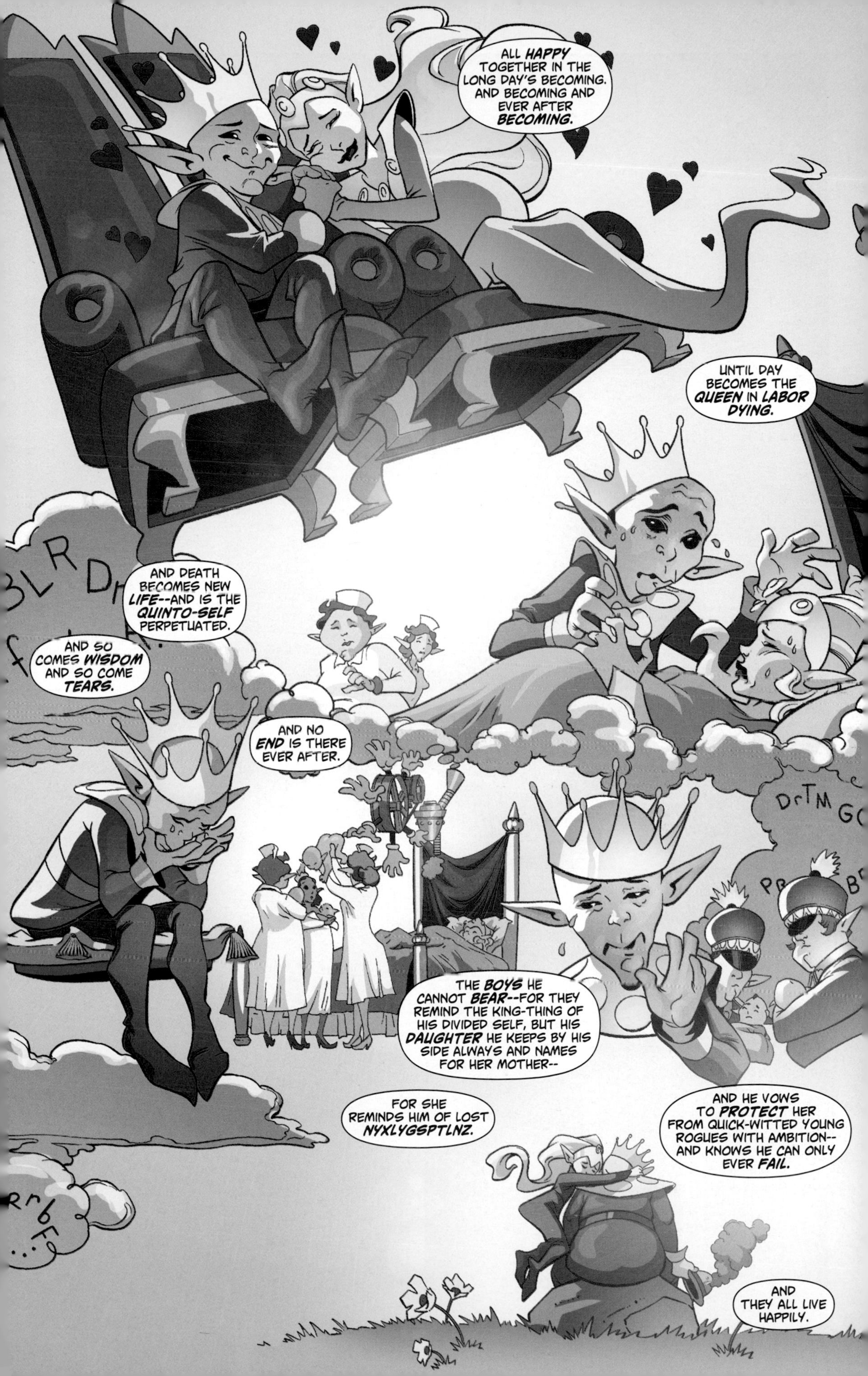
ALL HAPPY TOGETHER IN THE LONG DAY'S BECOMING. AND BECOMING AND EVER AFTER BECOMING.
UNTIL DAY BECOMES THE QUEEN IN LABOR DYING.
AND DEATH BECOMES NEW LIFE--AND IS THE QUINTO-SELF PERPETUATED.
AND SO COMES WISDOM AND SO COME TEARS.
AND NO END IS THERE EVER AFTER.
THE BOYS HE CANNOT BEAR--FOR THEY REMIND THE KING-THING OF HIS DIVIDED SELF, BUT HIS DAUGHTER HE KEEPS BY HIS SIDE ALWAYS AND NAMES FOR HER MOTHER--
FOR SHE REMINDS HIM OF LOST NYXLYGSPTLNZ.
AND HE VOWS TO PROTECT HER FROM QUICK-WITTED YOUNG ROGUES WITH AMBITION--AND KNOWS HE CAN ONLY EVER FAIL.
AND THEY ALL LIVE HAPPILY.

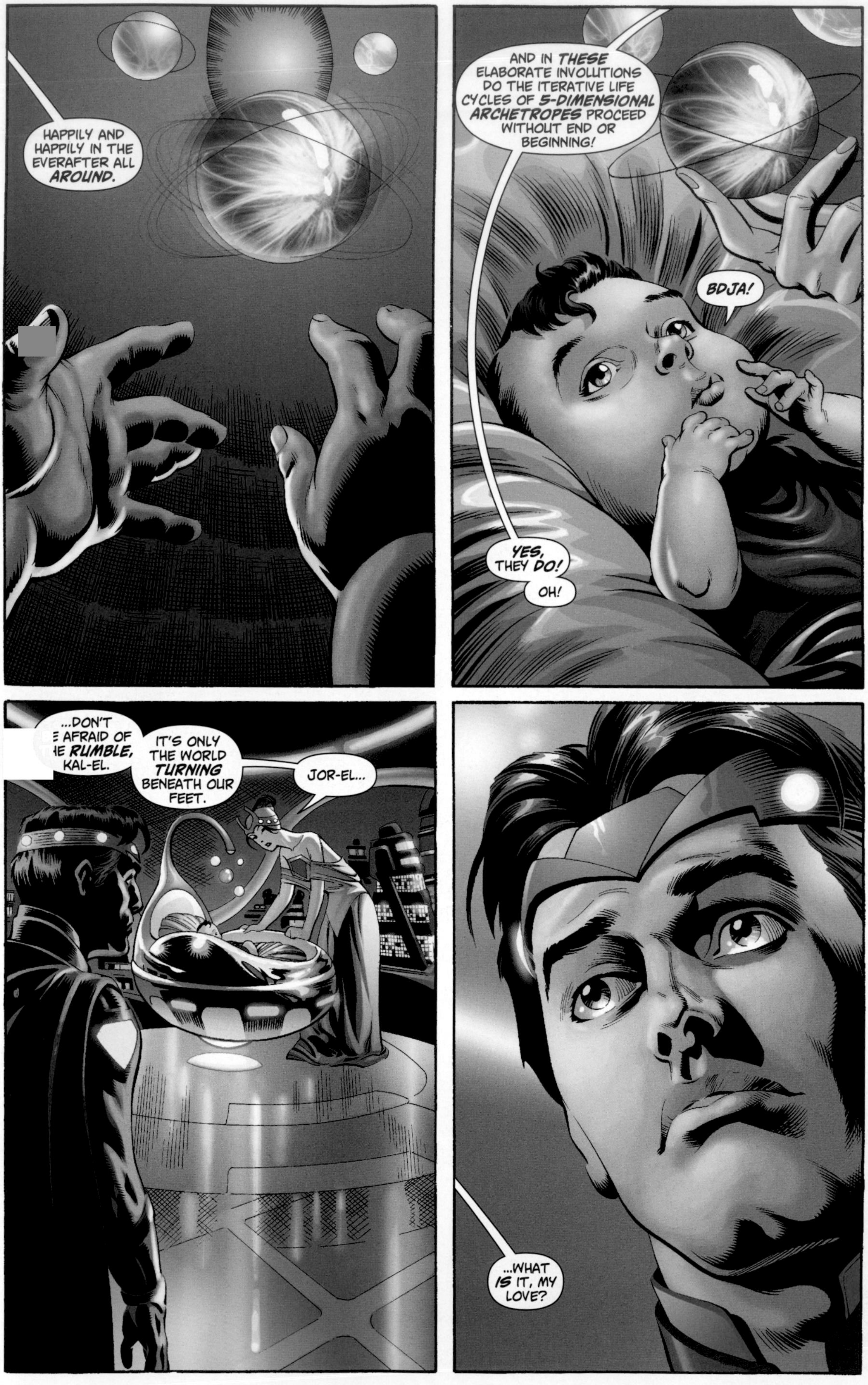
HAPPILY AND HAPPILY IN THE EVERAFTER ALL AROUND.
AND IN THESE ELABORATE INVOLUTIONS DO THE ITERATIVE LIFE CYCLES OF 5-DIMENSIONAL ARCHETROPES PROCEED WITHOUT END OR BEGINNING!
BDJA!
YES, THEY DO!
OH!
...DON'T
AFRAID OF
RUMBLE, KAL-EL.
IT'S ONLY THE WORLD TURNING BENEATH OUR FEET.
JOR-EL...
...WHAT IS IT, MY LOVE?

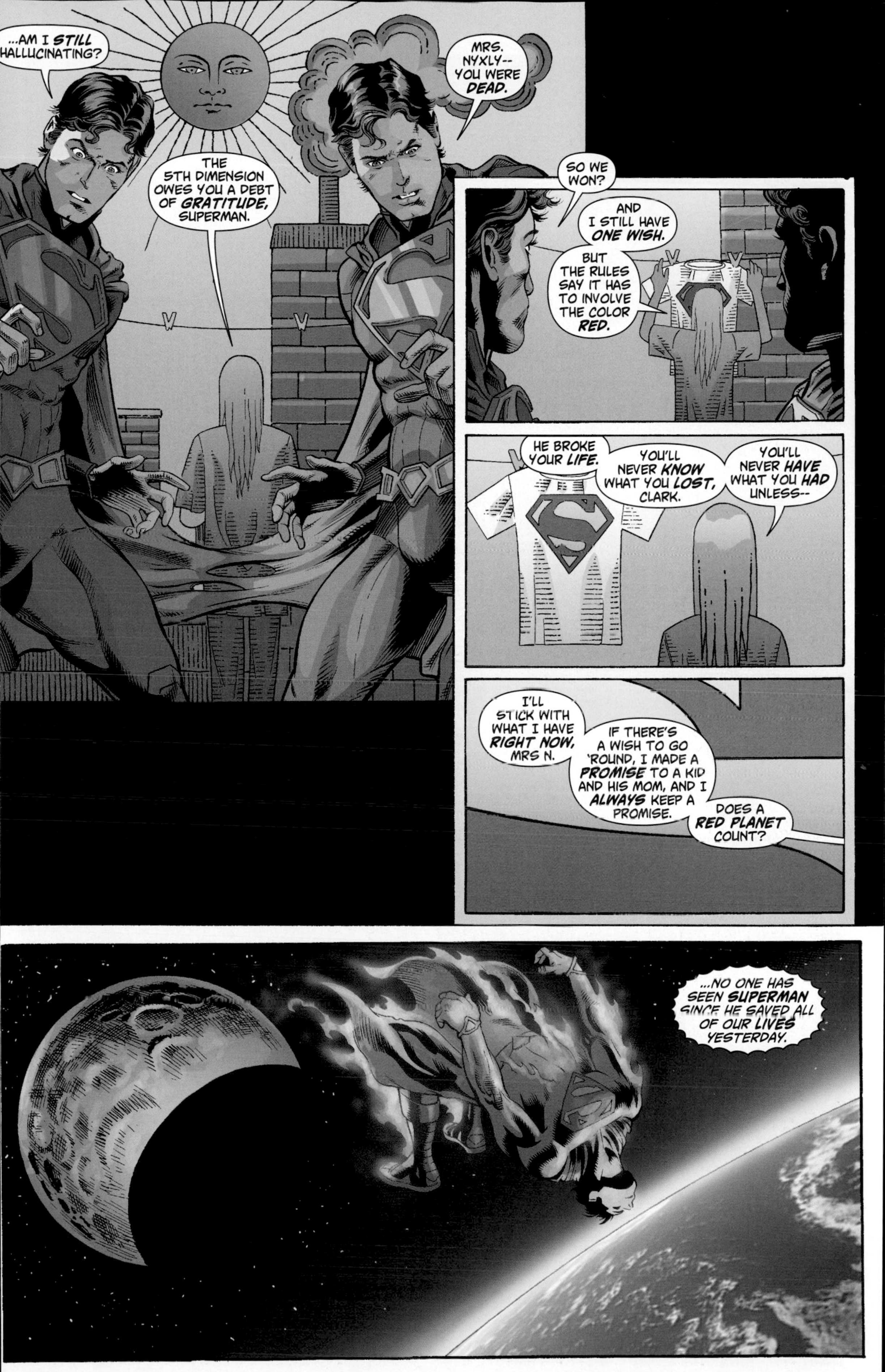
...AM I STILL HALLUCINATING?
MRS. NYXLY-- YOU WERE DEAD.
THE 5TH DIMENSION OWES YOU A DEBT OF GRATITUDE, SUPERMAN.
SO WE WON?
AND I STILL HAVE ONE WISH.
BUT THE RULES SAY IT HAS TO INVOLVE THE COLOR RED.
HE BROKE YOUR LIFE.
YOU'LL NEVER KNOW WHAT YOU LOST, CLARK.
YOU'LL NEVER HAVE WHAT YOU HAD UNLESS--
I'LL STICK WITH WHAT I HAVE RIGHT NOW, MRS N.
IF THERE'S A WISH TO GO 'ROUND, I MADE A PROMISE TO A KID AND HIS MOM, AND I ALWAYS KEEP A PROMISE.
DOES A RED PLANET COUNT?
...NO ONE HAS SEEN SUPERMAN SINCE HE SAVED ALL OF OUR LIVES YESTERDAY.

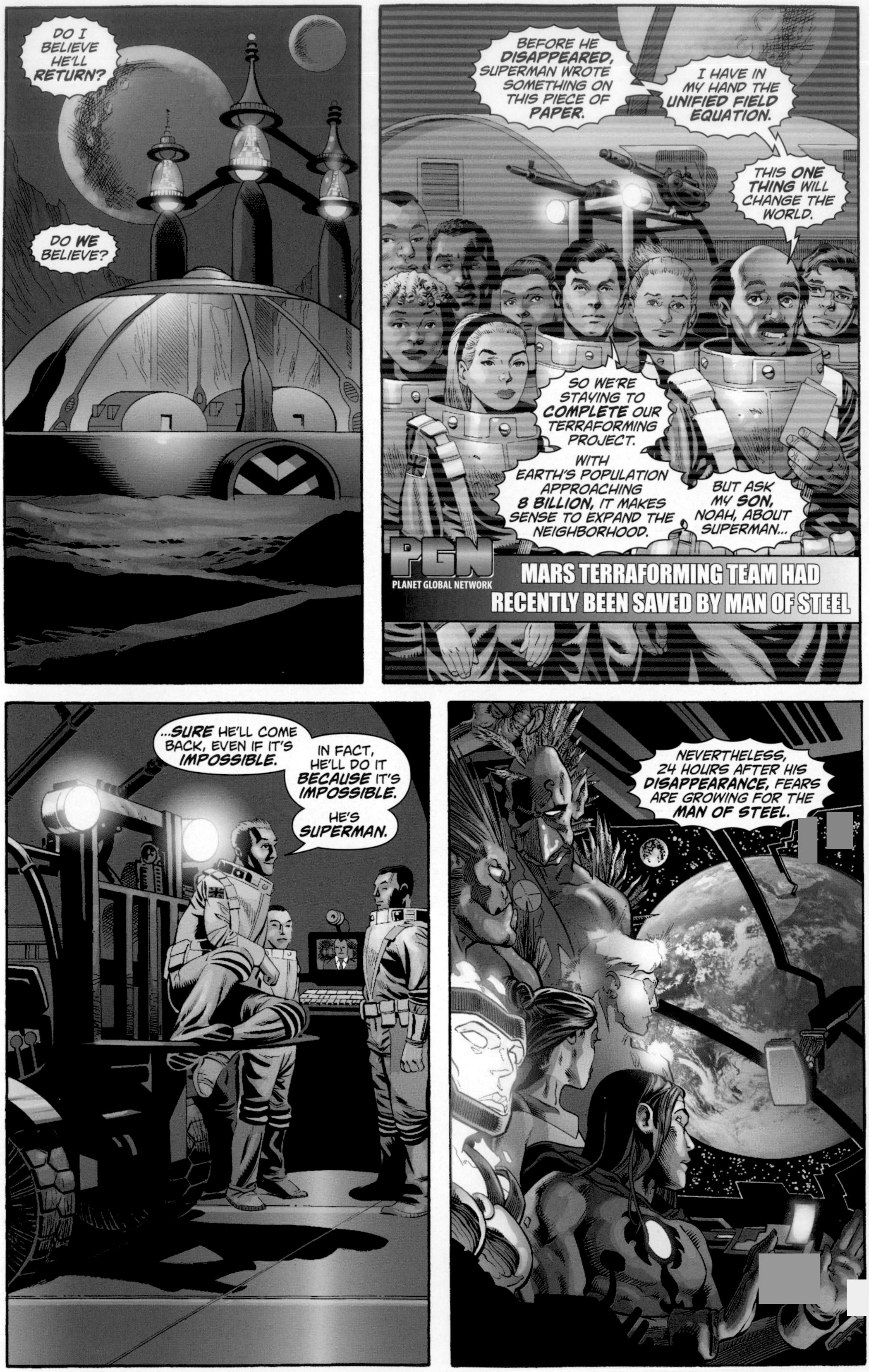
DO I BELIEVE HE'LL RETURN?
DO WE BELIEVE?
BEFORE HE DISAPPEARED, SUPERMAN WROTE SOMETHING ON THIS PIECE OF PAPER.
I HAVE IN MY HAND THE UNIFIED FIELD EQUATION.
THIS ONE THING WILL CHANGE THE WORLD.
SO WE'RE STAYING TO COMPLETE OUR TERRAFORMING PROJECT.
WITH EARTH'S POPULATION APPROACHING 8 BILLION, IT MAKES SENSE TO EXPAND THE NEIGHBORHOOD.
BUT ASK MY SON, NOAH, ABOUT SUPERMAN...
PGN
PLANET GLOBAL NETWORK
MARS TERRAFORMING TEAM HAD RECENTLY BEEN SAVED BY MAN OF STEEL
...SURE HE'LL COME BACK, EVEN IF IT'S IMPOSSIBLE.
IN FACT, HE'LL DO IT BECAUSE IT'S IMPOSSIBLE.
HE'S SUPERMAN.
NEVERTHELESS, 24 HOURS AFTER HIS DISAPPEARANCE, FEARS ARE GROWING FOR THE MAN OF STEEL.

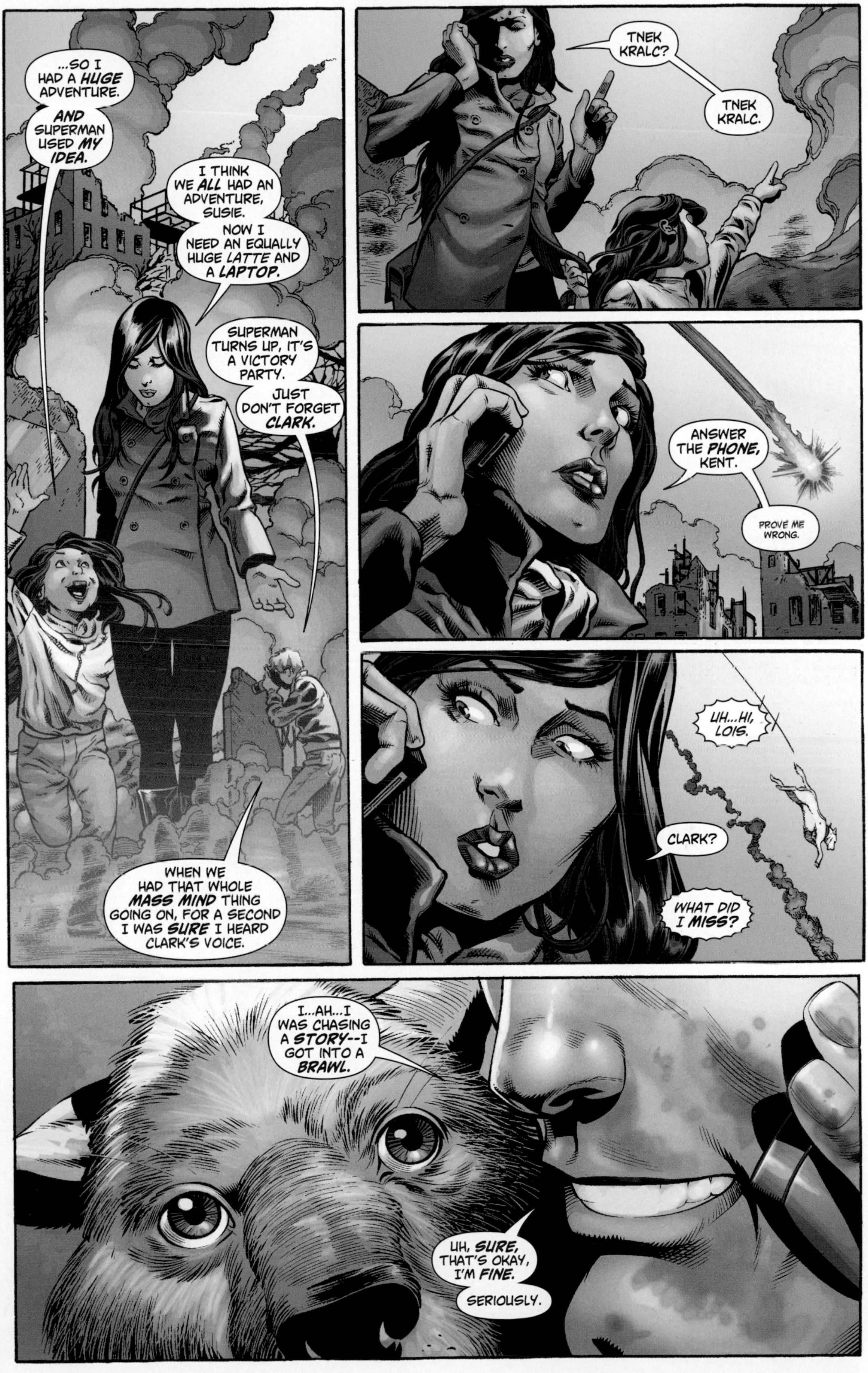

...SO I HAD A HUGE ADVENTURE.
AND SUPERMAN USED MY IDEA.
I THINK WE ALL HAD AN ADVENTURE, SUSIE.
NOW I NEED AN EQUALLY HUGE LATTE AND A LAPTOP.
SUPERMAN TURNS UP, IT'S A VICTORY PARTY.
JUST DON'T FORGET CLARK.
WHEN WE HAD THAT WHOLE MASS MIND THING GOING ON, FOR A SECOND I WAS SURE I HEARD CLARK'S VOICE.
TNEK KRALC?
TNEK KRALC.
ANSWER THE PHONE, KENT.
PROVE ME WRONG.
UH...HI, LOIS.
CLARK?
WHAT DID I MISS?
I...AH...I WAS CHASING A STORY--I GOT INTO A BRAWL.
UH, SURE, THAT'S OKAY, I'M FINE.
SERIOUSLY.

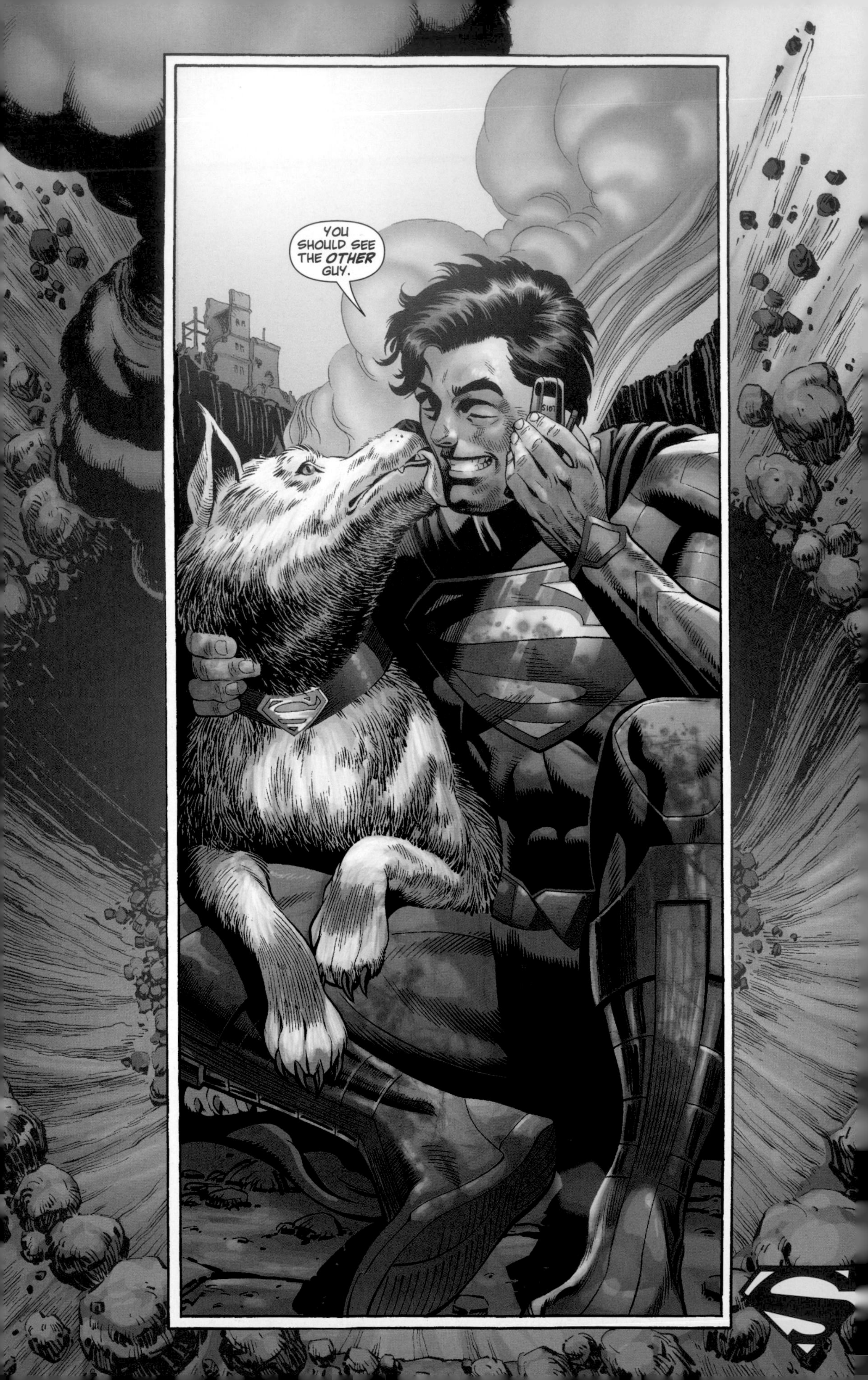
YOU SHOULD SEE THE *OTHER* GUY.

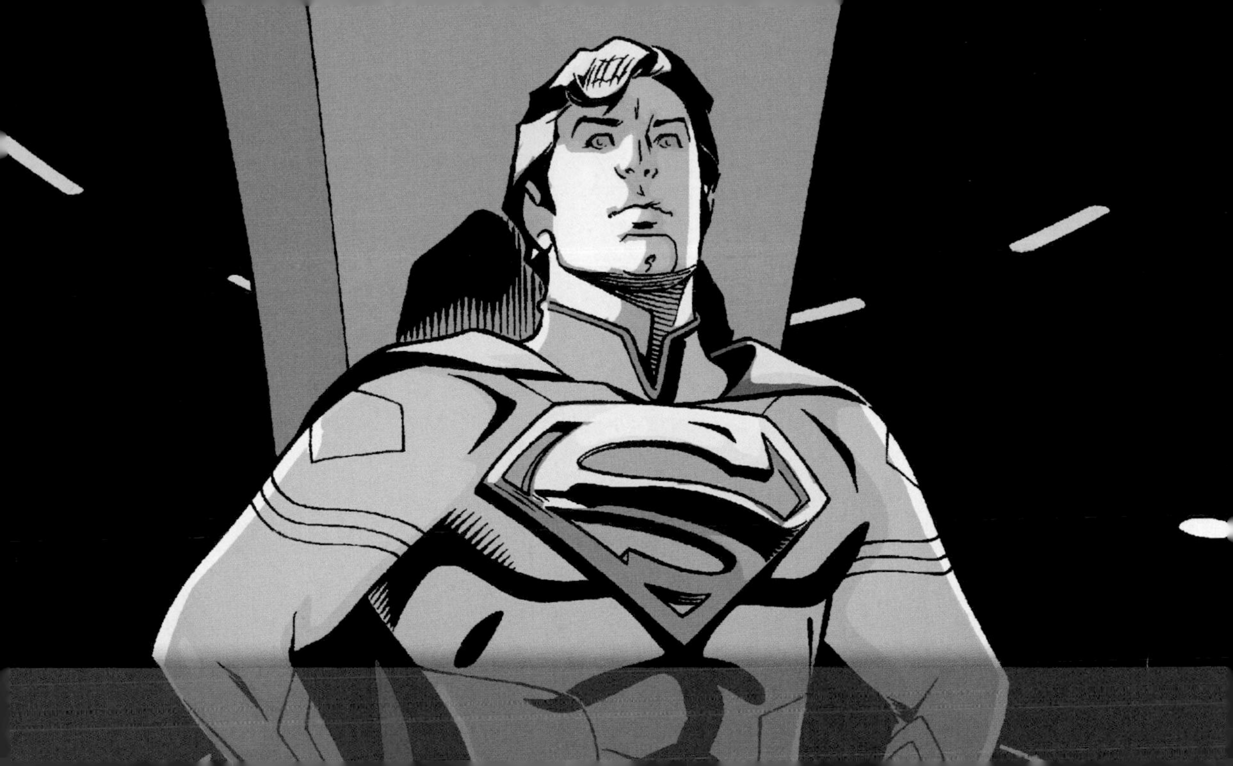

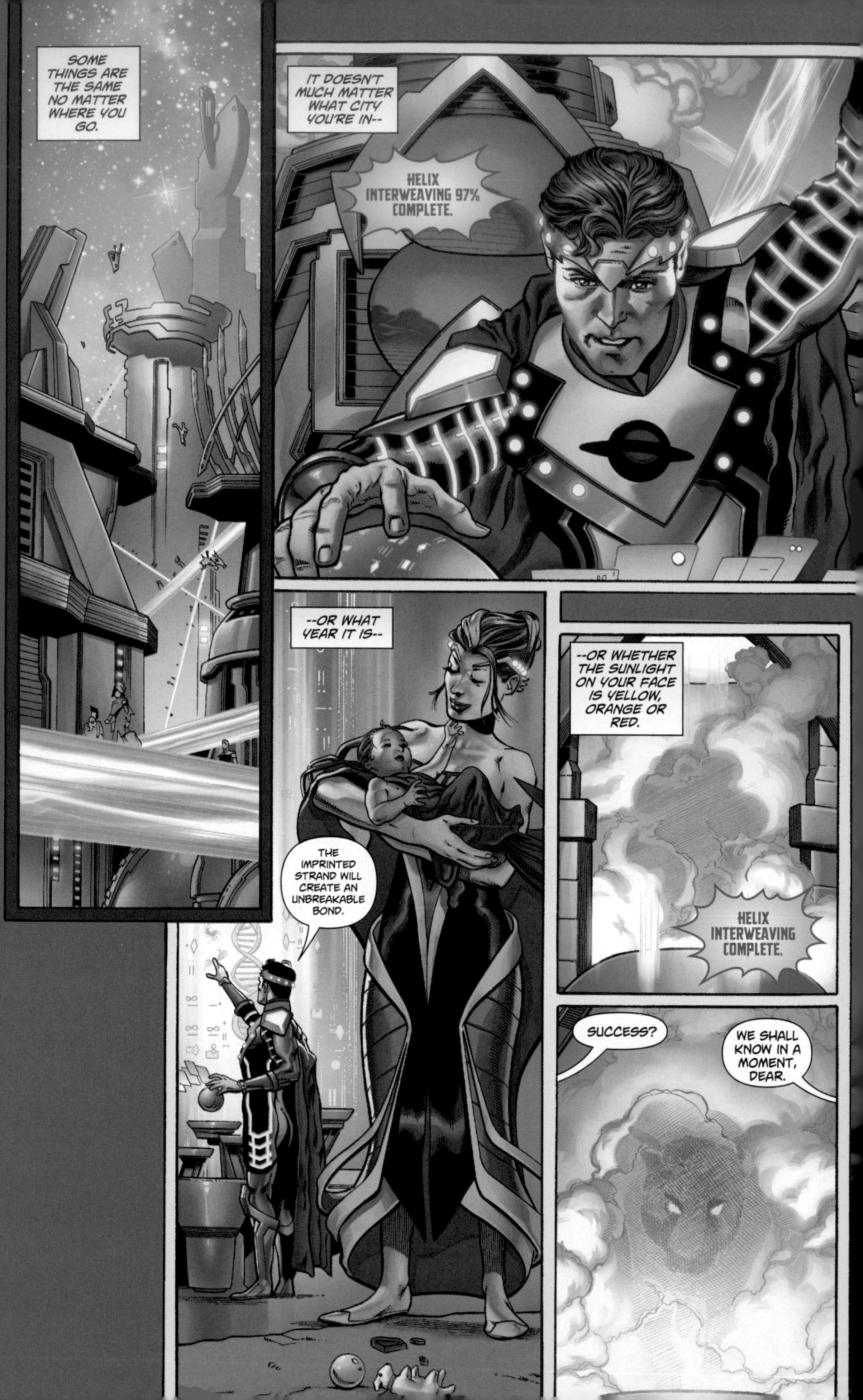
SOME THINGS ARE THE SAME NO MATTER WHERE YOU GO.
IT DOESN'T MUCH MATTER WHAT CITY YOU'RE IN--
HELIX INTERWEAVING 97% COMPLETE.
--OR WHAT YEAR IT IS--
THE IMPRINTED STRAND WILL CREATE AN UNBREAKABLE BOND.
--OR WHETHER THE SUNLIGHT ON YOUR FACE IS YELLOW, ORANGE OR RED.
HELIX INTERWEAVING COMPLETE.
SUCCESS?
WE SHALL KNOW IN A MOMENT, DEAR.

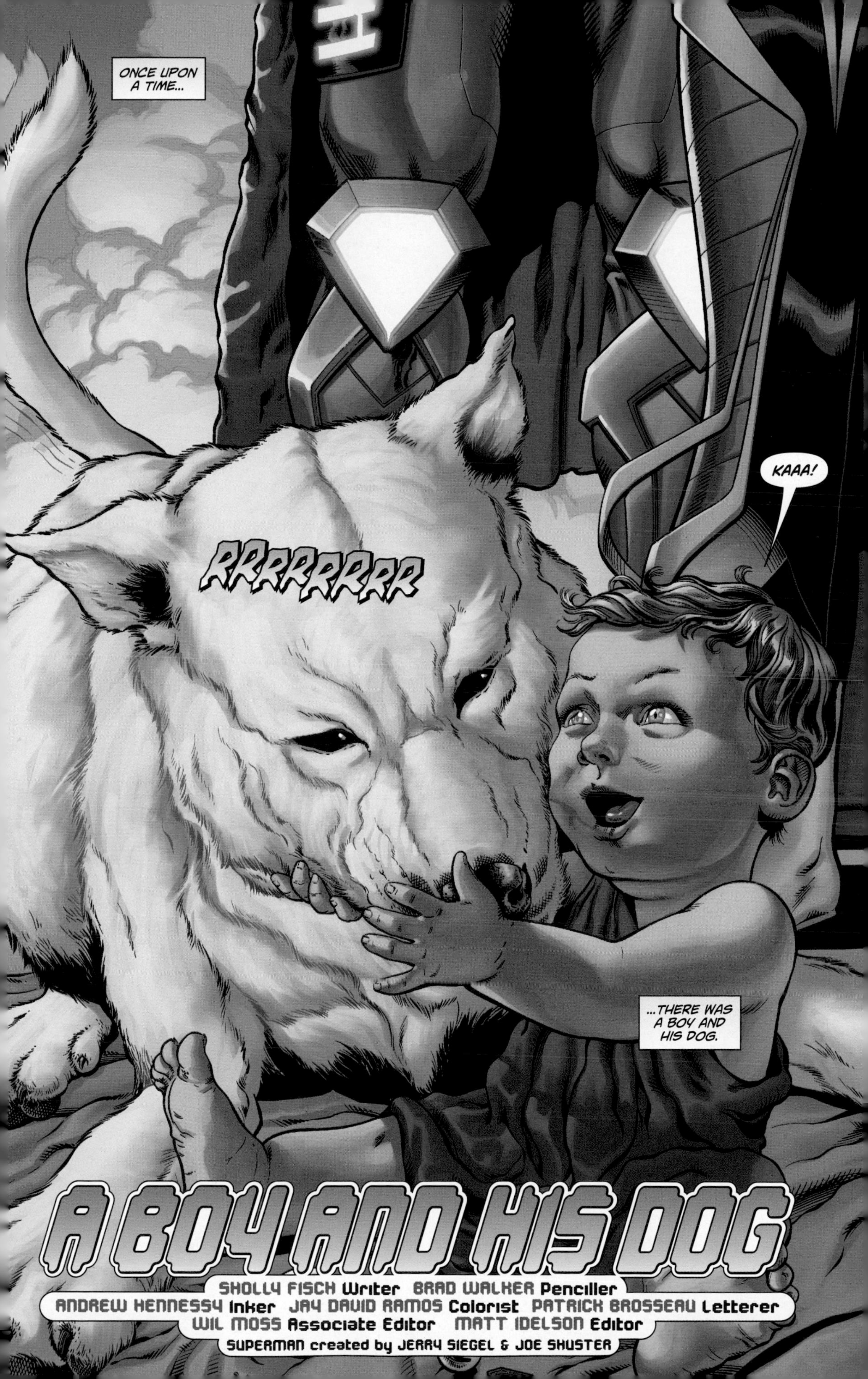
ONCE UPON A TIME...
RRRRRRRR
KAAA!
...THERE WAS A BOY AND HIS DOG.
A BOY AND HIS DOG
SHOLLY FISCH Writer BRAD WALKER Penciller
ANDREW HENNESSY Inker JAY DAVID RAMOS Colorist PATRICK BROSSEAU Letterer
WIL MOSS Associate Editor MATT IDELSON Editor
SUPERMAN created by JERRY SIEGEL & JOE SHUSTER

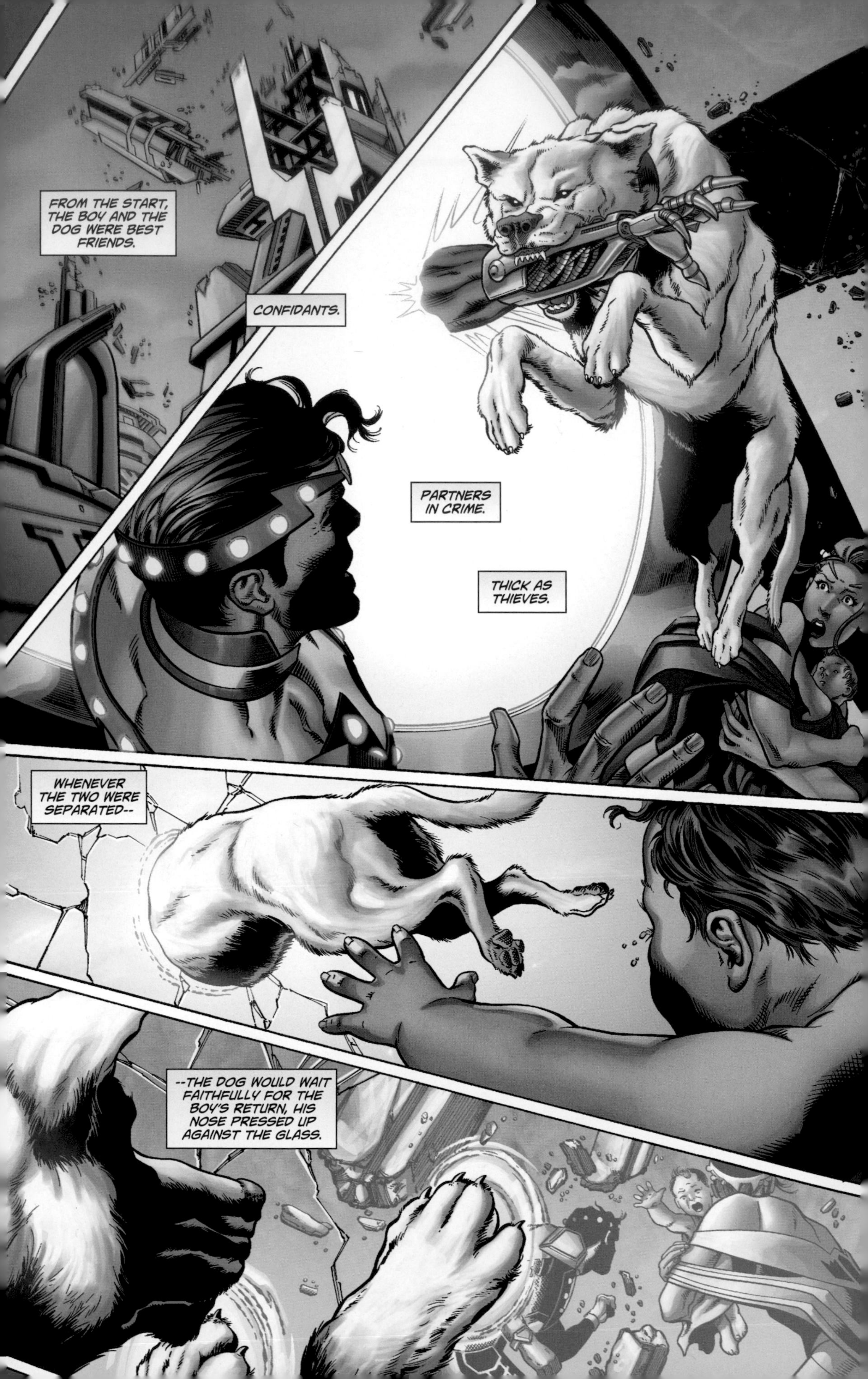
FROM THE START, THE BOY AND THE DOG WERE BEST FRIENDS.
CONFIDANTS.
PARTNERS IN CRIME.
THICK AS THIEVES.
WHENEVER THE TWO WERE SEPARATED--
--THE DOG WOULD WAIT FAITHFULLY FOR THE BOY'S RETURN, HIS NOSE PRESSED UP AGAINST THE GLASS.

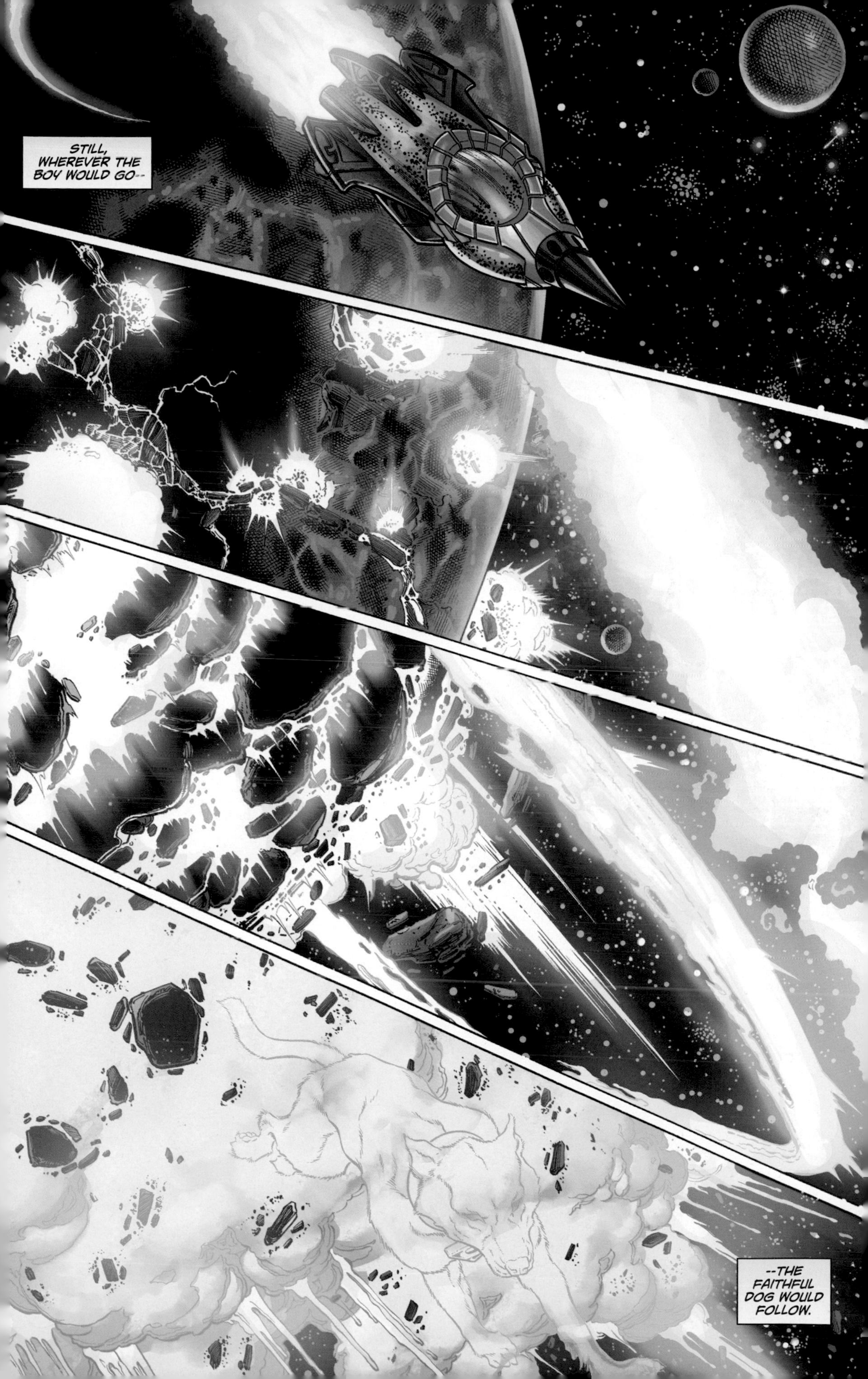
STILL, WHEREVER THE BOY WOULD GO--
--THE FAITHFUL DOG WOULD FOLLOW.

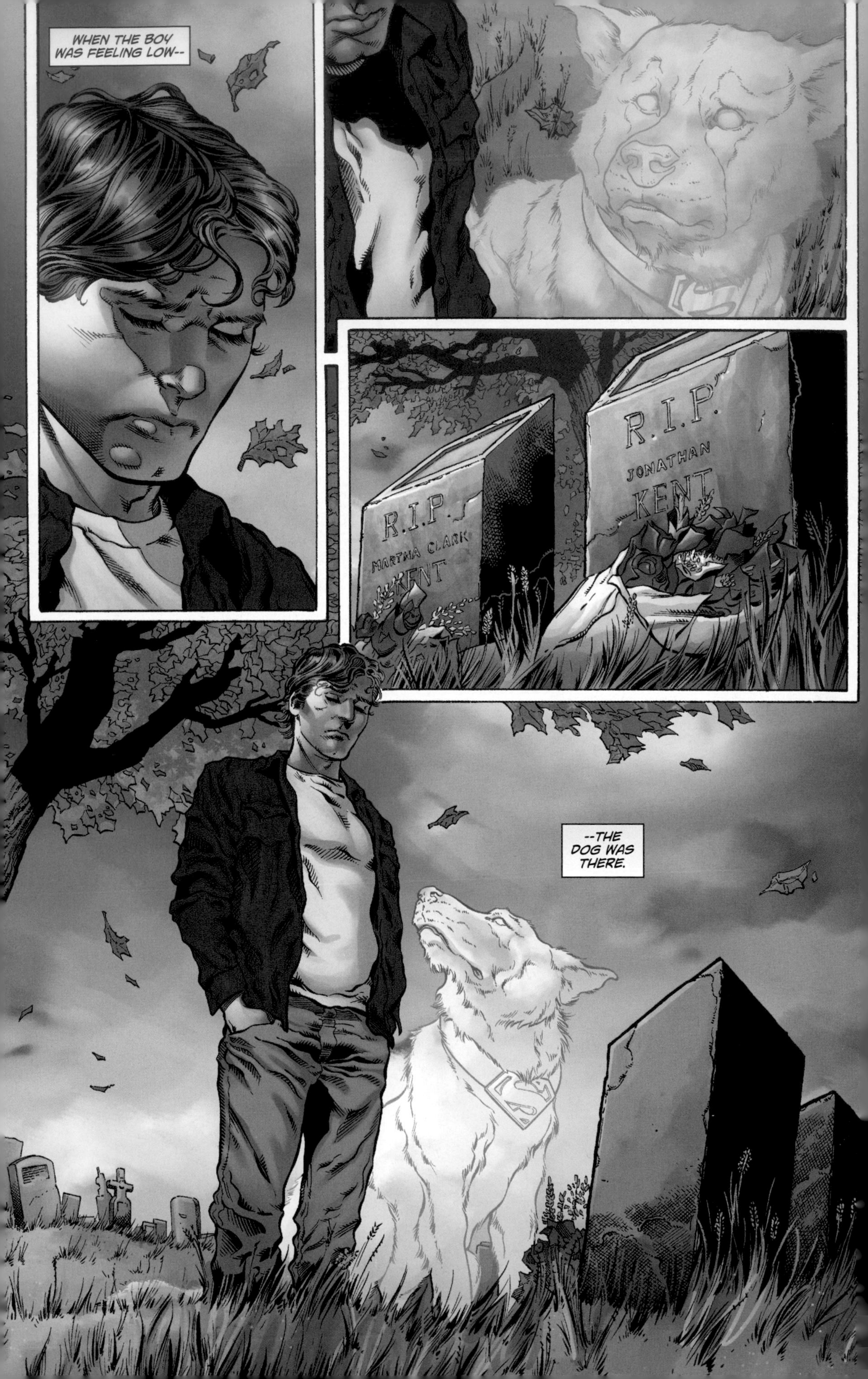
WHEN THE BOY WAS FEELING LOW--
R.I.P.
MARTHA CLARK KENT
R.I.P.
JONATHAN KENT
--THE DOG WAS THERE.

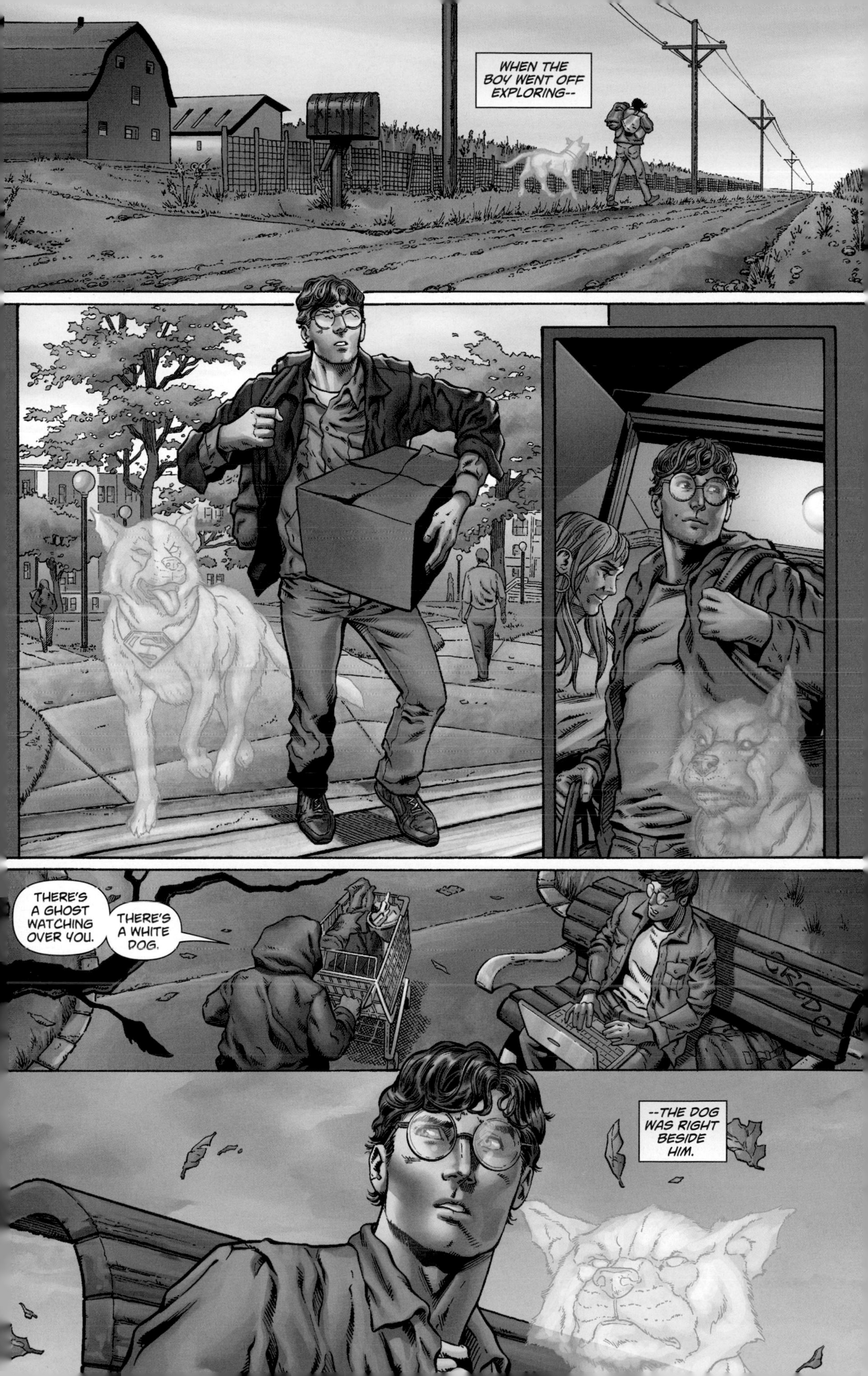

WHEN THE BOY WENT OFF EXPLORING--
THERE'S A GHOST WATCHING OVER YOU.
THERE'S A WHITE DOG.
--THE DOG WAS RIGHT BESIDE HIM.

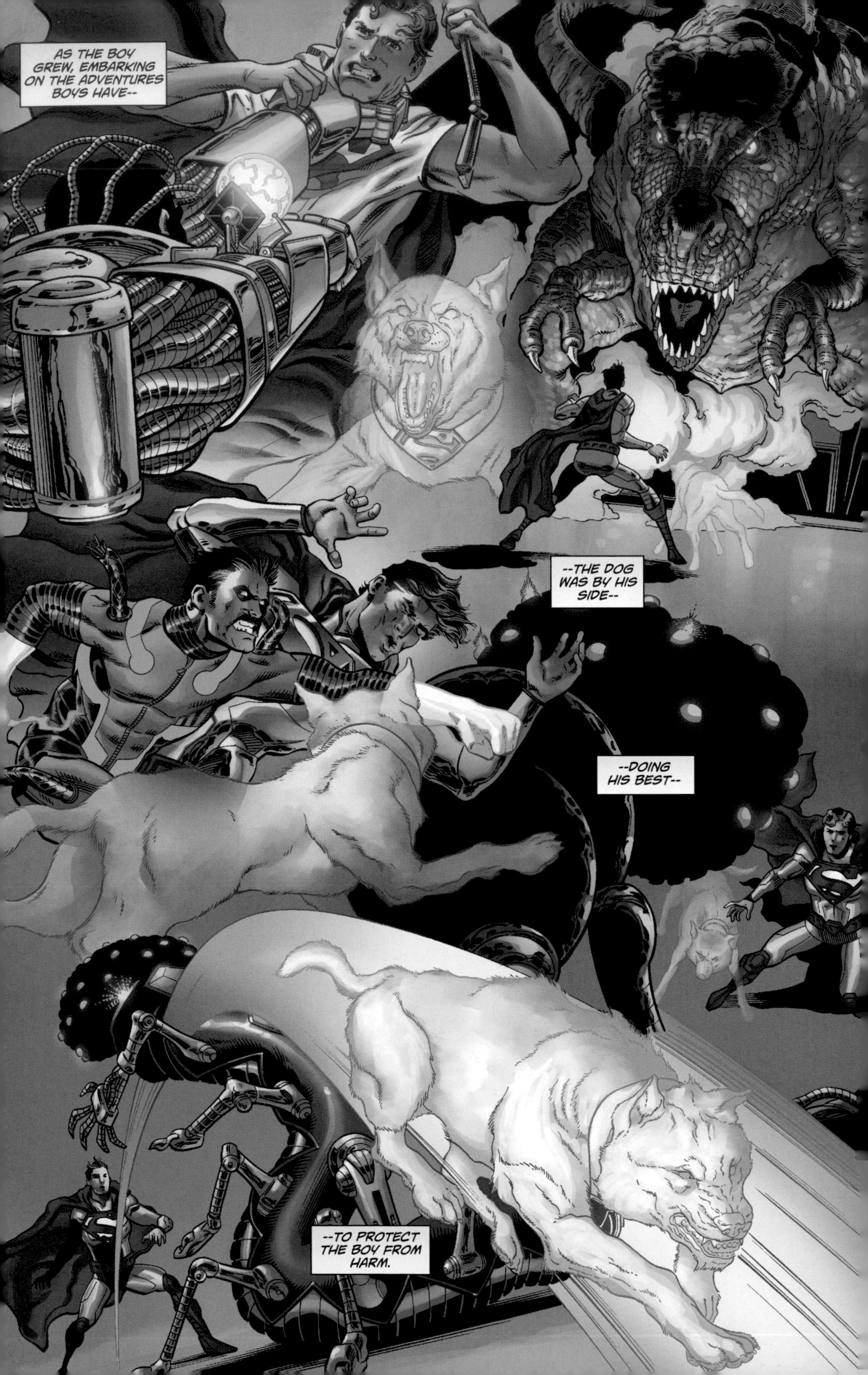
AS THE BOY GREW, EMBARKING ON THE ADVENTURES BOYS HAVE--
--THE DOG WAS BY HIS SIDE--
--DOING HIS BEST--
--TO PROTECT THE BOY FROM HARM.

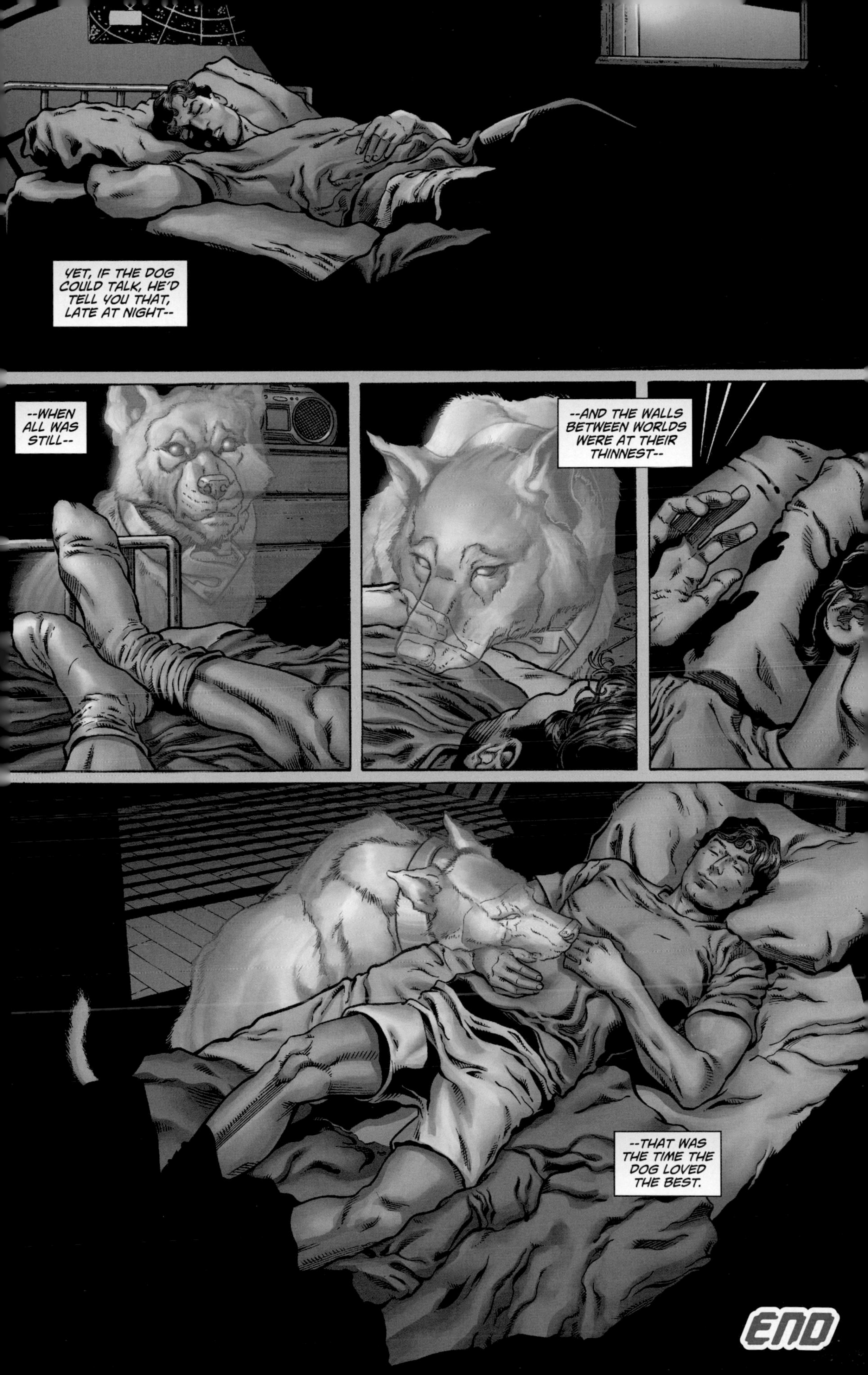

YET, IF THE DOG COULD TALK, HE'D TELL YOU THAT, LATE AT NIGHT--
--WHEN ALL WAS STILL--
--AND THE WALLS BETWEEN WORLDS WERE AT THEIR THINNEST--
--THAT WAS THE TIME THE DOG LOVED THE BEST.
END

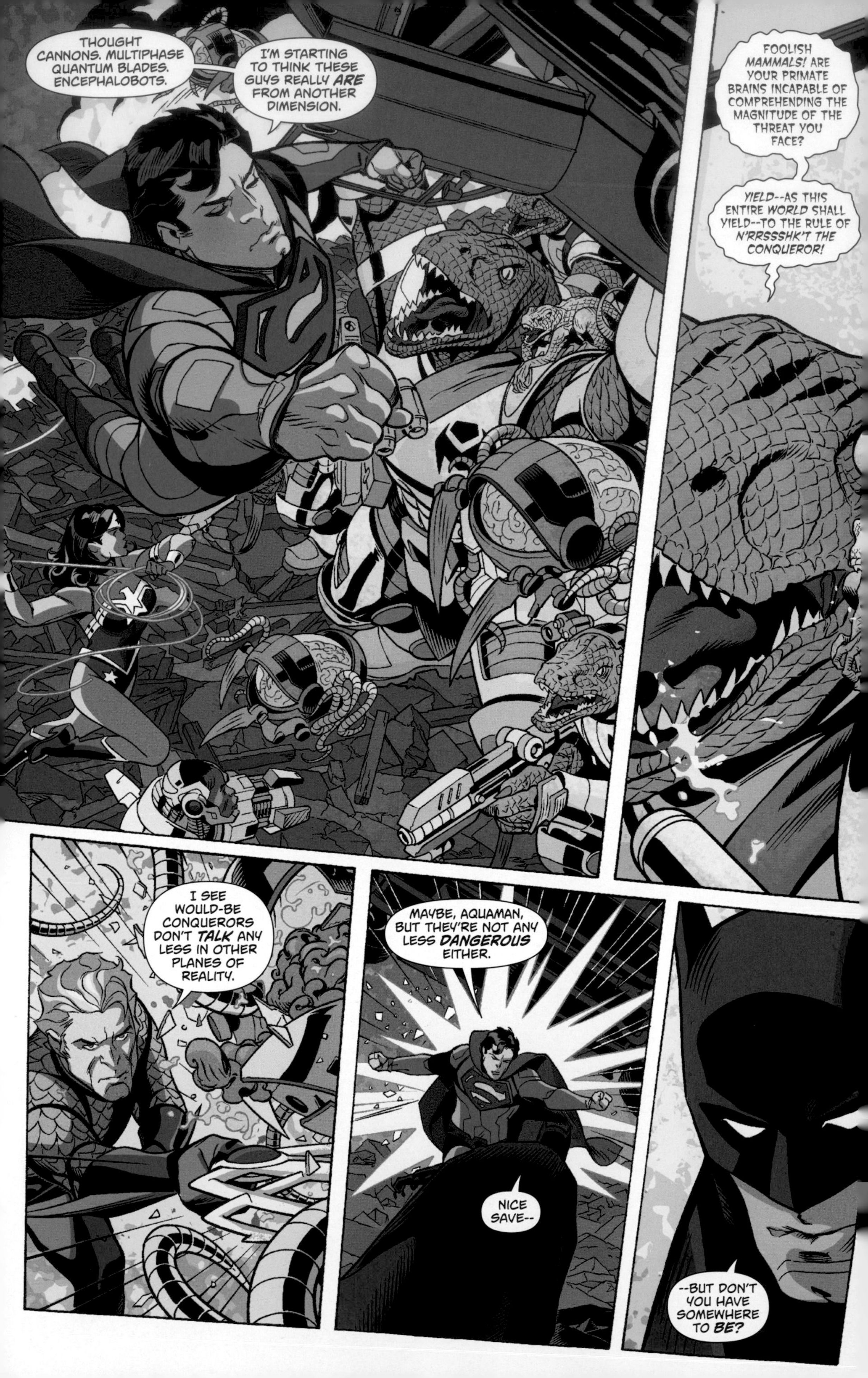
THOUGHT CANNONS. MULTIPHASE QUANTUM BLADES. ENCEPHALOBOTS.
I'M STARTING TO THINK THESE GUYS REALLY ARE FROM ANOTHER DIMENSION.
FOOLISH MAMMALS! ARE YOUR PRIMATE BRAINS INCAPABLE OF COMPREHENDING THE MAGNITUDE OF THE THREAT YOU FACE?
YIELD--AS THIS ENTIRE WORLD SHALL YIELD--TO THE RULE OF N'RRSSSHK'T THE CONQUEROR!
I SEE WOULD-BE CONQUERORS DON'T TALK ANY LESS IN OTHER PLANES OF REALITY.
MAYBE, AQUAMAN, BUT THEY'RE NOT ANY LESS DANGEROUS EITHER.
NICE SAVE--
--BUT DON'T YOU HAVE SOMEWHERE TO BE?

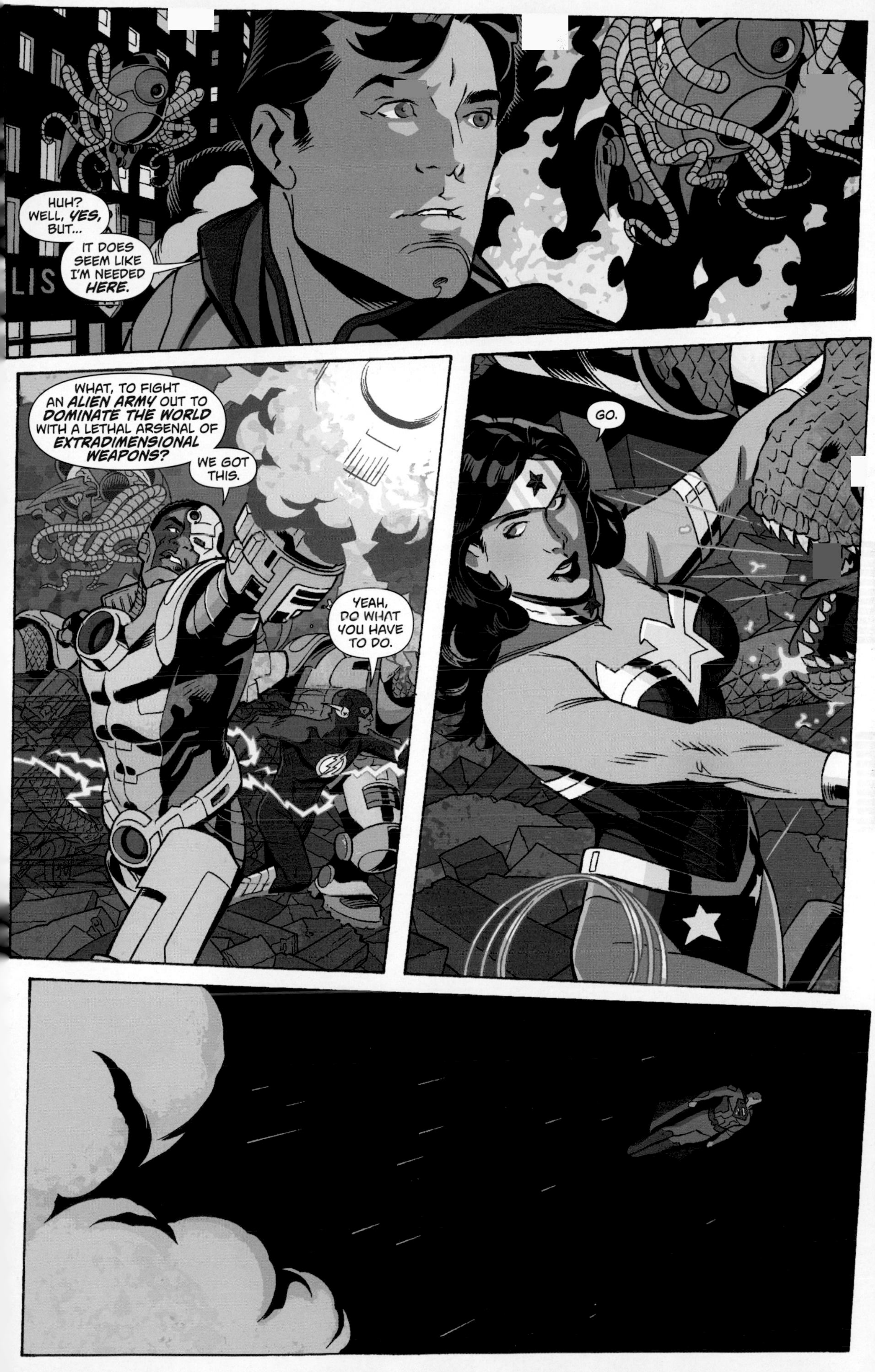
HUH? WELL, YES, BUT...
IT DOES SEEM LIKE I'M NEEDED HERE.
WHAT, TO FIGHT AN ALIEN ARMY OUT TO DOMINATE THE WORLD WITH A LETHAL ARSENAL OF EXTRADIMENSIONAL WEAPONS?
WE GOT THIS.
YEAH, DO WHAT YOU HAVE TO DO.
GO.

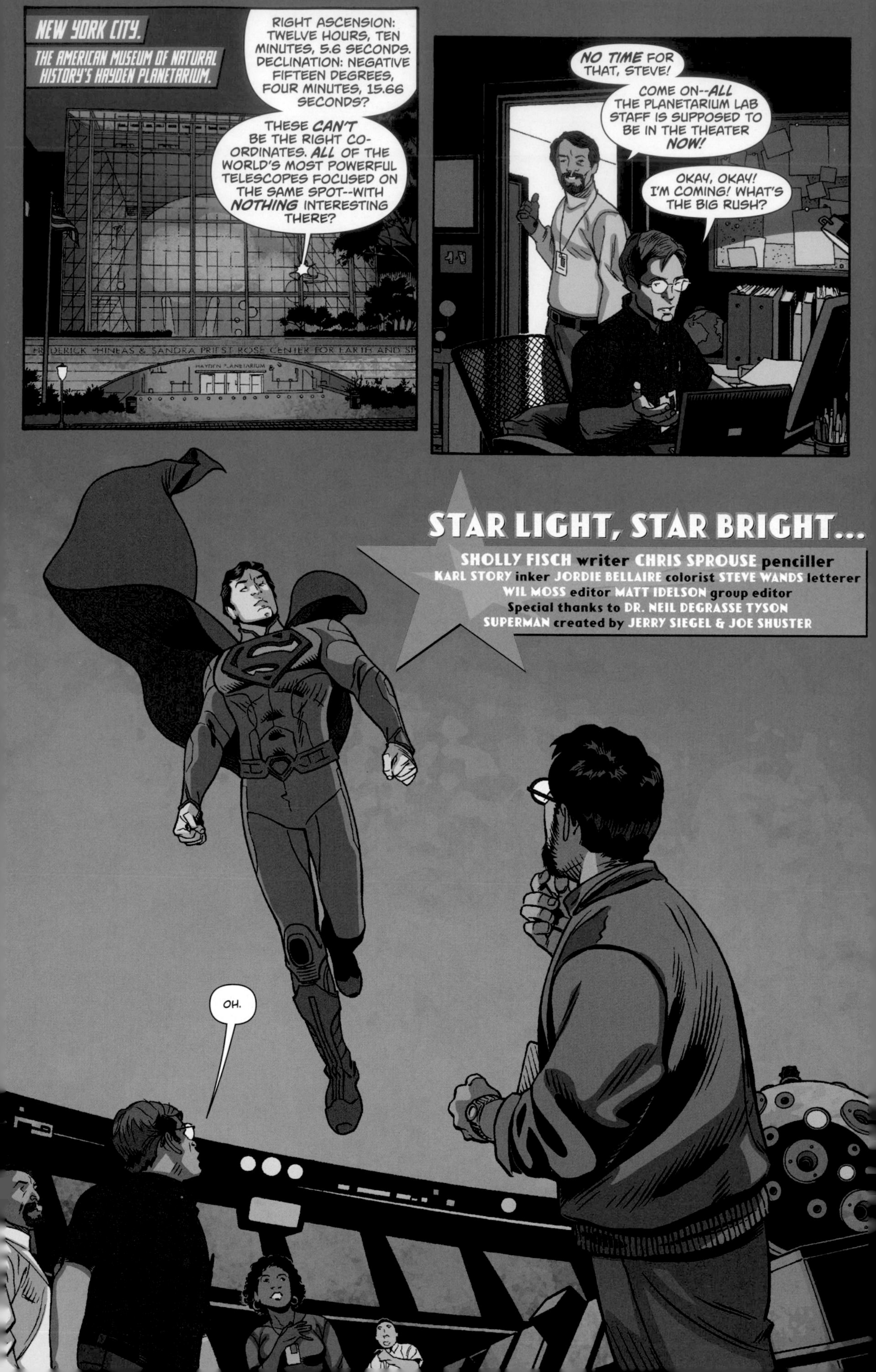
NEW YORK CITY.
THE AMERICAN MUSEUM OF NATURAL HISTORY'S HAYDEN PLANETARIUM.
RIGHT ASCENSION: TWELVE HOURS, TEN MINUTES, 5.6 SECONDS. DECLINATION: NEGATIVE FIFTEEN DEGREES, FOUR MINUTES, 15.66 SECONDS?
THESE CAN'T BE THE RIGHT CO-ORDINATES. ALL OF THE WORLD'S MOST POWERFUL TELESCOPES FOCUSED ON THE SAME SPOT--WITH NOTHING INTERESTING THERE?
HAYDEN PLANETARIUM
NO TIME FOR THAT, STEVE!
COME ON--ALL THE PLANETARIUM LAB STAFF IS SUPPOSED TO BE IN THE THEATER NOW!
OKAY, OKAY! I'M COMING! WHAT'S THE BIG RUSH?
STAR LIGHT, STAR BRIGHT...
SHOLLY FISCH writer CHRIS SPROUSE penciller
KARL STORY inker JORDIE BELLAIRE colorist STEVE WANDS letterer
WIL MOSS editor MATT IDELSON group editor
Special thanks to DR. NEIL DEGRASSE TYSON
SUPERMAN created by JERRY SIEGEL & JOE SHUSTER
OH.

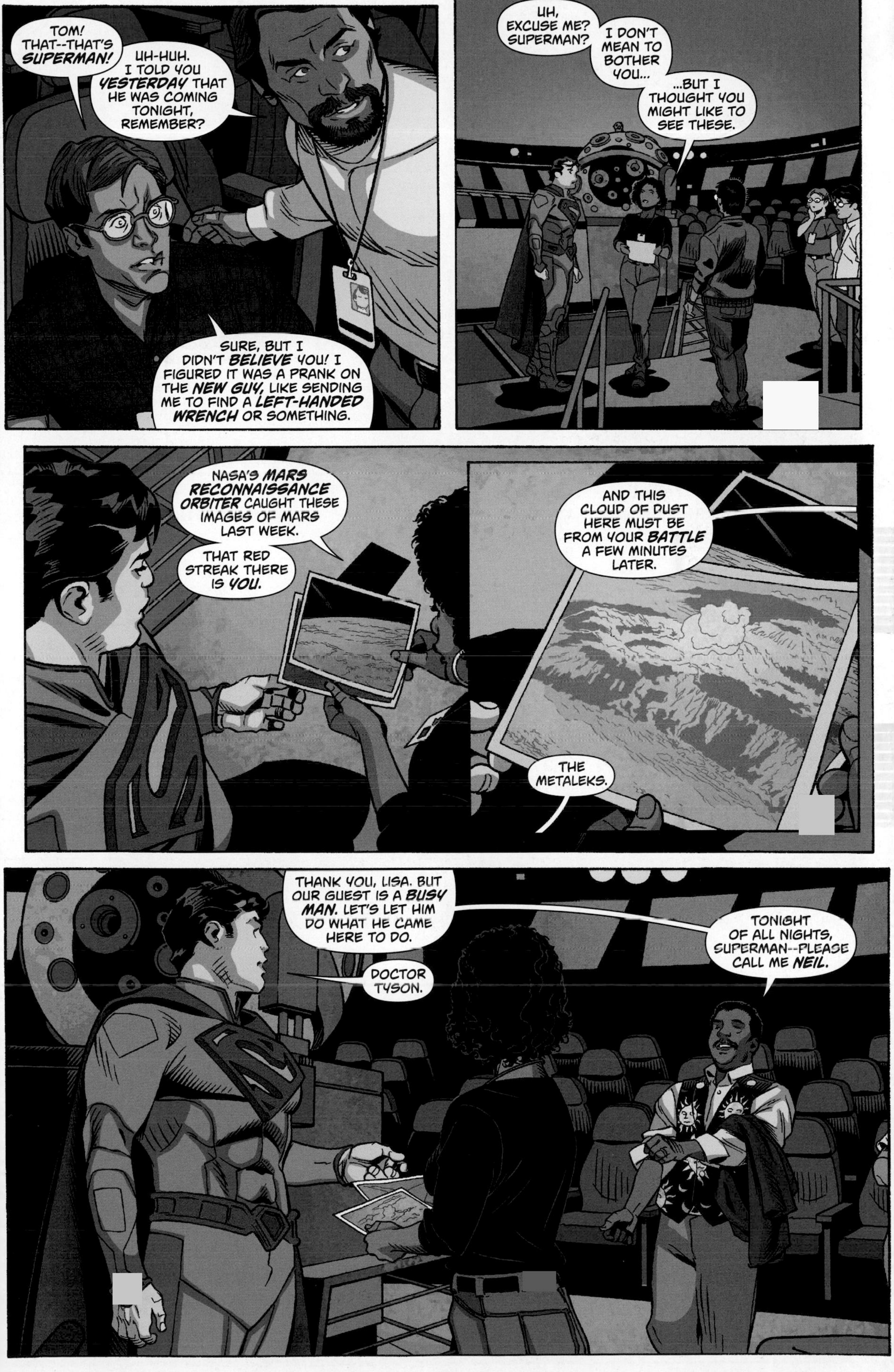
TOM! THAT--THAT'S *SUPERMAN!*
UH-HUH. I TOLD YOU *YESTERDAY* THAT HE WAS COMING TONIGHT, REMEMBER?
SURE, BUT I DIDN'T *BELIEVE* YOU! I FIGURED IT WAS A PRANK ON THE *NEW GUY,* LIKE SENDING ME TO FIND A *LEFT-HANDED WRENCH* OR SOMETHING.
UH, EXCUSE ME? SUPERMAN?
I DON'T MEAN TO BOTHER YOU...
...BUT I THOUGHT YOU MIGHT LIKE TO SEE THESE.
NASA'S *MARS RECONNAISSANCE ORBITER* CAUGHT THESE IMAGES OF MARS LAST WEEK.
THAT RED STREAK THERE IS *YOU.*
AND THIS CLOUD OF DUST HERE MUST BE FROM YOUR *BATTLE* A FEW MINUTES LATER.
THE METALEKS.
THANK YOU, LISA. BUT OUR GUEST IS A *BUSY MAN.* LET'S LET HIM DO WHAT HE CAME HERE TO DO.
DOCTOR TYSON.
TONIGHT OF ALL NIGHTS, SUPERMAN--PLEASE CALL ME *NEIL.*

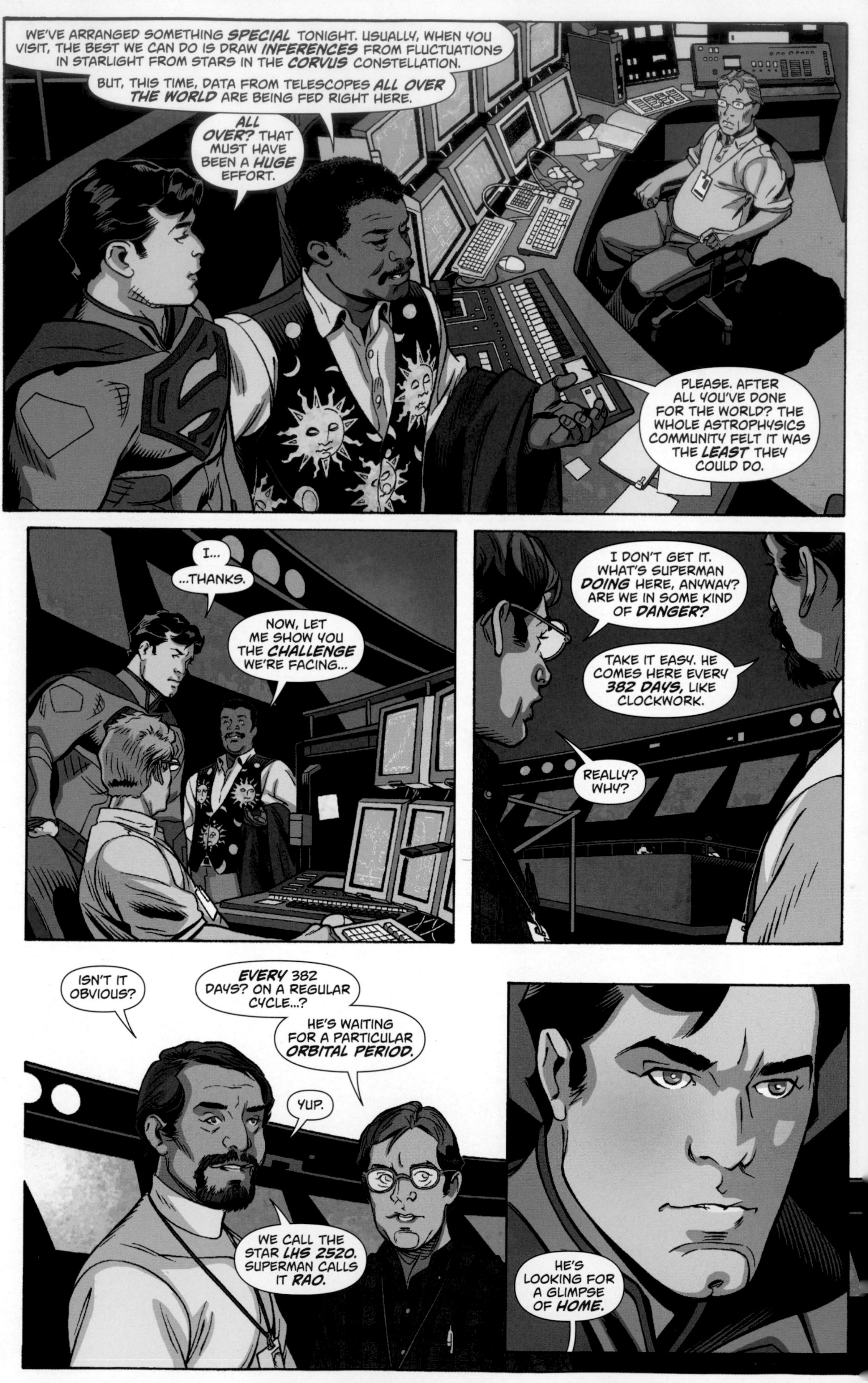
WE'VE ARRANGED SOMETHING SPECIAL TONIGHT. USUALLY, WHEN YOU VISIT, THE BEST WE CAN DO IS DRAW INFERENCES FROM FLUCTUATIONS IN STARLIGHT FROM STARS IN THE CORVUS CONSTELLATION.
BUT, THIS TIME, DATA FROM TELESCOPES ALL OVER THE WORLD ARE BEING FED RIGHT HERE.
ALL OVER? THAT MUST HAVE BEEN A HUGE EFFORT.
PLEASE. AFTER ALL YOU'VE DONE FOR THE WORLD? THE WHOLE ASTROPHYSICS COMMUNITY FELT IT WAS THE LEAST THEY COULD DO.
I...
...THANKS.
NOW, LET ME SHOW YOU THE CHALLENGE WE'RE FACING...
I DON'T GET IT. WHAT'S SUPERMAN DOING HERE, ANYWAY? ARE WE IN SOME KIND OF DANGER?
TAKE IT EASY. HE COMES HERE EVERY 382 DAYS, LIKE CLOCKWORK.
REALLY? WHY?
ISN'T IT OBVIOUS?
EVERY 382 DAYS? ON A REGULAR CYCLE...?
HE'S WAITING FOR A PARTICULAR ORBITAL PERIOD.
YUP.
WE CALL THE STAR LHS 2520. SUPERMAN CALLS IT RAO.
HE'S LOOKING FOR A GLIMPSE OF HOME.

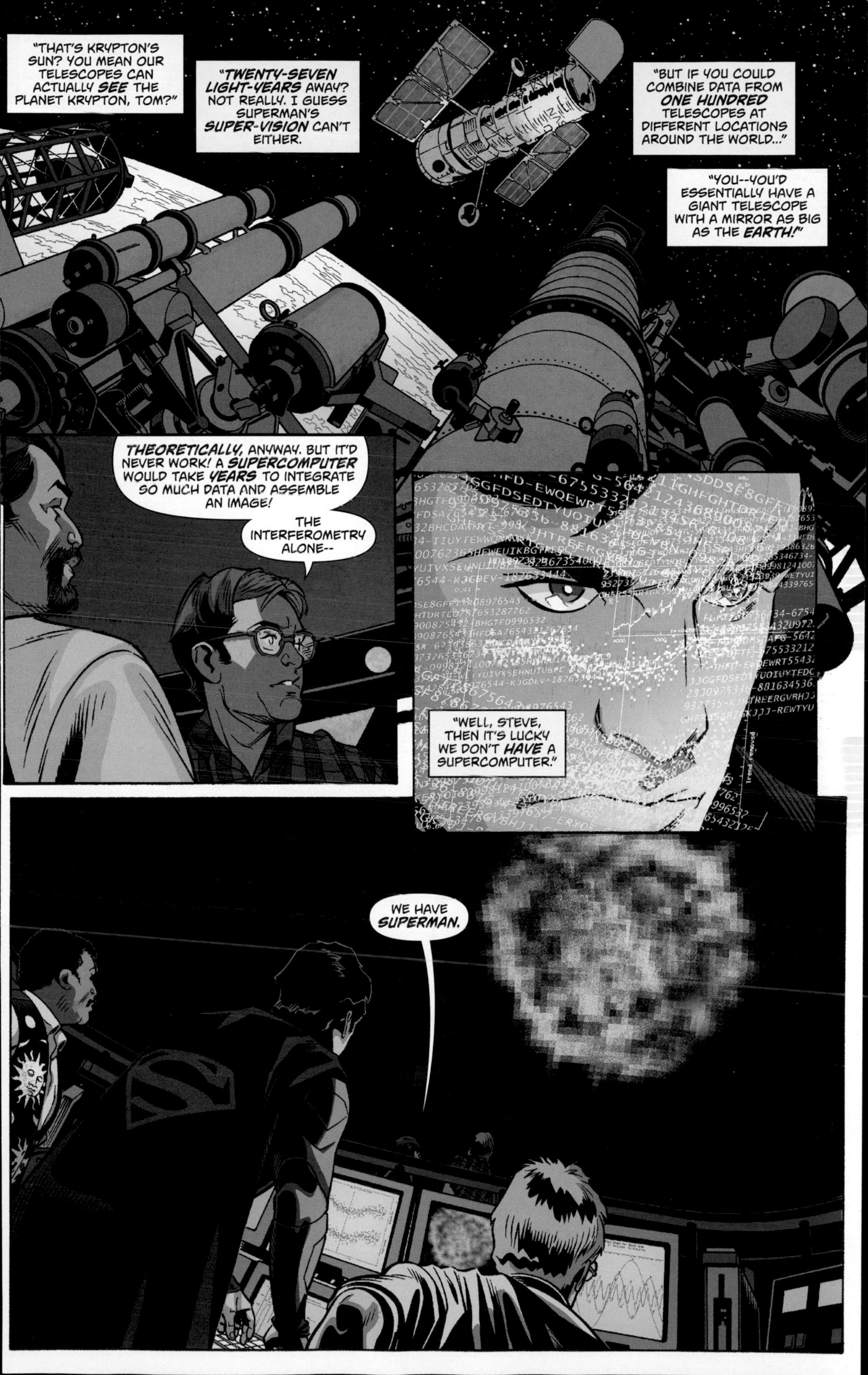
"THAT'S KRYPTON'S SUN? YOU MEAN OUR TELESCOPES CAN ACTUALLY SEE THE PLANET KRYPTON, TOM?"
"TWENTY-SEVEN LIGHT-YEARS AWAY? NOT REALLY. I GUESS SUPERMAN'S SUPER-VISION CAN'T EITHER.
"BUT IF YOU COULD COMBINE DATA FROM ONE HUNDRED TELESCOPES AT DIFFERENT LOCATIONS AROUND THE WORLD..."
"YOU--YOU'D ESSENTIALLY HAVE A GIANT TELESCOPE WITH A MIRROR AS BIG AS THE EARTH!"
THEORETICALLY, ANYWAY. BUT IT'D NEVER WORK! A SUPERCOMPUTER WOULD TAKE YEARS TO INTEGRATE SO MUCH DATA AND ASSEMBLE AN IMAGE!
THE INTERFEROMETRY ALONE--
"WELL, STEVE, THEN IT'S LUCKY WE DON'T HAVE A SUPERCOMPUTER."
WE HAVE SUPERMAN.

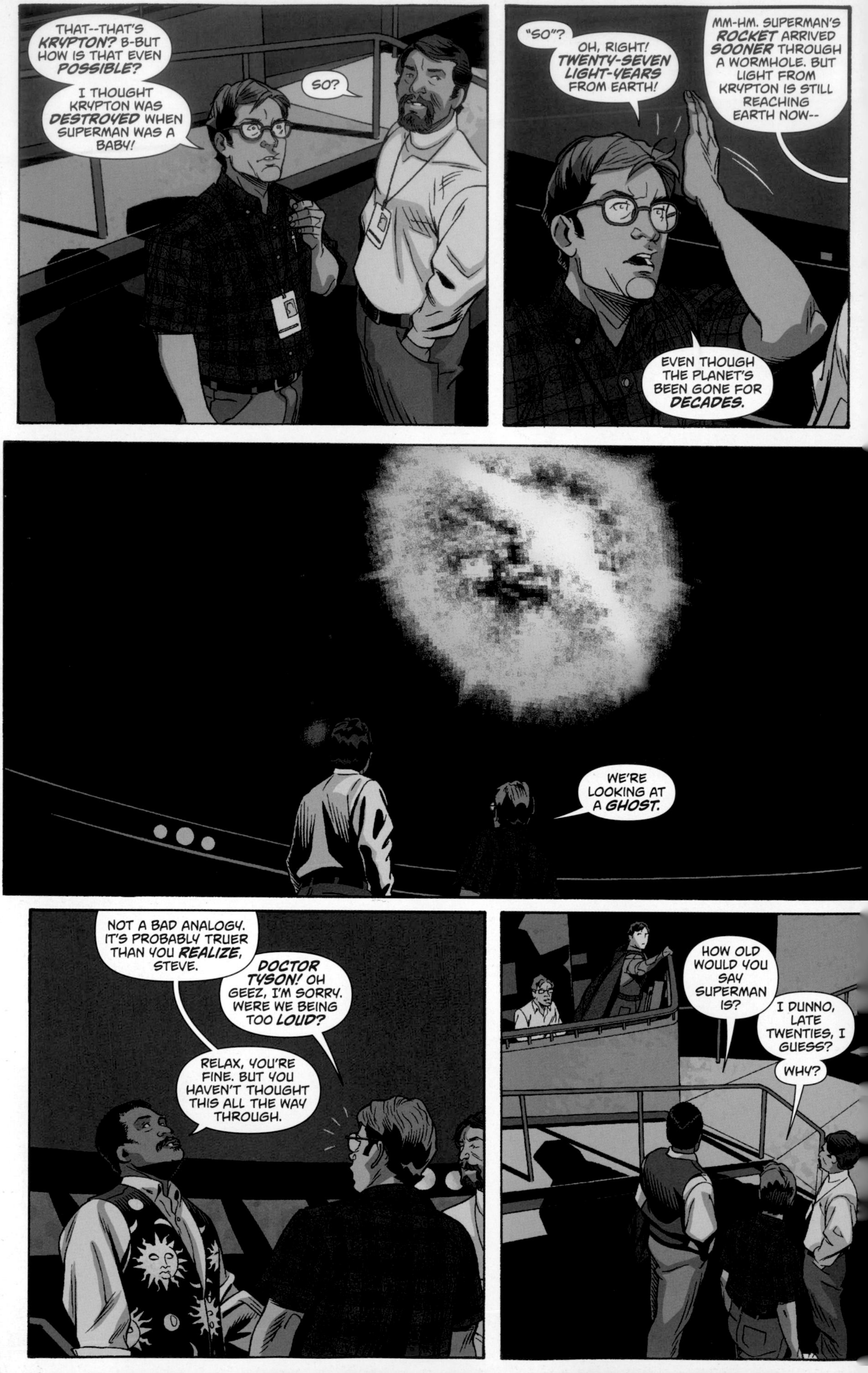
THAT--THAT'S KRYPTON? B-BUT HOW IS THAT EVEN POSSIBLE?
I THOUGHT KRYPTON WAS DESTROYED WHEN SUPERMAN WAS A BABY!
SO?
"SO"?
OH, RIGHT! TWENTY-SEVEN LIGHT-YEARS FROM EARTH!
MM-HM. SUPERMAN'S ROCKET ARRIVED SOONER THROUGH A WORMHOLE. BUT LIGHT FROM KRYPTON IS STILL REACHING EARTH NOW--
EVEN THOUGH THE PLANET'S BEEN GONE FOR DECADES.
WE'RE LOOKING AT A GHOST.
NOT A BAD ANALOGY. IT'S PROBABLY TRUER THAN YOU REALIZE, STEVE.
DOCTOR TYSON! OH GEEZ, I'M SORRY. WERE WE BEING TOO LOUD?
RELAX, YOU'RE FINE. BUT YOU HAVEN'T THOUGHT THIS ALL THE WAY THROUGH.
HOW OLD WOULD YOU SAY SUPERMAN IS?
I DUNNO, LATE TWENTIES, I GUESS?
WHY?

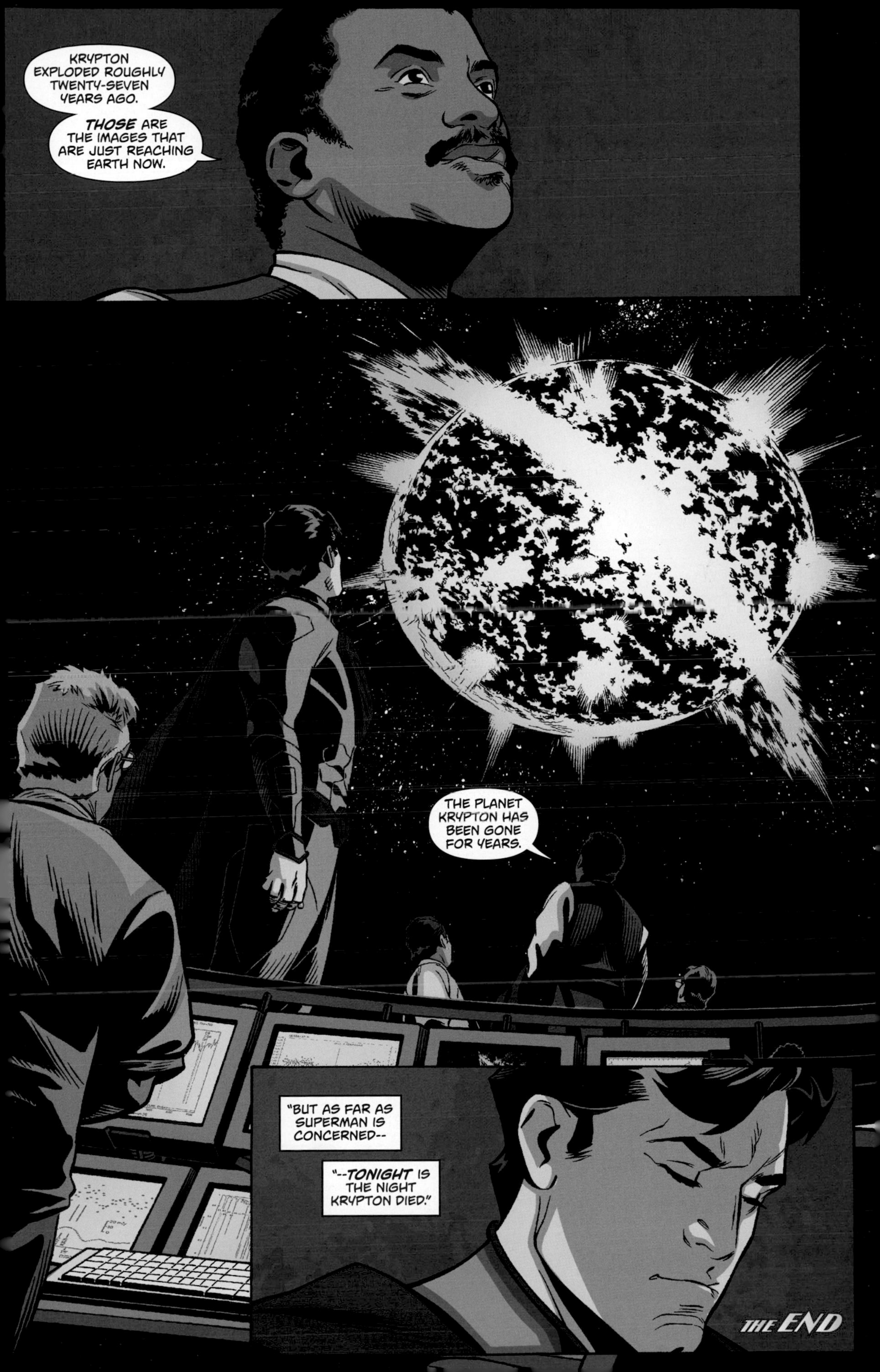
KRYPTON EXPLODED ROUGHLY TWENTY-SEVEN YEARS AGO.
THOSE ARE THE IMAGES THAT ARE JUST REACHING EARTH NOW.
THE PLANET KRYPTON HAS BEEN GONE FOR YEARS.
"BUT AS FAR AS SUPERMAN IS CONCERNED--
"--*TONIGHT* IS THE NIGHT KRYPTON DIED."
THE END

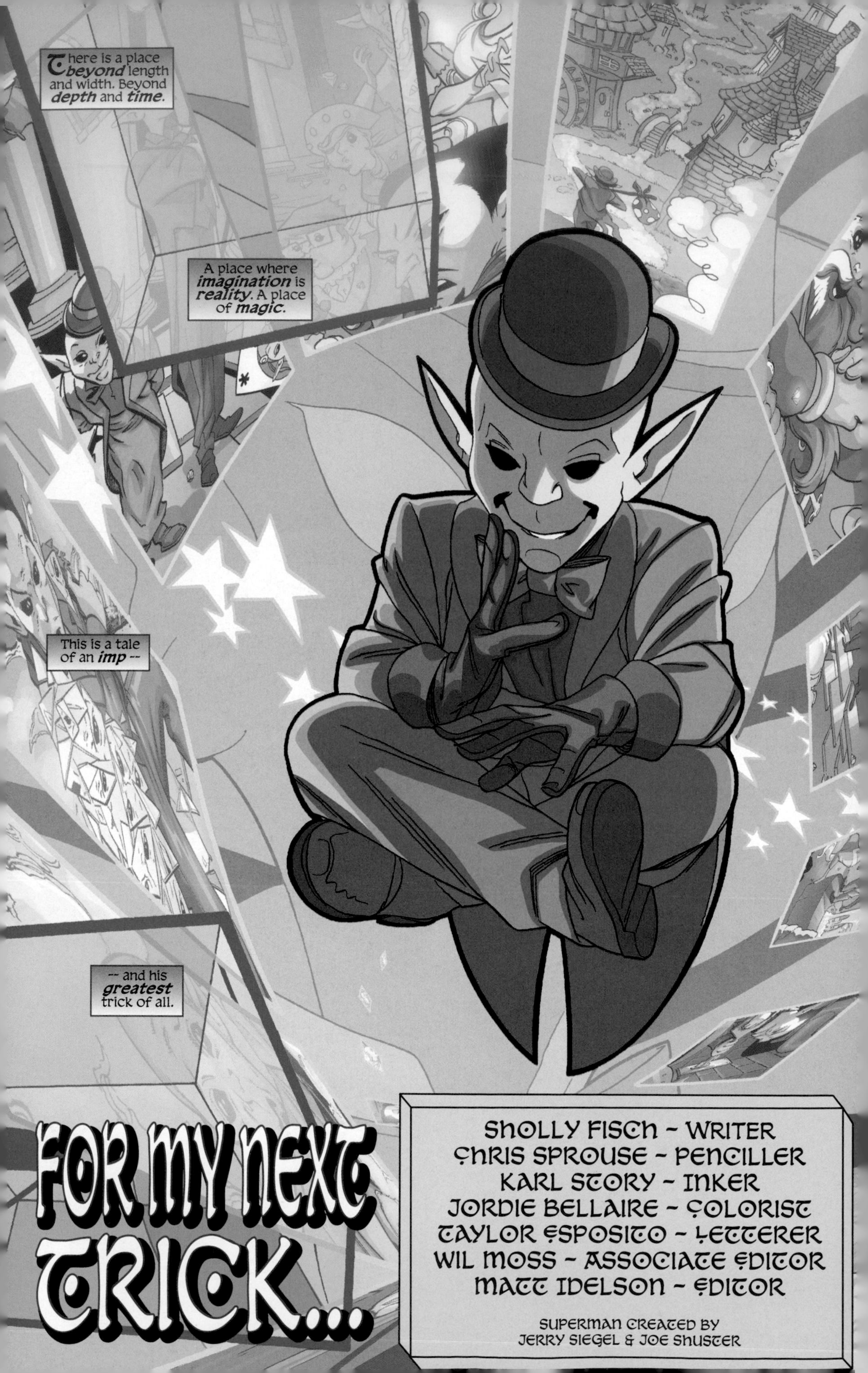
There is a place beyond length and width. Beyond depth and time.
A place where imagination is reality. A place of magic.
This is a tale of an imp --
-- and his greatest trick of all.
FOR MY NEXT TRICK...
SHOLLY FISCH – WRITER
CHRIS SPROUSE – PENCILLER
KARL STORY – INKER
JORDIE BELLAIRE – COLORIST
TAYLOR ESPOSITO – LETTERER
WIL MOSS – ASSOCIATE EDITOR
MATT IDELSON – EDITOR
SUPERMAN CREATED BY
JERRY SIEGEL & JOE SHUSTER

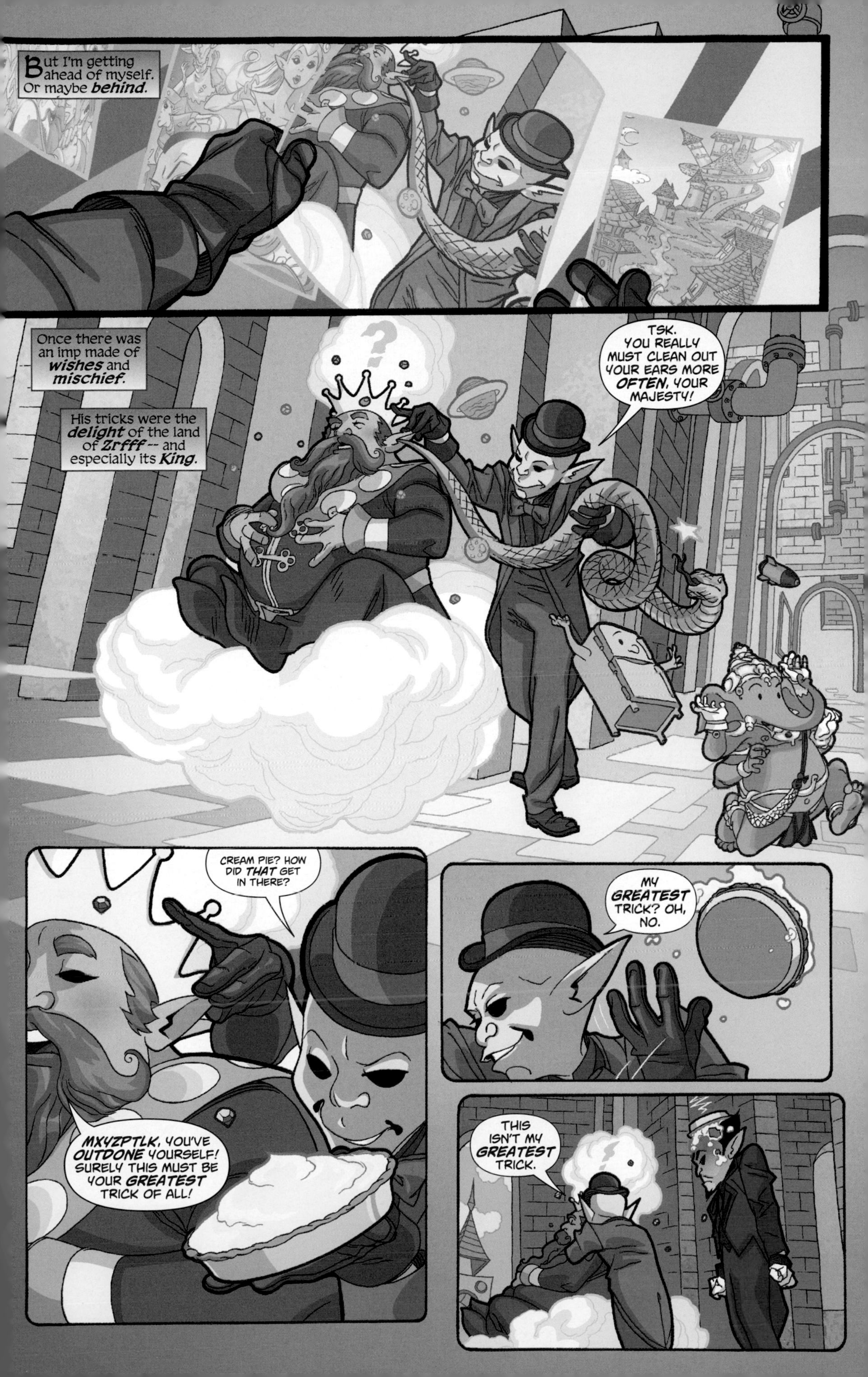
But I'm getting ahead of myself. Or maybe **behind**.
Once there was an imp made of **wishes** and **mischief**.
His tricks were the **delight** of the land of **Zrfff** -- and especially its **King**.
TSK. YOU REALLY MUST CLEAN OUT YOUR EARS MORE **OFTEN**, YOUR MAJESTY!
CREAM PIE? HOW DID **THAT** GET IN THERE?
MXYZPTLK, YOU'VE **OUTDONE** YOURSELF! SURELY THIS MUST BE YOUR **GREATEST** TRICK OF ALL!
MY **GREATEST** TRICK? OH, NO.
THIS ISN'T MY **GREATEST** TRICK.

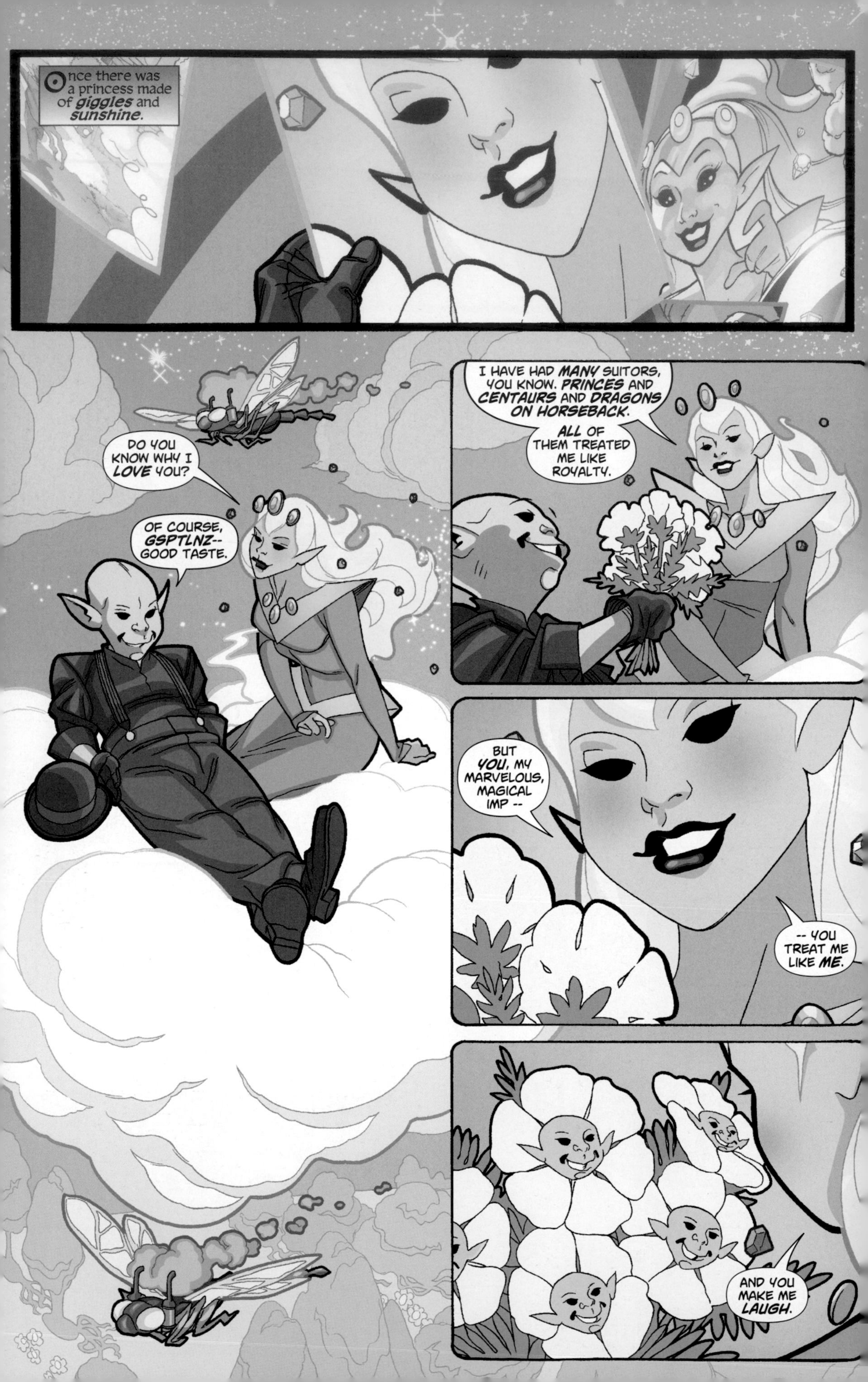
Once there was a princess made of giggles and sunshine.
DO YOU KNOW WHY I LOVE YOU?
OF COURSE, GSPTLNZ-- GOOD TASTE.
I HAVE HAD MANY SUITORS, YOU KNOW. PRINCES AND CENTAURS AND DRAGONS ON HORSEBACK.
ALL OF THEM TREATED ME LIKE ROYALTY.
BUT YOU, MY MARVELOUS, MAGICAL IMP --
-- YOU TREAT ME LIKE ME.
AND YOU MAKE ME LAUGH.

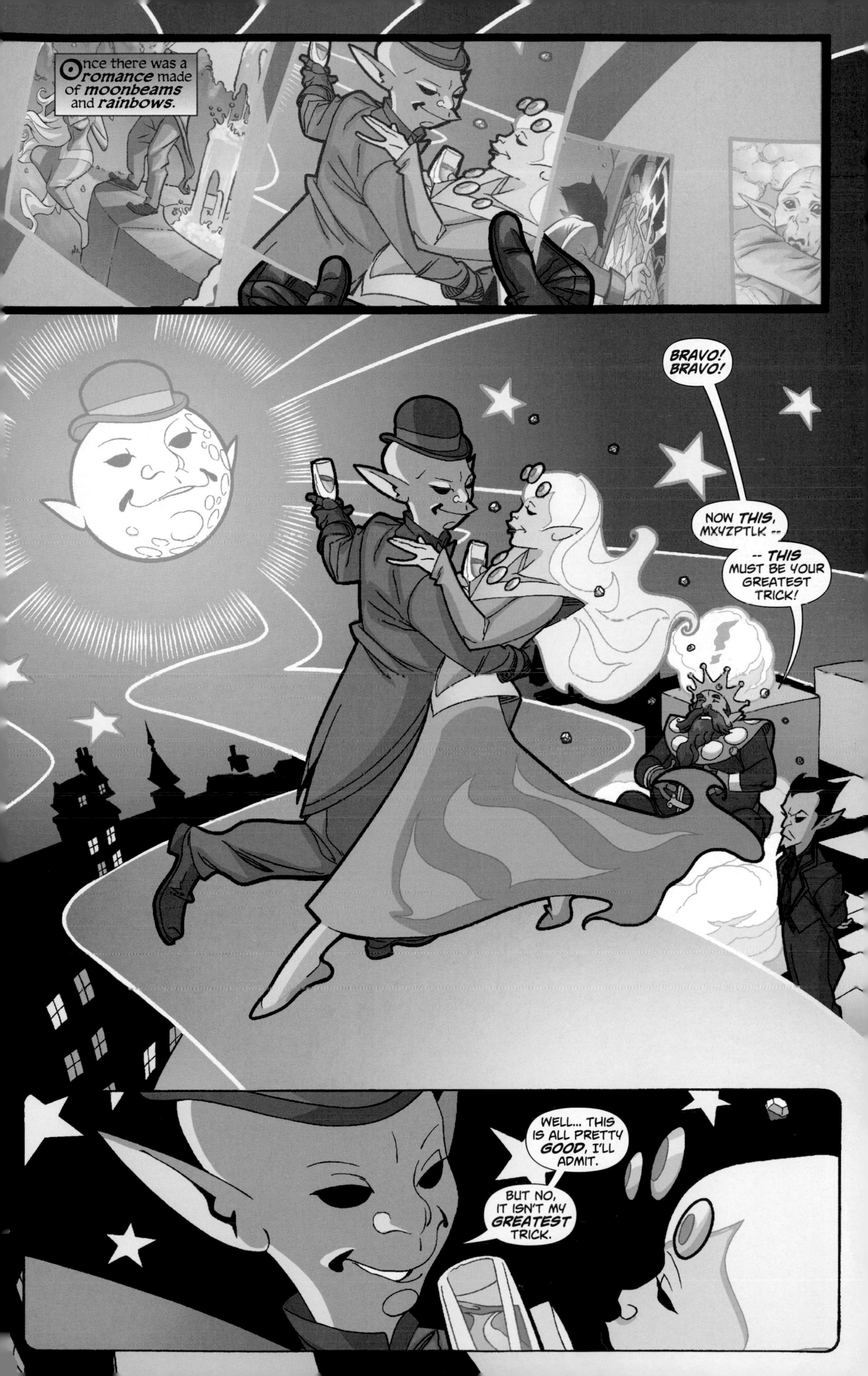
Once there was a romance made of moonbeams and rainbows.
BRAVO! BRAVO!
NOW THIS, MXYZPTLK --
-- THIS MUST BE YOUR GREATEST TRICK!
WELL... THIS IS ALL PRETTY GOOD, I'LL ADMIT.
BUT NO, IT ISN'T MY GREATEST TRICK.

Once there was a *villain* made of *spite* and *malice*.

Vyndktvx took himself so *seriously* that the imp couldn't resist giving his nose an occasional *tweak*.

Perhaps he *shouldn't* have.

The magician was determined to tear *everything* away from the imp. His *love* --

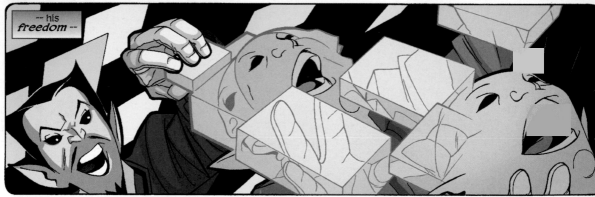

-- his *freedom* --

-- and even his *greatest trick*.

But the joke was on the villain. Because the Man of Steel was the imp's *favorite* trick --

-- not his *greatest*

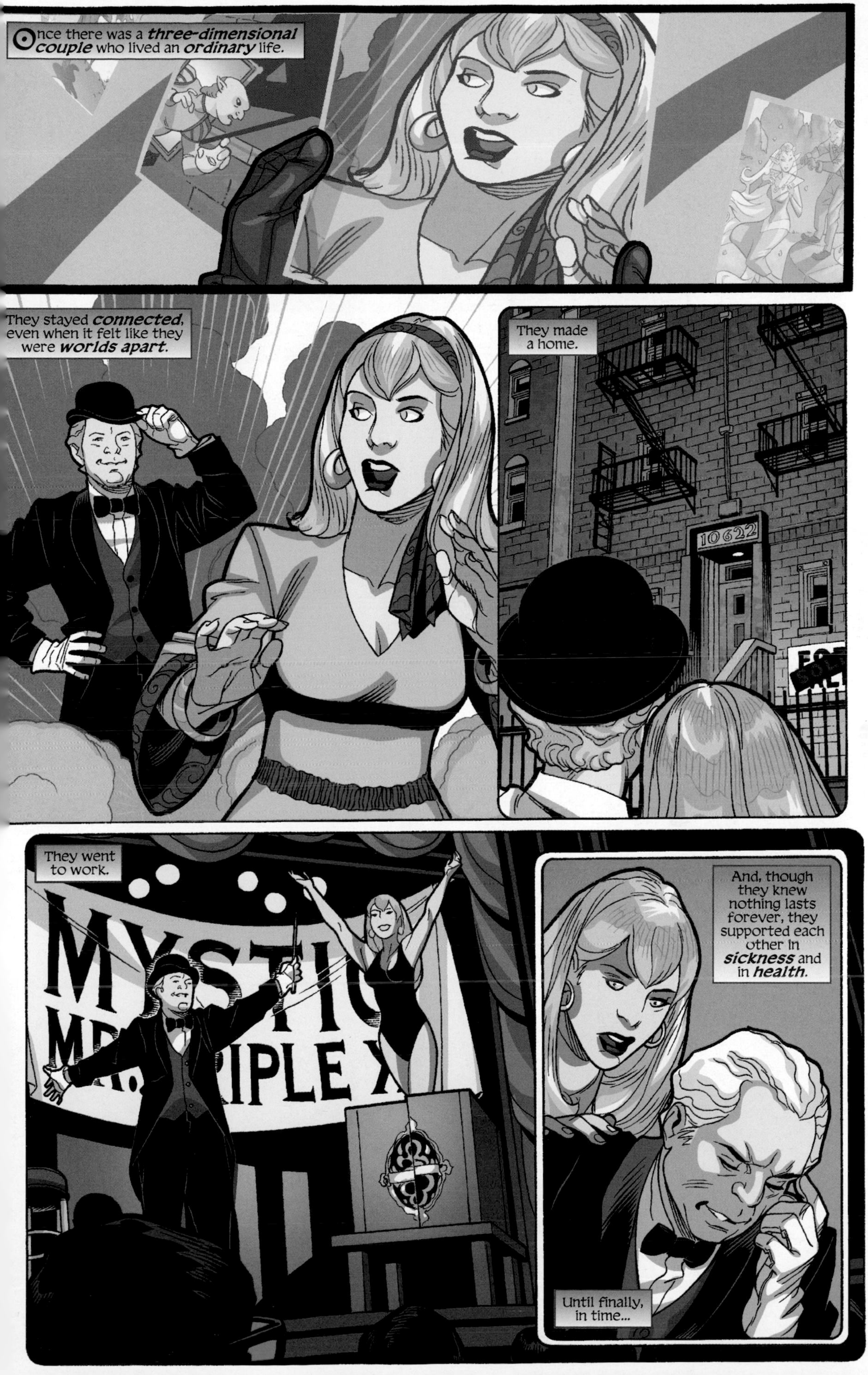
Once there was a *three-dimensional couple* who lived an *ordinary* life.
They stayed *connected*, even when it felt like they were *worlds apart*.
They made a home.
10622
They went to work.
MYSTIC
And, though they knew nothing lasts forever, they supported each other in *sickness* and in *health*.
Until finally, in time...

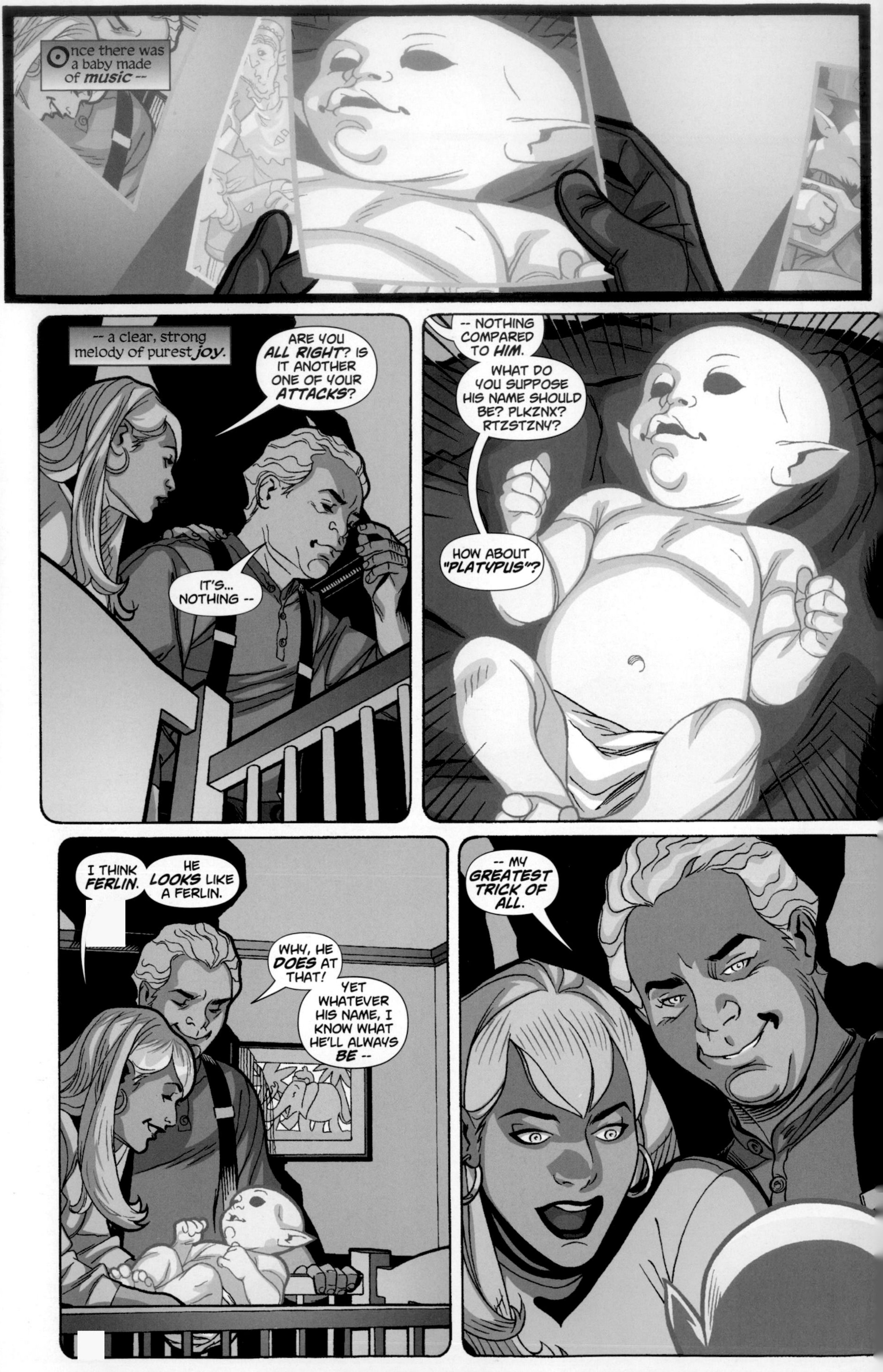
Once there was a baby made of music --
-- a clear, strong melody of purest joy.
ARE YOU ALL RIGHT? IS IT ANOTHER ONE OF YOUR ATTACKS?
IT'S... NOTHING --
-- NOTHING COMPARED TO HIM.
WHAT DO YOU SUPPOSE HIS NAME SHOULD BE? PLKZNX? RTZSTZNY?
HOW ABOUT "PLATYPUS"?
I THINK FERLIN.
HE LOOKS LIKE A FERLIN.
WHY, HE DOES AT THAT!
YET WHATEVER HIS NAME, I KNOW WHAT HE'LL ALWAYS BE --
-- MY GREATEST TRICK OF ALL.

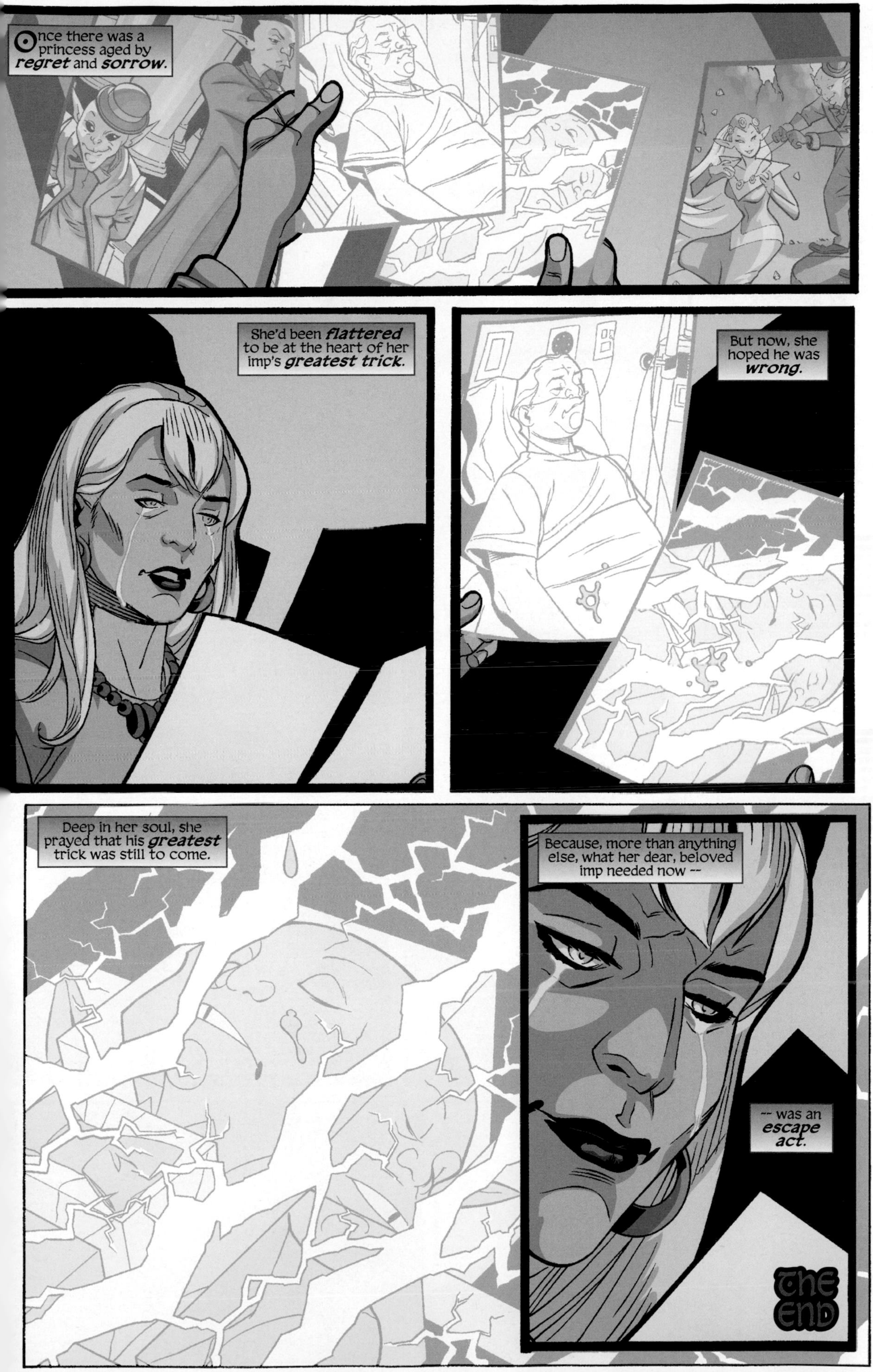
Once there was a princess aged by regret and sorrow.
She'd been flattered to be at the heart of her imp's greatest trick.
But now, she hoped he was wrong.
Deep in her soul, she prayed that his greatest trick was still to come.
Because, more than anything else, what her dear, beloved imp needed now --
-- was an escape act.
THE END

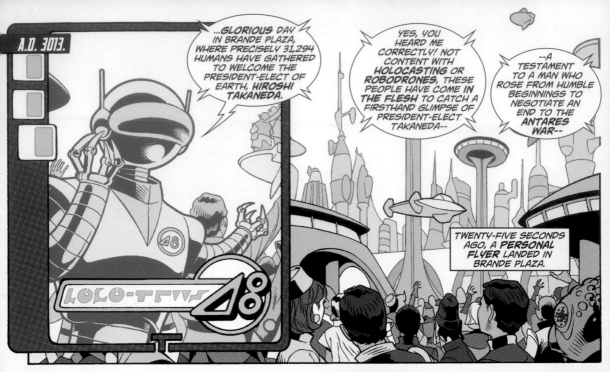

A.D. 3013.

...GLORIOUS DAY IN BRANDE PLAZA, WHERE PRECISELY 31,294 HUMANS HAVE GATHERED TO WELCOME THE PRESIDENT-ELECT OF EARTH, HIROSHI TAKANEDA.

YES, YOU HEARD ME CORRECTLY! NOT CONTENT WITH *HOLOCASTING* OR *ROBODRONES*, THESE PEOPLE HAVE COME IN *THE FLESH* TO CATCH A FIRSTHAND GLIMPSE OF PRESIDENT-ELECT TAKANEDA--

--A TESTAMENT TO A MAN WHO ROSE FROM HUMBLE BEGINNINGS TO NEGOTIATE AN END TO THE *ANTARES WAR*--

TWENTY-FIVE SECONDS AGO, A *PERSONAL FLYER* LANDED IN BRANDE PLAZA.

--AND WHOM THE LATEST *COMPUMODELS* PROJECT AS 86 PERCENT LIKELY TO BECOME THE NEXT LEADER OF THE *UNITED PLANETS.*

SEVEN YEARS FROM NOW, THE EARTH IS UNDER *MARTIAL LAW.*

EVEN THE LEGENDARY *LEGION OF SUPER-HEROES* HAS TURNED OUT FOR PRESIDENT-ELECT TAKANEDA!

WE'RE BEING *WASTED* AT THIS RALLY. SURELY THE SCIENCE POLICE CAN HANDLE SECURITY ON THEIR OWN.

THEY ASKED FOR OUR *HELP.* BESIDES, I WANT TO SEE TAKANEDA TOO!

GUYS, *PLEASE!* IT'S HARD ENOUGH SCANNING THOUSANDS OF MINDS FOR THREATS WITHOUT *DISTRACTIONS.*

NINE YEARS FROM NOW, WORLDS BEGIN TO *SECEDE* FROM THE UNITED PLANETS. HALF THE UNIVERSE SINKS INTO *GENOCIDE.*

AND HERE COMES THE PRESIDENT-ELECT...

THREE-POINT-FIVE MINUTES FROM NOW, THERE IS *DEATH.*

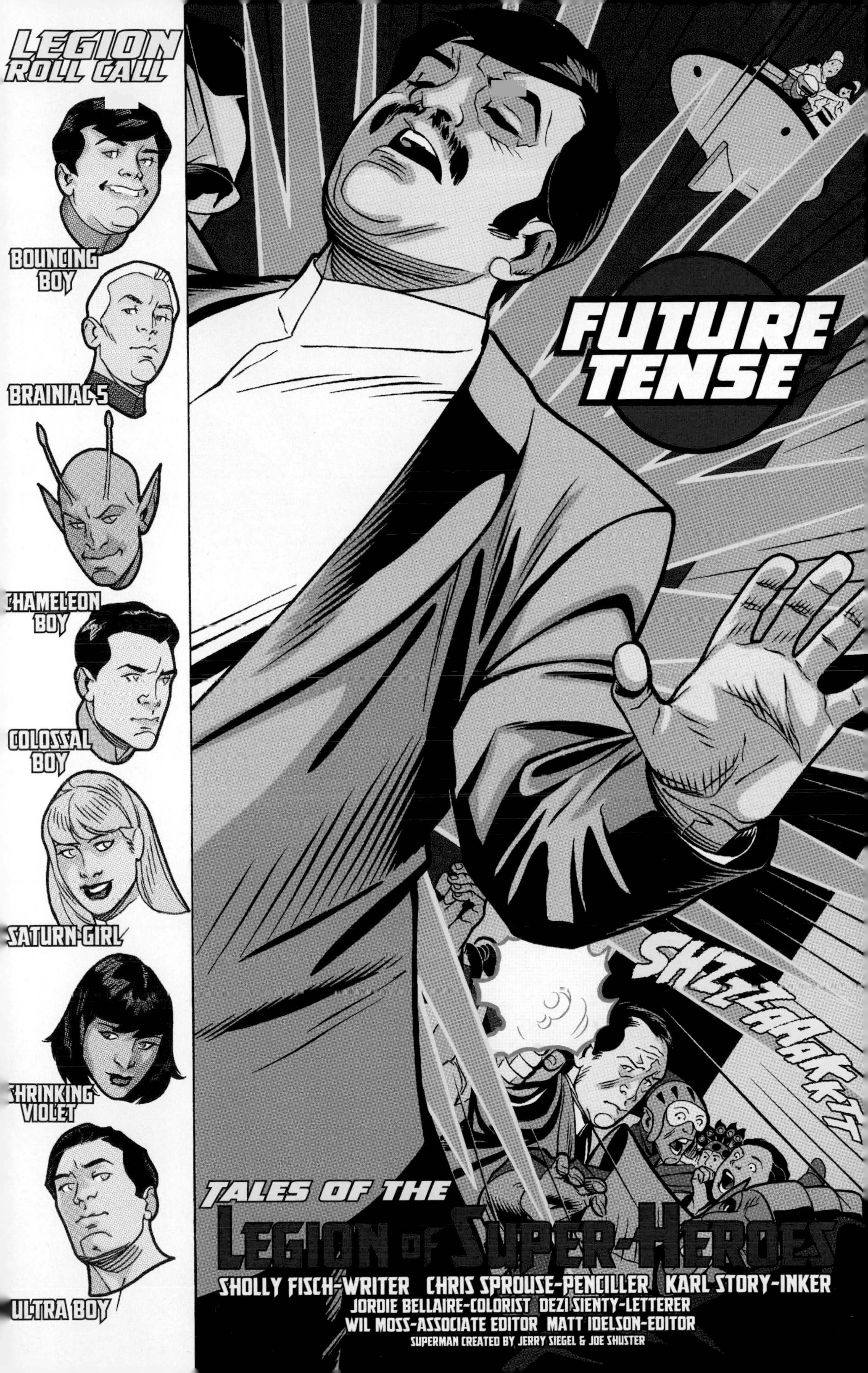
LEGION ROLL CALL
BOUNCING BOY
BRAINIAC 5
CHAMELEON BOY
COLOSSAL BOY
SATURN GIRL
SHRINKING VIOLET
ULTRA BOY
FUTURE TENSE
SHZZZAAAKKT
TALES OF THE LEGION OF SUPER-HEROES
SHOLLY FISCH-WRITER CHRIS SPROUSE-PENCILLER KARL STORY-INKER
JORDIE BELLAIRE-COLORIST DEZI SIENTY-LETTERER
WIL MOSS-ASSOCIATE EDITOR MATT IDELSON-EDITOR
SUPERMAN CREATED BY JERRY SIEGEL & JOE SHUSTER

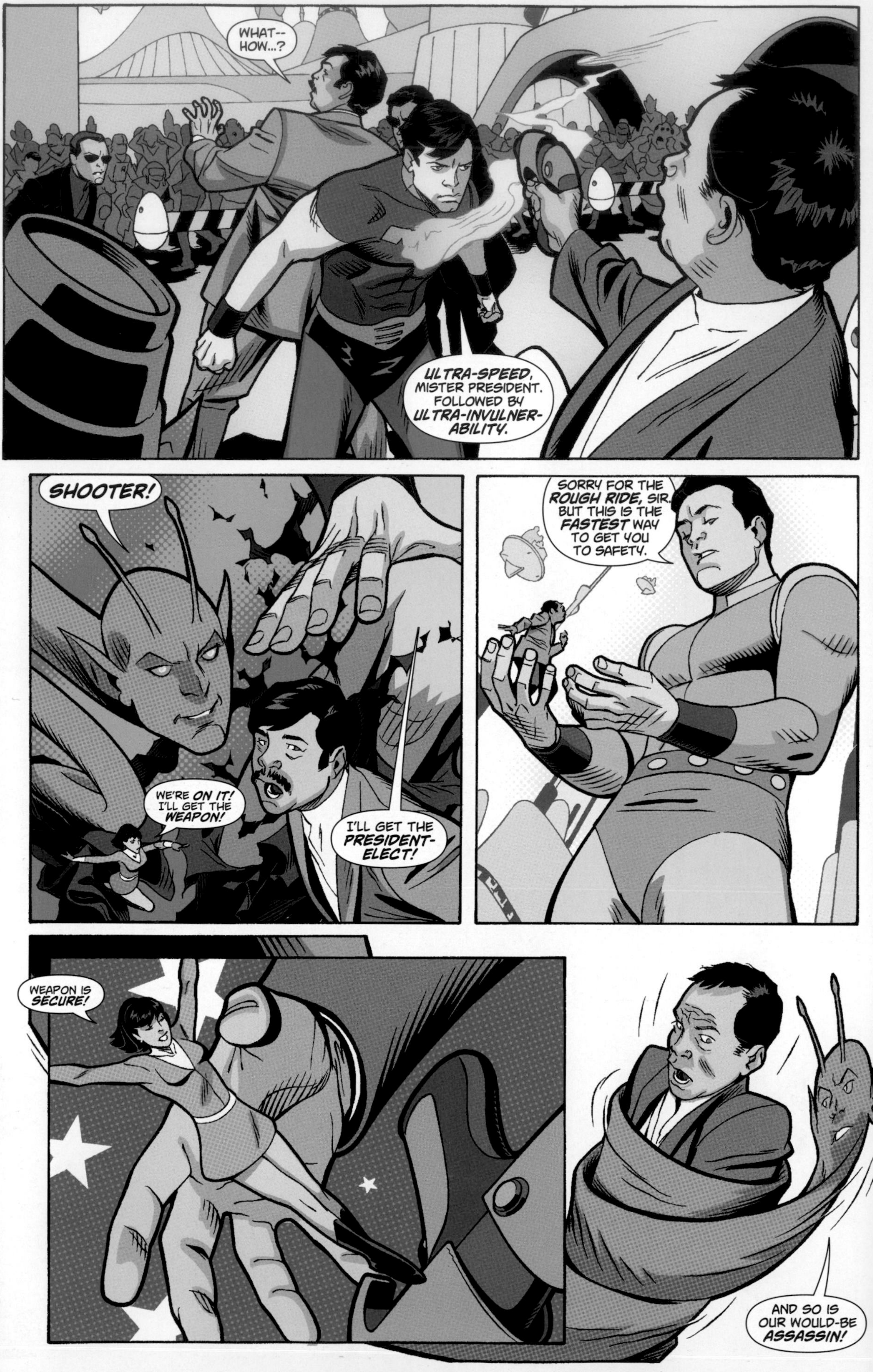
WHAT-- HOW...?
ULTRA-SPEED, MISTER PRESIDENT. FOLLOWED BY ULTRA-INVULNER-ABILITY.
SHOOTER!
WE'RE ON IT! I'LL GET THE WEAPON!
I'LL GET THE PRESIDENT-ELECT!
SORRY FOR THE ROUGH RIDE, SIR. BUT THIS IS THE FASTEST WAY TO GET YOU TO SAFETY.
WEAPON IS SECURE!
AND SO IS OUR WOULD-BE ASSASSIN!

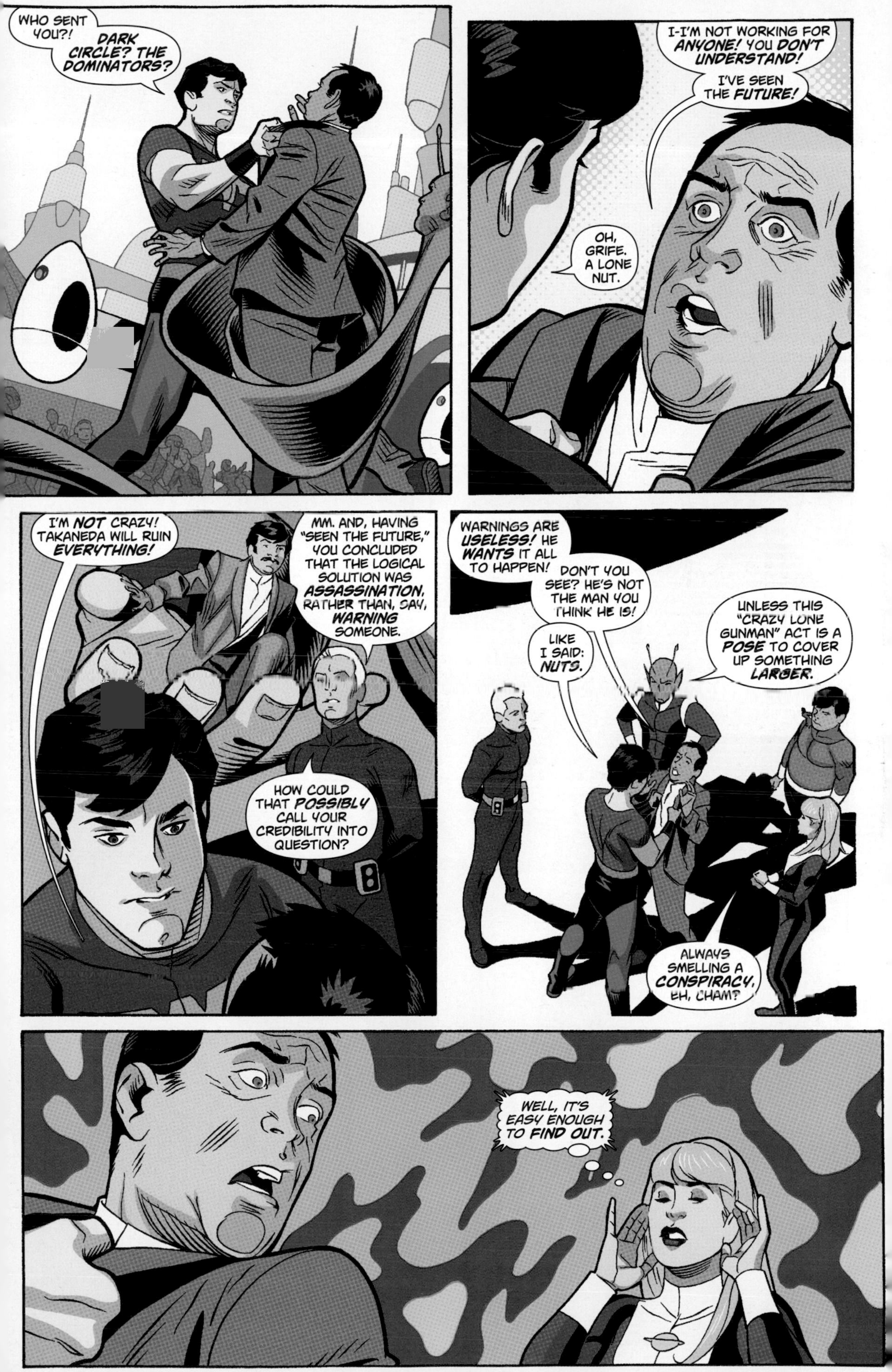
WHO SENT YOU?!
DARK CIRCLE? THE DOMINATORS?
I-I'M NOT WORKING FOR ANYONE! YOU DON'T UNDERSTAND!
I'VE SEEN THE FUTURE!
OH, GRIFE. A LONE NUT.
I'M NOT CRAZY! TAKANEDA WILL RUIN EVERYTHING!
MM. AND, HAVING "SEEN THE FUTURE," YOU CONCLUDED THAT THE LOGICAL SOLUTION WAS ASSASSINATION, RATHER THAN, SAY, WARNING SOMEONE.
HOW COULD THAT POSSIBLY CALL YOUR CREDIBILITY INTO QUESTION?
WARNINGS ARE USELESS! HE WANTS IT ALL TO HAPPEN!
DON'T YOU SEE? HE'S NOT THE MAN YOU THINK HE IS!
LIKE I SAID: NUTS.
UNLESS THIS "CRAZY LONE GUNMAN" ACT IS A POSE TO COVER UP SOMETHING LARGER.
ALWAYS SMELLING A CONSPIRACY, EH, CHAM?
WELL, IT'S EASY ENOUGH TO FIND OUT.

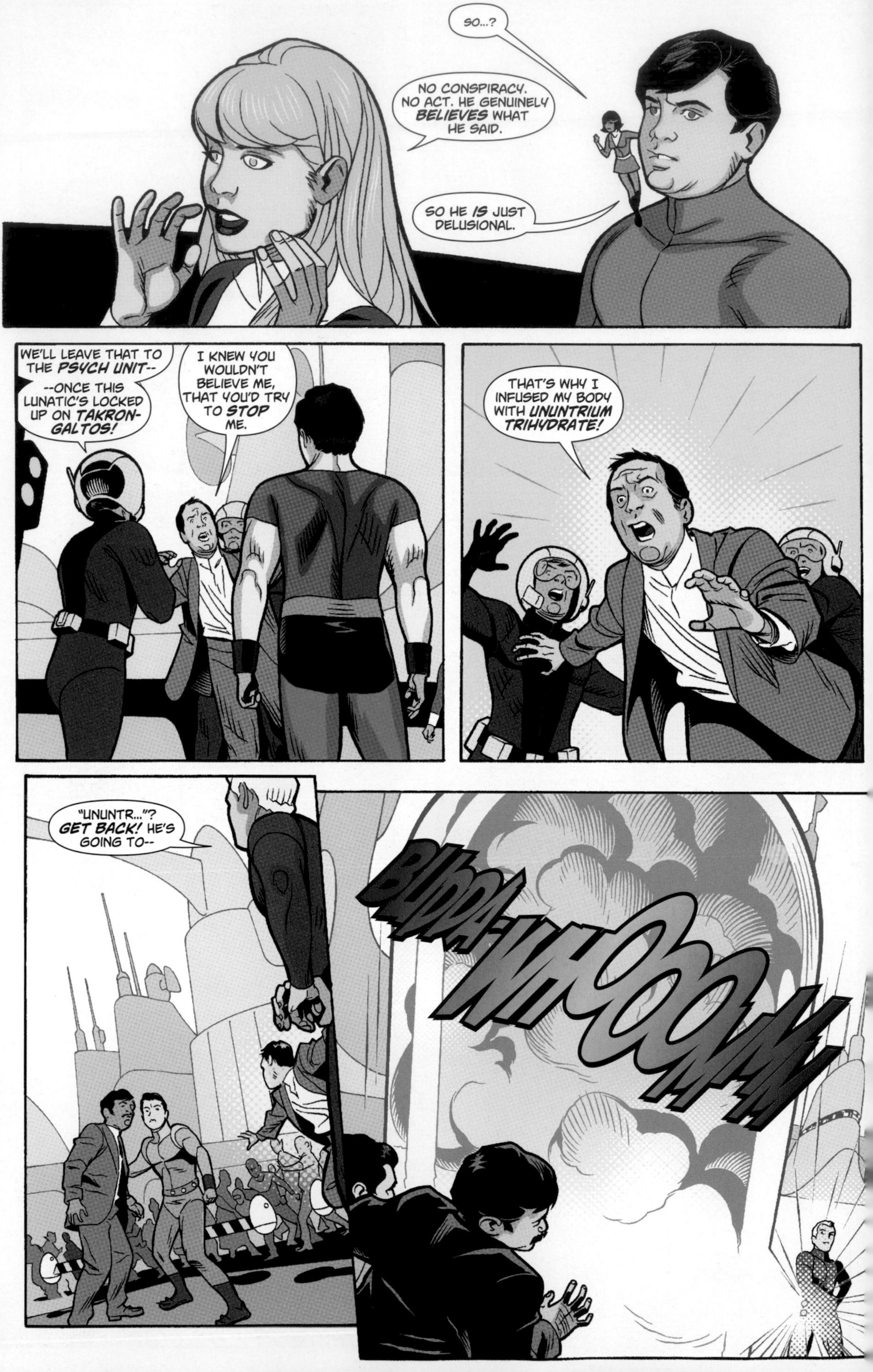
SO...?
NO CONSPIRACY. NO ACT. HE GENUINELY BELIEVES WHAT HE SAID.
SO HE IS JUST DELUSIONAL.
WE'LL LEAVE THAT TO THE PSYCH UNIT--
--ONCE THIS LUNATIC'S LOCKED UP ON TAKRON-GALTOS!
I KNEW YOU WOULDN'T BELIEVE ME, THAT YOU'D TRY TO STOP ME.
THAT'S WHY I INFUSED MY BODY WITH UNUNTRIUM TRIHYDRATE!
"UNUNTR..."? GET BACK! HE'S GOING TO--
BUDDA-WHOOOM

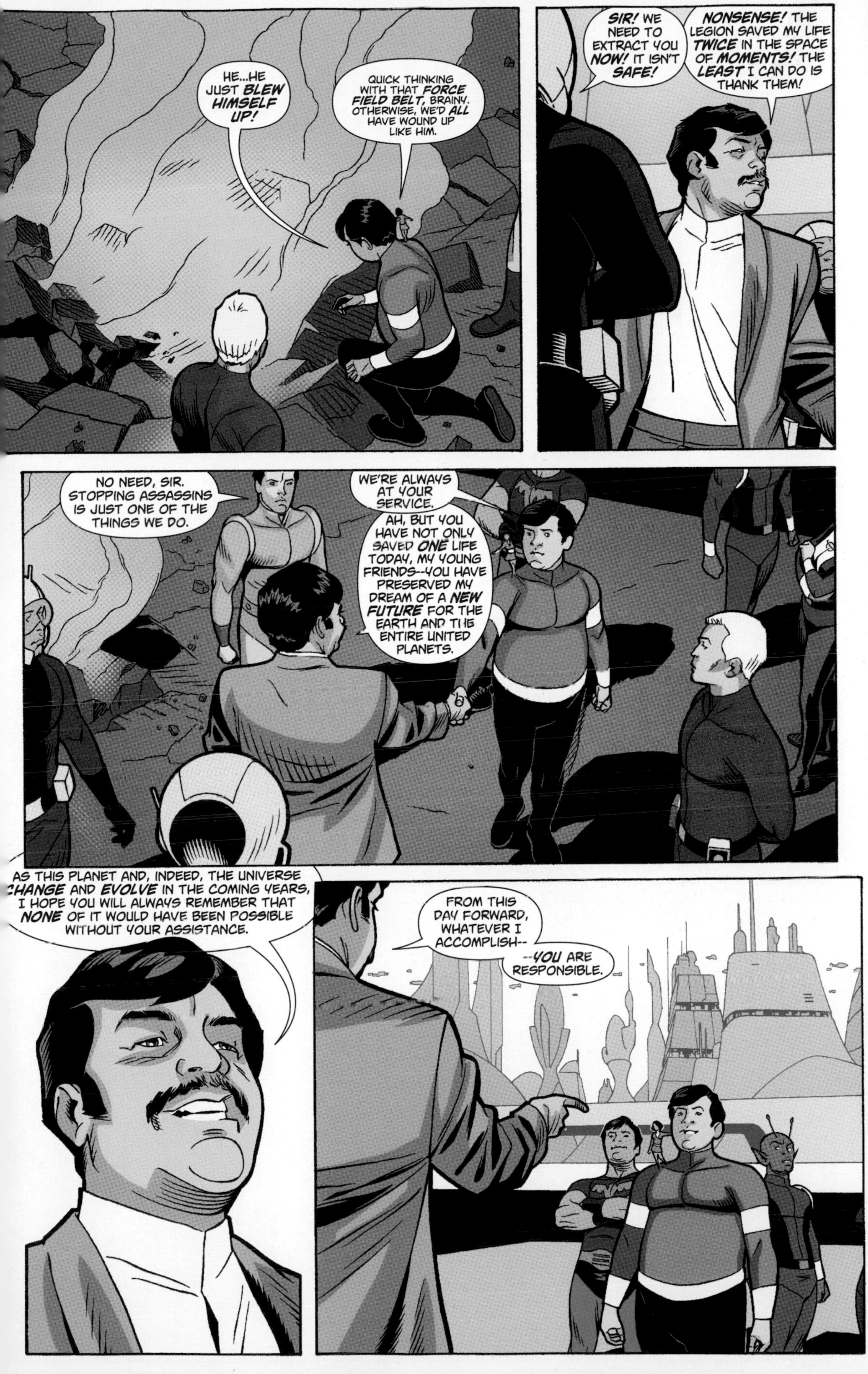
HE...HE JUST BLEW HIMSELF UP!
QUICK THINKING WITH THAT FORCE FIELD BELT, BRAINY. OTHERWISE, WE'D ALL HAVE WOUND UP LIKE HIM.
SIR! WE NEED TO EXTRACT YOU NOW! IT ISN'T SAFE!
NONSENSE! THE LEGION SAVED MY LIFE TWICE IN THE SPACE OF MOMENTS! THE LEAST I CAN DO IS THANK THEM!
NO NEED, SIR. STOPPING ASSASSINS IS JUST ONE OF THE THINGS WE DO.
WE'RE ALWAYS AT YOUR SERVICE.
AH, BUT YOU HAVE NOT ONLY SAVED ONE LIFE TODAY, MY YOUNG FRIENDS--YOU HAVE PRESERVED MY DREAM OF A NEW FUTURE FOR THE EARTH AND THE ENTIRE UNITED PLANETS.
AS THIS PLANET AND, INDEED, THE UNIVERSE CHANGE AND EVOLVE IN THE COMING YEARS, I HOPE YOU WILL ALWAYS REMEMBER THAT NONE OF IT WOULD HAVE BEEN POSSIBLE WITHOUT YOUR ASSISTANCE.
FROM THIS DAY FORWARD, WHATEVER I ACCOMPLISH--
--YOU ARE RESPONSIBLE.

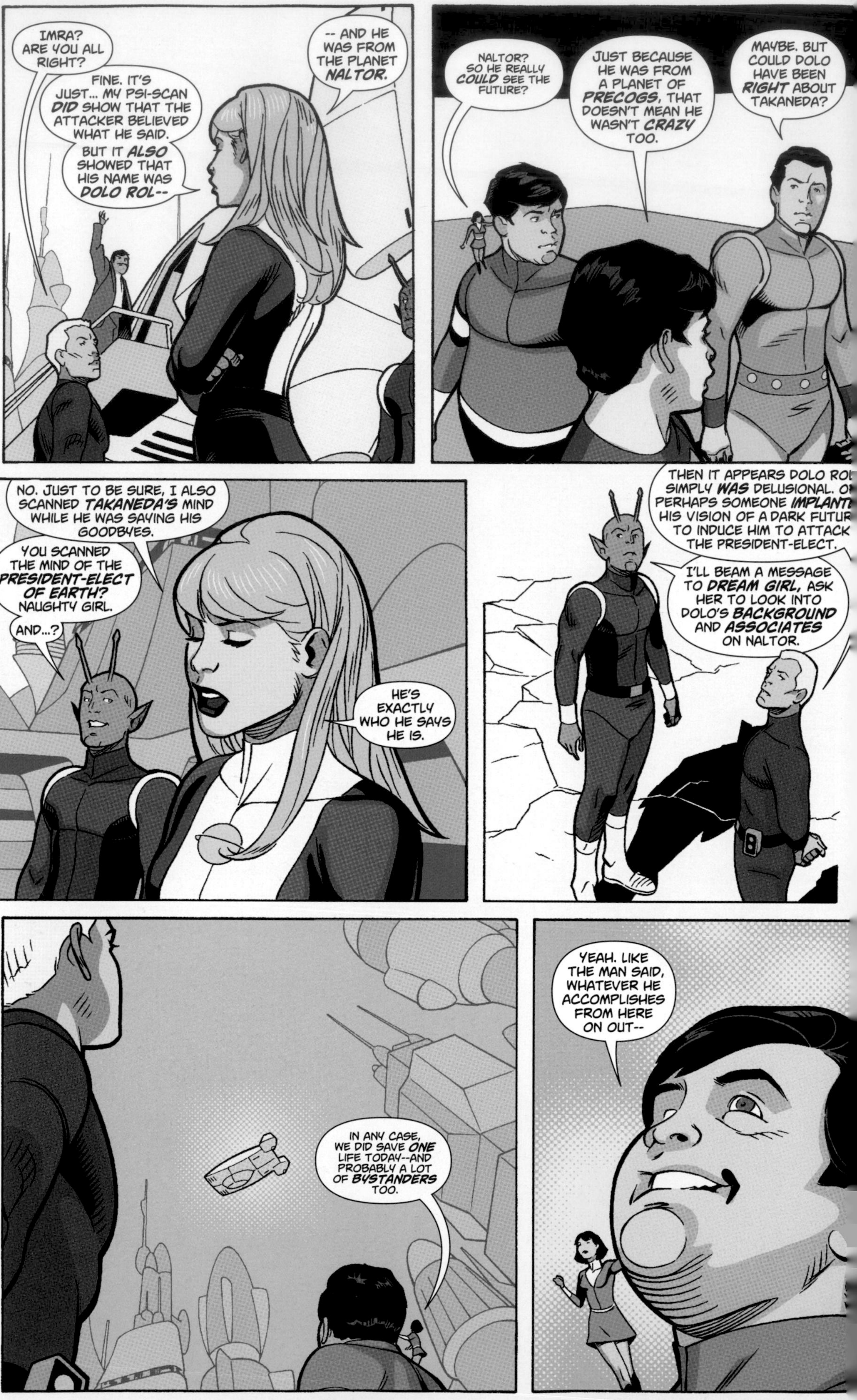
IMRA? ARE YOU ALL RIGHT?
FINE. IT'S JUST... MY PSI-SCAN DID SHOW THAT THE ATTACKER BELIEVED WHAT HE SAID.
BUT IT ALSO SHOWED THAT HIS NAME WAS DOLO ROL--
-- AND HE WAS FROM THE PLANET NALTOR.
NALTOR? SO HE REALLY COULD SEE THE FUTURE?
JUST BECAUSE HE WAS FROM A PLANET OF PRECOGS, THAT DOESN'T MEAN HE WASN'T CRAZY TOO.
MAYBE. BUT COULD DOLO HAVE BEEN RIGHT ABOUT TAKANEDA?
NO. JUST TO BE SURE, I ALSO SCANNED TAKANEDA'S MIND WHILE HE WAS SAYING HIS GOODBYES.
YOU SCANNED THE MIND OF THE PRESIDENT-ELECT OF EARTH? NAUGHTY GIRL.
AND...?
HE'S EXACTLY WHO HE SAYS HE IS.
THEN IT APPEARS DOLO ROL SIMPLY WAS DELUSIONAL. OR PERHAPS SOMEONE IMPLANTED HIS VISION OF A DARK FUTURE TO INDUCE HIM TO ATTACK THE PRESIDENT-ELECT.
I'LL BEAM A MESSAGE TO DREAM GIRL, ASK HER TO LOOK INTO DOLO'S BACKGROUND AND ASSOCIATES ON NALTOR.
IN ANY CASE, WE DID SAVE ONE LIFE TODAY--AND PROBABLY A LOT OF BYSTANDERS TOO.
YEAH. LIKE THE MAN SAID, WHATEVER HE ACCOMPLISHES FROM HERE ON OUT--

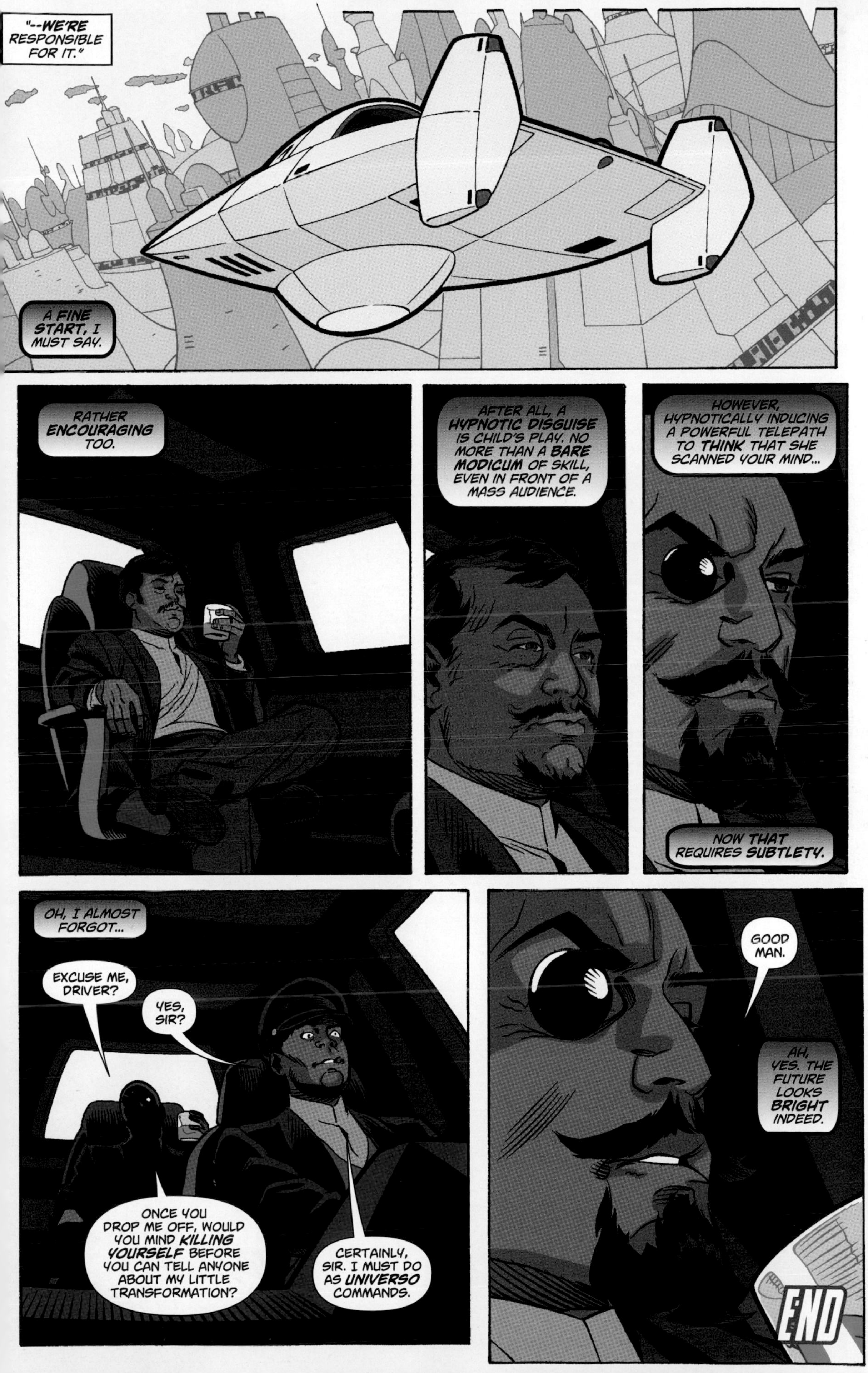
"--WE'RE RESPONSIBLE FOR IT."
A FINE START, I MUST SAY.
RATHER ENCOURAGING TOO.
AFTER ALL, A HYPNOTIC DISGUISE IS CHILD'S PLAY. NO MORE THAN A BARE MODICUM OF SKILL, EVEN IN FRONT OF A MASS AUDIENCE.
HOWEVER, HYPNOTICALLY INDUCING A POWERFUL TELEPATH TO THINK THAT SHE SCANNED YOUR MIND...
NOW THAT REQUIRES SUBTLETY.
OH, I ALMOST FORGOT...
EXCUSE ME, DRIVER?
YES, SIR?
ONCE YOU DROP ME OFF, WOULD YOU MIND KILLING YOURSELF BEFORE YOU CAN TELL ANYONE ABOUT MY LITTLE TRANSFORMATION?
CERTAINLY, SIR. I MUST DO AS UNIVERSO COMMANDS.
GOOD MAN.
AH, YES. THE FUTURE LOOKS BRIGHT INDEED.
END

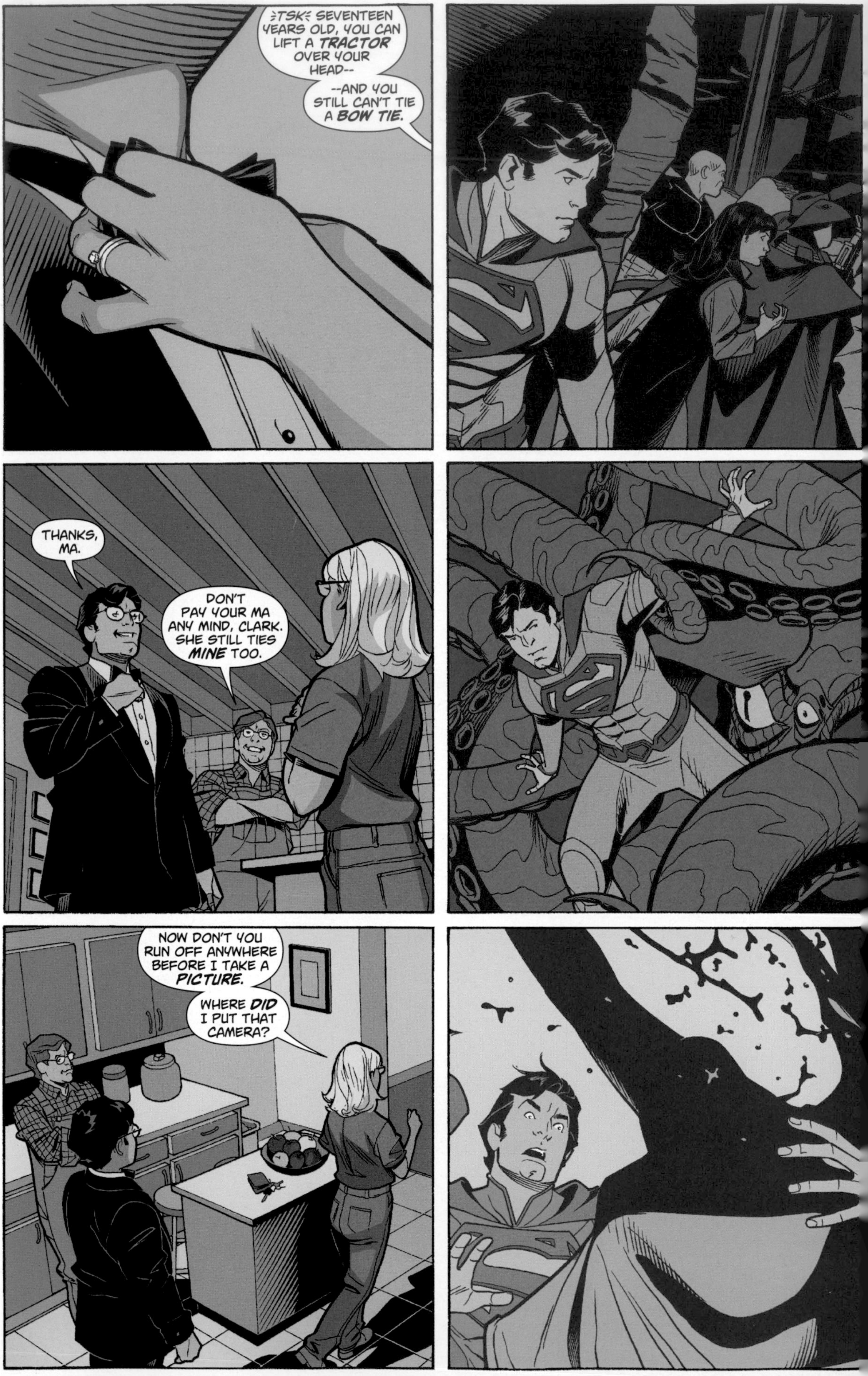

TSK SEVENTEEN YEARS OLD, YOU CAN LIFT A TRACTOR OVER YOUR HEAD--
--AND YOU STILL CAN'T TIE A BOW TIE.
THANKS, MA.
DON'T PAY YOUR MA ANY MIND, CLARK. SHE STILL TIES MINE TOO.
NOW DON'T YOU RUN OFF ANYWHERE BEFORE I TAKE A PICTURE.
WHERE DID I PUT THAT CAMERA?

SENIOR PROM. GUESS THAT MEANS *GRADUATION'S* RIGHT AROUND THE CORNER.

WON'T BE LONG NOW BEFORE YOU'RE OFF MAKING YOUR OWN WAY IN THE WORLD.

PRETTY EXCITING.

YEAH.

I GUESS.

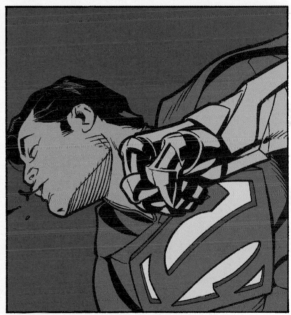

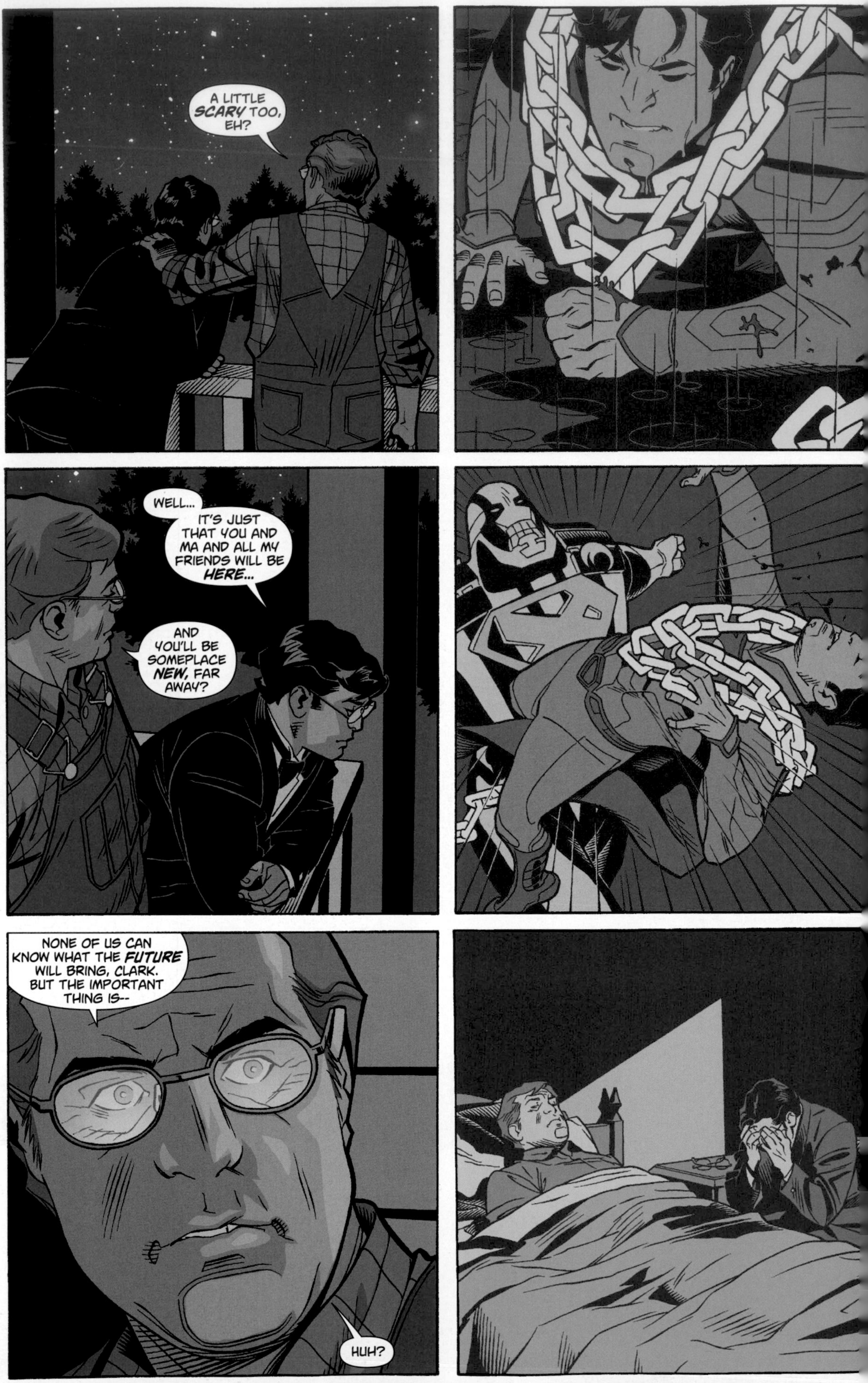
A LITTLE SCARY TOO, EH?
WELL... IT'S JUST THAT YOU AND MA AND ALL MY FRIENDS WILL BE HERE...
AND YOU'LL BE SOMEPLACE NEW, FAR AWAY?
NONE OF US CAN KNOW WHAT THE FUTURE WILL BRING, CLARK. BUT THE IMPORTANT THING IS--
HUH?

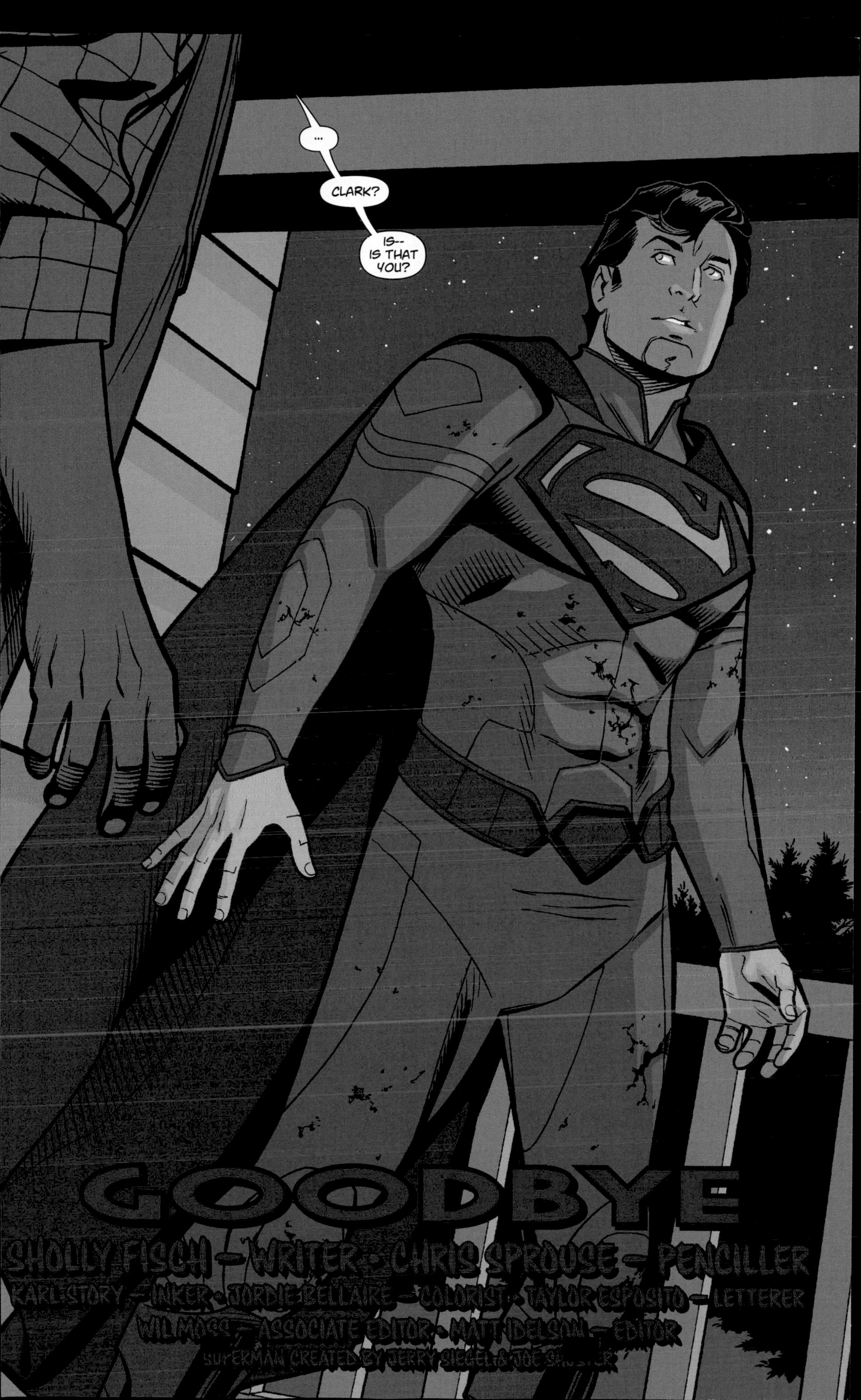
...
CLARK?
IS-- IS THAT YOU?
GOODBYE
SHOLLY FISCH - WRITER • CHRIS SPROUSE - PENCILLER
KARL STORY - INKER • JORDIE BELLAIRE - COLORIST • TAYLOR ESPOSITO - LETTERER
WIL MOSS - ASSOCIATE EDITOR • MATT IDELSON - EDITOR
SUPERMAN CREATED BY JERRY SIEGEL & JOE

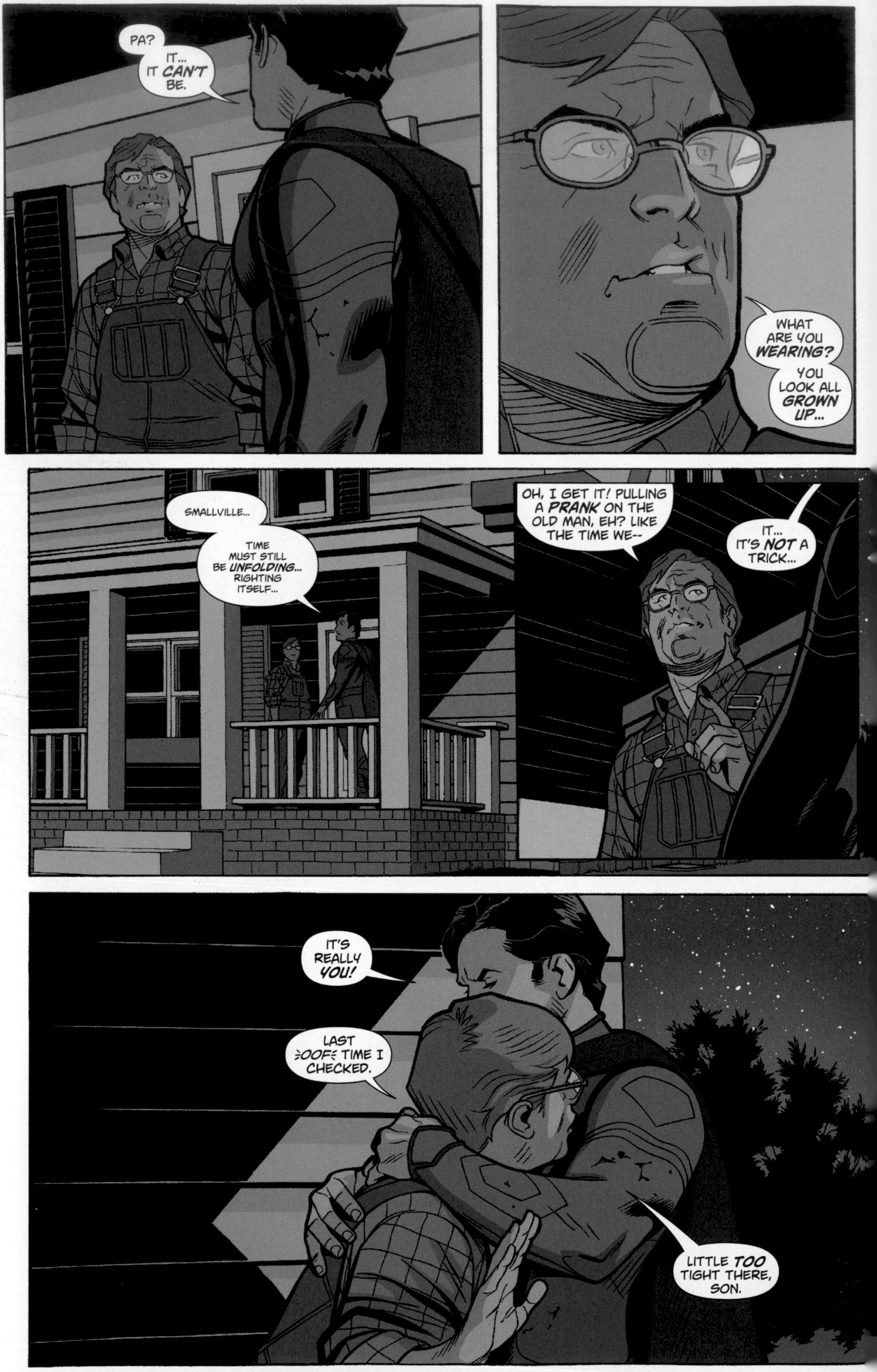
PA?
IT... IT CAN'T BE.
WHAT ARE YOU WEARING?
YOU LOOK ALL GROWN UP...
SMALLVILLE...
TIME MUST STILL BE UNFOLDING... RIGHTING ITSELF...
OH, I GET IT! PULLING A PRANK ON THE OLD MAN, EH? LIKE THE TIME WE--
IT... IT'S NOT A TRICK...
IT'S REALLY YOU!
LAST ≶OOF≷ TIME I CHECKED.
LITTLE TOO TIGHT THERE, SON.

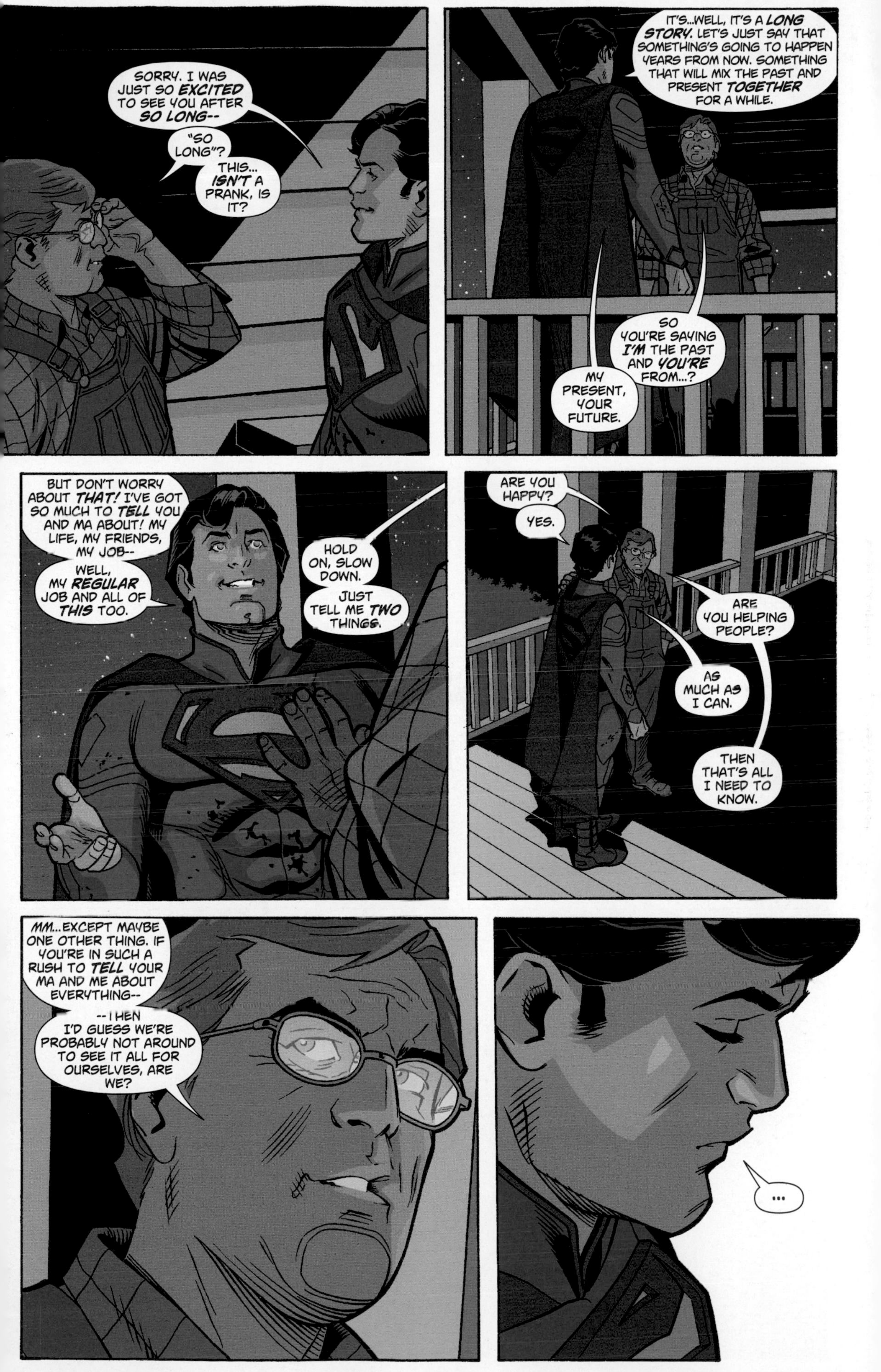
SORRY. I WAS JUST SO EXCITED TO SEE YOU AFTER SO LONG--
"SO LONG"? THIS... ISN'T A PRANK, IS IT?
IT'S...WELL, IT'S A LONG STORY. LET'S JUST SAY THAT SOMETHING'S GOING TO HAPPEN YEARS FROM NOW. SOMETHING THAT WILL MIX THE PAST AND PRESENT TOGETHER FOR A WHILE.
SO YOU'RE SAYING I'M THE PAST AND YOU'RE FROM...?
MY PRESENT, YOUR FUTURE.
BUT DON'T WORRY ABOUT THAT! I'VE GOT SO MUCH TO TELL YOU AND MA ABOUT! MY LIFE, MY FRIENDS, MY JOB--
WELL, MY REGULAR JOB AND ALL OF THIS TOO.
HOLD ON, SLOW DOWN.
JUST TELL ME TWO THINGS.
ARE YOU HAPPY?
YES.
ARE YOU HELPING PEOPLE?
AS MUCH AS I CAN.
THEN THAT'S ALL I NEED TO KNOW.
MM...EXCEPT MAYBE ONE OTHER THING. IF YOU'RE IN SUCH A RUSH TO TELL YOUR MA AND ME ABOUT EVERYTHING--
--THEN I'D GUESS WE'RE PROBABLY NOT AROUND TO SEE IT ALL FOR OURSELVES, ARE WE?
...

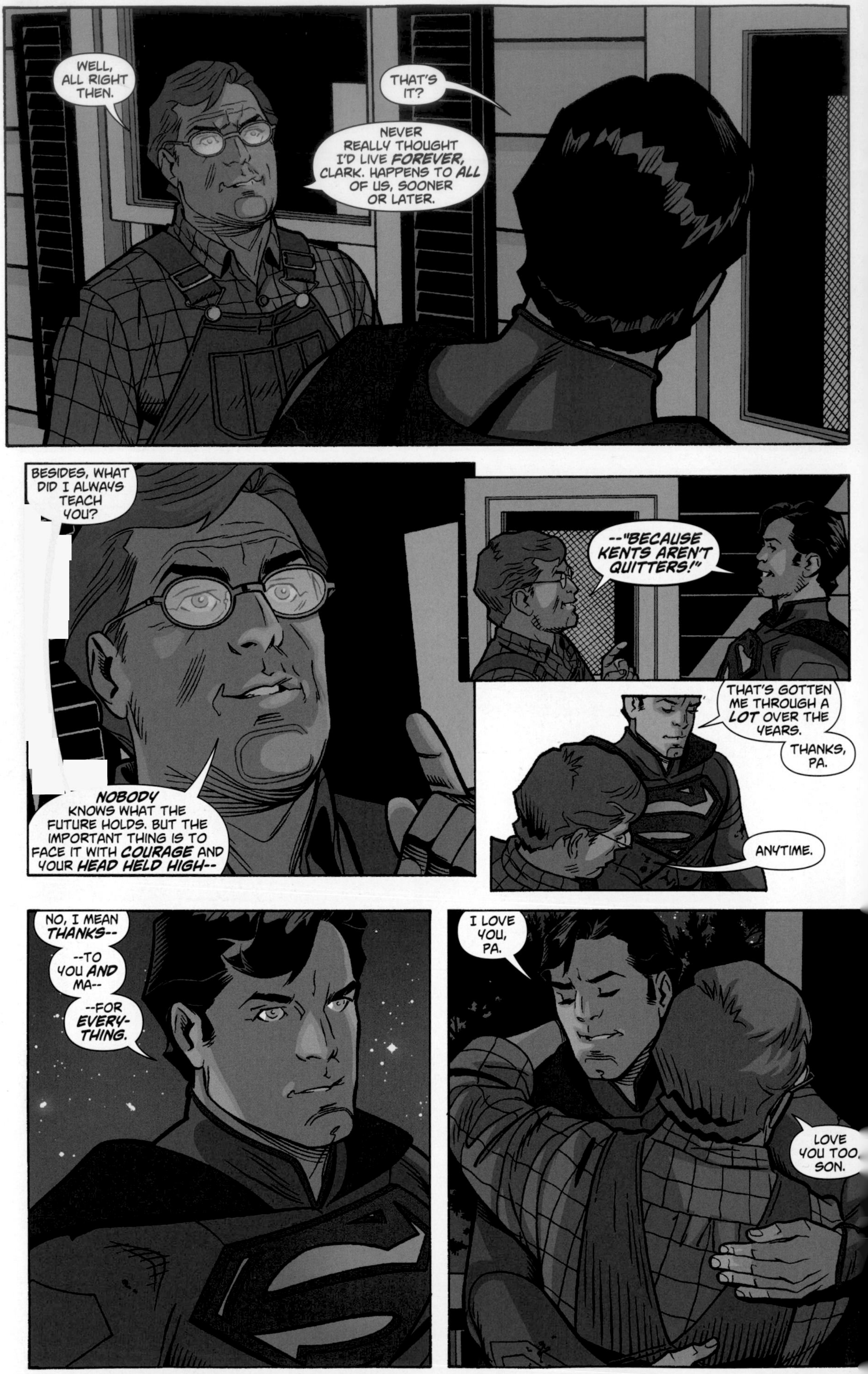
WELL, ALL RIGHT THEN.
THAT'S IT?
NEVER REALLY THOUGHT I'D LIVE FOREVER, CLARK. HAPPENS TO ALL OF US, SOONER OR LATER.
BESIDES, WHAT DID I ALWAYS TEACH YOU?
NOBODY KNOWS WHAT THE FUTURE HOLDS. BUT THE IMPORTANT THING IS TO FACE IT WITH COURAGE AND YOUR HEAD HELD HIGH--
--"BECAUSE KENTS AREN'T QUITTERS!"
THAT'S GOTTEN ME THROUGH A LOT OVER THE YEARS.
THANKS, PA.
ANYTIME.
NO, I MEAN THANKS--
--TO YOU AND MA--
--FOR EVERY-THING.
I LOVE YOU, PA.
LOVE YOU TOO, SON.

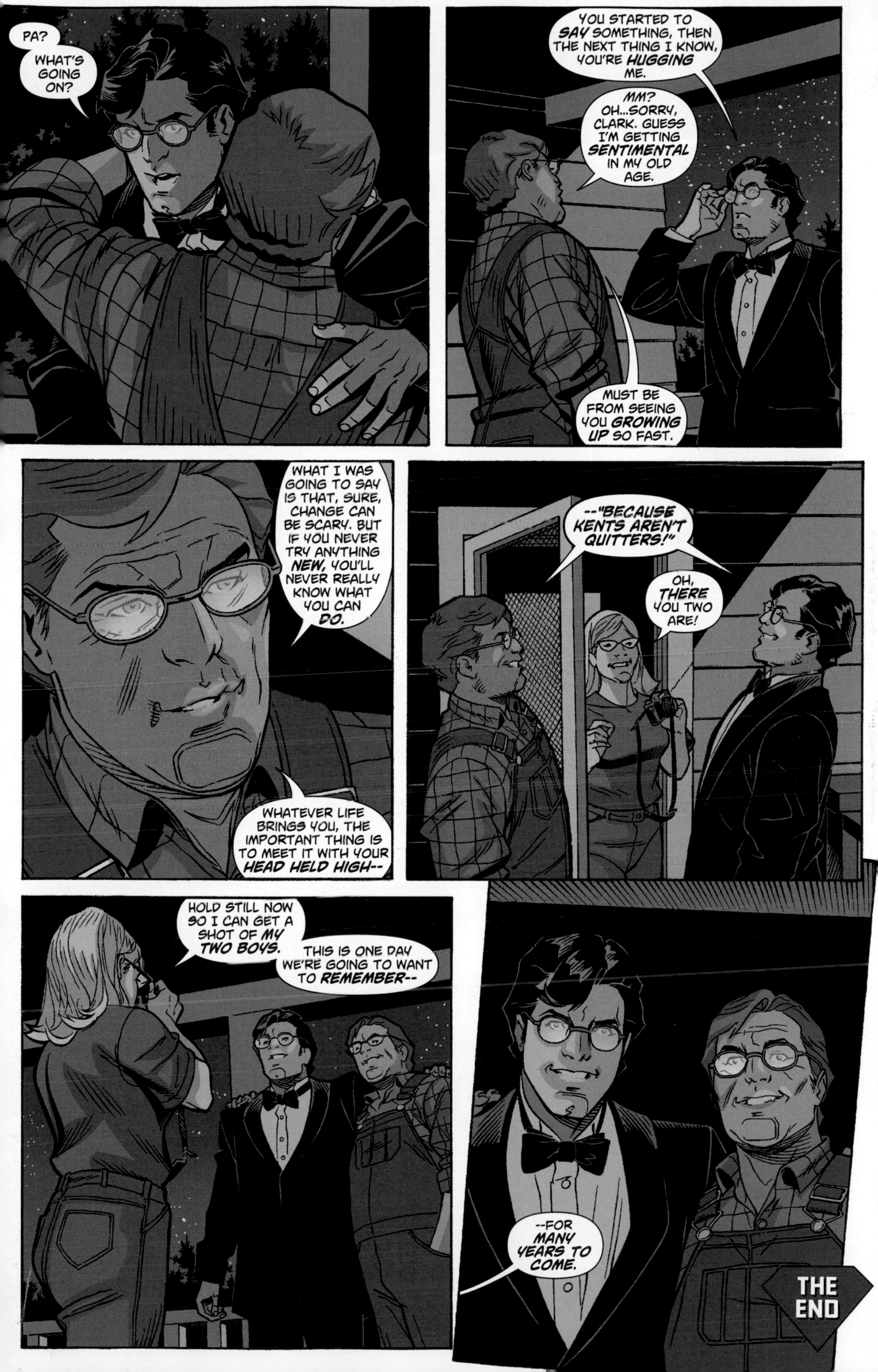
PA?
WHAT'S GOING ON?
YOU STARTED TO SAY SOMETHING, THEN THE NEXT THING I KNOW, YOU'RE HUGGING ME.
MM? OH...SORRY, CLARK. GUESS I'M GETTING SENTIMENTAL IN MY OLD AGE.
MUST BE FROM SEEING YOU GROWING UP SO FAST.
WHAT I WAS GOING TO SAY IS THAT, SURE, CHANGE CAN BE SCARY. BUT IF YOU NEVER TRY ANYTHING NEW, YOU'LL NEVER REALLY KNOW WHAT YOU CAN DO.
WHATEVER LIFE BRINGS YOU, THE IMPORTANT THING IS TO MEET IT WITH YOUR HEAD HELD HIGH--
--"BECAUSE KENTS AREN'T QUITTERS!"
OH, THERE YOU TWO ARE!
HOLD STILL NOW SO I CAN GET A SHOT OF MY TWO BOYS.
THIS IS ONE DAY WE'RE GOING TO WANT TO REMEMBER--
--FOR MANY YEARS TO COME.
THE END

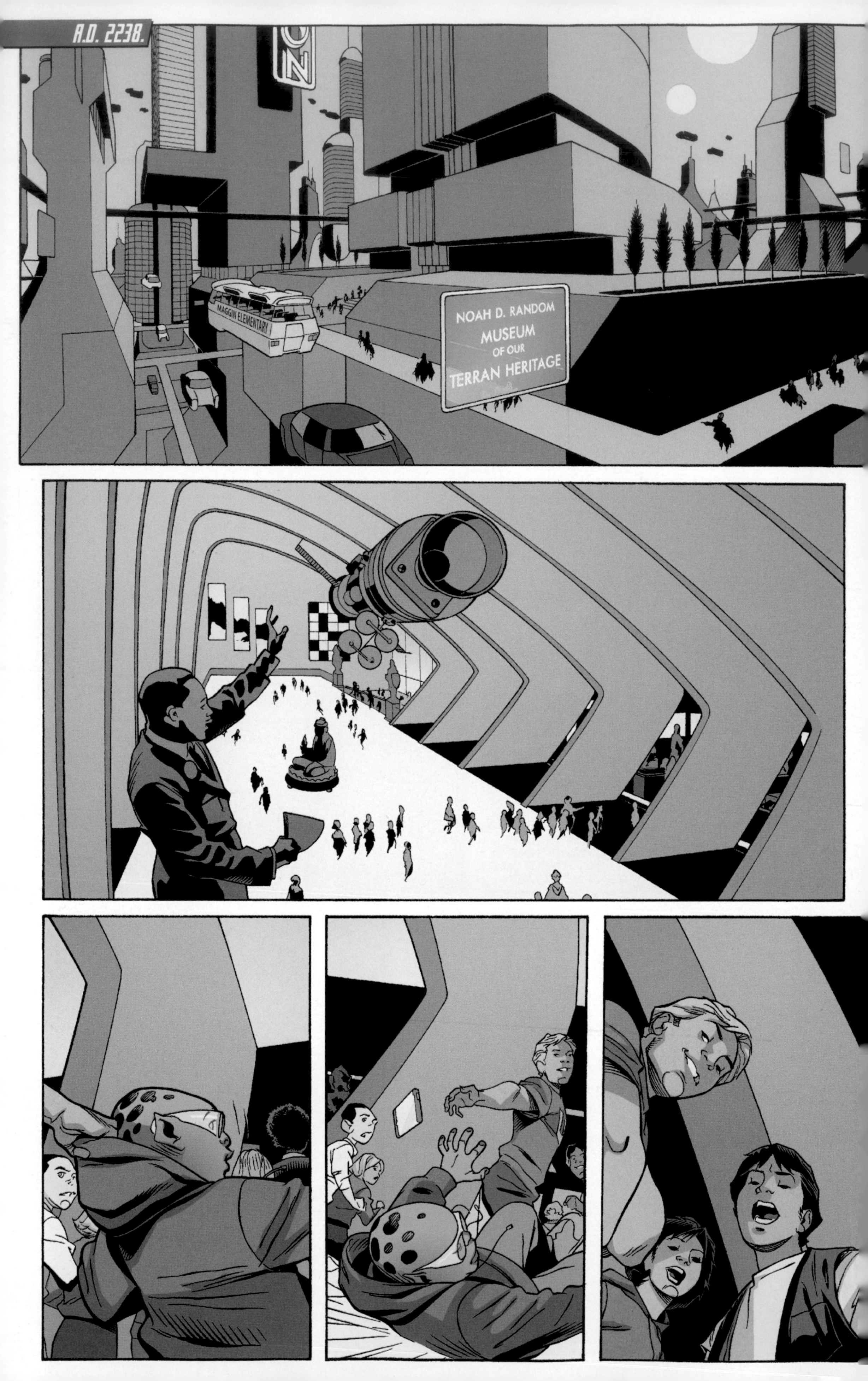
A.D. 2238.
MAGGIN ELEMENTARY
NOAH D. RANDOM
MUSEUM
OF OUR
TERRAN HERITAGE

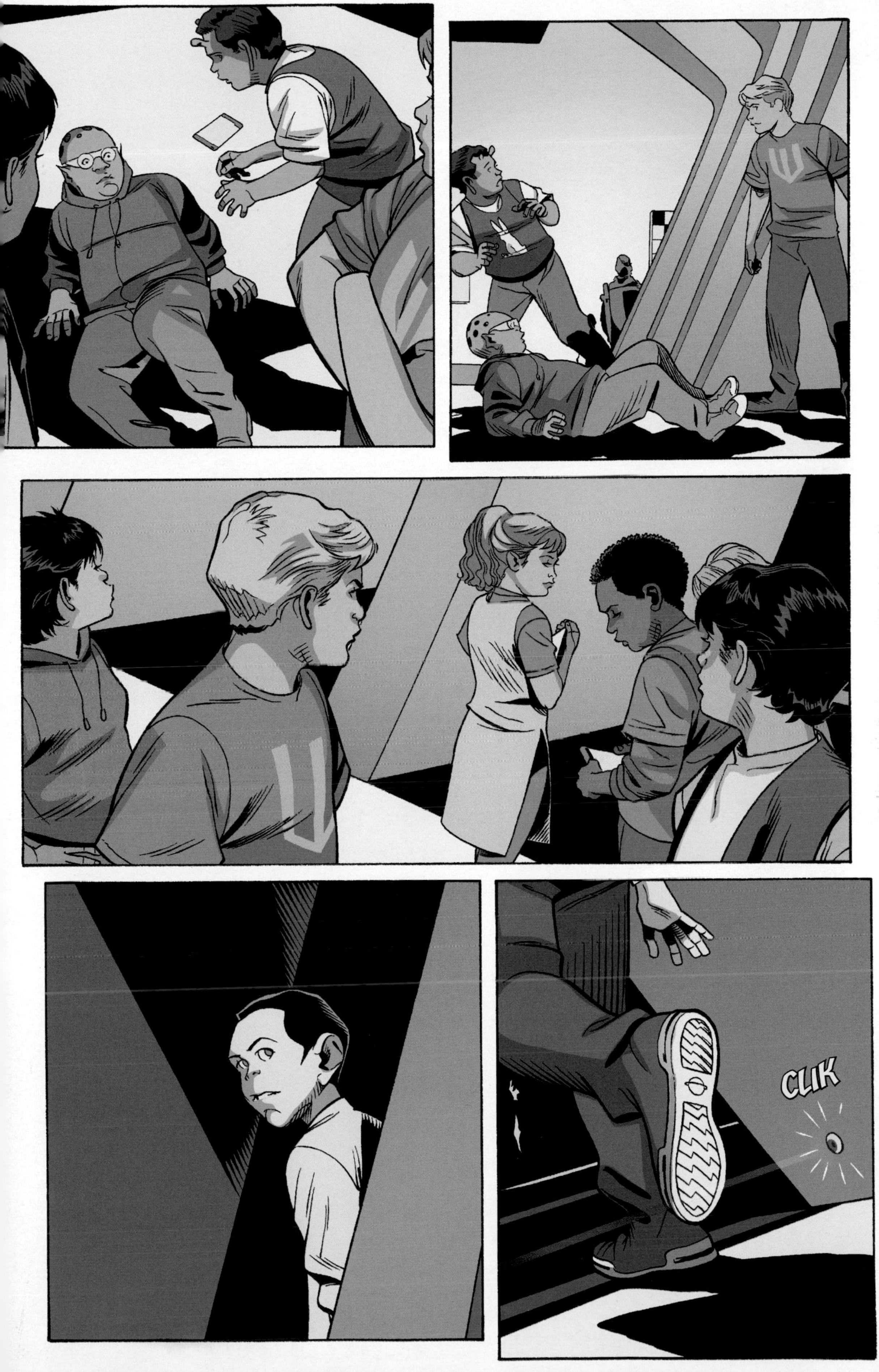
CLIK

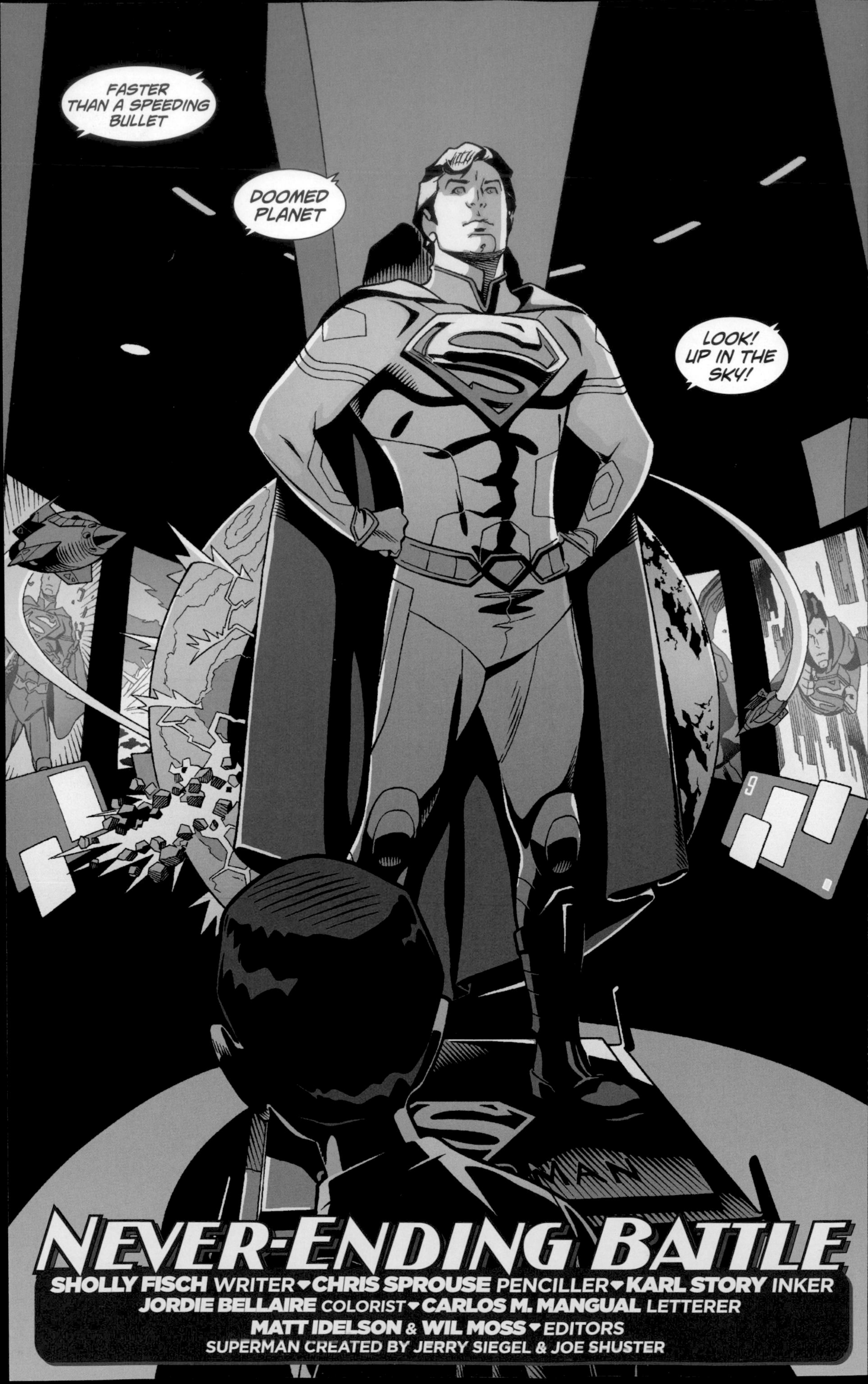
FASTER THAN A SPEEDING BULLET
DOOMED PLANET
LOOK! UP IN THE SKY!
NEVER-ENDING BATTLE
SHOLLY FISCH WRITER • CHRIS SPROUSE PENCILLER • KARL STORY INKER
JORDIE BELLAIRE COLORIST • CARLOS M. MANGUAL LETTERER
MATT IDELSON & WIL MOSS • EDITORS
SUPERMAN CREATED BY JERRY SIEGEL & JOE SHUSTER

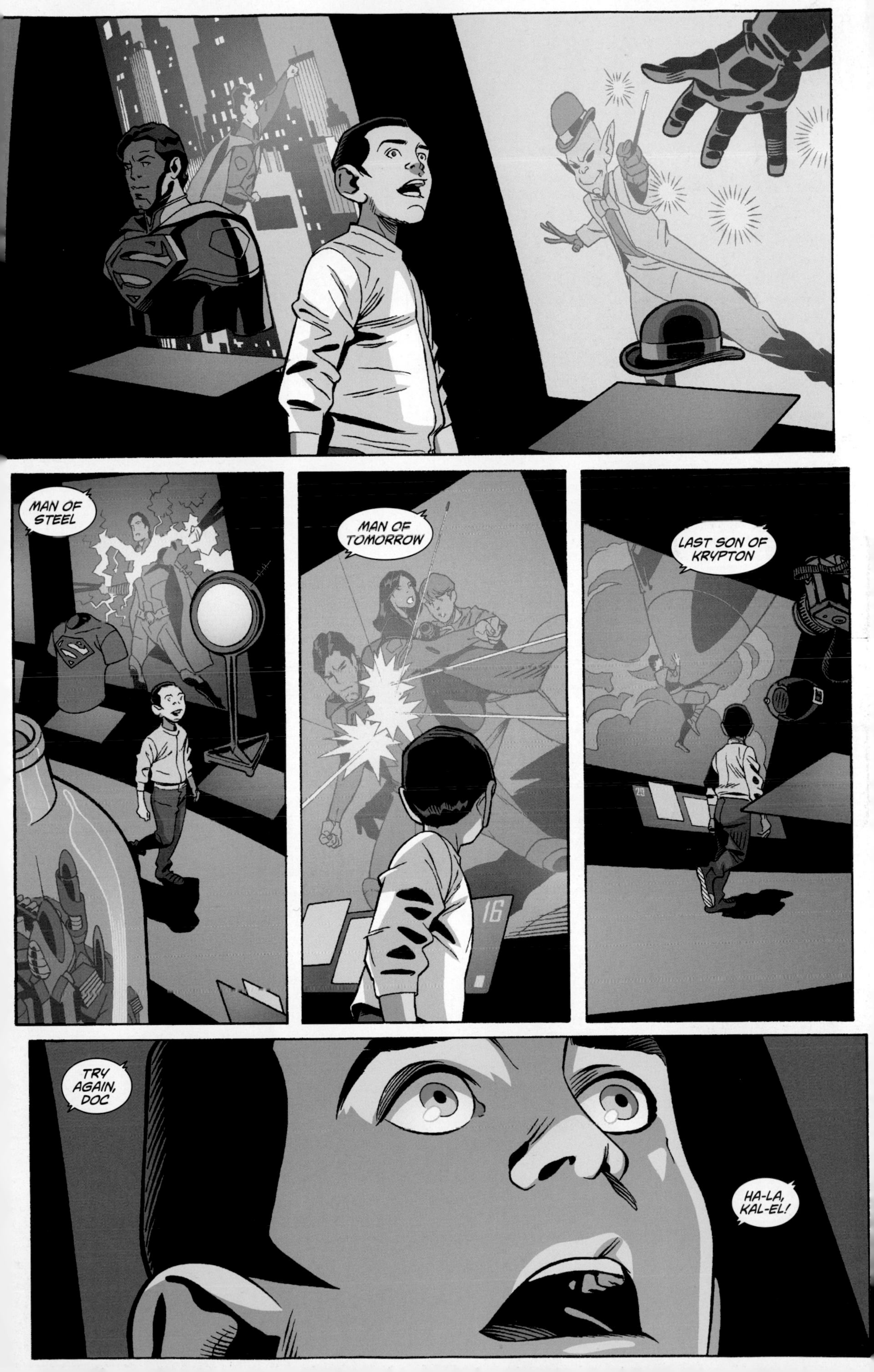
MAN OF STEEL
MAN OF TOMORROW
LAST SON OF KRYPTON
TRY AGAIN, DOC
HA-LA, KAL-EL!

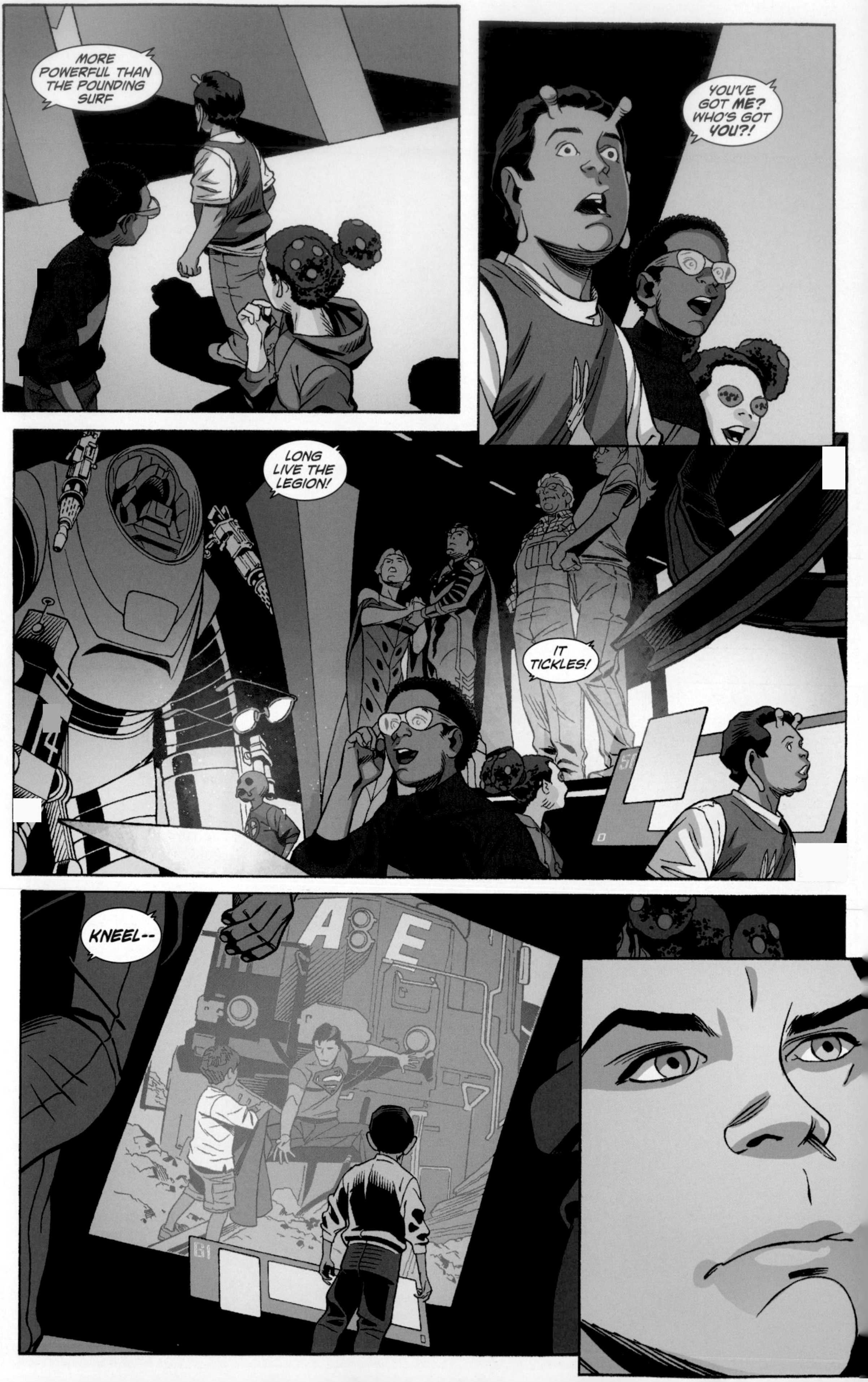
MORE POWERFUL THAN THE POUNDING SURF
YOU'VE GOT ME? WHO'S GOT YOU?!
LONG LIVE THE LEGION!
IT TICKLES!
KNEEL--

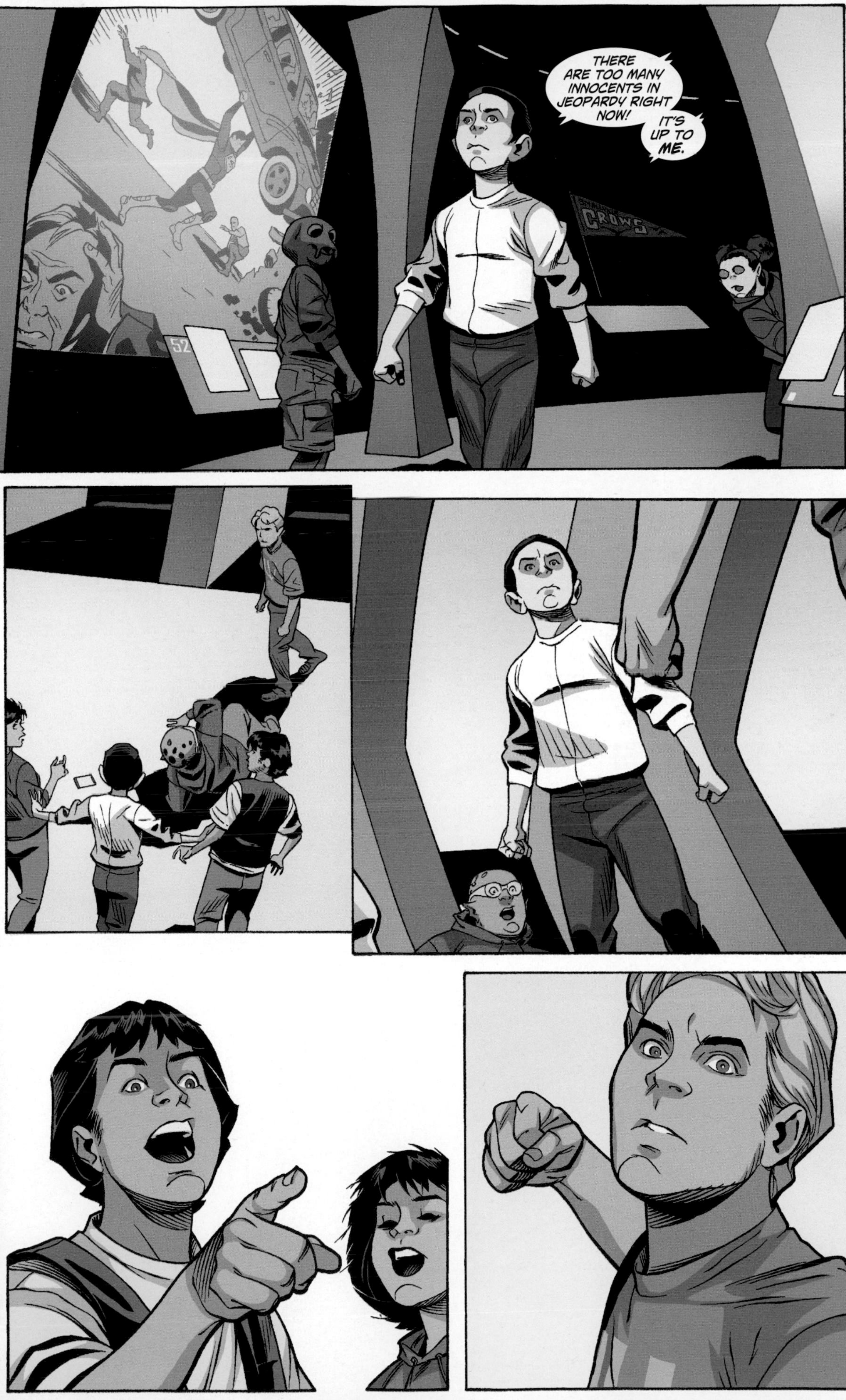
THERE ARE TOO MANY INNOCENTS IN JEOPARDY RIGHT NOW!
IT'S UP TO ME.
CROWS
52

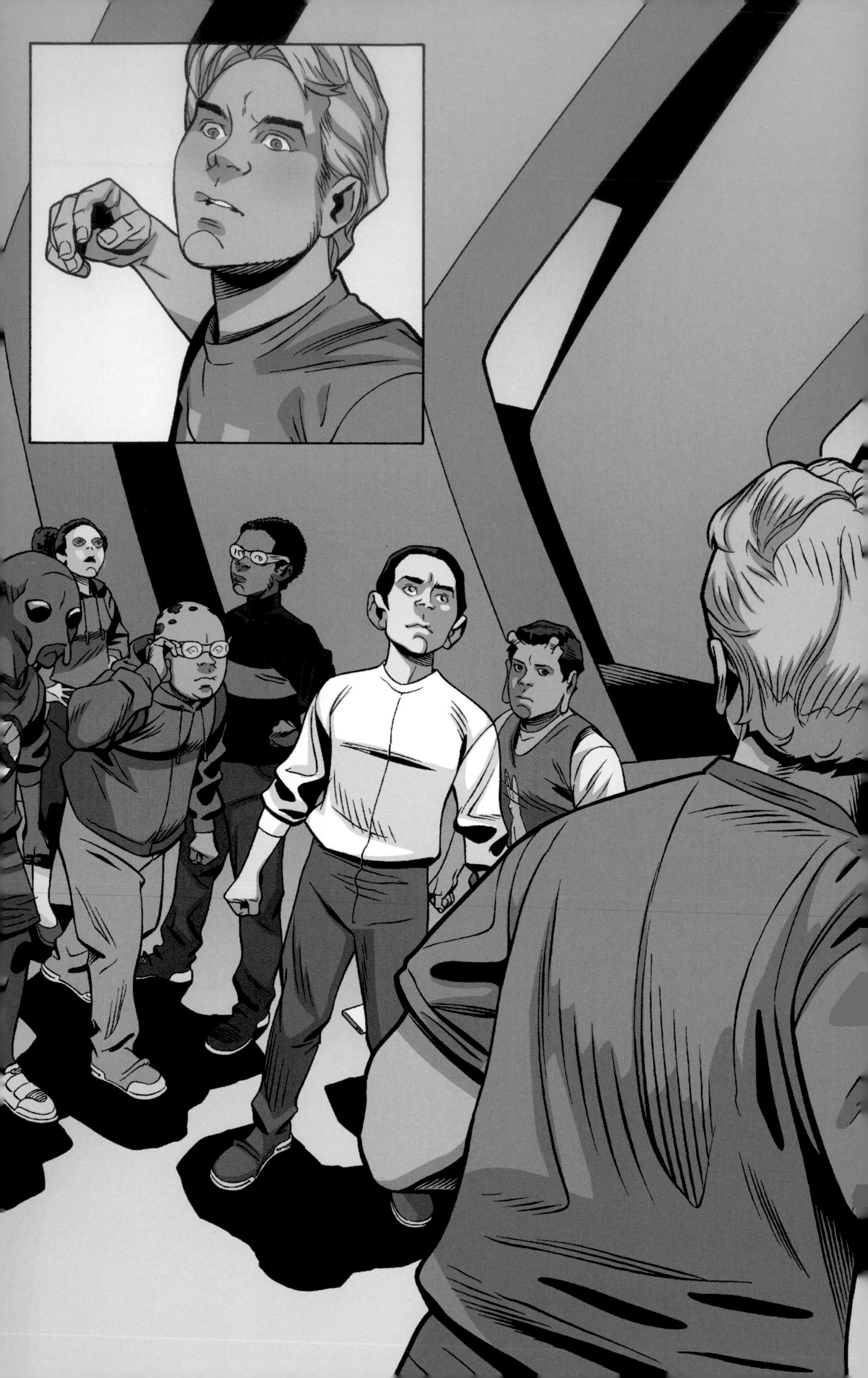

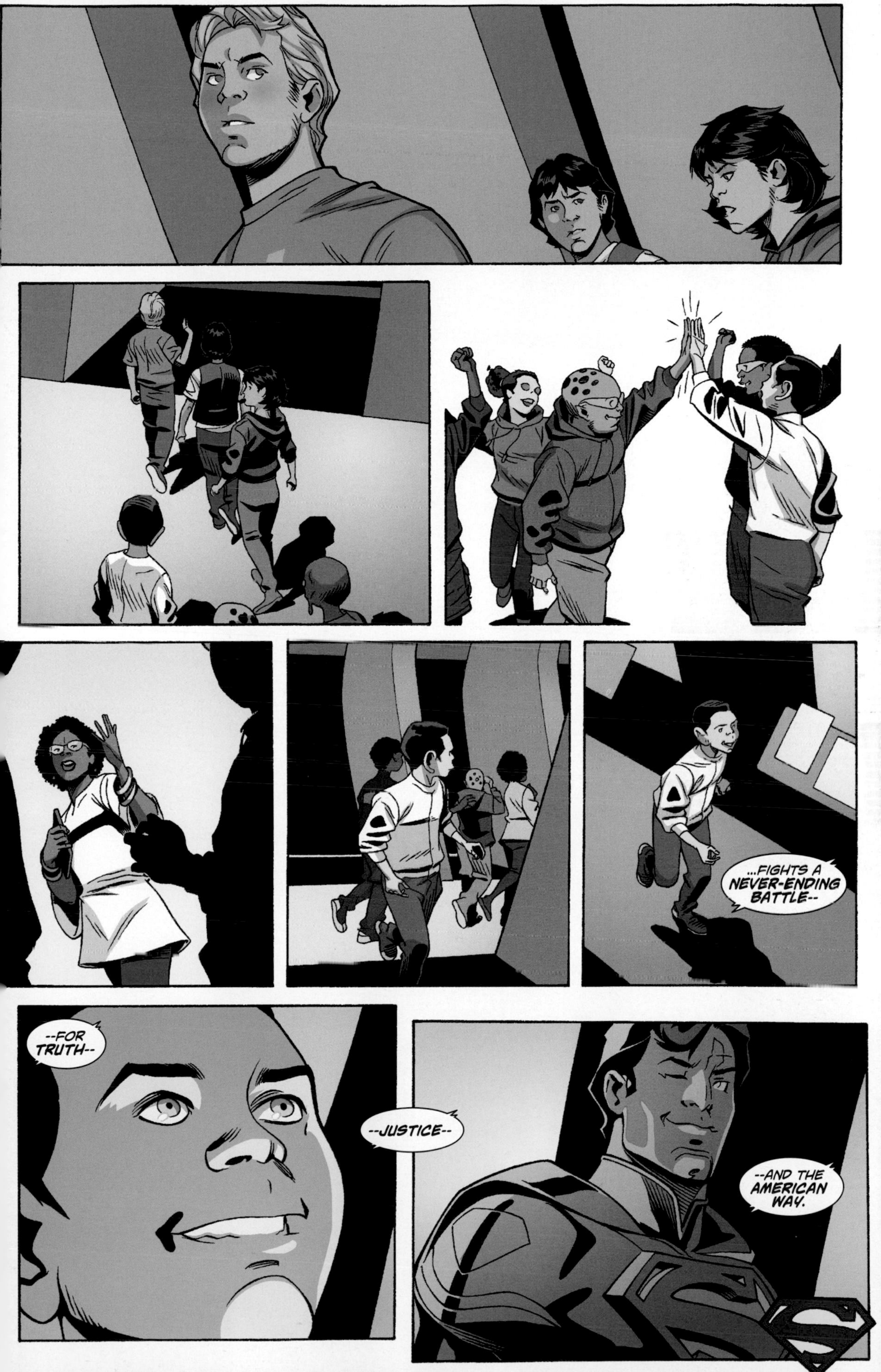
...FIGHTS A NEVER-ENDING BATTLE--
--FOR TRUTH--
--JUSTICE--
--AND THE AMERICAN WAY.

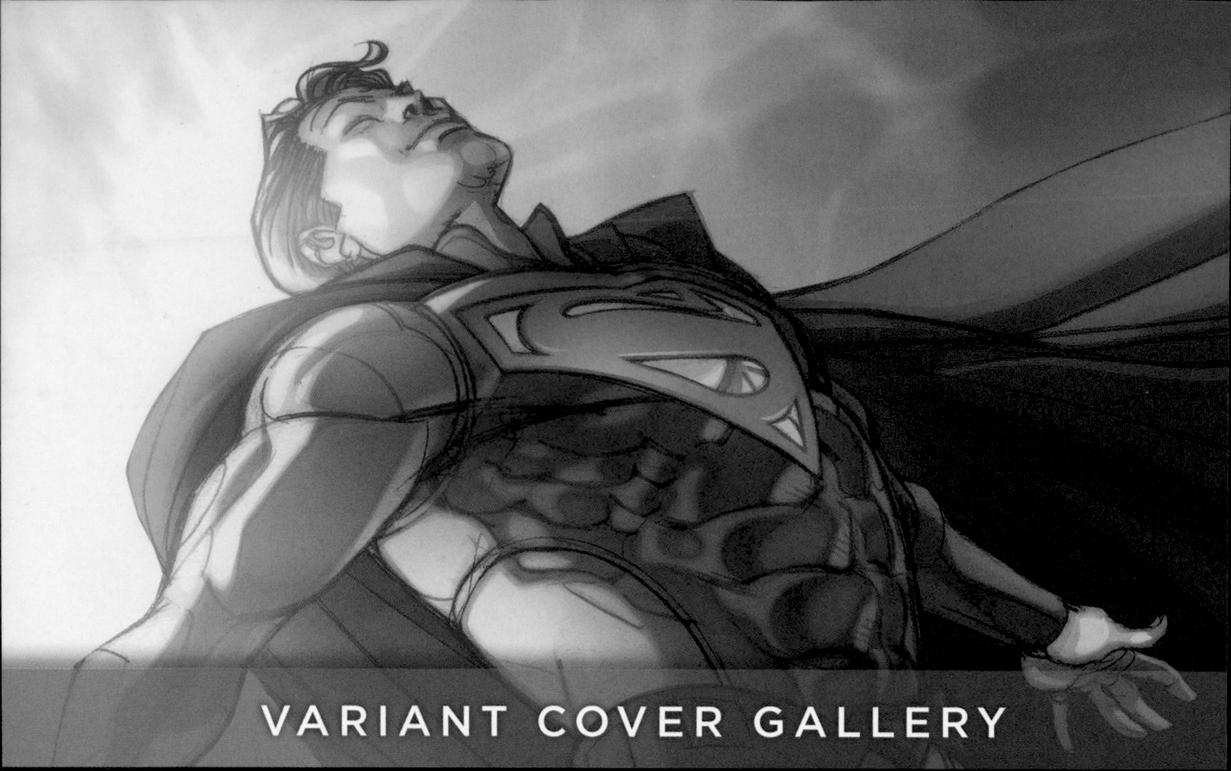

VARIANT COVER GALLERY

ACTION COMICS #13
Art by Rags Morales & Brad Anderson

ACTION COMICS #14
Art by Steve Skroce & Jason Keith

ACTION COMICS #15
Art by Fiona Staples

ACTION COMICS #16
Art by Pasqual Ferry & Dave McCaig

ACTION COMICS #17
Art by Terry Dodson & Rachel Dodson

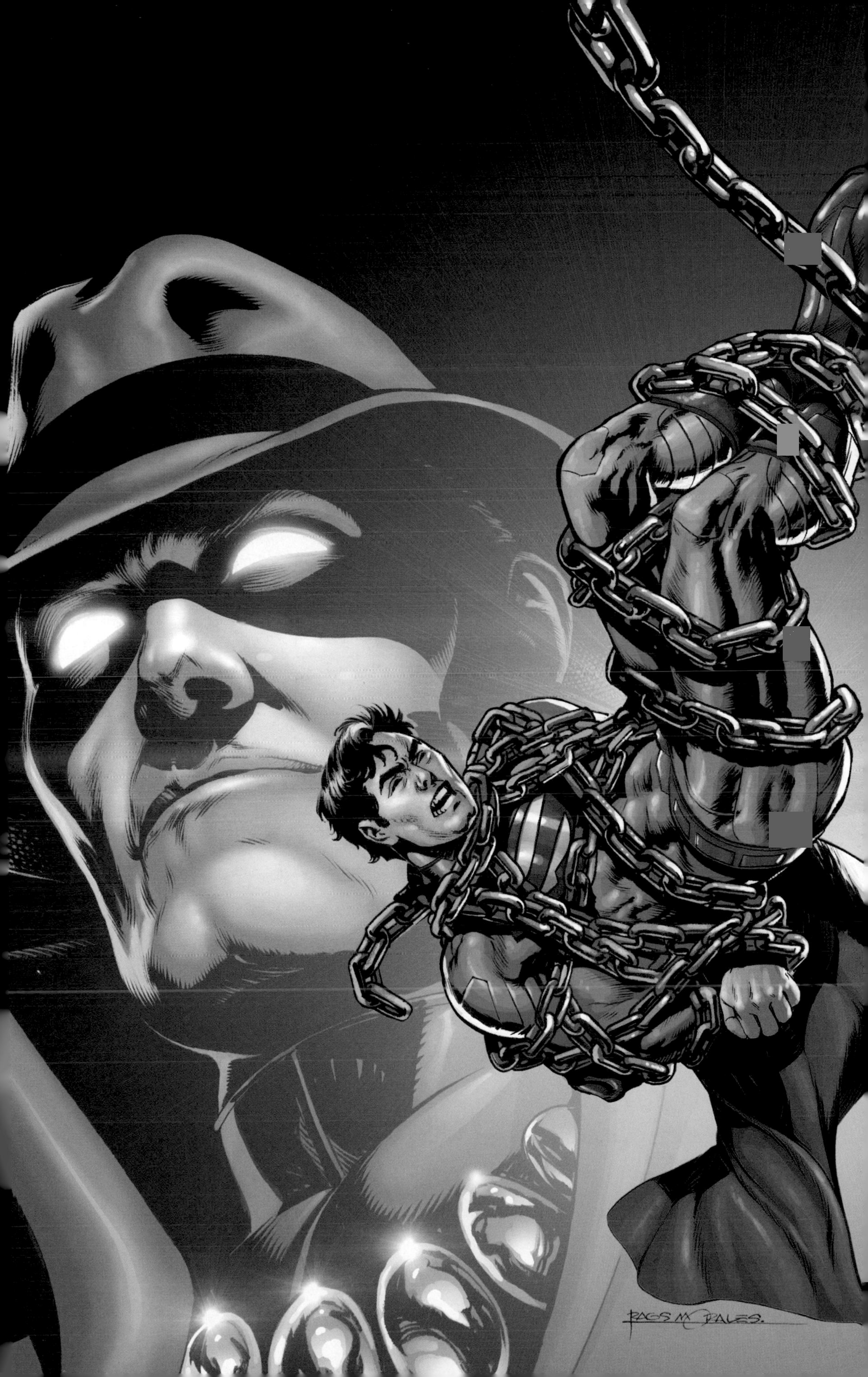

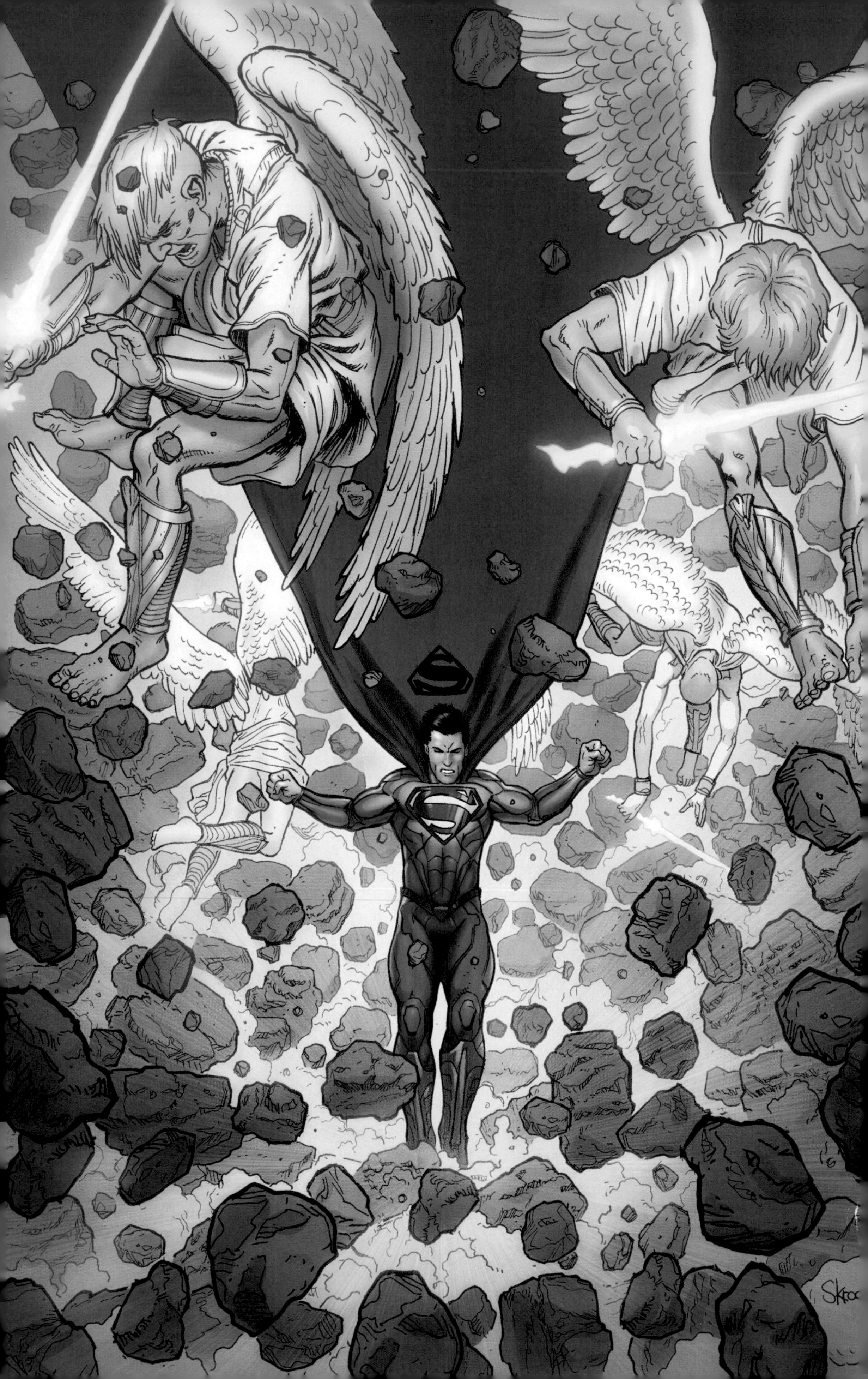

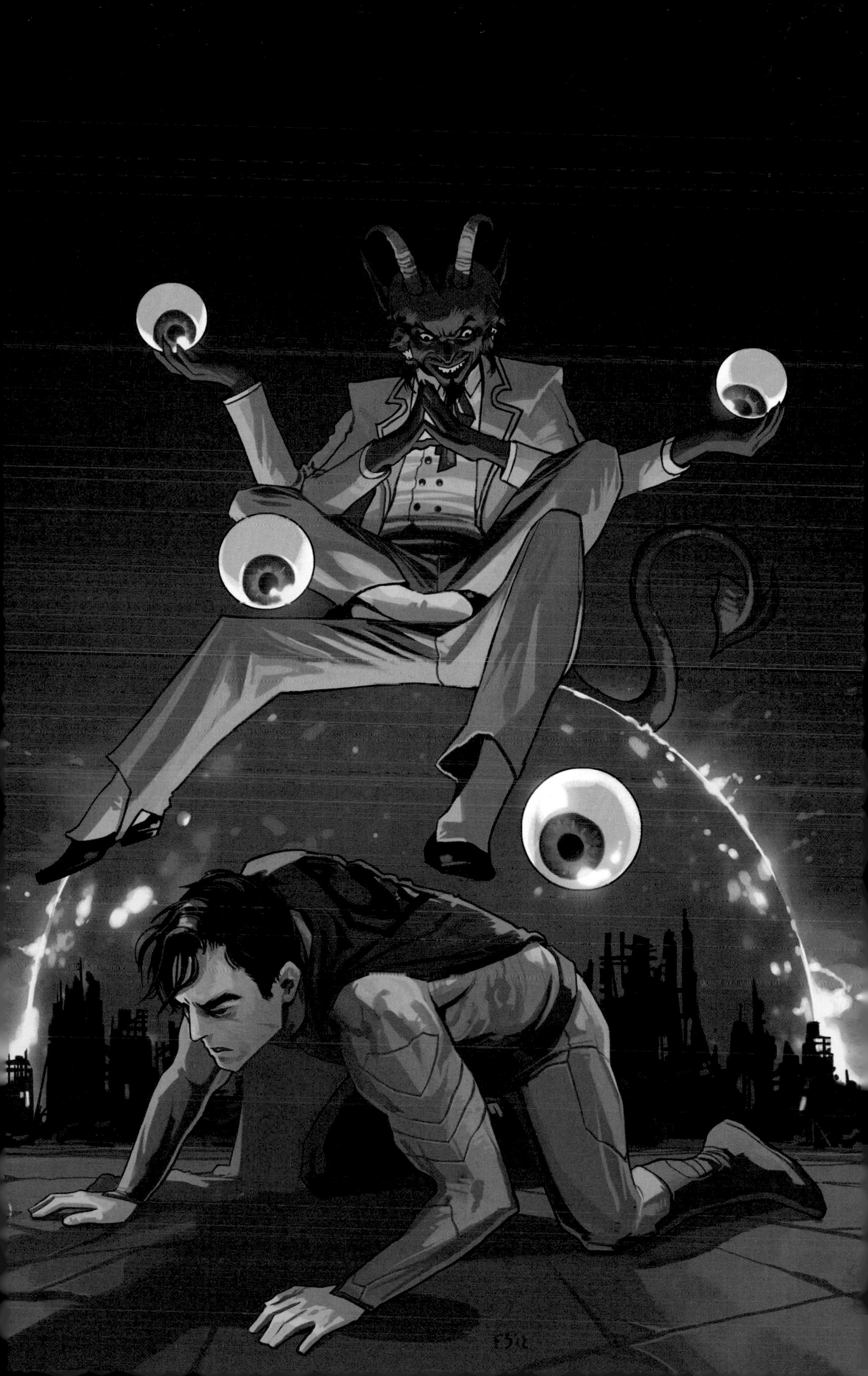

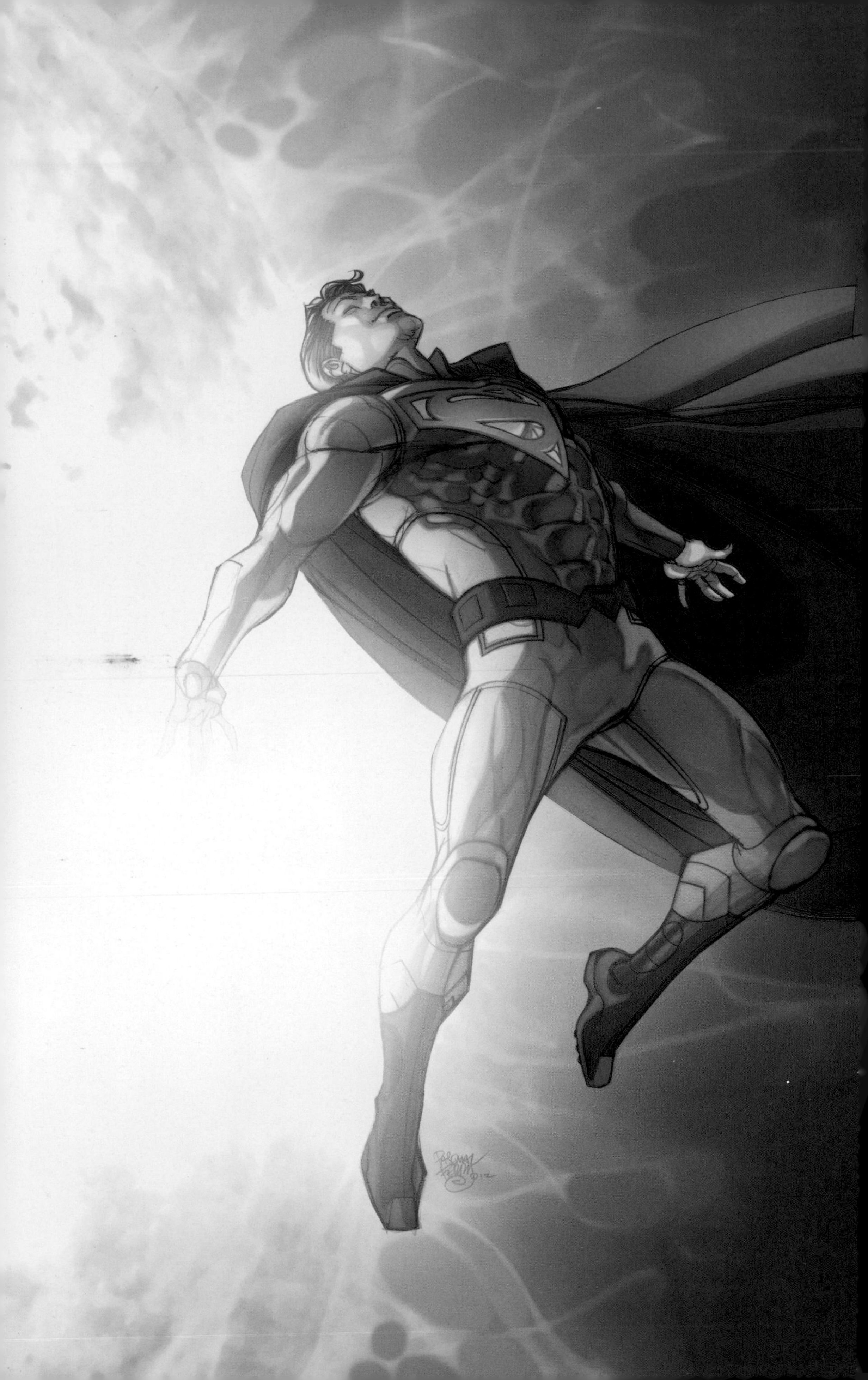

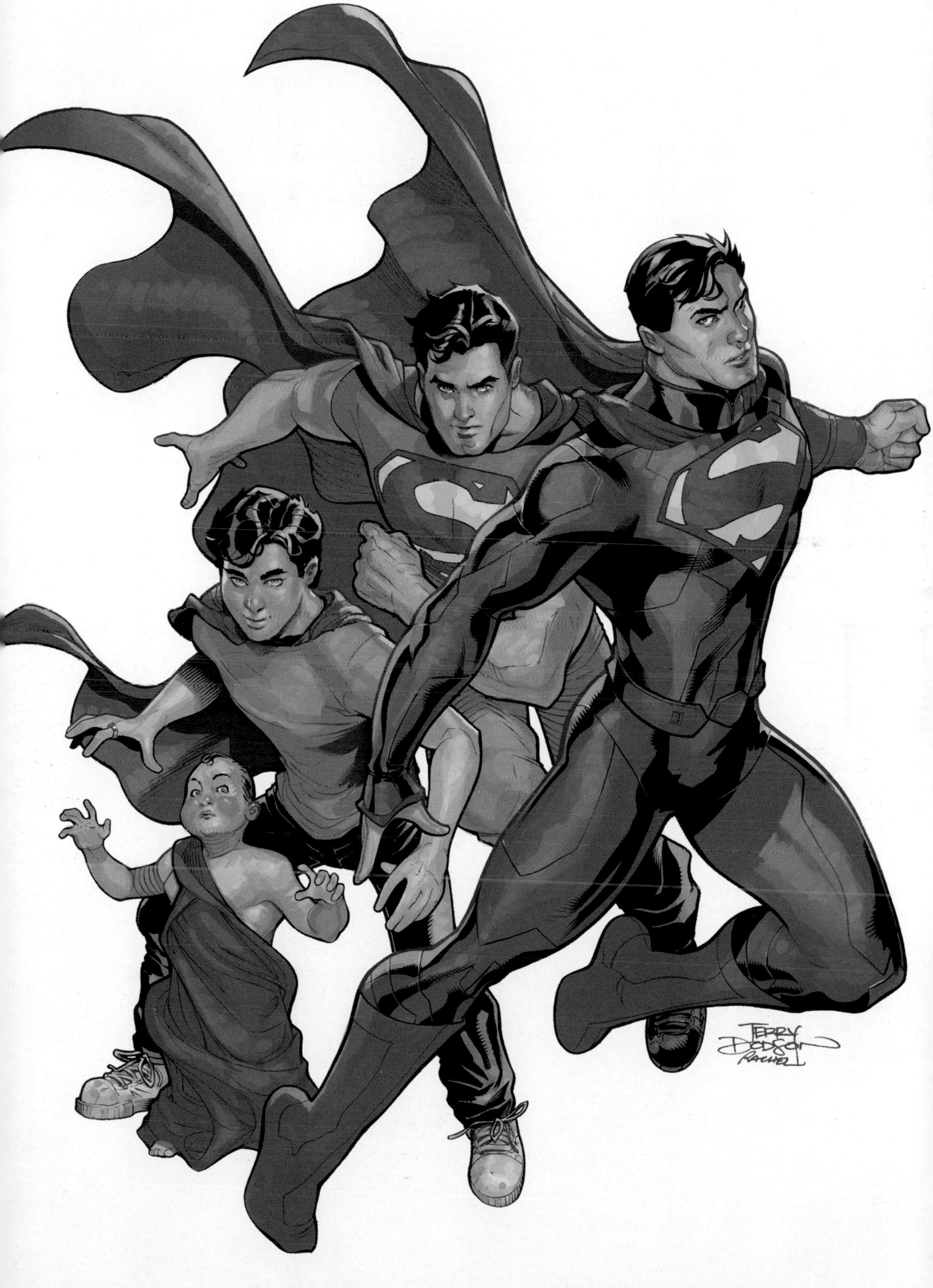
TERRY DODSON
RACHEL

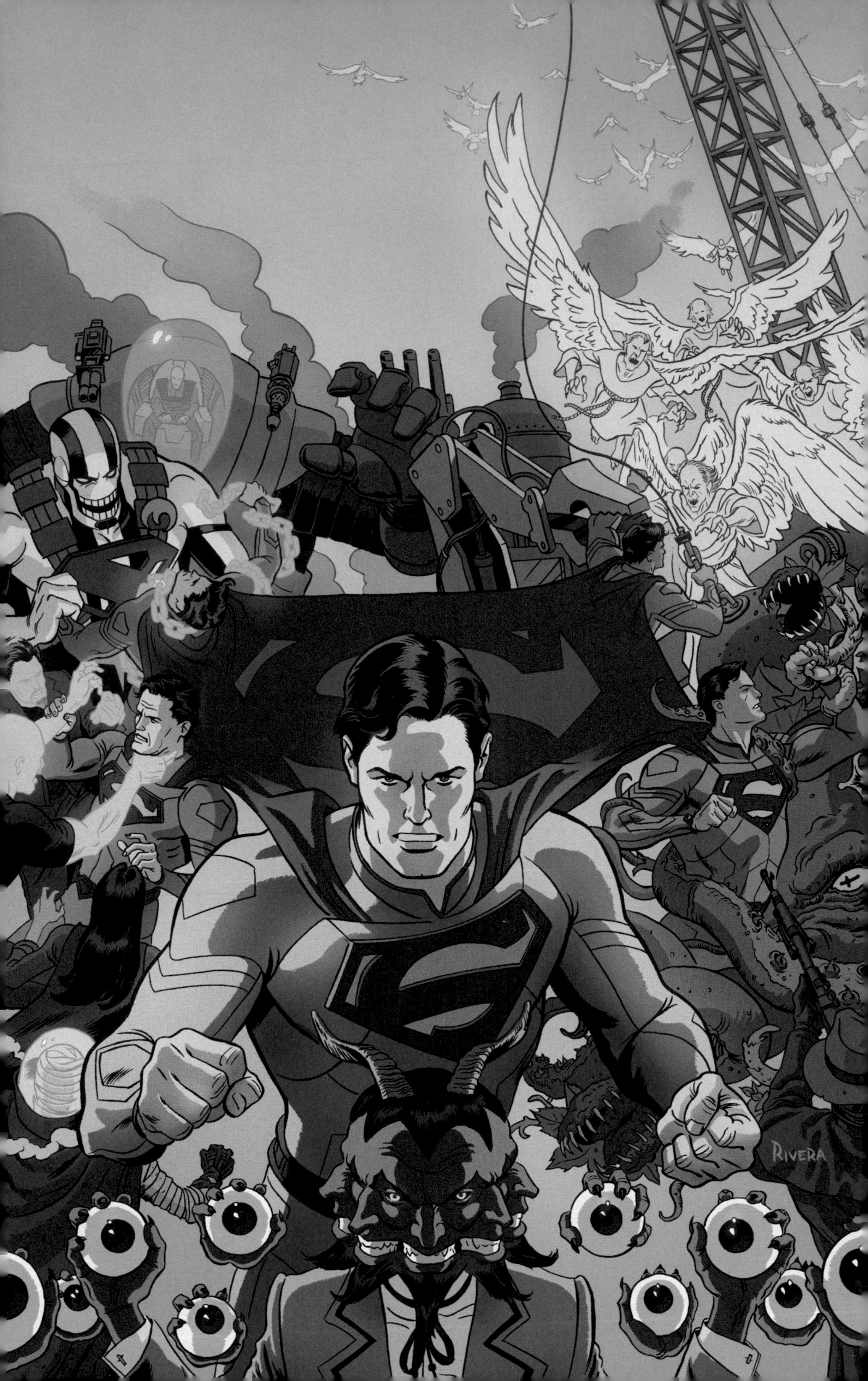
RIVERA

Action Comics #13 cover sketch by Grant Morrison

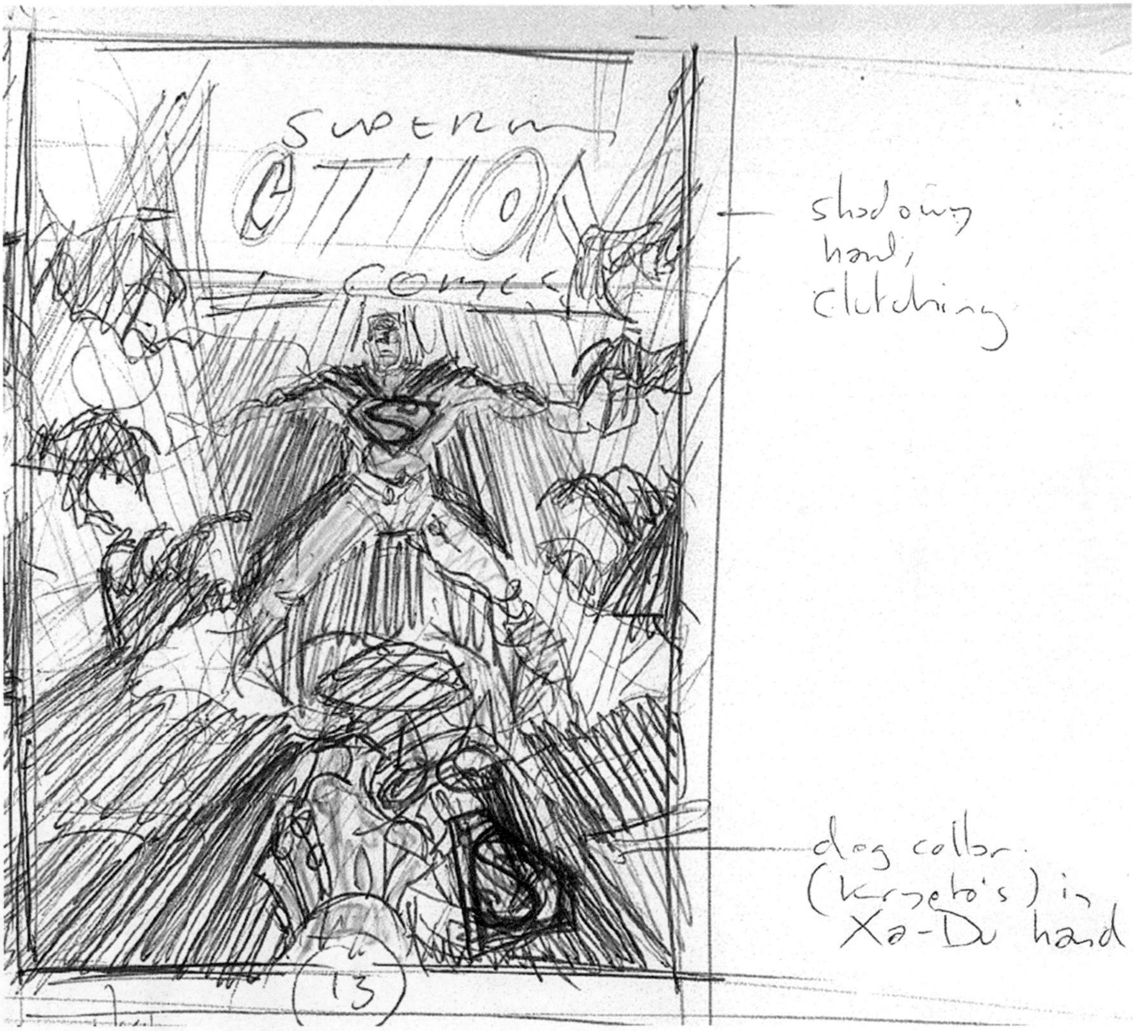
shadowy hand, clutching
dog collar (Krypto's) in Xa-Du hand
13

Action Comics #14 cover sketch by Grant Morrison

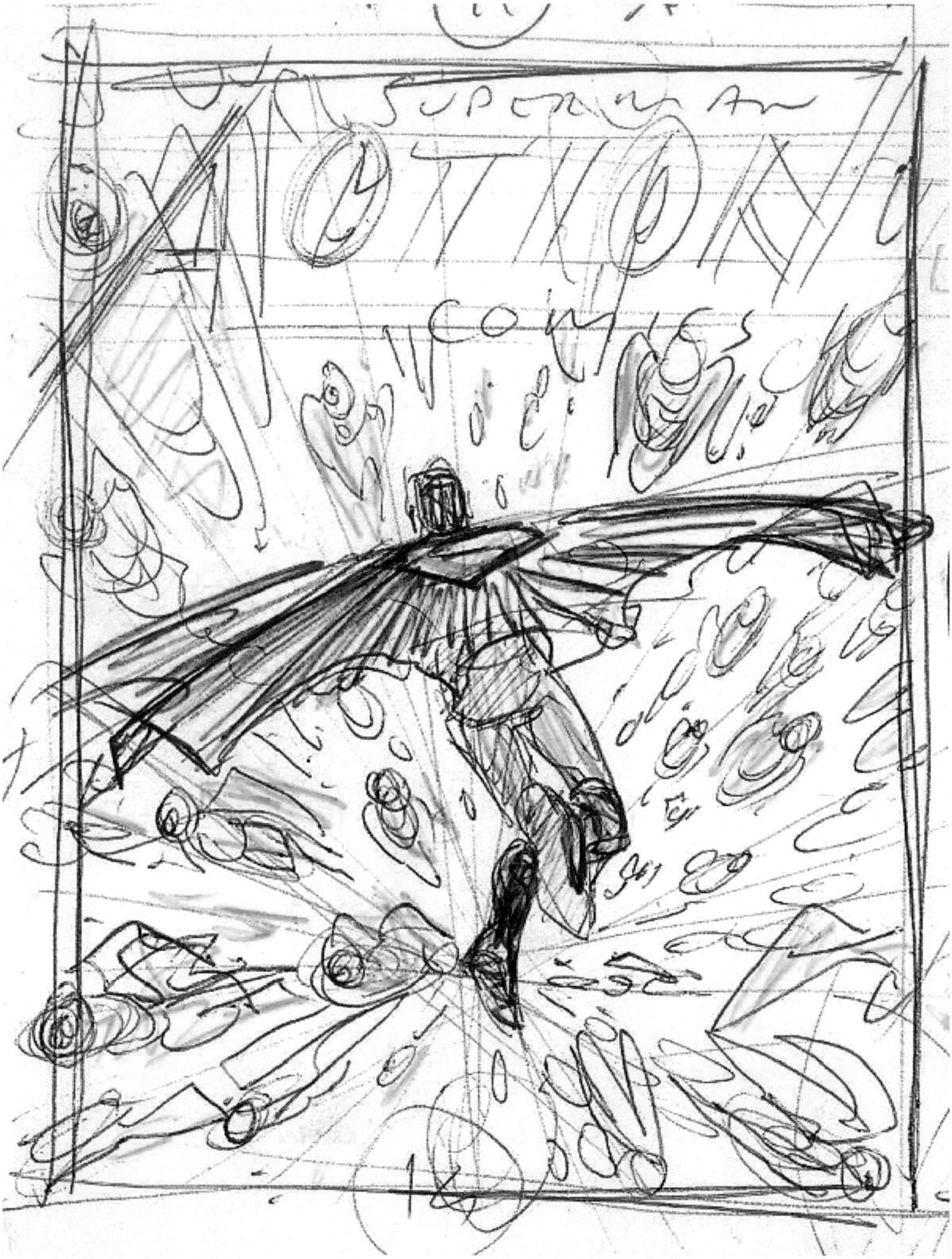

Action Comics #15 cover sketch by Rags Morales

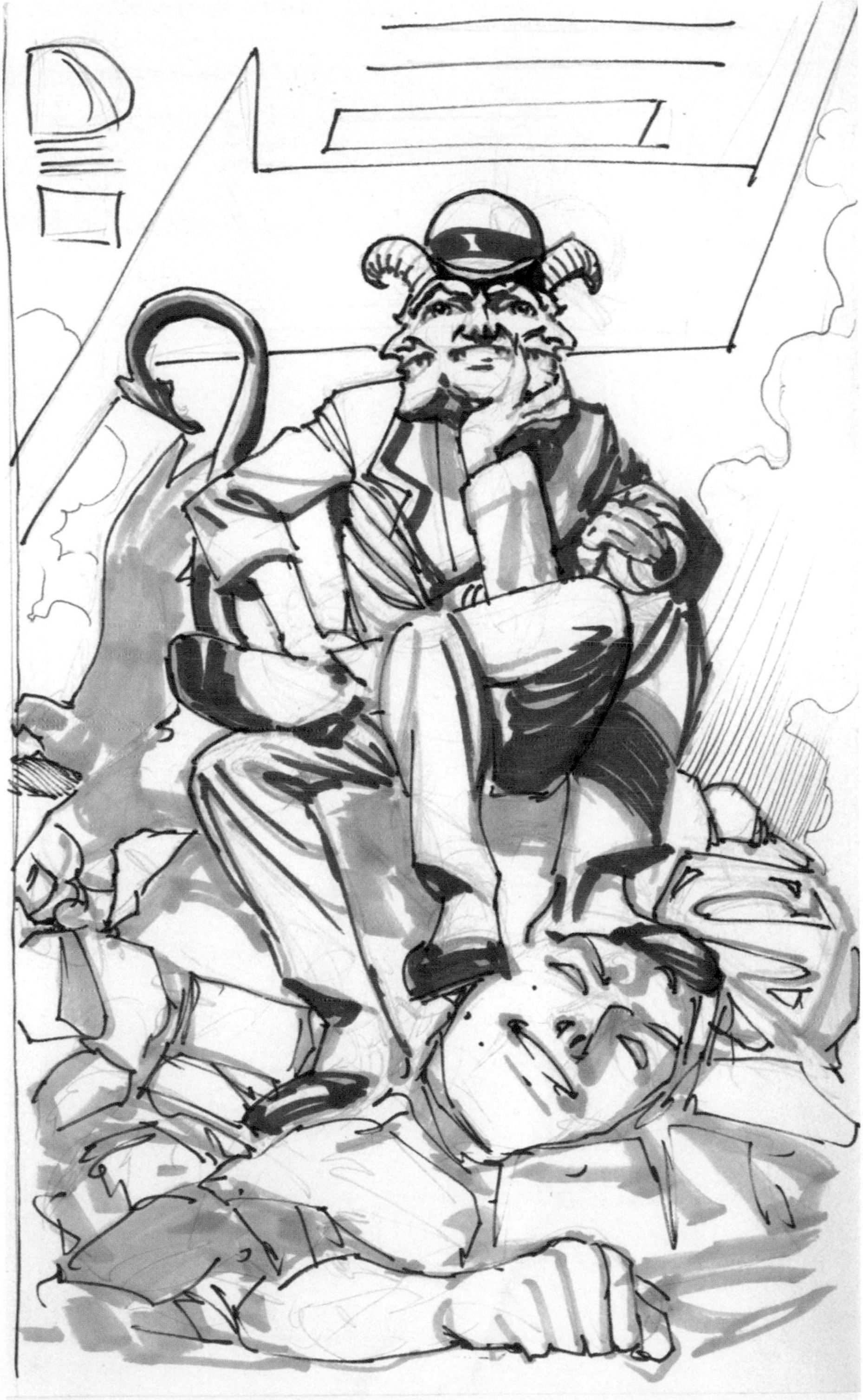

Action Comics #18 cover sketch by Grant Morrison

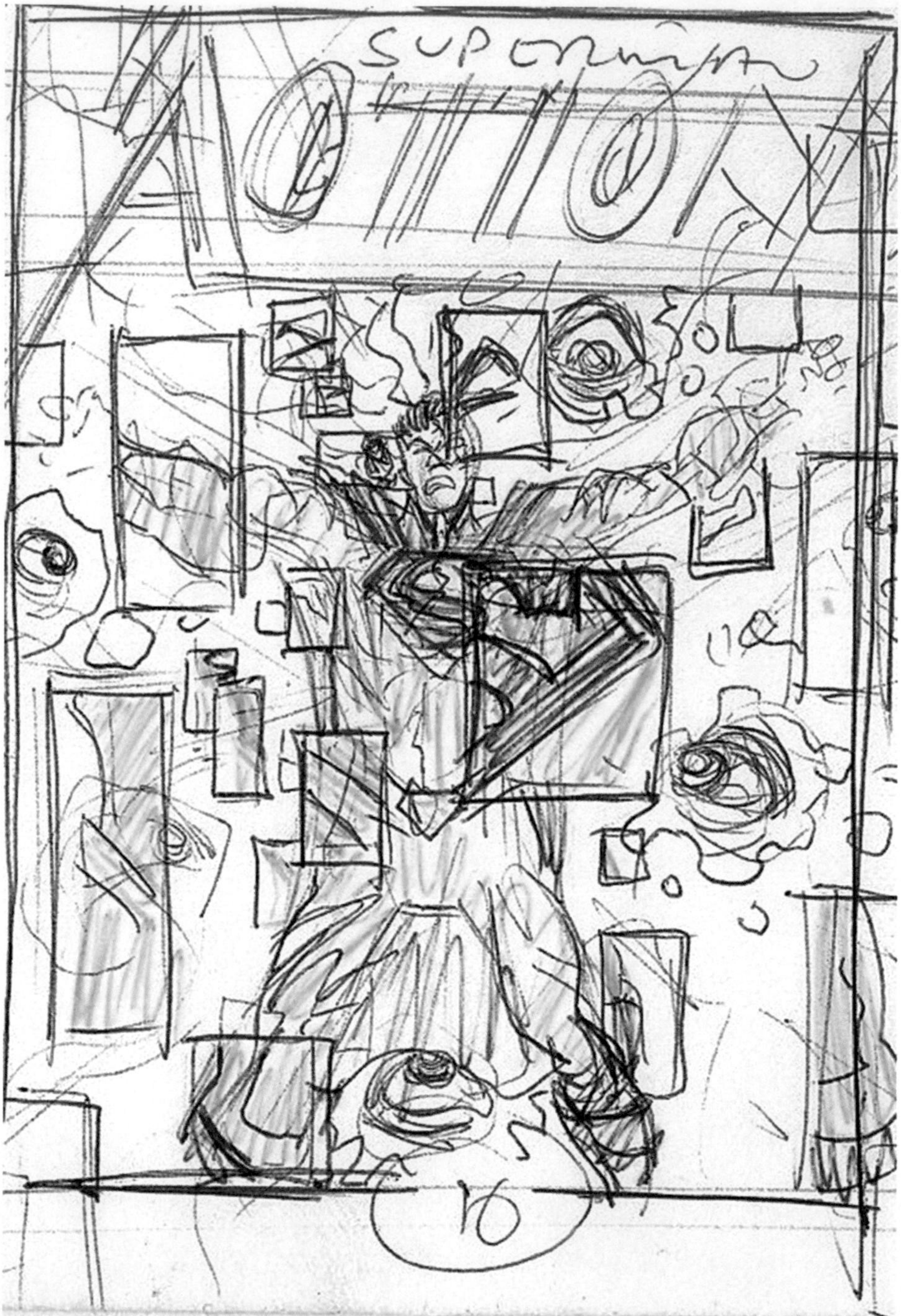

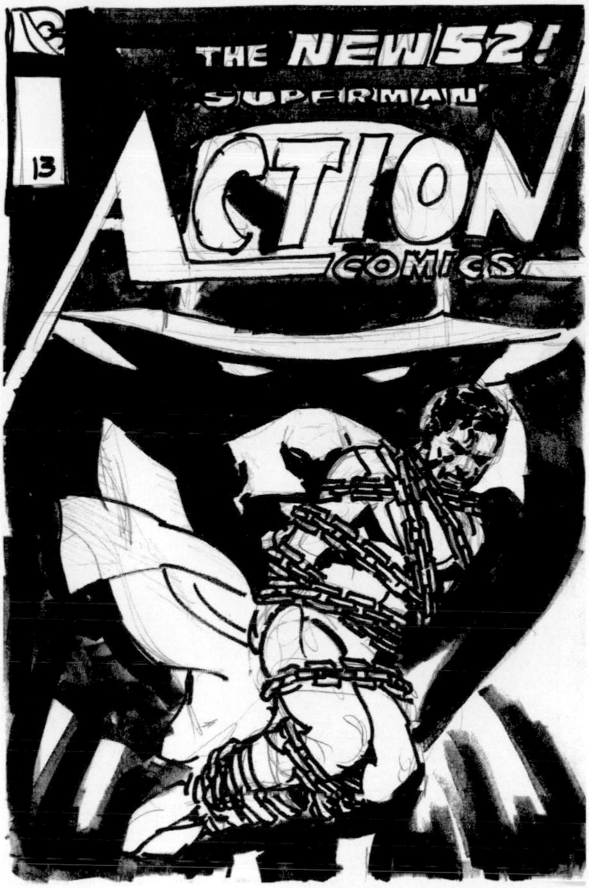
THE NEW 52!
SUPERMAN
ACTION
COMICS
13

Action Comics #13
variant cover sketch
by Rags Morales

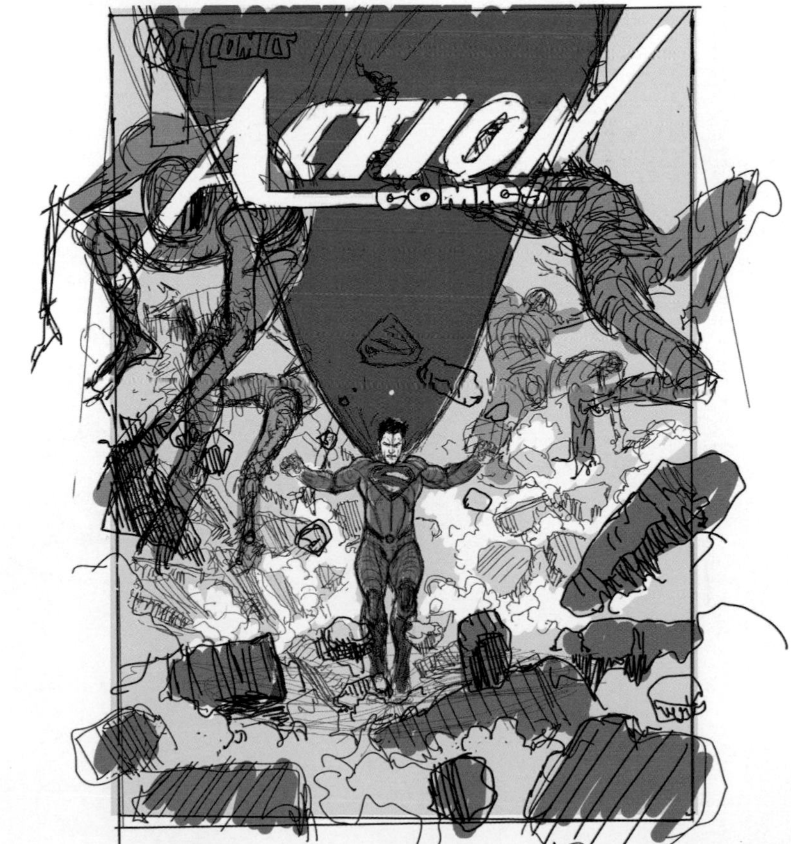
DC COMICS
ACTION
COMICS

Action Comics #14
variant cover sketch
by Steve Skroce

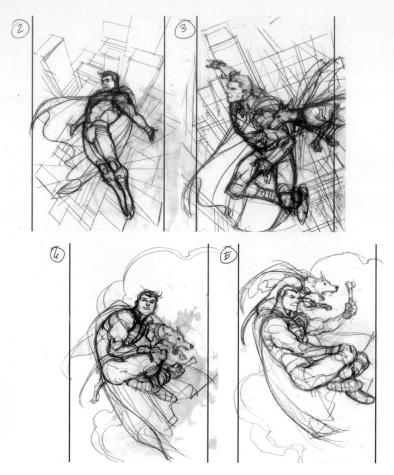

Action Comics #16
variant cover sketches
by Pasqual Ferry

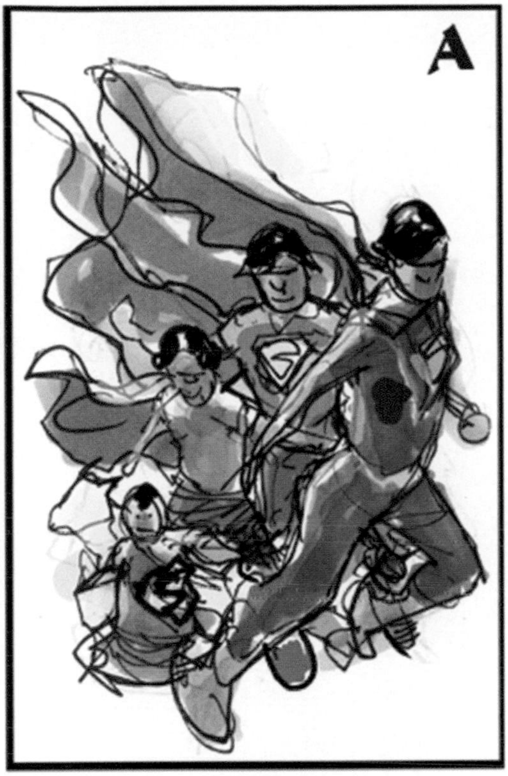
A

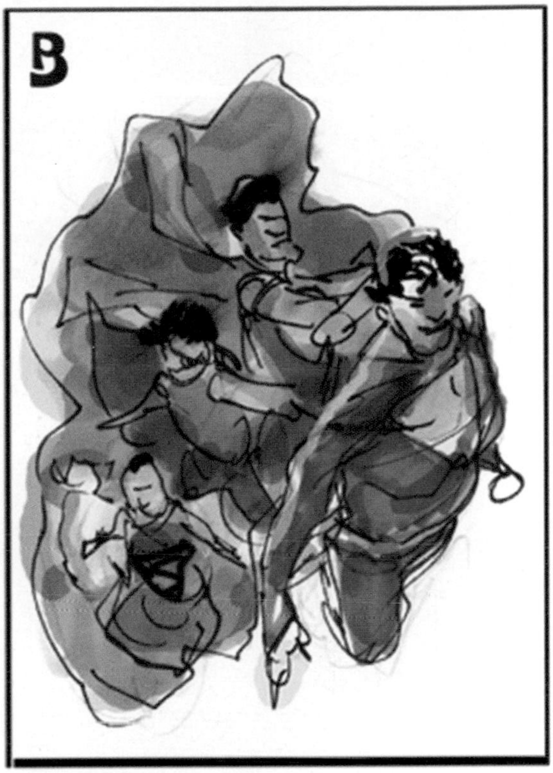
B

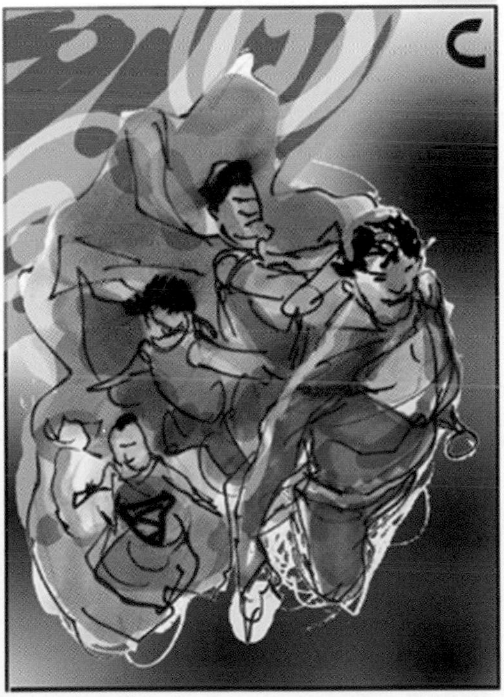
C

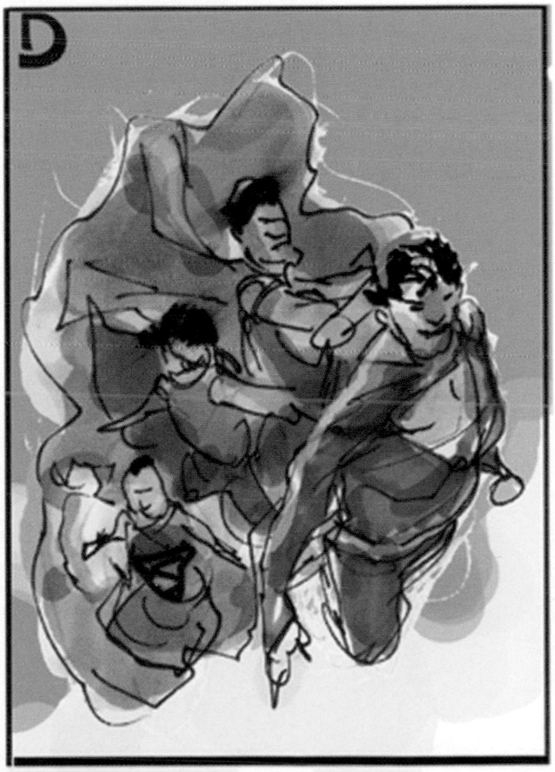
D

Action Comics #17 variant cover
sketches by Terry Dodson

Action Comics #18 variant cover sketch by Paolo Rivera

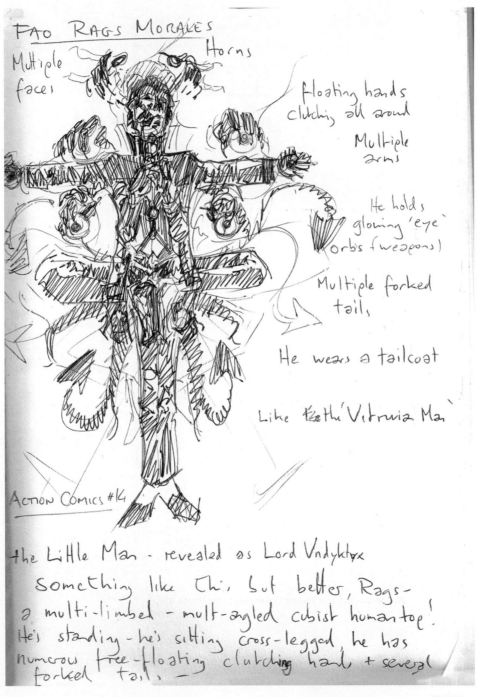

FAO RAGS MORALES

Multiple faces

Horns

Floating hands clutching all around

Multiple arms

He holds glowing 'eye' orbs (weapons)

Multiple forked tails

He wears a tailcoat

Like 'Vitruvia Man'

Action Comics #14

the Little Man - revealed as Lord Vndyktvx
Something like this, but better, Rags -
a multi-limbed - mult-angled cubist human top!
He's standing - he's sitting cross-legged, he has
numerous free-floating clutching hands + several
forked tails. —

Vyndktvx
character sketch by Grant Morrison

The Cometeers
character sketch by Grant Morrison

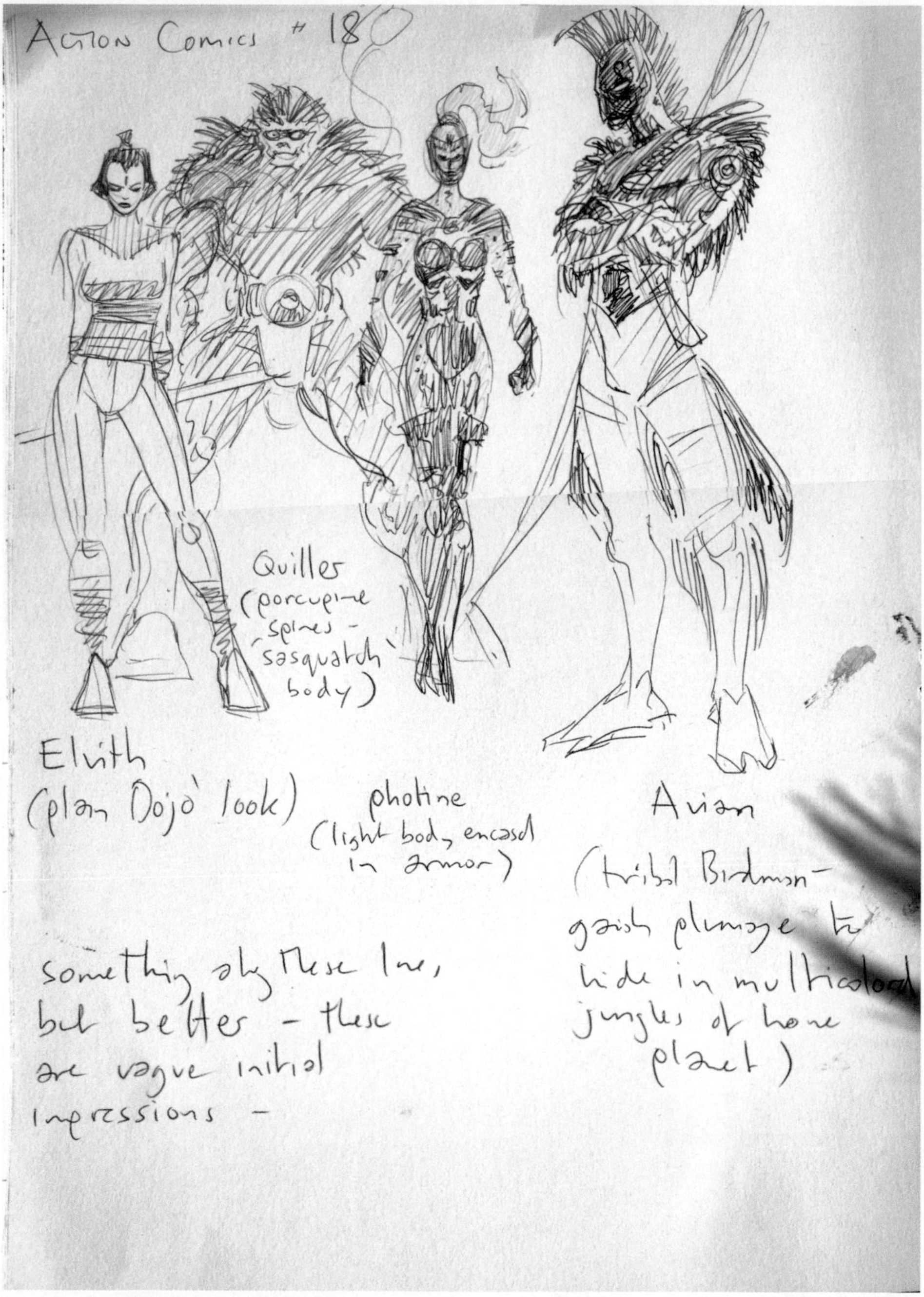

Action Comics #18
Quiller
(porcupine spines - 'sasquatch' body)
Elvith
(plain 'Dojo' look)
photine
(light body, encased in armor)
Avian
(tribal Birdman - garish plumage to hide in multicolored jungles of home planet)
something along these lines, but better - these are vague initial impressions -

"It's fresh air. I like this all-too-human Superman, and I think a lot of you will, too."
—SCRIPPS HOWARD NEWS SERVICE

START AT THE BEGINNING!

SUPERMAN: ACTION COMICS VOLUME 1: SUPERMAN AND THE MEN OF STEEL

SUPERMAN VOLUME 1: WHAT PRICE TOMORROW?

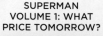

SUPERGIRL VOLUME 1: THE LAST DAUGHTER OF KRYPTON

SUPERBOY VOLUME 1: INCUBATION

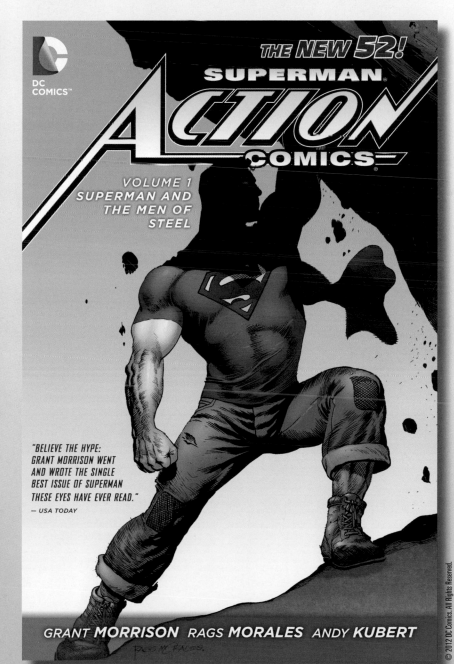

"BELIEVE THE HYPE: GRANT MORRISON WENT AND WROTE THE SINGLE BEST ISSUE OF SUPERMAN THESE EYES HAVE EVER READ."
— USA TODAY

GRANT MORRISON   RAGS MORALES   ANDY KUBERT

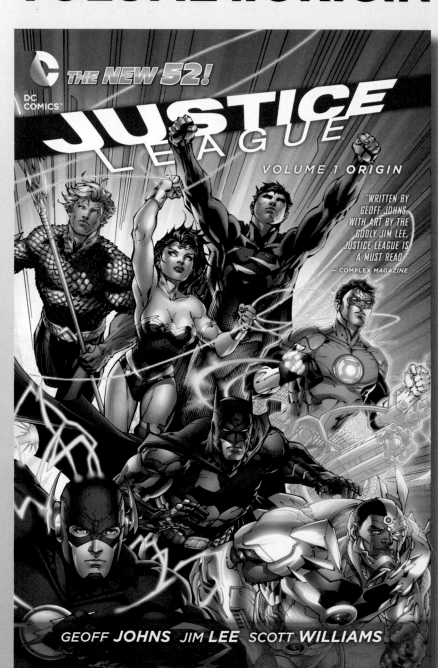

"Maniacally brilliant."
—THE NEW YORK TIMES

"A stirringly mythic, emotionally resonant, and gloriously alternative take on the Man of Steel."
—ENTERTAINMENT WEEKLY

"Taking the Man of Steel back to his roots and into the future at the same time, All Star Superman is exciting, bold and supercool...all the makings of a classic."
—VARIETY

GRANT MORRISON
ALL-STAR SUPERMAN
with FRANK QUITELY

FINAL CRISIS

with J.G. JONES, CARLOS PACHECO & DOUG MAHNKE

BATMAN: ARKHAM ASYLUM

with DAVE McKEAN

SEVEN SOLDIERS OF VICTORY VOLS. 1 & 2

with J.H. WILLIAMS III & Various Artists

ALL ★ STAR
SUPERMAN

"A stirringly mythic, emotionally resonant, and gloriously alternative take on the Man of Steel."
—ENTERTAINMENT WEEKLY

GRANT MORRISON
FRANK QUITELY
JAMIE GRANT